Studying Hasidism

Studying Hasidism

Sources, Methods, Perspectives

Edited by Marcin Wodziński

RUTGERS UNIVERSITY PRESS
NEW BRUNSWICK, CAMDEN, AND NEWARK,
NEW JERSEY, AND LONDON

Library of Congress Cataloging-in-Publication Data

Names: Wodziński, Marcin, editor.
Title: Studying Hasidism: sources, methods, perspectives / edited by Marcin Wodziński.
Description: New Brunswick, New Jersey : Rutgers University Press, [2019] | Includes bibliographical references and index.
Identifiers: LCCN 2018039640 | ISBN 9781978804227 (cloth) | ISBN 9781978804210 (pbk.)
Subjects: LCSH: Hasidism—History.
Classification: LCC BM198.3 .S78 2019 | DDC 296.8/332072—dc23
LC record available at https://lccn.loc.gov/2018039640

A British Cataloging-in-Publication record for this book is available from the British Library.

⊗ The paper used in this publication meets the requirements of the American National Standard for Information Sciences—Permanence of Paper for Printed Library Materials, ANSI Z39.48-1992.

www.rutgersuniversitypress.org

Manufactured in the United States of America

Contents

A Note on Transcription and Place Names

The transcription of Hebrew in this book reflects the pronunciation of modern Hebrew rather than Ashkenazi pronunciation used by the Hasidim themselves. No attempt is made to indicate the distinctions between *alef* and *'ayin* (both represented by apostrophe), *tet* and *taf*, *kaf* and *kuf*, and *sin* and *samekh*. However, the distinction between *ḥet* and *khaf* has been retained, using *ḥ* for the former and *kh* for the latter. The *dagesh* is not indicated except where it affects pronunciation. However, transcriptions that are well established have been retained even when they are not consistent with the system adopted. On similar grounds, the *tsadi* (usually represented by *ts*) is rendered by *tz* in such familiar words as *bar mitzvah* or when it could create a confusion before *h* or *ḥ*; hence, *Yitzḥak* instead of *Yitsḥak*. The final *heh* is indicated too, though numerous exceptions appear. Prefixes, prepositions, and conjunctions are followed by hyphens: *be-toledot ha-'am*. *Sheva na'* is represented by *e*.

The transcription of Yiddish follows the YIVO system.

In both Yiddish and Hebrew, capital letters are used only in cases of proper names and for words that are capitalized in English, for example, *r. Yisra'el mi-Ruzhin u-mekomo be-toledot ha-ḥasidut*. For names of people in both Yiddish and Hebrew, the spellings that they used or that became common in popular use—for example, *Assaf* (not *Asaf*), *Peretz* (not *Perets*)—have been retained.

With regard to place names, I have used the Polish form for all localities in territories of the former Polish-Lithuanian Commonwealth; Hungarian for the territory of the Kingdom of Hungary; and Romanian for Moldavia, Wallachia, Bessarabia, and Bukovina, excepting cities that have well-known English names (e.g., Warsaw, not Warszawa) and post-Holocaust contexts, for which I use contemporary forms. Where the Yiddish form is markedly different from its Polish/Hungarian/Romanian/Ukrainian/Belarussian/Lithuanian equivalent, I add a transcription of the Yiddish name in the standard northeast dialect in parentheses: *Mstów* (*Amstov*). The rule is reversed in the case of Hasidic courts and several personalities (e.g., the Maiden of Ludmir), for which transcription of the Yiddish name typically associated with the court, tsadik, or other personality residing there is followed by its Polish/Hungarian/Romanian equivalent: *Amshinov* (*Mszczonów*), *Ger* (*Góra Kalwaria*). However, when the Yiddish form differs from the Polish/Hungarian/Romanian one only by omission of diacriticals or very minor alteration, I use the latter only: *Słonim*, not *Slonim*; *Radomsko*, not *Radomsk*.

Studying Hasidism

Ad fontes

INTRODUCTION

Marcin Wodziński

Hasidism is undoubtedly one of the most powerful phenomena informing the modern history of European Jewry, and its historical and present roles have significant impacts on current public opinion and academic discourse.[1]

Its eighteenth-century beginnings did not necessarily foretell such a train of events. Its acknowledged founding father is the kabbalist, mystic, and folk healer R. Israel ben Eliezer (c. 1700–1760), known as the Baal Shem Tov (literally "the owner of the good name"), which was contracted to the Besht. He began his career as a preacher and healer around 1736 in Podolia in the southeastern part of the Polish-Lithuanian Commonwealth. The group of kabbalists associated with him, as well as their disciples and disciples of the disciples, became the genesis of a new movement named Hasidism (from the Hebrew word *ḥasid*—pious). However, the transformation of this initial group into a real mass movement did not take place before the end of the eighteenth century.

Like other mystical Jewish confraternities of the time, Hasidism drew extensively on earlier kabbalistic traditions, especially as developed in Palestinian Safed, the so-called Lurianic Kabbalah, but also those from other Jewish esoteric traditions. However, this was not the hallmark of Hasidism. The elements that fundamentally distinguished the new Hasidism from related mystical groupings were an emphatic antiascetic attitude and an interest in the broad propagation of mystical ideals. It can be assumed that it was precisely such an egalitarian ideology and its associated social platform that were decisive in Hasidism's eventual success (of course, premodern egalitarianism needs to be understood in its context and limitations, i.e., with exclusion of the poor, women, and many other underprivileged groups). In the face of the liquidation or significant weakening of the *kehalim* (local Jewish communities), in the face of their disempowerment by the state with replacement religious supervision, in the face of constant control—often harassment—of all official social and religious structures, Hasidism offered alternative, autonomous structures of Jewish collective life. The charismatic Hasidic leader, the tsadik, gradually replaced the state-nominated rabbi; the tsadik's court replaced the kahal that had been disbanded by the civil authorities; the social safety net focused on the tsadik replaced the disbanded confraternities and disempowered charitable associations. With time, as Hasidim managed to gain a dominant position in many local Jewish communities in Galicia, Ukraine, and the Kingdom of Poland (Congress Poland), Hasidic institutions began to fill a supplementary position vis-à-vis the kahal, instead of creating alternative structures. Significantly, Hasidism operated as a completely voluntary and transterritorial structure, not limited by local or city boundaries or by the control of state institutions. In this sense Hasidism was a voluntary modern movement par excellence: it skillfully used the opportunities created by the modern states to escape from the coercive power of the premodern kahal (a quintessentially feudal structure) and to create a transterritorial and voluntary association not limited by premodern privileges. In the course of the nineteenth century, Hasidism also developed into a skillful political player, effectively defending its rights and interests with the means provided by the modern states. In other words, Hasidism, even if ideologically antimodernist, became an active, fully engaged, and savvy participant of the modernizing processes that the Jewish community of Eastern Europe underwent in the long nineteenth century.[2]

We cannot precisely state how extensive Hasidism was at any period of its existence. The widely repeated estimates that supposedly it had conquered almost all of Eastern Europe by the end of the eighteenth century are undoubtedly a great exaggeration. Initially, its adherents formed a small mystical group active in the southeastern border regions of the commonwealth, in Podolia and Volhynia, and then in Galicia, in southern Belarus, and in central Poland. It appears that the apogee of Hasidic influence occurred around the mid- to late nineteenth century, when in Galicia and some regions of central Poland Hasidim represented more than half the local Jewish population. At the same time, Hasidism expanded the sphere of its influence into Hungary and Romania. While of course not all Jews living in Eastern Europe were followers of the movement, the attractiveness of its social platform meant that it affected the lifestyles not only of its followers and their families but also of just about all the other Jews in the region. Over the course of a great many succeeding decades, the Hasidic image, norms of behavior, system of values and meaning, and even folk tales, tunes, and highbrow and lowbrow literature intensively combined to create the culture of East European Jewry.

The end of the nineteenth century, and especially the time of World War I, created a crisis for the movement. New political challenges, industrialization, urbanization, and mass migration led to a gradual decline in numbers. However, the influence of Hasidism remained very distinct, and the greatest Hasidic leaders of the time, especially the tsadikim of Ger (Góra Kalwaria) and Alexander (Aleksandrów), supposedly had more than 100,000 followers between the wars.

The tragic end of East European Hasidism, as indeed of almost the whole of Jewish life in Europe, was the Holocaust. Humiliated, brutalized, and finally murdered en masse, Hasidim were often the first victims of Nazi crimes, due to their traditional appearance. The overwhelming majority of Hasidim perished. Despite this, the Hasidic world survived and managed to revive. After 1945, small, decimated, and scattered groups began to gather again around handfuls of surviving tsadikim or their descendants. Over time the Hasidic movement managed to create vibrant centers in the United States, Israel, Canada, and several European enclaves. Today, New York, with the largest population, is home to around 190,000 Hasidim, about 90,000 live in Jerusalem, and close to 30,000 are in London. Altogether, the current global Hasidic community is estimated at 700,000 to 750,000 people. Thanks to its followers' distinctive dress, visibility, and political influence, Hasidism is without a doubt the most visible and recognizable Jewish religious group, and perhaps one of the most recognizable religious groups in the world.

It is, therefore, understandable that Hasidism is one of the most intensively studied aspects of the history and culture of Jewish Eastern Europe, and now also of Judaism in the United States and Israel. Indeed, today academic monographs published in English, Hebrew, and other languages on virtually all aspects of Hasidism are legion.[3]

The first academic works dealing with the history of Hasidism were already appearing in the early phase of Jewish German historiography in the first half of the nineteenth century, above all in the works of Marcus Jost (1793–1860) and Heinrich Graetz (1817–1891).[4] The context of this early interest was the anti-Hasidic polemics emanating from the circle of *mitnagedim* (rabbinical opponents of Hasidism), as well as from the *maskilim* (supporters of the Jewish Enlightenment). For both groups Hasidism represented a radically different vision of the world and the social order; hence, they used hyperbolic attacks to represent it as a real threat. The works of German Jewish authors of the Wissenschaft des Judentums group drew heavily on this tradition. They also staked out a basic direction for the first phase of the historiography of Hasidism. These historians' modest sources were mainly the anti-Hasidic writings of the *mitnagedim* and maskilim. The violently anti-Hasidic writings of the Belarusian preacher Israel Löbel and the Galician maskil Josef Perl defined the image of Hasidism in the first two generations of historians of Hasidism.[5] Other sources, for instance Hasidic rabbinical literature (sermons, tracts), were not widely used, and it seems that in place of these texts the aforementioned historians studied instead excerpts provided by East European maskilim. The natural result of this use of the sources was a rather one-sided, negative picture of the Hasidic movement, and the speculative nature of the analysis presented by Jost and Graetz. The long-term result was also that anti-Hasidic diatribes became one of the basic sources of knowledge of Hasidism for succeeding generations of historians, and to a certain extent they have shaped the methodological approach toward Hasidism to this day. In chapters 4 and 5 we will reinvestigate these *mitnagedic* and maskilic sources, seeking ways to understand their usefulness and their limitations, and to use them without falling into the trap of their polemical nature.

A real shift in academic interest in Hasidism is associated above all with the work of Simon Dubnow (1860–1941).[6] Dubnow's most acknowledged innovation in relation to the earlier German writers was an interpretation of Jewish history, including the history of Hasidism, along the nationalist (although not Zionist) lines of Jewish historiography. This feature became the trademark of many subsequent historians of Hasidism.[7] But no less important was Dubnow's methodological awareness of source criticism in general and the nature and implications of the sources used for the research of Hasidism in particular. His critical analysis of the sources, to which he devoted a separate section of his monumental *Toledot ha-ḥasidut*, has become the most important discussion of sources in the study of Hasidism to this day.[8] Starting with Dubnow, sources typical of modern historiography (archival material, including archives of Hasidic groups, documents from local Jewish communities, state archives) are gradually beginning to appear more frequently in research into Hasidism. In addition, Dubnow and his successors used Hasidic literature, including hagiographical and Hasidic folk tales, as well as—following in their predecessors' footsteps—anti-Hasidic literature.

Alongside the studies of Graetz, Dubnow, and their successors, research into the history of Hasidic doctrine has been developing. They have often been perceived as in competition with the methodological line represented by the historians mentioned above, which we now understand as early attempts at social history. Criticism of Graetz's and Dubnow's grand narratives and of their simplified cause-and-effect models was in any event well justified. Historians of ideas have rightly indicated that Hasidism is above all a religious system, and that a description of it should take into account categories appropriate to religious studies, and should avoid simple, mechanistic interpretive models. At the same time, this type of criticism has shaped the divide in studies of Hasidism between intellectual history and social history that exists to this day, as well as the accompanying methodological, source, and even institutional divides.

The common features of research under the banner of intellectual history have been a shift toward Hasidic doctrine, an analysis of it in the context of traditional Jewish religious literature, especially the mystical and messianic tradition, and an interest in the teachings (and to a certain extent the lives) of the most eminent representatives of Hasidic thought, among them R. Shneur Zalman of

Lady, R. Naḥman of Bratslav (Bracław), and R. Menaḥem Mendel of Kock. (The biographical approach was a perspective common to the different schools of research into Hasidism.)[9] In this sense the "Hasidism" of historians of ideas was closer to Hasidism's own image of itself than was the "Hasidism" of the social historians, which was to a large extent shaped by polemical writings.

The most distinguished representative and symbol of the work on Hasidism by the intellectual history school was Gershom Scholem (1897–1982).[10] His unquestioned authority as the greatest expert on Jewish mystical movements, and also as an influential intellectual, undoubtedly forged a path for similar work under the banner of intellectual history. Despite this, as has rightly been pointed out, this school's decisive breakthroughs have also become its limitations. Above all, focusing on Jewish religious tradition has unprofitably limited interest in the broader sociopolitical context of the Hasidic movement, whether within the Jewish community or, more generally, within the context of the non-Jewish world of Eastern Europe, and in the twentieth century also of Israel and the United States. The same applies to the methodologies used in research into Hasidism. Hasidism's clearly religious character does not mean that the movement has no social, political, cultural, or economic features extending beyond its religious character, and thus no measurable tools appropriate to disciplines other than intellectual history. Finally, perhaps the most important unhelpful tendency has been (and often is) to limit the field of studied sources principally to printed Hebrew and Yiddish religious, Hasidic, and anti-Hasidic texts, thus to sources typical of scholars of intellectual history. This has resulted in a one-sided and fragmentary image of the studied phenomenon, not just plucked from its natural historical context but also locked into a circle of the rabbinical cultural elite's texts and ideas.[11]

Current research into Hasidism aims to identify and fill these gaps. The result has been a wave of publications devoted to Hasidism in the nineteenth century or during the Holocaust, to the sociology and anthropology of modern Hasidism, to the Hasidic movement's political characteristics, or to an analysis of its gender framework. Although each of these approaches is fragmentary and one-sided, all of them together aim to erase an essentially artificial distinction between interests under the banners of intellectual and social history.[12] New research investigates, for example, the correlation between social forms of the Hasidic movement and its ideology, or between economic theory and practice of the Hasidic communities, strongly pointing to their mutual dependence. A good example is the prosopographic study by Uriel Gellman, who analyzed Hasidic leadership in central Poland between the 1780s and the 1830s, focusing on the interrelation of the teachings and social structures adopted by Hasidism in Poland.[13] Similarly, new studies of the performative aspect of Hasidism underlie the significance of religious practices as a form of religious teaching.[14] The most important and most frequently emphasized element of current research is the integration of various approaches to what is after all the many-faceted phenomenon of Hasidism.[15]

A similar goal inspired this volume. We hope that a systematic discussion of the sources and methods typical of both the intellectual and the social history, as well as of many other disciplines, will allow for better inclusion of the research methods avoided by many practitioners of these two competitive approaches, or at least will allow for their better mutual understanding. What is more, we hope that the introduction of new sources and methods will permit researchers to overpass the artificial binary opposition between these two approaches and to take into account other perspectives, characteristic of, inter alia, literary studies, historical sociology, or digital humanities.

A good example of such an overpassing of methodological limitations is the contemporary study of the gender structure of the Hasidic world and the role of women in Hasidism. As I discussed extensively in another place, until the beginning of the twentieth century, women were systematically excluded from the institutionally defined Hasidic community. But this, as in many other traditional cultures, did not exclude other forms of their alternative association.[16] Some women were evidently interested in and sympathetic to at least some aspects of Hasidic life. The best examples of this are women who adopted or introduced into their homes certain customs that can be shown to be distinctly Hasidic, or those who visited the courts of the tsadikim, or those who urged their husbands to travel to the tsadik and become a Hasid. The phenomenon is so far unexplored. Until recently, scholars believed that sources that would allow for any reliable analyses of this phenomenon did not exist. However, the tools of feminist analysis, women's studies, and gender studies have shown how widespread the possibilities are, if only one asks the right questions. Studies by Ada Rapoport-Albert show, for example, the changing role of women in twentieth-century Chabad Hasidism, from total exclusion, through women as full-fledged Hasidim, up to the ideal of a female tsadik.[17] Of all topics, the women who reached for the power of the tsadik were possibly the single most appealing research object to the scholars of the female constituency in Hasidism.[18] This, however, seems to me a somewhat misguided approach to the study of the gender structure of the Hasidic movement. The fact that some exceptional women occasionally played atypical roles tells us nothing about the position of most women within the overall structure of the movement, or their share in the experience of its numerous adherents within their own places of residence, far away from the centers of Hasidism. Much more instructive to me are the examples analyzed in this volume, which explore the ways women informed their different roles in and attitudes toward the Hasidic world. The ego-documents discussed in chapter 6 show, for example, Pauline Wengeroff completely indifferent to her husband's Hasidic affiliation, and by implication they show that the Hasidic husband's affiliation did not have to affect his wife's religious attitude. Similarly, the iconography analyzed by Maya Balakirsky Katz (chapter 10) allows for insight into the gender divisions of the Hasidic world: both where gender lines run within the Hasidic world, and where they ran for the Hasidim when they looked at the world external. A meticulous analysis of Hasidic material culture (chapter 12) reveals the differences between female and male prayer rooms, burial spaces, and dress. Many other analyses reveal the gender patterns of Hasidic narrations, roles assigned permanently to women and men in the Hasidic world, such as that which we see in chapter 7, on folk narratives. Similarly, one finds a number of gender categories that define Hasidic roles in a fascinating narrative by Puah Rakovsky telling the family story of a Hasidic attack on her grandfather and a transgender masquerade to compromise him (see more in chapter 6).

A no less significant trend of current work on Hasidism as the drive to employ new methodologies is an attempt to expand the source base. Most current work tries to use a differentiated body of sources, from the most typical Hasidic tales and rabbinical literature by way of polemical writings and belles lettres, to archival sources, the press, memoirs, and so on. It is not just a question of individual sources, but rather of new categories of sources, hitherto entirely neglected. While of course this does not cover all works and all types of sources, it appears that this shift is potentially the most significant. It is indeed the primary inspiration for this work.

By far the greatest number of studies hitherto done on Hasidism have been shaped by recurrent methodological and source approaches. Social historians naturally reach for the tools of social history, and, in terms of sources, mainly for archival materials, the press, and if need be memoirs. Historians of ideas use that discipline's methodology, making religious tracts by the Hasidic rabbinical elite, polemical texts, and—least frequently—popular literature the objects of analysis. Both of them to a very minor degree use halakhic literature, iconographical materials, and cartographical sources.[19] Anthropologists and sociologists use above all surveys, field research, and census data. But, like historians of ideas and social historians, they barely use folklore or musical sources, visual materials, or material artifacts. And so on. Each of these approaches is to some extent limiting. This is precisely the main theme of this textbook: source possibilities in the study of Hasidism are still vast, and past research has not used many first-rate types of sources.

A fuller introduction of new sources into the methodological approach to Hasidism is essential not just for building a more complete source base, and thus supplementing the factual element. As we shall try to show in this volume, new sources also reveal new issues, new avenues of research, and, more importantly, possibilities of new methodological approaches. A good example is the ostensibly minor discovery made by Moshe Rosman in the archives in 1979 that had spectacular methodological consequences for the historiography of Hasidism. Among the entries in the tax files for the town of Międzybóż, Rosman discovered among others "Doktor Balszam"—that is, the Besht, the putative founder of Hasidism.[20] This apparently modest finding allowed for a radical revaluation of the basic ideas about the Besht and early Hasidism. Lodged in the community's house at the expense of the kahal, titled "doctor," the Besht certainly was not a poor outsider or a rebel fighting against existing religious structures. On the contrary, he was a respected member of the rabbinical elite, and the kabbalistic group gathered around him was no different from other such groups (*kloyzn*) existing in many communities of the Polish-Lithuanian Commonwealth. Further, as Rosman points out clearly, Międzybóż was not a small shtetl, but an important trade center and a large Jewish community. The conclusions from this discovery drawn by Rosman, and even more from a critical analysis of the remaining sources on the Besht's life, were criticized by many scholars opting for traditional methods of source analysis.[21] The debate concerned, in particular, the credibility of the late and hagiographical sources that Rosman essentially questioned and proposed to be treated as auxiliary sources for other, more credible testimonies. In essential disagreement, more traditional researchers have seen in them, first of all, a late record of authentic traditions dating back to the time of the Besht. For them, these late materials are not only the nineteenth-century reworking of the images of the historic Besht, but also his actual life stories. Disagreement notwithstanding, these polemical voices were indebted to Rosman in their problematizing the source analysis and engagement into the discussion of the relation between source basis and research results. More importantly, however, Rosman's work has led to a number of fundamental questions being asked on the research tools used in studies of Hasidism, on these studies' source bases, on methods for critiquing the sources, and above all on ways of using hagiographical literature and late sources. It showed, too, that new sources of decisive significance continue to be accessible, and that they may exist in the most obvious places, to which no scholar has hitherto turned.[22]

Over the last twenty years, many new studies have followed a similar path. The change has in part a natural generational character (new researchers reach for new sources), and also a geographic one that is associated with a greater openness of these younger scholars to possible resources in Eastern Europe. The changes they have collectively introduced can be summarized in four points.

First, scholars have made an effort to deconstruct successive stereotypes present in studies of Hasidism, for instance on the subject of events invented by later Hasidic hagiography. These studies' principal thrust is to verify late and hagiographical sources, re-creating the process of building legends and thus getting to their roots.[23] In terms of methodology, these studies are inspired by a postmodernist awareness of the textuality of sources and the constructed nature of discourse, but they also ultimately refer to a neopositivist vision of historiography as a discipline embedded in an empirical reality beyond the text, which the scholar is aiming to discover.

Second, in recent years a methodological effort has also been underway, which aims to develop tools to enhance the ability to use the sources called into question by Rosman, above all Hasidic stories, in a technically reliable way. Rosman has proposed abandoning the principle of reliability of sources and asking instead about their usability.[24] In other words, he proposes departure from the classical categories of the historical source criticism, pointing out that "every source is biased."[25] This observation, clearly inspired by postmodern criticism of sources' textuality, leads Rosman to conclude that "there is no such thing as a typical source, and certainly no platonic ideal source. Every source genre and each source have limitations and strengths,"[26] thus every source is by nature limited in its reliability. The fundamental question of the historical craft is, thus, how can we use a source that we know is inherently unreliable? In response, Rosman suggests we should not look for "reliable" sources, but rather for ways to use them as they are, despite their limitations.

Similar debates are taking place on the usability of archival sources, discredited en bloc by some scholars as unreliable "official sources."[27] Here, criticism of "official sources" resorts to the ethnic stereotypes according to which state authorities, or any non-Jewish representatives for that matter, have been essentially driven by their inherent antisemitism and ignorance in matters of Jewish life and culture, which should render all the sources they generate irrelevant. Even if the antisemitism of many of those figures is unquestionable, this oversimplified reasoning does not give justice to the variety of sources and their varying utility. As I have written more extensively elsewhere, archival documents related to Hasidism may be divided into a number of very distinct categories. There are official correspondences generated in connection with formal administrative proceedings, protocols of administrative investigations that record relatively autonomous statements by interrogated individuals, various sorts of letters or memos received from Jewish institutions and individuals, such as formal petitions from kehalim or self-appointed representatives of the Jewish community, official curricula vitae and applications or petitions, government-commissioned reports, and a number of anonymous letters, petitions, and denunciations. Lastly, one can find numerous documents produced by Jewish community representatives for their community's internal use, without relation to the public administration. Some documents of this type, among them tax letters, lampoons, and rabbinic contracts, would fall into state officials' hands, whether through the agency of offended rivals or merely as extra pieces of documentation attached to other official materials. This variety of genres and communicative contexts defines the differing status of these documents, which cannot be summarized under an oversimplifying category of "official records." The archival documents represent almost any and all of the possible standpoints regarding the Hasidic movement and all possible sources of origin. Each such piece of documentation should be subject to analysis in its appropriate context.[28] We will return to this topic in greater detail in chapter 8. Here let me only mention the fascinating research by Agnieszka Jagodzińska, who proved that sources as biased and unreliable as reports by the Protestant missionaries aiming to convert Polish Jews bring invaluable insights into the life, customs, and beliefs of nineteenth-century Polish Hasidim, insights that no other source can offer.[29]

Third, new research recalls the significance of classic tools of critical editing of sources and linguistic analysis of texts. Hitherto, relatively few classic Hasidic sources, whether rabbinical literature, Hasidic tales, or others, have appeared in critical editions, while often editions purporting to be academic do not meet the criteria of a real critical edition. Effectively, many basic Hasidic texts are used by scholars in popular editions, and even in editions modified by Hasidic publishers for modern religious needs. Academic conclusions drawn on the basis of such editions naturally cannot be fully reliable. An excellent example of this is the startling discovery by Daniel Reiser, who subjected to critical analysis a manuscript by the tsadik of Piaseczno, R. Kalonymos Kalman Shapira, of the most famous collection of sermons from the Warsaw ghetto. Reiser proves that all studies made hitherto of R. Shapira's sermons used an edition that did not take advantage of the tools of textual analysis, thus collating the sermons incorrectly, and in many places reading the text against its actual meaning. Meanwhile, the surviving manuscript had been freely available in the archives of the Jewish Historical Institute in Warsaw, and scholars of R. Shapira had shown no interest whatsoever in it. Reiser shows that a critical edition of these sermons takes us back to the start of research into R. Shapira's thinking. If sermons were written in a different order than previously assumed, it calls into question nearly all the prevailing opinions on the subject of the dynamics of the intellectual development of this important Hasidic author.[30]

Finally, the fourth thread of changes in awareness and knowledge of sources by modern scholars of Hasidism aims to expand the range of categories of sources used. Among the works illustrating this trend, we can name the studies of Levi Cooper and others on halakhic texts.[31] This discovery is striking given that rabbinical literature appears hitherto to have been the most intensively exploited Hasidic source. Despite this, as Cooper demonstrates, within it there are categories that have until now almost in their entirety escaped scholars' attention, despite their obvious value to research into Hasidism. Somewhat more generally, Cooper's work can be included in this growing literary awareness of rabbinical genres: a wave of analyses of Hasidic texts as conditioned by their genre. His research also demonstrates how new sources and new research exceed the artificial opposition of the intellectual and social history: Cooper convincingly shows that rabbinic decisions reflect both on the theology of Hasidic leaders and on everyday practices and lives of many rank-and-file Hasidim.

But Cooper is certainly not alone. The work of Maya Balakirsky Katz on the visual culture of Chabad is an even more radical innovation in terms of types of sources used.[32] Her work illustrates well that new types of sources are linked to new questions and, above all, to the introduction of new research methods, in this case an anthropological analysis of image.

My own work on the geography of Hasidism belongs to this same current. Although the actual question about the spatial dimensions of the Hasidic movement is not new, the tools introduced into the humanities by the spatial turn, and especially the tools of the digital humanities, allow us to ask the question again and to turn to radically new methods of research. And this suggests completely new types of quantitative sources. The largest database created for the needs of a historical atlas of Hasidism records almost 130,000 Hasidic households in twelve hundred locations on six continents (for more on this see chapter 13). Similarly, one microlevel map of pilgrims who traveled to one investigated Hasidic court is based on a collection of around sixty-three hundred petitions delivered to a particular Hasidic leader in the 1870s. In other words, rich and valuable historical resources might be easily available for research.[33]

Furthermore, as has been emphasized above, new sources not only supplement the existing database with new detail but also indicate new, hitherto unknown aspects of the phenomenon being studied. Quantitative sources on the subject of the geography of Hasidism demonstrate, for instance, the dependence of the Hasidic movement on its spatial conditions not only in its social organization and political context but also in its spiritual life, type of religious leadership, and cultural articulation—that is, in the movement's most intimate inner characteristics.

This precise thread of source-based thinking appears to be the most promising, for it opens up the greatest number of new paths: to new, unknown materials and information but also to new perspectives and new research methodologies. This textbook sets itself a task: to assemble and tidy up knowledge of existing sources for studying the history and culture of Hasidism with regard to their types, associated research practices, methodologies, and research approaches used and not used.

Of course, no book is able to discuss all sources. Here, in thirteen chapters we have collected information about the most typical, most frequently used, and—in our opinion—the most important, most sizable, and potentially groundbreaking source materials for historical research of Hasidism. The book starts with a discussion of sources traditionally used most frequently in studies on Hasidism, above all homiletic literature. This chapter is supplemented by another one devoted to halakhic writing. As has been already mentioned, this chapter is in some respects surprising: although rabbinic literature has long been the most typical source in the study of Hasidism, chapter 2 shows that some genres of rabbinic literature by the Hasidic masters, in this case halakhic literature, remain almost unknown. The following chapter, on Hasidic stories, returns to canonical sources, as do the two subsequent chapters, which are devoted to the literature by the *mitnagedim* and the maskilim as the two types of non-Hasidic texts that informed the image of Hasidism in the most persuasive way.

Starting from chapter 6, we discuss slightly less obvious types of sources, although many of them are by no means obscure. These are chapters about ego-documents, folklore narratives, archival materials, press, iconography, music, material culture, and big data. The list is not complete, of course. It does not contain, for example, the types of sources used intensively in sociological or anthropological research but poorly incorporated into historical research. The most prominent example of this is field work. Some potential chapters have not been written for the simple fact that there was no one to write them. This happened with a chapter on intra-Hasidic archival collections: four researchers refused to write about it, arguably due to the particular difficulty of summarizing the state of knowledge in the area. Despite these shortcomings, this book discusses almost all the most important types of sources used so far in historical studies on Hasidism and those that are still used insufficiently, but contemporary historians have special hopes for them. In this sense, the book is complete with regard to sources so far typically used in historical Hasidic studies and those that in recent years have emerged as important and promising.

Certainly, in the future, researchers will investigate new types of sources and will expand this list. Already today we can imagine several such types: correspondence, the non-Jewish press, non-Jewish literature. Among the prominent examples of the latter, one can list fascinating descriptions of the Hasidic court in Sadagura penned by the well-known Austrian writer Leopold Sacher-Masoch, or equally fascinating descriptions of Hasidism in the first novel in Polish literature on Jewish themes, *Lejbe and Sióra* (1822), by Julian Ursyn Niemcewicz, an almost perfect paraphrase of the most famous anti-Hasidic text of the Haskalah: an epistolary novel titled *Megale temirin* (1821), by Josef Perl.[34] All these and many other unmentioned literary texts are excellent sources for the reconstruction of non-Jewish perceptions of Hasidism, but also for the verification of knowledge about aspects of Hasidic life, customs, and beliefs (although using them requires reaching for the tools and methods of literary analysis, still an uncharted path for many traditional historians).

I do not think, however, that expanding the list of chapters with new types of sources, which may become important in the future, would be worthwhile at the moment. First, as mentioned on a number of occasions, it is simply impossible to list all possible sources. Any attempt at making the list complete, or even comprehensive, would deserve rightful criticism about omitting still more obscure types of sources. Second, a unique feature of this volume is that it shows not only types of sources but much more: it shows how sources treated as irrelevant become relevant when approached with proper research questions and proper methodologies. Each of the chapters in this volume provides one or more such explication of the innovative use of the sources. Without this, the list would be meaningless. We are not yet at the stage to show such relevance for any significant group of materials that this volume has not covered.

The book is aimed at two types of readers. First, it is an aid for students to find their way around the basic kinds of sources for the history of Hasidism, their usability, accessibility, limitations, and hitherto untapped potential; it thus aims to show possibilities for future directions of research. In this sense the textbook is a source-based teaching aid aimed at students at all levels of academic education. It can be used equally for studying the history of Hasidism and of other related subjects, as well as for source-based exercises to bring students closer to the secrets for using a range of historical sources. Providing information on types of sources, their specifics, and the possible ways of using them, this work aims to help in tidying up this knowledge, as well as in a more general way to help in changing Hasidism's image and the ways we teach about it.

This is done, too, by an analysis of a chosen source—an important part of each chapter. Each chapter contains at least one document that illustrates the cognitive possibilities of the type of source covered therein. Each small case study demonstrates some interesting and instructive example from the history of Hasidism and can also be used as instructional material for teaching both about Hasidism itself and about the specific category of source. The accompanying commentary helps in using the case study.

We are also convinced that this textbook will be a useful resource for advanced scholars of Hasidism, Jewish culture, and Judaism. Doubtless many scholars will have much more to say about one or several types of sources that they typically use in their academic work—much more than we can present in a book with thirteen necessarily short chapters. The research segmentation referred to earlier between intellectual history, social history, anthropology, and sociology means, however, that scholars typically use on a day-to-day basis only one type of source, or maybe a few types, skipping a great many others. This often means that even when they would like to use other types of sources, these are not readily accessible, their usability is not apparent, and the tools needed to analyze them are not obvious. This textbook's aim is to make these other types and ways of using them accessible to those who hitherto have not used them. Thus, each chapter presents information on the specifics of the type of source, its most important collections, significant publications of critical editions, typical and atypical ways of using the source in research on Hasidism, its major limitations, both general and specifically for research on Hasidism, and—finally—exemplary scholarly publications based on the type of source in research on Hasidism and related areas. An emphasis on atypical use aims to indicate the possibilities of using sources precisely where typically they are not used, and thus aims to expand their application. Furthermore, part of the chapters discuss sources hitherto poorly represented, or in fact skipped, in research into Hasidism, hence new also for many advanced scholars of Hasidism. Each chapter is also equipped with a short annotated bibliography.

We hope that all of this means that the book we are offering the reader will be a valuable teaching and academic resource. We trust that it will introduce new students to the secrets of using sources on the history of Hasidism, and that it will illuminate for experienced scholars new ways of expanding their source base and of bringing in new sources, methods, and research perspectives, or will at least provide tools for attaining better insight into other methods of studying Hasidism.

NOTES

1. For the best introduction to the history and culture of Hasidism, see Shimon Dubnow, *Toledot ha-ḥasidut* (Tel Aviv: Dvir, 1967); Jean Baumgarten, *La naissance du hassidisme, Mystique, rituel et société (XVIIIe–XIXe siècles)* (Paris: Presses Universitaires de France, 2006); David Biale et al., *Hasidism: A New History* (Princeton, NJ: Princeton University Press, 2017); Marcin Wodziński, *Hasidism: Key Questions* (New York: Oxford University Press, 2018); Wodziński, *Historical Atlas of Hasidism* (Princeton, NJ: Princeton University Press, 2018).

2. On this, see Biale et al., *Hasidism: A New History*, 1–11; Moshe Rosman, "Hasidism as a Modern Phenomenon: The Paradox of Modernization without Secularization," *Jahrbuch des Simon-Dubnow-Instituts* 6 (2007), 215–224; Marcin Wodziński, "How Modern Is an Anti-Modernist Movement? The Emergence of Hasidic Politics in Congress Poland," *AJS Review* 31 (2007), 2:221–240.

3. Bibliographical essays summarizing the state of research can be found in Biale et al., *Hasidism: A New History*, 813–846; David Biale, "Hasidism," in *Oxford Bibliographies in Jewish Studies*, ed. N. Seidman (New York, 2015); Marcin Wodziński, "Hasidism in Poland," in *Oxford Bibliographies in Jewish Studies*, ed. N. Seidman (New York: Oxford University Press, 2016). Both are available online: http://www.oxfordbibliographies.com.

4. For the most influential of those, see Peter Beer, *Geschichte, Lehren und Meinungen aller bestandenen und noch bestehenden religiösen Sekten der Juden und der Geheimlehre oder Kabbalah* (Brünn: Trassler, 1823), 2:197–259; I[saak] M[arcus] Jost, *Geschichte der Israeliten seit der Zeit der Maccabäer bis auf unsere Tage* (Berlin: Schlesinger'sche Buch- und Musikhandlung, 1828), 9:40–57, 158–162; Jost, *Allgemeine Geschichte des Israelitischen Volkes, sowohl seines zweimaligen Staatslebens alsauch der zerstreuten Gemeinden und Secten, bis in die neueßte Zeit* (Berlin: Amelang, 1832), 2:467–486; H[einrich] Graetz, *Geschichte der Juden von den ältesten Zeiten bis auf die Gegenwart. Aus den Quellen neu bearbeitet von . . .*; vol. 11: *Geschichte der Juden vom Beginn der Mendelssohn'schen Zeit (1750) bis in die neueste Zeit (1848)* (Leipzig: O. Leiner, 1870), 102–126.

5. See Israel Löbel, "Glaubwürdige Nachricht von der in Polen und Lithauen befindlichen Sekte: Chasidim genannt," *Sulamith* 1/2 (1807), 5:308–333; Josef Perl, *Uiber das Wesen der Sekte Chassidim*, ed. A. Rubinstein (Jerusalem: The Israel Academy of Sciences and Humanities, 1977). On Israel Löbel, see Rachel Manekin, "A Jewish Lithuanian Preacher in the

Context of Religious Enlightenment: The Case of Israel Löbel," *Jewish Culture and History* 13 (2012), 134–152. See also Uriel Gellman, "Mitnagedim," in this volume.

6. Hebrew edition Dubnow, *Toledot ha-ḥasidut*; German edition *Geschichte des Chassidismus* (Berlin: Jüdischer Verlag, 1931).

7. Alongside Dubnow's still relevant research, the work of Benzion Dinur (1884–1973) and Raphael Mahler (1899–1977), who introduced Zionist and Marxist elements into analysis and descriptions of Hasidism, belongs to the most distinguished and also most distinctive achievements of this school. See, e.g., Benzion Dinur, *Be-mifneh ha-dorot* (Jerusalem: Mosad Bialik, 1972); partial English translation in Dinur, "The Origins of Hasidism and Its Social and Messianic Foundations," in *Essential Papers on Hasidism: Origins to Present*, ed. G. D. Hundert (New York: New York University Press, 1991), 86–208; Rafael Mahler, *Ha-ḥasidut veha-haskalah (be-Galitsyah uve-Polin ha-kongresa'it ba-maḥatsit ha-rishonah shel ha-me'ah ha-tesha-esre, ha-yesodot ha-sotsyaliyim veha-medinayim* (Merḥavia: Kibuts ha-artsi ha-shomer ha-tsa'ir, 1961); incomplete English translation in Raphael Mahler, *Hasidism and the Jewish Enlightenment: Their Confrontation in Galicia and Poland in the First Half of the Nineteenth Century*, trans. E. Orenstein, A. Klein, J. Machlowitz Klein (Philadelphia: Jewish Publication Society, 1985).

8. See Dubnow, *Toledot ha-ḥasidut*, 375–483.

9. See Naftali Loewenthal, *Communicating the Infinite: The Emergence of the Habad School* (Chicago: Chicago University Press, 1990); Rachel Elior, *The Paradoxical Ascent to God: The Kabbalistic Theosophy of Habad Hasidism*, trans. J. M. Green (Albany: State University of New York, 1993); Arthur Green, *Tormented Master: A Life of Rabbi Nahman of Bratslav* (Tuscaloosa: University of Alabama Press, 1979); Abraham Joshua Heschel, *A Passion for Truth* (New York: Sanhedrin Press, 1974).

10. Despite the fact that Scholem has left no concise work on Hasidism, many of his articles have had a key influence on the field; see, e.g., Gershom Scholem, "Devekut, or Communion with God," in *Essential Papers on Hasidism: Origins to Present*, 275–298; Scholem, "The Neutralisation of the Messianic Element in Early Hasidism," in *The Messianic Idea in Judaism and Other Essays on Jewish Spirituality* (New York: Scocken Books, 1971), 176–202; for the collected writing of Scholem on Hasidism, see Scholem, *Ha-shelav ha-aharon*, ed. D. Assaf and E. Liebes (Jerusalem: Am Oved, Magness Press, 2008). Together with Scholem, one should list Isaiah Tishby (1908–1992), Joseph Weiss (1918–1969), Joseph Dan (b. 1935), and Moshe Idel (b. 1947). See, e.g., Isaiah Tishby, "The Messianic Idea and Messianic Trends in the Growth of Hasidism," *Zion* 32 (1967), 1–45; Joseph Dan, *Ha-sipur ha-ḥasidi* (Jerusalem, 1975); Joseph George Weiss, *Studies in East European Jewish Mysticism and Hasidism*, ed. D. Goldstein (London: The Littman Library of Jewish Civilization, 1997); Moshe Idel, *Hasidism: Between Ecstasy and Magic* (Albany: State University of New York, 1995).

11. For more on this, see Wodziński, *Hasidism: Key Questions*, xxi–xxxi.

12. For a prominent expression of such a dichotomous view and, simultaneously, the call to overcome it, see Yohanan Petrovsky-Shtern, "*Hasidei de'ar'a* and *Hasidei dekokhvaya*': Two Trends in Modern Jewish Historiography," *AJS Review* 32 (2008), 1:141–167.

13. Uriel Gellman, *Ha-shevilim ha-yots'im mi-Lublin: Tsemiḥata shel ha-ḥasidut be-Polin* (Jerusalem: Zalman Shazar Center, 2018).

14. Gadi Sagiv, "Hasidism and Cemetery Inauguration Ceremonies: Authority, Magic, and Performance of Charismatic Leadership," *Jewish Quarterly Review* 103 (2013), 3:328–351; Tsippi Kauffman, "Hasidic Performance: Establishing a Religious (Non)Identity in the Tales about Rabbi Zusha of Annopol," *The Journal of Religion* 95 (2015), 51–71.

15. Particularly valuable in this regard are new studies integrating thoughts on the ideological nature of leadership with research into the social workings of the tsadik and the Hasidic leadership structure. For an early study of this kind, see Immanuel Etkes, "The Zaddik: The Interrelationship between Religious Doctrine and Social Organization," in

Hasidism Reappraised, ed. A. Rapoport-Albert (London: The Littman Library of Jewish Civilization, 1996), 159–167. For most contemporary approaches of this kind, see, e.g., Gadi Sagiv, *Ha-shoshelet: Bet Chernobyl u-mekomo be-toledot ha-ḥasidut* (Jerusalem: Zalman Shazar Center, 2014). For a sociological attempt at similar integration of doctrinal and institutional perspectives, see Justin Jaron Lewis and William Shaffir, "Tosh, between Earth and Moon: A Hasidic Rebbe's Followers and His Teachings," in *From Antiquity to the Postmodern World: Contemporary Jewish Studies in Canada*, ed. D. Maoz and A. Gondos (Newcastle upon Tyne: Cambridge Scholars Publishing, 2011), 139–170.

16. See Wodziński, *Hasidism: Key Questions*, 43–85.

17. Ada Rapoport-Albert, "On Women in Hasidism: S. A. Horodecky and the Maid of Ludmir Tradition," in *Jewish History: Essays in Honour of Chimen Abramsky*, ed. A. Rapoport-Albert and S. J. Zipperstein (London: Halban, 1988), 495–525; Rapoport-Albert, "The Emergence of a Female Constituency in Twentieth-Century Habad Hasidism," in *Yashan mi-penei ḥadash: Shai le-Immanuel Etkes*, 1: *Ḥasidim u-va'alei musar*, ed. D. Assaf and A. Rapoport-Albert (Jerusalem: Zalman Shazar Center, 2009), English section [denoted by *], 7–68*; Rapoport-Albert, "From Woman as Hasid to Woman as 'Tsadik' in the Teachings of the Last Two Lubavitcher Rebbes," *Jewish History* 27 (2013), 2–4:435–473.

18. Yoram Bilu, "The Woman Who Wanted to Be Her Father: A Case Analysis of Dibbuk Possession in a Hasidic Community," *Journal of Psychoanalytical Anthropology* 8 (1985), 1:11–27; Justin Jaron Lewis, "'Eydele, the Rebbe': Shifting Perspectives on a Jewish Gender Transgressor," *Journal of Modern Jewish Studies* 6 (2007), 1:21–40; Nathaniel Deutsch, *The Maiden of Ludmir: A Jewish Holy Woman and Her World* (Berkeley: University of California Press, 2003).

19. For a rare example of an interesting insight into the intellectual history of Hasidism drawn from a cartographical discovery, see Nathaniel Deutsch, "New Archival Sources on the Maiden of Ludmir," *Jewish Social Studies* 9 (2002), 1:164–172.

20. See Moshe Rosman, *Founder of Hasidism: A Quest for the Historical Baal Shem Tov*, 2nd ed. (Oxford: The Littman Library of Jewish Civilization, 2013 [originally published in 1996]).

21. See, e.g., Immanuel Etkes, "The Historical Besht: Reconstruction or Deconstruction?" *Polin* 12 (1999), 297–306; Haviva Pedaya, "Bikoret al M. Rosman *Ha-Besht: Meḥadesh ha-ḥasidut*," *Zion* 69 (2004), 515–524.

22. Rosman's own summing up of the debate in Moshe Rosman, "Introduction to the Paperback Edition," in *Founder of Hasidism*, XIII–LXI.

23. For a good illustration, see Uriel Gellman, 'Ha-ḥatunah ha-gedolah be-Ustila: Gilgulav shel mitos ḥasidi," *Tarbiz* 80 (2013), 4:567–594. Compare, too, the extensive literature on the subject of an anti-Hasidic investigation in 1824 in Ezriel N. Frenk, "Yekhezkel Hoge oder 'Haskel Meshumad,'" in Frenk, *Meshumadim in Poylen in 19ten yohrhundert* (Warsaw: Freid, 1923), 38–110; Mahler, *Hasidism and the Jewish Enlightenment*, 317–337; Beth-Zion Lask Abrahams, "Stanislaus Hoga: Apostate and Penitent," *Jewish Historical Society of England. Transactions* 15 (1939–1945), 121–149; Yehudah Menaḥem Boim, *Ha-rabi rebe Bunem mi-Peshisḥah: Toledot ḥayav, sipurim, minhagim, siḥot* (Bnei Brak: Torat Simcha, 1997), 2:633–636; Marcin Wodziński, *Hasidism and Politics: The Kingdom of Poland, 1815–1864* (Oxford and Portland: The Littman Library of Jewish Civilization, 2013). For a hagiographical image of R. Yitzḥak Kalisz of Warka confronted with historical reality, see Marcin Wodziński, "Hasidism, *Shtadlanut*, and Jewish Politics in Nineteenth Century Poland: The Case of Isaac of Warka," *Jewish Quarterly Review* 96 (2005), 2:290–320.

24. See Moshe Rosman, "Hebrew Sources on the Baal Shem Tov: Usability vs. Reliability," *Jewish History* 27 (2013), 153–169; Rosman, "In Praise of the Ba'al Shem Tov: A User's Guide to the Editions of *Shivḥei haBesht*," *Polin* 10 (1997), 183–199. See also Glenn Dynner, "The Hasidic Tale as a Historical Source: Historiography and Methodology," *Religion Compass* 3 (2009), 4:655–675.

25. Rosman, "Hebrew Sources on the Baal Shem Tov," 154.

26. Ibid.

27. See, e.g., Petrovsky-Shtern, "*Hasidei de'ar'a* and *Hasidei dekokhvaya*'"; Glenn Dynner, "How Many *Hasidim* Were There Really in Congress Poland? A Response to Marcin Wodziński," *Gal-ed* 20 (2006), 91–104.

28. *Źródła do dziejów chasydyzmu w Królestwie Polskim, 1815–1867, w zasobach polskich archiwów państwowych*, ed. M. Wodziński (Kraków: Wydawnictwo Austeria, Institute for the History of Polish Jewry and Israel-Poland Relations, Tel Aviv University, 2011), 529.

29. Agnieszka Jagodzińska, "'English Missionaries' Look at Polish Jews: The Value and Limitations of Missionary Reports as Source Material," *Polin* 27 (2014), 89–116.

30. Daniel Reiser, "*Esh Kodesh*: A New Evaluation in Light of a Philological Examination of the Manuscript," *Yad Vashem Studies* 44 (2016), 1:65–97; see also Kalonymos Kalman Shapira, *Derashot mi-shenot ha-za'am: Derashot ha-admor mi-Piasechno be-geto Varsha*, ed. D. Reiser (Jerusalem: Miklalat ha-akademit Herzog, 2017).

31. See, e.g., Levi Cooper, *Ha-admor me-Munkach ha-rav Ḥayim Ele'azar Shapira: Ha-posek ha-ḥasidi* (Ramat Gan: Bar Ilan University Press, 2011); Cooper, "Bitter Herbs in Hasidic Galicia," *Jewish Studies Internet Journal* 12 (2013), 1–40. See also chapter 2 in this volume.

32. See Maya Balakirsky Katz, *The Visual Culture of Chabad* (New York and Cambridge: Cambridge University Press, 2010). See, too, studies of Hasidic material culture: Batsheva Goldman Ida, *Hasidic Art and the Kabbalah* (Leiden and Boston: Brill, 2017) and chapter 10 in this volume.

33. See Wodziński, *Historical Atlas of Hasidism.*

34. See Biale et al., *Hasidism: A New History*, 524–529.

CHAPTER 1

Homilies

Gadi Sagiv

Texts attributed to Hasidic leaders are major sources for the study of Hasidism, for they are the most explicit sources for our knowledge of the spiritual world of the tsadikim, as well as for the religious messages they conveyed to their followers. Those messages were in the domains of theology, ethics, and religious praxis. Texts attributed to the tsadikim are of various genres—epistles, conduct literature, legalistic (halakhic) writing, commentaries, autobiographies, systematic theological-ethical treatises, and homilies. This essay focuses on homilies, the most widespread and most representative genre of all the above. However, in order to put homilies in the contexts of other texts attributed to the tsadikim, we will first touch upon the other genres.

Genres

Hasidic homilies should be understood in the context of other literary genres attributed to the tsadikim:

> *Letters.* There are letters written by the tsadikim, either to individual addressees or to groups of people. The most celebrated of these is "The Holy Epistle" that the Besht wrote to Gershon of Kuty, his brother-in-law. In that epistle, termed by Simon Dubnow a "manifesto of Hasidism," the Besht reports on the spiritual journeys he experienced and also gives spiritual recommendations to the addressee.
>
> *Conduct Literature.* Conduct material was usually published as short tractates, each containing numbered brief practical recommendations (*hanhagot* in the plural, or *hanhagah* in the singular) for pious religious life. As such, they were accessible to wide circles of Hasidim. The *hanhagot* were usually delivered as written tractates attributed to par-

ticular tsadikim. However, Hasidic *hanhagot* do not always distinctively characterize the tsadik to whom they were attributed, and they often lack any Hasidic content. For example, research by Zeev Gries has shown that the formulations of the *hanhagot* by the disciples of the Maggid of Mezrich (Międzyrzecz) have kabbalistic content that is not specifically Hasidic, and were quite similar across different disciples.[1] The most famous collection of *hanhagot* is entitled *Tsava'at ha-rivash* (Heb.: The Will of the Besht). However, research proves that the *hanhagot* included in this book, first printed in 1794, originated in the school of the Maggid of Mezrich and were falsely attributed to the Besht. Many *hanhagot* were taken from homilies delivered by the Maggid or his close disciples.

Legalistic Writing. Although most of the early Hasidic leaders were neither rabbis nor experts in halakhah, several tsadikim engaged in halakhic creation. This became more widespread from the nineteenth century, when many tsadikim were also community rabbis. The relevant subgenres are halakhic monographs as well as responsa. As an example, we can point to the works of the Galician tsadik R. Ḥayim of Sanz (for more on this genre see chapter 2).

Commentaries. Some tsadikim engaged in hermeneutics and wrote commentaries to the Jewish canon, in particular the Zohar and the Lurianic kabbalah. This kind of Hasidic writing is virtually neglected by scholars. Examples can be found in the writings of R. Israel of Kozienice.

Autobiographies. Hardly any autobiographies were written by tsadikim. The most famous example is *Megilat setarim*, by R. Yitzḥak Aizik Yehudah Yeḥiel Safrin, the tsadik of Komarno (on this see chapter 6).

Systematic Theological-Ethical Treatises. Few instances of systematic treatises focus on theology and ethics in the Hasidic way. The most famous example is the book *Likutei amarim* (Heb.: A Collection of Discourses), by the founder of Chabad Hasidism, R. Shneur Zalman of Lady. This book, also titled *Sefer shel beynonim* (Heb.: A Book of Average People), but generally known as *Tanya* (a title that includes other material as well), is a systematic elaborate discussion of the recommended way of worship and of achieving spiritual perfection. Other examples can be found, for instance, in the literature of the Żydaczów-Komarno dynasty.

Homilies. Homilies are discourses that depart from interpreting biblical verses, or phrases from rabbinic literature such as the Mishnah or

Babylonian Talmud, but continue to more elaborate discussions of themes the author considers relevant. Hasidic homilies can be thus seen as part of Jewish homiletical literature (*sifrut ha-derush*), whose ancestor is ancient midrash. But Hasidic homilies are also part of Jewish ethical literature (*sifrut ha-musar*), which is characterized by its purpose to convey relatively practical values to the daily lives of its audience. Scholars hence disagree on the degree of innovation of Hasidic teachings; for example, Joseph Weiss argues for innovation, while others, such as Mendel Piekarz, highlight continuity. At the same time, Hasidic homilies can be seen as part of Jewish mystical-kabbalistic literature, and here, too, scholars disagree on its relationship to earlier instances of kabbalistic literature. While Gershom Scholem presents it as reacting to sixteenth-century Lurianic kabbalah, Moshe Idel highlights its relations with a wide array of sources, including the medieval ecstatic kabbalah of Abraham Abulafia and Renaissance kabbalah influenced by European occultism.

Compared to the other genres of writing by tsadikim, homilies differ in various features but also share some. Compared to *hanhagot*, which usually contain a few lines of practical recommendation, homilies are relatively long texts and include observations that require some rabbinic education to be understood. At the same time, formulations in *hanhagot* are sometimes intertwined with homilies, and some *hanhagot* are similar in length and content to homilies. Some were even taken from books of homilies. Compared to commentaries, homilies indeed contain interpretation of canonic texts, but the interpretation was but the first step in a lengthy discussion. Concurrently, there were commentaries on canonic sources that look similar to homilies in the elaborate discussion and free style of exegesis. Compared to halakhic writing, although the homily was not meant to express a practical halakhic opinion or decision, tsadikim sometimes address halakhic issues in their homilies.

The Life Cycle of a Hasidic Homily

Prior to discussing the homilies as sources, it is essential to discuss how they were created. While some homilies were written from the outset, it seems that the origins of the majority of Hasidic homiletical literature are in oral teachings, namely live sermons. Hence, whereas Hasidic homilies are part of Jewish homiletical literature, the delivery of these homilies is part of Jewish preaching. Hasidic homilies were delivered not by a professional preacher but by the tsadik himself; the audience comprised not the occasional visitors to a particular synagogue but the group of followers of that tsadik, his Hasidim; and the event occurred not before or after a regular prayer but often as part of a ceremonial setting centered around a ritualistic meal, which was called a *tish* (Yiddish for "table"). The delivery of Hasidic homilies often took place on Shabbat or a holiday. The tsadik spoke in Yiddish, the vernacular that was usually used in the communication between the tsadik and his followers, as it was by virtually all Jews of Eastern Europe. The text was not read but delivered from the tsadik's memory or created at the moment of its delivery, sometimes as part of a spiritual experience. That sort of performance included various gestures of voice and body language. There are thousands of printed homilies, and there are numerous first-person accounts of events surrounding the delivery of a homily. However, only rarely can we associate the two, that is, get to know what was said at a particular occasion at which a Hasidic homily was delivered.

An oft-quoted personal account of a delivery of a sermon was given by Salomon Maimon, an eighteenth-century Lithuanian Jew who was drawn to German Enlightenment and wrote his memoirs recalling episodes from his early life. Although his standpoint is biased, as a proponent of Enlightenment who opposed irrationality and mysticism, scholars consider his description to reflect some historical realities of early Hasidism. Maimon attended the sermon of the Maggid of Mezrich after he had met an emissary of the Maggid, who invited him to the Shabbat ceremonial meal at the Maggid's table. Maimon then described the ceremonial meal and delivery of the sermon:

> Accordingly, on Sabbath I went to this solemn meal, and found there a large number of respectable men who had gathered from various quarters. At length the awe-inspiring great man appeared, clothed in white satin. Even his shoes and snuffbox were white, this being among the Kabbalists the color of grace. He gave every newcomer his greeting. We sat down to table and during the meal a solemn silence reigned. After the meal was over, the superior struck up a solemn inspiring melody, held his hand for some time upon his brow, and then began to call out, "Z___ of H___, M___ of R___," and so on. Every newcomer was thus called by his own name and the name of his residence, which excited no little astonishment. Each recited, as he was called, some verse of the Holy Scriptures. Thereupon the superior commenced to deliver a sermon for which the verses served as a text, so that although they were disconnected verses taken from different parts of the Holy Scriptures they were combined with as much skill as if they had formed a single whole. What was still more extraordinary, every one of the newcomers believed that he had discovered, in that part of the sermon which was founded on his verse, something that had reference to the facts of his own spiritual life. At this we were of course greatly astonished.[2]

Several striking characteristics are to be noted in the event: First, the auditory and visual characteristics of the music as well as the color white of the garment and other objects. Second, the impression that the Maggid had a mystical-ecstatic experience prior to delivering the sermon. Third, the virtuoso sermon that tailored together all independent verses. And finally, the emphasis on the personal reference to every attendant.

Maimon's description represents the fundamental lively oral and interpersonal nature of Hasidism, which somewhat contrasts with the written character of the homilies. Maimon also conveys the sense of unusual impression that the sermon had on the Hasidim. Interpreted by the Hasidim as mystical moments for the tsadikim, oral teachings were often described as peak experiences during the encounters between Hasidim and tsadikim, in which the performance of the text included various visual and audial effects.

Whereas the sermon was delivered orally in Yiddish, most of the homilies are available in written Hebrew. The transition from Yiddish to Hebrew actually marks the transition from the oral to the literary. The descendants or disciples of tsadikim often wrote down what they had heard in Yiddish, rendering it in Hebrew. As Hasidism flourished in the nineteenth century we see more and more instances in which it was the tsadik himself who wrote down his homilies. The rendering made by a disciple of the tsadik from his memory occurred at least several hours after the actual delivery of the discourse because Jewish law forbids writing during Shabbat and holidays. That transcription-translation of the oral discourse was usually checked and at times edited by an authoritative figure, such as a close disciple, a descendant of the tsadik, or the tsadik himself. The books of homilies that are available to us are thus collections of that sort of adapted transcription of oral teachings ascribed to a particular tsadik.

The books of homilies were usually published by the descendants or disciples of the tsadik. A major purpose for printing the books of collections of teachings was to preserve and foster the spiritual legacy of a specific tsadik. Hence, many of these books were published posthumously or a short time before the tsadik died. In rare cases they were published in the middle of the tsadik's lifetime, to promote his active leadership.

As is often the case in religious literature, the specific formulation of a printed homily is sometimes but one of several options available to the publisher. Research shows that some homilies have several transcriptions, each recorded by a different disciple. Each of these disciples remembered differently the oral discourse and emphasized different religious ideas and demands.[3]

It should also be noted that the books of homilies are not the only reservoir of Hasidic homilies. Homilies can also be embedded in sources of other genres, such as a quotation from a homily in a story about a tsadik, or can be included in volumes with collections of various materials, not just homilies.

Books of Hasidic Homilies: Structure, Style, Inventory

The structure of a typical book of homilies with a life cycle as described above is a collection of independent textual units attributed to a particular tsadik, often divided into sections according to the weekly Torah reading cycle (*parashat ha-shavua*), a Jewish holiday, or tractates of the Talmud. These textual units are in Hebrew, each spanning from a few lines to several pages.

A typical Jewish homily begins with a quotation: a biblical verse or a citation from rabbinic literature. The biblical verse usually belongs to the weekly Torah portion of the week in which the discourse was delivered. Other opening quotes were usually also related to the time and place in which the discourse was delivered, such as a holiday or wedding ceremony. The opening quote was only a point of departure for a discussion not necessarily tightly related to the citation, centering around the religious point the tsadik would like to make. So, in addition to exegesis of verses, these teachings introduce theology and ethical demands.

The religious message of Hasidic homilies often refers to themes considered "Hasidic," such as striving to mystical union (*devekut*) with God or attachment to the tsadik. Theologically, homilies are often thus based on the premise of the ubiquitous immanence of God in the world, often communicating that the Hasid is required to attach himself to the manifestation of God that exists in every layer of reality, sanctifying all his deeds, religious and nonreligious alike. The tsadik himself is often presented in homilies as a metaphysical entity, a mediatory layer through which it was possible to attach to God.

However, homilies rarely unfold systematically. Importantly, the nature of a homily as a free-style elaboration on a verse, though self-explicatory, did not allow for the development of consistent lines of argument, longer narrative, or discursive strategies, and so on. Tsadikim, being spiritual guides rather than philosophers or theologians, usually jumped from one subject to another, attempting to connect ideas and relevant verses. Even in cases of well-structured homilies, the focal point of most tsadikim was the religious ethical message of sanctification rather than exegesis of relevant verses or theology of divine immanence.

As is the case with many genres of Jewish religious literature, homilies contain numerous references to earlier sources, from the Bible, through rabbinic literature, to earlier Hasidic masters. Thus, Hasidic homilies are often sources not only for the religious message of the tsadik to which the book is ascribed but also for the worldviews of other tsadikim who are cited or to whom he refers in his homilies. In fact, since no book of homilies is ascribed to the Besht, our knowledge of his spiritual message is primarily based on citations of him in the books ascribed to his disciples, as we shall see later on.

As part of the traditional genre of homiletical literature, it is of no surprise that the first Hasidic book to be published was a book of Hasidic homilies. That book, published in 1780, entitled *Toledot Ya'akov Yosef*, is a collection of homilies by R. Ya'akov Yosef of Polnoe (Połonne), a prominent disciple of the Besht. R. Ya'akov Yosef wrote three other books of discourses.

Another prominent disciple of the Besht—maybe the most famous—was R. Dov Ber of Mezrich. Over time, his homilies were published in various editions. The earliest was *Magid devarav le-Ya'akov*, published in 1781 by one of his disciples.

The most famous (actually "classical") are the books by these two students of the Besht as well as by the disciples of the Maggid of Mezrich, such as *Noam Elimelekh*, by R. Elimelekh of Leżajsk; *Meor Eynaim*, by R. Naḥum of Czarnobyl; and *Kedushat Levi*, by R. Levi Yitzḥak of Berdyczów.

Surprisingly, there are very few critical editions of books of Hasidic teachings, namely editions that incorporate variants of the text, either in manuscript or printed form, attempting to reach the "original" or "authentic" teaching delivered by the tsadik. A notable exception is Rivka Schatz Uffenheimer's edition of the abovementioned *Magid devarav le-Ya'akov*, by the Maggid of Mezrich.[4] A more recent notable example is Daniel Reiser's edition of the teachings by R. Kalonymos Kalman Shapira, the tsadik of Piaseczno, from the Warsaw ghetto.[5] While many books of homilies lack variants in manuscripts, many other homilies are still in manuscript, and many are not found in public archives but rather in the private archives of the relevant courts, owned by descendants of the tsadikim. Consequently, for some books the best copies available are annotated editions of previously printed editions (such as Gedaliah Nigal's edition of *Noam Elimelekh*), while for others accessibility to the archives in the courts is difficult. In addition to the dearth of critical editions, there are actually no comprehensive bibliographical tools to assist in finding the hundreds of available editions of the homilies.

Whereas we have Hasidic hagiographical writings about almost every major tsadik, this is not the case with Hasidic homilies; some tsadikim avoided delivering oral teachings, and some delivered such teachings but their materials were not collected or published. As noted, there are also teachings of tsadikim that were quoted by other tsadikim and then embedded in their books of teachings. This is how we are acquainted with the religious message of the Besht. There is neither a book of homilies nor a tractate of *hanhagot* that can be reliably attributed to the Besht himself. We have acquaintance with his teachings through his above-mentioned "Holy Epistle," but more extensive examples are found in the printed teachings of his disciples. In these teachings the disciples sometimes provided short statements in the name of their master. Accordingly, important collections of the "teaching of the Besht" are actually collections of such quotations.

An important such collection is *Keter shem tov*. First published in 1794, it is a collection of teachings that were quoted in the books of the aforementioned prominent disciple of the Besht, R. Ya'akov Yosef of Polnoe. This collection is considered the first of its kind, but it is limited by the fact that all of its teachings were taken from the sayings of a single disciple. A single disciple, prominent though he might have been, reflects only what he heard during his period of closeness to his master (a period that could have been relatively short), and what he transcribes is shaped by his own understanding, which is not necessarily identical to that of other disciples.

Another important collection, much more comprehensive, is *Sefer Ba'al Shem Tov al ha-Torah*.[6] Published in 1938 in Poland, this is a collection of a wider array of quotes from books of tsadikim who are considered direct disciples of the Besht as well as disciples of those direct disciples. It is organized according to the weekly Torah reading cycle, like the "real" collections of homilies attributed to other tsadikim. This collection is very useful because it apparently saves readers the need to delve through dozens of books to find sayings of the Besht. However, like any anthology, it should be treated cautiously for several reasons. First, it cannot be considered comprehensive but rather contains sources that the editors could reach. Second, every source should be checked for authenticity. Some sources are more reliable, such as those quoted by direct disciples of the Besht, but those quoted by tsadikim who did not know the Besht should be treated with extra care. Third, the editors might have uprooted a quotation from the homily in which it was embedded. Often, to understand that statement, it is essential to go back to the source book of homilies to check the entire homily for context.

Challenges and Limitations

The complex life cycle of numerous Hasidic homilies—from independent oral teaching delivered in Yiddish on various occasions to written and edited texts in Hebrew collected in books—generates significant challenges to the researcher of Hasidism. A major problem is found in the gap between the original oral teaching in Yiddish and the extant written homily in Hebrew.

The language gap seems significant. Research by Ariel Evan Mayse and Daniel Reiser of the homilies of one of the leaders of the Ger Hasidism, a rare instance in which we have Yiddish transcriptions, shows that the Yiddish version differs in many ways from the Hebrew one. The Yiddish was more accessible to laypeople, whereas the written (which in this case was made by the tsadik himself) was somewhat more scholarly.

In addition to the change of language, the fact that the homily was written down several hours after its delivery—by a person who could have forgotten some of the details or could have misunderstood others—might have resulted in significant changes between the oral original and the written rendering.

Moreover, often the original text delivered by the tsadik deliberately underwent a process of editing. That process was not unique to Hasidism but rather can be found the entire corpus of Jewish homiletical literature; homilies were sometimes expanded, sometimes cut. Sometimes the cuts were an act of internal censorship that deleted expressions that might be understood as being hostile to non-Jewish authorities or non-Jews in general. Another characteristic of published homilies was the deletion of particularities of time and place, in order, perhaps, to disconnect the book from the burdens of a specific time, thereby making it more generally appealing and relevant for future generations and for those who dwelled in other places.

It is therefore important, when analyzing a Hasidic homily, to try to locate the Yiddish originals. However, only in rare cases do we have that sort of material. In most cases all we have is the printed homily in Hebrew.

Next, even if we do know something about the original text of the sermon, the text available to us is usually stripped of all the nontextual aspects of that teaching. That is, all physical gestures, such as movements of the body and changes in the voice, could not have been captured in print. This is true not only in the case of Hasidim but in all sermon literature, not necessarily Jewish. Only a report by a witness to the event could tell us about what was seen and heard, but in the context of Hasidism there are few examples of that sort of testimony, and we have very few cases containing such testimony along with the text (even edited) that was delivered concurrently. For example, we do not know the text of the homily that the Maggid of Mezrich delivered in front of Maimon in the event described above. Conversely, we do not have any description of the event of the delivery of any of the printed homilies by the Maggid.

Another issue is the question of representability: to what extent do Hasidic teachings indeed reflect the thought, ideas, or spiritual world of the tsadik? Employing a minimalist or rather pessimistic approach, the only assumption that can be made is that a homily represents the *particular message* the tsadik wanted to convey to the *particular audience* at a *particular event*. Indeed, one can find in a single book discourses that are inconsistent and that even contradict one another. This is clearly a result of the situational nature of the genre: the sermon is to speak to the specific audience in a specific time and place. Another obstacle to the representability is the fact that a book of homilies can be a random collection of homilies written down and adapted by a disciple, sometimes even by several people, who are not the tsadik himself. In effect, books of homilies were sometimes criticized for being a distortion of the "real" message of the tsadik by a student or students. Naturally, this is a motif common to virtually all other religions.

A less pessimistic approach would claim that those contradictions are easily explained by the fact that they were delivered in different and often distant points in time, that they reflect changes in the opinions of the tsadik, and that they correctly show his overall general ways of thinking. Such an approach would suggest that it is usually possible to point to themes that exist in several discourses and hence can be described in vague terms, such as alluding to the "thought," "worldview," or "spiritual world" of the tsadik. This spiritual world has components unique to that tsadik, but often it shares components with other tsadikim.

The fact that books of homilies consist of discourses from various points in time may raise hope that the development of the tsadik's ideas over time can be reconstructed. Unfortunately, with some notable exceptions (such as the book *Sefat emet*, by R. Aryeh Yehudah Leib Alter of Ger), the vast majority of Hasidic teachings are undated. They are grouped according to the applicable weekly Torah reading cycle and were probably delivered at that point of time in the year, but the year is rarely mentioned. In the rare cases in which we do have dates of delivery, it is possible to ask whether a particular homily reflects the opinion of the tsadik on contemporaneous issues. For example, a sermon in *Sefat emet* emphasizing that the entering into Canaan was not done by human force but was based on divine intervention might be an implicit reaction to a pamphlet in support of Zionism published around that time by the tsadik's grandson.[7] Dated sermons can also help portray spiritual, intellectual, emotional, and ideological changes the tsadik experienced over the years. An example of this is the growing despair during the Holocaust reflected in the sermons of R. Kalonymos Kalman Shapira of Piaseczno.

Another limitation of Hasidic homilies, which actually characterizes Jewish homiletical literature in general, is the limited possibility of drawing information about historical reality from these teachings. By definition, they provide the normative aspect of Hasidic life; that is, they tell what the Hasidim are expected or advised to do. However, although original sermons sometimes included references to contemporaneous reality (as noted by observers), such references are usually cleansed from printed homilies, as noted. Still, in many cases the homilies do contain indirect evidence about issues that were pressing at the time of their delivery. The reminiscent issues are in the domain of ethics and religious life, and less so in the domain of external politics. Thus, for example, if a tsadik were consistently warning against the sexual sin of masturbation, then it might be that this was a pressing issue in his congregation or at least in his personal worldview. And if a tsadik did not stop preaching against rational explorations and readings of books of philosophy, then this might indicate that such books and investigations had become dangerously popular among his followers.

Against the backdrop of these challenges, we will point to four notable scholarly approaches to the study of Hasidic homilies:

1. A theological-mystical approach focusing on homilies as sources of religious ideas and practices. This sort of approach characterizes the school of Gershom

Scholem, with notable studies by other scholars such as Rivka Schatz Uffenheimer, Isaiah Tishby, Moshe Idel, and their disciples. Those studies often relate Hasidic ideas to sources of Jewish thought of earlier periods—rabbinic, kabbalistic, and philosophical.

2. A historical approach attempting to isolate historical conclusions from homilies with implicit references to historical reality, mostly social or cultural. An example is Benzion Dinur's research on early Hasidism. Basing himself on Hasidic homiletic literature, Dinur argued that early Hasidism had a distinct messianic element.[8] Dinur's methodology was criticized by scholars of Scholem's school as well as by social historians. Both camps pointed to the problems in drawing sweeping historical conclusions from fragments of texts that are extracted, as noted above, from historical context. Social historians after Dinur, such as Immanuel Etkes and David Assaf, use homiletical literature much more cautiously, usually regarding homilies as an aspect of the biography of the tsadik to whom they were attributed.

3. A philological approach focusing mainly on the life cycle of a homily from its Yiddish transcriptions by different disciples, and then on its translation to Hebrew and its editing toward its publication in a book of sermons. This sort of approach involves locating manuscripts of teachings and making a comparative analysis between the various versions, in both manuscript and printed form. Examples include the studies of Zeev Gries on Hasidic conduct literature, and of Ariel Evan Mayse and Daniel Reiser on the teachings of Rabbi Aryeh Yehudah Leib Alter, the tsadik of Ger, whose book of teaching is *Sefat emet* (for literature, see the bibliography at the end of the chapter).

4. A performative approach focusing on the homily in the context of the event of the delivery of the sermon. Keeping in mind the life cycle of homilies described above, this sort of approach attempts to bring together historical evidence on the delivery of the original sermon and the content of the homily. However promising this approach, the relatively limited sources on the events of sermons prevent its application to the majority of available homilies.

These approaches do not exclude each other. Rather, each of them highlights a different aspect of Hasidic teaching and life. Although scholars tend to focus on a single approach based on their training and interest, a comprehensive investigation of the lives and creations of Hasidic leaders calls for adopting more than a single approach.

Example: A Teaching by the Maggid of Mezrich (Międzyrzecz)

The following example of a homily, attributed to the Maggid of Mezrich, exemplifies both how Hasidic homilies are major windows into Hasidic thought and how scholarly debates develop around them:

"Make for yourself two trumpets of silver" (Num. 10:2)

The phrase *shetey ḥatsotserot*, two trumpets, is to be read as linked with "On the image of the throne was an image with the appearance of a man, from above" (Ezek. 1:26).

A person is really only made up of *dalet* and *mem*, two letters that may be taken to stand for *dibur*, speech, and *malkhut*, God's kingship that dwells within it [but together also composing *dam*, or "blood"]. But when you attach yourself to the blessed Holy One who is the cosmic *aleph* [representing the oneness of all being], you become *adam*, a full human being [i.e., the divine presence turns "flesh and blood" into humanity].

The blessed Holy One entered into multiple contractions of His own self, coming through various worlds, in order to become one with humans, who could not have withstood God's original brightness. Now the person has to leave behind all corporeality, also traveling across many worlds, in order to become One with God. Then our own existence is itself negated. Such a person is truly called *adam*, the one on the image of the throne, or *kisse*. That word can also refer to "hiding," for God Himself is hidden (*kisui*) there. This follows the prophet's description of "cloud and crackling fire." At first the person is in a "cloudy" state, filled with darkness, unable to pray with enthusiasm. But then along comes the "crackling fire," when we attain ecstasy. This is the "image of the throne," where our blessed God is hidden. We discover it in a *mar'eh* ("appearance"), a word that can also mean "mirror." Whatever is awakened in us is awakened also within God. If love is aroused in the *tsadik*, so too is it aroused above. The same can be true of any quality. This is true of those who are very pure, rising across all those worlds to become one with God. . . .

These are the two *ḥatsotserot* (trumpets) of *kesef* (silver). A person is only a *ḥatsi tsurah*, a half of the whole form—*dam*, or blood. But the *aleph* by itself, as it were, is also an incomplete form. But only when attached to one another are they made whole. *Kesef* can mean "longing." When you long for the blessed Holy One, God loves you as well.[9]

This is part of a homily (with some omissions denoted by the ellipsis sign) on a verse from the book of Numbers. The original discourse was probably delivered on the Shabbat in which the relevant chapter from Numbers was read within the weekly Torah cycle. The point of departure is a biblical verse in which God requires Moses to produce two silver trumpets that should be used for various purposes, such as announcing the movement of the Israelite camp or announcing an attack by enemies. The homily is built upon linguistic similarities: the Hebrew word for *trumpets* is *ḥatsotserot*, which sounds like *ḥatsi tsurot*, which means "half form" in Hebrew. The Hebrew word for *silver* is *kesef*, which sounds like *kisuf*, which means "yearning" in Hebrew. Hence, the verse "Make for yourself two trumpets of silver" can be understood as hinting to two half forms that yearn to unite. On the basis of these linguistic associations, the Maggid applies the directive to create two trumpets to the letters of the Hebrew alphabet, which in turn signify the spiritual world of the worshipper. The worshipper has to yearn to unite the first letter of the Hebrew alphabet, *aleph*, on the one hand, with the two letters *dalet* and *mem*, on the other. The *aleph* represents God, the spiritual aspect of the world; the *dalet* and *mem* together are the word *dam*, or blood, signifying the corporeal aspect of the world. The demand to unite the *aleph* and the *dalet-mem* is the unification of the two forms, of which the result is the word with the letters *aleph-dalet-mem*: *adam*, or human being. Hence, the Maggid demands the worshipper to unite his material self with God, thereby to become a full human being. This is the very basic content of the homily. It is evident that the Maggid did not seek to convey theology to his followers but rather to transmit an ethical message about the preferred way of life. But questions that remain include determining the meaning of that unification, and learning how exactly this should be done. To understand this we will refer to scholars' discussions of the homily.

This homily is one of the most popular Hasidic texts among scholars. But since it lacks any reference to historical reality, and since we do not have any transcriptions in Yiddish or a personal account of its delivery, the discussion of this homily focused on the printed Hebrew version, as carried out by scholars of Jewish thought. Of these discussions, we will limit ourselves to a few instructive interpretations by Rivka Schatz Uffenheimer, Gershom Scholem, Moshe Idel, and Arthur Green.

Rivka Schatz Uffenheimer interpreted Hasidism as a striking example of quietist mysticism, that is, "the path towards God via the abandonment of the self," with parallels in the Christian quietist movement in seventeenth-century Europe.[10] From that point of view, the Maggid's homily intended "to stress the activist motif of God within the spirit of the human being who empties himself of all his substance." That dwelling of God within the human being is based on the "ontic identity between God and man."[11]

Gershom Scholem discussed this homily in his seminal essay "Devekut, or Communion with God,"[12] discussing *devekut* as a central concept representing mystical experiences as well as the ways to attain such experiences. Scholem claims that the Maggid's homily "goes as far as anything in early Hasidism," and he explains the Maggid's demand thus:

> If man casts off all earthly or material elements and ascends through all the worlds and becomes one with God to the degree of losing the feeling of separate existence, then will he be rightly called *adam*, Man, "being transformed into the cosmic figure of the primordial man whose likeness upon the throne Ezekiel beheld." This, according to Baer [the Maggid of Mezrich], is the trans-

> figuration of man which is reached through, or in, the state of *devekut*: man finds himself by losing himself in God, and by giving up his identity he discovers it on a higher plane. Hence, and in many other sayings of Rabbi Baer, *devekut* is said to lead not only to communion, but to *ahdut*, union. But this union is, in fact, not at all the pantheistic obliteration of the self within the divine mind which he likes to call the Naught [*Ayin*], but pierces through this state on to the rediscovery of man's spiritual identity.[13]

Scholem argues that the Maggid's homily should not be understood as introducing "the pantheistic obliteration of the self within the divine mind" but as espousing a position that keeps separate the personal existence of the self—a position he calls "Jewish." This argument regarding the Maggid's homily is actually an example of an argument regarding Jewish mysticism in general. According to Scholem, mystical experiences in Judaism are relatively restrained and usually do not reach a full union between man and God, a union that means the annihilation of the human being inside God. Whereas Christian mystics introduced the notion of *unio mystica*, which entails the erasure of the self within God, the Jewish mystic always keeps a minimal separation between God and himself. As Scholem wrote, the Jewish *devekut* is not *union* with God but *communion*. How, then, does Scholem resolve this gap between his general argument and this specific homily? He warned his readers before his analysis that "it may be wise not to lose ourselves in his [the Maggid's] terminology, which is radical indeed, but to consider the context of his thought."[14] Presumably, Scholem assumes that there is a coherent system of the Maggid's ideas that is reflected in his homilies, and that they should be interpreted as such a coherent system. This is not an obvious assumption.

Moshe Idel disagrees with Scholem's argument that Jewish mystics did not reach for or preach union with God. The Maggid's radical formulation serves him as an example of the opposite position. Idel actually claims that Scholem chooses to interpret the Maggid's homily in a particular way that fits his general approach rather than simply reading his words. For example, Idel claims against Scholem that "it is equally valid to assume that 'Adam' refers not to the mystic who has returned from the annihilative experience but to what remained absorbed in the depth of the Godhead. The reference to union as a step preceding annihilation is evidence that the unitive experience culminates with the total loss of individuality."[15] Moreover, Idel claims that besides formulations that conform with Scholem, there are numerous other examples that go in tandem with an interpretation as union.

Idel's position is not the same as Schatz Uffenheimer's, either. Whereas Schatz Uffenheimer frames the union discussed in the Maggid's homily in the context of quietist annihilation, in which God dwells inside the worshipper, Idel understands this union in a Neoplatonic way, in which the human soul is absorbed in its divine source.[16]

Arthur Green, in his collection of Hasidic homilies from which the translation of the Maggid's homily was taken, interprets this one in a different direction than the scholars mentioned above:

> The theological statement here is quite a bold one: both God and the human are "*hatsi tsures*," as it was pronounced; they are both "half forms," each needing the other in order to be complete. We humans may be mere flesh, needing God's presence to be whole. But God without us is "merely" an *aleph*, not yet a whole word, unable to be manifest in speech or to bring about God's earthly kingdom. We thus need to long for one another, in order to make for wholeness both "above" and "below."[17]

Unlike Schatz Uffenheimer, Scholem, and Idel, who differ in the specific characterization of the mystical experience, Green does not frame this homily in the context of "mysticism." His explanation is existential, even dialogic, focusing on the requirement for the full existence not only of the human being but also of God himself. God is missing a critical aspect of himself without the connection to human beings.

In the analysis above we can distinguish between the basic investigation of the homily and the study of its broader meaning and significance. The basic analysis, with which all scholars seem to agree, is a challenge in itself when dealing with Hasidic homilies, for it requires significant acquaintance with traditional Jewish literature, rabbinic and kabbalistic in particular. Only after deciphering the basic text is it possible to move to the broader aspects. The scholars mentioned above actually agree on the basic layer but disagree on the broader issues. Each of them interpret the Maggid's homily according to a general understanding of Hasidism. For Schatz Uffenheimer it is a quietist system of thought; Scholem understands it as a mystical movement featuring restrained mysticism; Idel also understands it as a mystical movement, but with much more radical formulations; and Green highlights the dialogic aspect. When Scholem feels that this homily is not very representative, he suggests interpreting it according to the general context of the Maggid's thought. Idel, from his side, argues that his interpretation goes in tandem with other homilies from the school of the Maggid. Hence, it is clear that when scholars analyze homilies, they also have in mind other homilies. Analysis of Hasidic homilies is always done in the context of other homilies the scholar is acquainted with.

As is the case for most Hasidic homilies, we have no information regarding the event or events surrounding the delivery of this one. As explained above, this is a major limitation of attempting to study the thousands of Hasidic homilies. Accordingly, as rich as the discussions by the four scholars are, each of those discussions employs only one of the four approaches described in this chapter.

Conclusion

The importance of written teachings has always been recognized by scholars of Hasidism, who have used them as almost exclusive sources for understanding Hasidic thought, namely the religious theory of Hasidism. Basic Hasidic ideas such as the immanence of God in the world, communion with God (*devekut*), the theory of prayer, and the theory of the tsadik—all of these and many other ideas are elaborated in these sources. The role these sources have played in the research of Hasidism is so central that social historians sometimes claim that Hasidic teachings were overemphasized by scholars of Hasidic thought, who often neglected other kinds of sources. Conversely, social historians are often accused of oversimplifying the religious message embedded in Hasidic homilies. It seems that a more balanced and integrative approach is recommended. The ideas conveyed in the discourses are crucial to understanding the ethos of Hasidism, but these ideas cannot be researched without paying heed to their historical and social contexts, to the extent that they can be reconstructed. In any event, Hasidic homilies are essential to the study of basic Hasidic ideas. Moreover, from a historical point of view, they are useful not only for the study of the history of Hasidic ideas but also for the study of other historical aspects of Hasidism, such as the social and cultural histories.

With all their limitations, homiletical Hasidic texts can be a source for various perspectives on the theological message or the resulting ethical demand, but also on the general nature of the spiritual experience in Hasidism. But perhaps more than other types of historical sources, Hasidic teachings are open to opposite interpretations.

SUGGESTED READING

As Hasidic teachings are part of Jewish homiletical literature, research on the latter is relevant to the study of the former. A classic but dated study in this context is Leopold Zunz, *Gottesdienstliche Vorträge der Juden historisch entwickelt* (Berlin: A. Asher, 1832), a history of Jewish sermons by one of the founding fathers of the Wissenschaft des Judentums movement. Concerning Hasidism, this book only mentions Hasidic preaching, and with much criticism. For updated scholarly contributions, see, for example, Israel Bettan, *Studies in Jewish Preaching* (Cincinnati: Hebrew Union College Press, 1939); Joseph Dan, *Sifrut ha-musar veha-derush* (Jerusalem: Keter, 1975); Marc Saperstein, *Jewish Preaching, 1200–1800: An Anthology* (New Haven, CT: Yale University Press, 1989); Kimmi Caplan, Carmi Horowitz, and Nahem Ilan, eds., *Doresh tov le'amo: Ha-darshan, ha-derashah, ve-sifrut ha-derush ba-tarbut ha-Yehudit* (Jerusalem: Merkaz Zalman Shazar, 2012).

A comprehensive and updated study of Hasidic sermons, exemplifying reading strategies on various books of homilies, is Ora Wiskind-Elper, *Hasidic Commentary on the Torah* (London: Liverpool University Press, 2018).

Zeev Gries has published numerous studies on the genres of Hasidic literature as well as on Jewish preaching in general. Most relevant to Hasidic discourses are *Sifrut ha-hanhagot: Toldotehah u-mekomah be-ḥayei ḥasidei rabi Israel Baal Shem Tov* (Jerusalem: Mossad Bialik, 1990); *Sefer, sofer ve-sipur be-reshit ha-ḥasidut* (Tel Aviv: Hakibutz ha-Meuhad, 1992); *Ha-sefer ha-ivri: Perakim le-toldotav* (Jerusalem: Mossad Bialik, 2015).

A seminal study on Hasidic preaching and sermons in light of pre-Hasidic preachers is Mendel Piekarz, *Bi-yemei tsemiḥat ha-ḥasidut: Megamot ra'ayoniot be-sifrei derush u-musar* (Jerusalem: Mossad Bialik, 1978).

A general updated discussion of Hasidic homilies is Arthur Green, "The Hasidic Homily: Mystical Performance and Hermeneutical Process," in *As a Perennial Spring: A Festschrift Honoring Rabbi Dr. Norman Lamm*, ed. B. Cohen (New York: Downhill Publishing, 2013), 237–265. A general discussion on the interface between Yiddish and Hebrew and the transformation of oral teachings to written homilies is Ariel Evan Mayse and Daniel Reiser, "Territories and Textures: The Hasidic Sermon as the Crossroads of Language and Culture," *Jewish Social Studies* 24 (2018), 127–160.

For other recent scholarly contributions on Hasidic discourses focusing on specific test cases, see Uriel Gellman, *Ha-shevilim ha-yots'im mi-Lublin: Tsemihata shel ha-ḥasidut be-Polin* (Jerusalem: Merkaz Zalman Shazar, 2018); Ariel Evan Mayse and Daniel Reiser, "*Sefer Sefat Emet*, Yiddish Manuscripts and the Oral Homilies of R. Yehudah Aryeh Leib of Ger," *Kabbalah* 33 (2015), 9–43; Gadi Sagiv, *Ha-shoshelet: Bet Chernobyl u-mekomo be-toledot ha-ḥasidut* (Jerusalem: Merkaz Zalman Shazar, 2014), 181–213.

The body of Hasidic teachings translated into English is not extensive. A sample of teachings of an eighteenth-century tsadik is *Menahem Nahum of Chernobyl: Upright Practices, the Light of the Eyes*, trans. A. Green (New York: Paulist Press, 1982). The above-mentioned *Tanya* is available in numerous languages; an English translation is *Liqquṭei Amarim [Tanya] by Rabbi Schneur Zalman of Liadi*, trans. N. Mindel (New York: Kehot, 1962). An English translation of another prominent book of teachings is *Likutei Moharan by Rabbi Nachman of Breslov*, 11 vols., trans. S. Bergman (vol. 1), M. Mykoff (vols. 2–11) (Jerusalem, New York: HaNachal Press, 1986–2000). A sample of teachings of an influential nineteenth-century tsadik is *The Language of Truth: The Torah Commentary of the Sefat Emet, Rabbi Yehudah Leib Alter of Ger*, trans. A. Green (Philadelphia: Jewish Publication Society, 1998).

A collection of teachings from various tsadikim, with a commentary, organized thematically, is Norman Lamm, *The Religious Thought of Hasidism: Text and Commentary* (New York: Yeshiva University Press, 1999). A more recent collection, organized around the weekly Torah reading cycle and accompanied by the Hebrew sources and by a commentary, is Arthur Green, ed., *Speaking Torah: Spiritual Teachings from around the Maggid's Table*, with Ebn Leader, Ariel Evan Mayse, and Or N. Rose, 2 vols. (Woodstock, VT: Jewish Light Pub, 2013).

NOTES

1. Zeev Gries, *Sifrut ha-hanhagot: Toledotehah u-mekomah be-ḥayei ḥasidei rabi Israel Ba'al Shem Tov* (Jerusalem: Mossad Bialik, 1989).

2. Solomon Maimon, *An Autobiography*, trans. J. Clark Murray (London: A. Gardner, 1888), 168–169.

3. See, for example, Ariel Evan Mayse and Daniel Reiser, "*Sefer Sefat Emet*, Yiddish Manuscripts and the Oral Homilies of R. Yehudah Aryeh Leib of Ger," *Kabbalah* 33 (2015): 9–43.

4. *Magid devarav le-Ya'akov la-magid Dov Ber mi-Mezerich*, ed. R. Schatz Uffenheimer (Jerusalem: Magness Press, 1976).

5. *Derashot mi-shenot ha-za'am: Derashot ha-admor mi-Piasechna be-geto Varsha [5]700–5[702] [1939–1942]*, ed. D. Reiser (Jerusalem: Ha-Mikhlalah ha-Akademit Herzog, 2017).

6. *Sefer Ba'al Shem Tov al ha-Torah* (Lodz, 1938).

7. David Biale et al., *Hasidism: A New History* (Princeton, NJ: Princeton University Press, 2017), 346.

8. Benzion Dinur, "Reshita shel ha-ḥasidut u-yesodotehah ha-sotsyaliyim ve-ha-meshiḥiyim," in *Be-mifne ha-dorot: Meḥkarim ve-iyunim be-reshitam shel ha-zemanim ha-ḥadashim be-toledot Yisra'el* (Jerusalem: Mossad Bialik, 1955), 83–227.

9. *Or Torah* (Koretz, 1804), Parashat Baha'alotekha. Translation taken from Arthur Green, *Speaking Torah: Spiritual Teachings from Around the Maggid's Table* (Woodstock,VT: Jewish Light Pub, 2013), 2:18–19, with minor editing modifications. The square brackets contain comments by the translators or editors of *Speaking Torah*.

10. Rivka Schatz Uffenheimer, *Hasidism as Mysticism: Quietistic Elements in Eighteenth-Century Hasidic Thought*, trans. J. Chipman (Princeton, NJ, and Jerusalem: Princeton University Press and Magnes Press, 1993), 65.

11. Ibid., 213–214.

12. Gershom Scholem, *The Messianic Idea in Judaism and Other Essays on Jewish Spirituality* (New York: Schocken Books, 1971), 203–227. The homily is discussed on 226–227.

13. Ibid., 226–227.

14. Ibid., 226.

15. Moshe Idel, *Kabbalah: New Perspectives* (New Haven, CT: Yale University Press, 1988), 65–66.

16. For this observation as well as a comparative discussion of the interpretations of Scholem, Schatz Uffenheimer, and Idel, see Ron Margolin, *Mikdash Adam: Ha-hafnama ha-datit ve-itsuv ḥayei ha-dat he-penimiyim be-reshit ha-ḥasidut* (Jerusalem: Magnes Press, 2005), 183.

17. Green, *Speaking Torah*, 2:19.

CHAPTER 2

Halakhah

Levi Cooper

Scholars often cast the Hasidic movement, its ethos, and its religious message in antinomian or anomian hues, suggesting that Hasidim either flouted halakhah (Jewish law) or ignored it. Yet, contrary to this image, Hasidic masters from the earliest days of the nascent movement have been active and interested in the world of Jewish law. The scholarly promise of this aspect of Hasidism has yet to be fully realized. This chapter demonstrates some of the fruitful potential of this academic frontier.

A Medley of Hasidic Law

Hasidic masters who served in official rabbinic capacities were central to the communal administration of Jewish law. Thus, for instance, R. Levi Yitzḥak of Berdichev (Berdyczów) (1740–1809)—author of the seminal Hasidic work *Kedushat Levi* and a beloved master in Hasidic lore—served as the rabbi of important cities: Ryczywół, Żelechów, Pinsk, and Berdyczów. In this role, R. Levi Yitzḥak was responsible for the day-to-day administration of Jewish law. Indeed, surviving documents attest to his juridical role in civil disputes.[1]

Hasidic masters and scholars who identified as Hasidim have also composed works of Jewish law. For example, R. Uziel Meisels (1744–1785), a colleague of R. Levi Yitzḥak, also served in the rabbinate of a number of towns: Ostrowiec, Ryczywół, and Nowe Miasto Korczyn. R. Meisels's work, *Tiferet 'uziel*, preserves early Hasidic teachings. He also wrote commentaries on portions of the Talmud, as well as *Menorah ha-tehora*—a commentary on the laws of Shabbat. This work was reportedly written at the behest of the second-most important figure in Hasidic collective memory, R. Dov Ber (d. 1772), the Maggid of Mezrich (Międzyrzecz).[2]

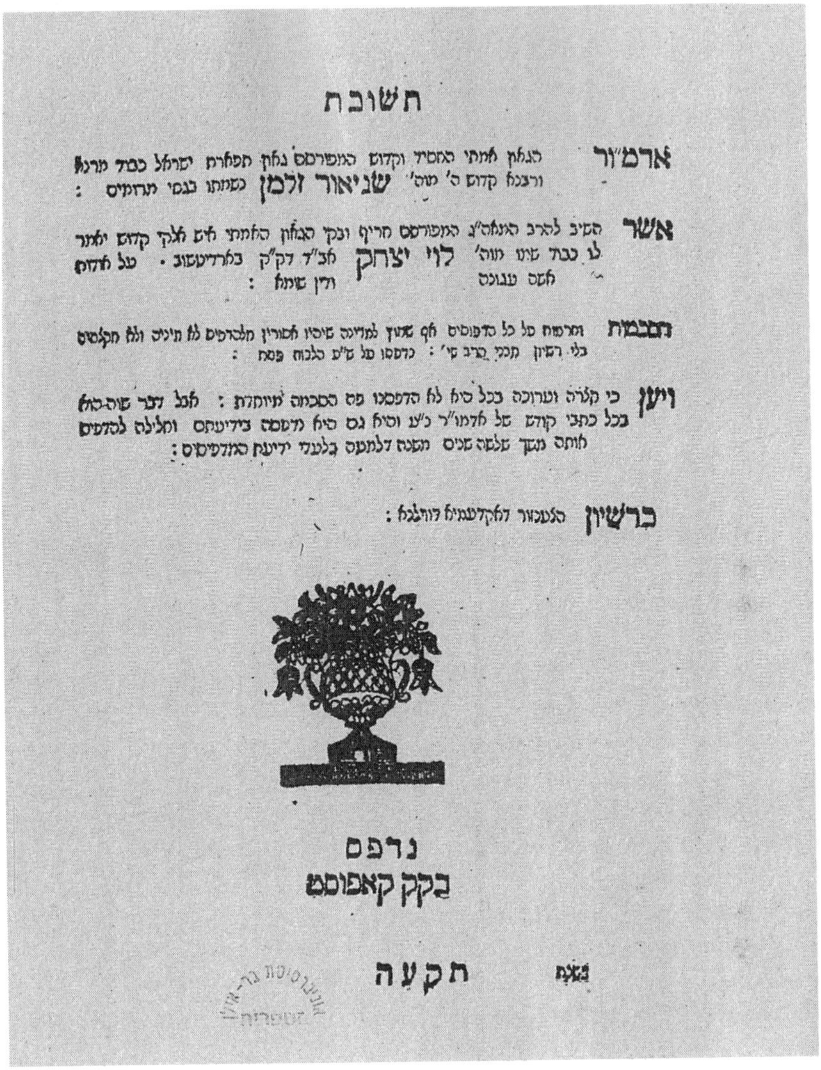
תשובת

אדמו"ר הגאון האמתי החסיד וקדוש המפורסם נאון תפארת ישראל כבוד מרנא
ורבנא קדוש ה' מוה' שניאור זלמן נשמתו בגנזי מרומים :

אשר השיב להרב המאה"ג המפורסם חריף ובקי הגאון האמתי איש אלקי קדוש יאמר
לו כבוד שמו מוה' לוי יצחק אב"ד דק"ק בארדיטשוב · על אדות
אשה עגונה ודין שומה :

הסכמות והרשות על כל המדפיסים אף שאינן למדינה שיהיו אסורין מלהדפיס לא תיכף ולא תכלעס
בלי רשיון מכל ברב סי' : נדפסו על ש"ע הלכות פסח :

ויען כי קצרה וערוכה בכל היא לא הדפסנו פה הסכמה מיוחדת : אבל דבר שוה-בכל
בכל כתבי קודש של אדמו"ר נ"ע והיא גם היא נדפסה בידיעתם וחלילה להדפיס
אותה משך שלשה שנים מעתה דלמטה בלעדי ידיעת המדפיסים :

ברשיון הצענזור דהקדעמיא דווילנא :

נדפס
בקק קאפוסט

בשנת תקעה

Figure 2.1. Title page of responsum penned by R. Shneur Zalman of Lady to R. Levi Yitzḥak of Berdyczów, printed in 1815 in Kopyś, Russian Empire. Source: Bar-Ilan University Library.

Hasidic involvement in the development of Jewish law extended to printing ventures that included the publication of classic tomes of Jewish law. While R. Shneur Zalman of Lady (c. 1745–1812) is famous as a Hasidic thinker, he was also an eminent author of legal texts whose writings were almost entirely published posthumously (see figure 2.1). In addition, R. Shneur Zalman served as an arbitrator in civil disputes, though we know little about his activity in this area. Moreover, R. Shneur Zalman was active in bringing classic works of Jewish law to the printing press. He was responsible for the publication of an edition of the Babylonian Talmud and an edition of *Arba'ah turim*, a leading fourteenth-century consolidation of Jewish law.[3] Publishing ventures, especially those involving multivolume works, entailed significant financial investment and risk.

Hasidic masters also had a hand in publishing enterprises by writing approbations that encouraged the public to purchase the books. Such approbations generally included a ban for a given period against publication of the work by another party, thereby assisting investors in recovering their costs and turning a profit. We have a solitary approbation from the Maggid of Mezrich, and this letter was given for a legal work.[4] R. Avraham Yehoshua Heshel (c. 1747–1825) is known for his posthumously published Hasidic work, entitled *Ohev yisra'el*. He did not bequeath legal writing, but served in the rabbinate in Kolbuszowa, Opatów, and Iaşi before retiring from the official rabbinate and moving to Międzybóż—the city famous as the hometown of the Besht (c. 1700–1760). We would be hard pressed to find a Hasidic master who matched R. Avraham Yehoshua Heshel for the sheer number of approbations he wrote, many of them for the publication of works in Jewish law.

The enduring interest in the legal sphere was also reflected in curricula that included the study of Jewish law. Thus, for example, when R. Levi Yitzḥak of Berdichev (Berdyczów) first published his *Kedushat levi* in 1798, he included selections from two of his children and from his father. One of his sons, R. Meir of Husaków (1760–1806), opened his contribution with a vignette about his father. R. Meir described how many people came to his father for inspiration in the service of God *and* in order to study Jewish law.[5] R. Meir had inherited the Husaków rabbinate from his paternal grandfather, and his two-volume work included Talmudic novellae and responses to those who disagreed with the rulings of the great twelfth-century codifier Maimonides.[6] In the first volume, R. Meir once again related to the curriculum of those who were under his father's tutelage, highlighting the prominence of Talmud and Jewish law.[7]

Even in their homilies, Hasidic masters—some who served in juridical roles and others who were not known as legal practitioners—theorized about Jewish law. For example, R. Shlomo of Łuck (c.1740–1813) recorded that his teacher the Maggid of Mezrich expounded a famous Talmudic maxim: "These and those"—referring to contradictory legal opinions—"are the words of the living God." The Maggid's homilies on this dictum present what could be understood as a consideration of legal pluralism in Jewish law from a mystical perspective.[8] While the extant materials do not allow us to paint a complete portrait of the Maggid's approach, the fact that he chose to expound on the multiplicity of opinions in Jewish law indicates that he was not disengaged from the legal realm.

This collage need not surprise us. From time immemorial, halakhah has guided and governed traditional Jewish life. Yet much of Hasidic scholarship has yet to mine the treasure trove of Jewish legal writing from the school of Hasidism. What might such a mining venture uncover? Before demonstrating such an undertaking, let us begin by fossicking: surveying the terrain of literary sources of Jewish law.

Literary Sources of Jewish Law

Jewish law from the late modern period can be found in an array of literary sources, including codes of law, glosses and commentaries, responsa, and to a lesser extent legislation. The *bet midrash* (study hall) of Hasidism—that is, an imaginary convocation spanning 250 years of learned scholarship from Hasidic masters and from people who identified as Hasidim—has contributed works to each of these genres of legal writing. I will briefly describe the principal genres and survey some of the Hasidic contributions to each of these. I will also indicate examples of what the student of Hasidism might gain from exploring these legal sources. At the outset, let me note that each writer I will discuss also made a contribution to Hasidic literature and served as the head of a Hasidic community; their Hasidic credentials, therefore, are unimpeachable.

Codes

In legal parlance, the term *code* has not been used consistently, and typologies for distinguishing between collections, compilations, consolidations, and codifications have been suggested. The unique circumstances of Jewish law in the late modern period—including a lack of defined jurisdictional boundaries and inconsistent instituted enforcement mechanisms—mean that terms associated with corpora of law in national, secular legal systems should be employed with caution. Despite the fact that many key codification features are missing in Jewish law, the term *codification* has been used by scholars to describe a particular genre of Jewish legal writing that has the following salient features: (1) The work seeks to set out law in a defined field; (2) it presages a range of scenarios, dictating conduct for each eventuality, and; (3) it presents itself as an exclusive statement of law, precluding the need to consult earlier sources. Admittedly, comprehensiveness and exclusivity are often more aspirations than achievements.

Important codifications of Jewish law include *Mishneh torah*, by Maimonides (1138–1204), the aforementioned *Arba'ah turim*, by R. Ya'akov ben Asher (c. 1269–1343), and *Shulḥan 'arukh*, by R. Yosef Karo (1488–1575). The most important Hasidic contribution to this genre of legal writing is the work known as *Shulḥan 'arukh ha-rav*, by R. Shneur Zalman of Lady. The popularity of this code went beyond the confines of the Hasidic community: it has been published more than fifty times, translated into English, and extensively annotated.[9] To this day, *Shulḥan 'arukh ha-rav* is avidly studied and regularly consulted by practitioners of Jewish law.

While scholars of Hasidic thought and scholars of Hasidic history have invested much effort in exploring R. Shneur Zalman's seminal contributions to Hasidism, his compilation of Jewish law and his other legal writing have gone virtually untouched.[10] One reason for the neglect is that the work does not demonstrate Hasidism in any apparent manner. This itself is striking: a leader of the nascent movement who produced a groundbreaking work in Hasidic thought also authored a legal tome bereft of overt Hasidic influence.[11] This may also partly explain how the work achieved popularity beyond Hasidic circles.

R. Yitzḥak Aizik Yehudah Yeḥiel Safrin of Komarno (1806–1874) also produced a code of Jewish law, entitled *Shulḥan ha-tahor*.[12] In contrast to R. Shneur Zalman's code, R. Safrin's code is barely known and seldom cited, despite its lucid style. This was because the work remained in manuscript until 1963–1965, when it was first published in Tel Aviv.[13] Even once the work became available to the wider public, it has rarely been considered in legal discourse because it is chock-full of kabbalistic considerations, making it inappropriate for mass consumption.

Thus, for example, R. Safrin discusses the order of precedence between *seliḥot* and *tikkun ḥatsot*—that is, penitentiary prayers in the lead up to the High Holy Days and the midnight rite of mourning for the exile.[14] While the question is no doubt legitimate, it is only the mystically committed who engage in *tikkun ḥatsot* and might be faced with such a dilemma. R. Safrin also discusses wearing white clothes on Shabbat, a mystical practice adopted by Hasidic leaders in the formative years of the movement that survived until the twentieth century but has since faded.[15] R. Safrin's commitment to Kabbalah is so pronounced that dictates based on Jewish mysticism are given greater weight than classic sources of Jewish law. Thus the work pushes the boundaries of legal discourse in the Jewish tradition.[16] This fascinating work suggests one particular permutation of how the gnostic world of Jewish mysticism was incorporated into daily Jewish practice by Hasidic masters.

Shulḥan ha-tahor might also be read on the backdrop of kabbalistic literature that translated the mystical *kavanot* (meditations) of R. Yitzḥak Luria (*Ari*, 1534–1572) into practical instructions that could be followed by all, especially people who were not adept in Lurianic mysticism. This reminds us that Hasidism should be seen—at least to some extent—as a continuation or development of the Jewish mystical tradition, rather than an entirely new phenomenon.

Glosses

Glosses and commentaries seek to elucidate, repudiate, or extrapolate earlier texts. Commentaries may have legal material, particularly when the base text is a legal work. This is the case, for instance, with commentaries on the Talmud. The commentator's goal is to explain the Talmud; since the Talmud includes much legal material, the commentary may be read as a legal text with normative implications. Commentaries on works of law are clearly legal works, as authors aim to rule on matters of law, using the earlier text as scaffolding. Like the manuscripts of the eleventh- and twelfth-century glossators, these works were often published as *glosa marginalis*—the base text is printed in the middle of the page, and the gloss is printed in the margins. Legal glosses are a significant phenomenon in Jewish law. Writing a gloss—even when the author argued with the base text—contributed to the standing, popularity, and lasting worth of the base text. Perhaps the most important legal gloss was written by the Kraków rabbi Moshe Isserles (*Remu*, c. 1530–1572), on Karo's *Shulḥan 'arukh*. Remu's gloss ensured that the composite work could be used by Jews from various diasporas, resulting in a work that remains a benchmark in Jewish law to this day.

Hasidism also contributed to this genre of legal writing. I already mentioned the commentary on the laws of Shabbat penned by R. Uziel Meisels; let me add three further examples. R. Avraham David Wahrman of Buczacz (1771–1840) wrote a commentary on each of the four sections of the *Shulḥan 'arukh*.[17] R. Tsevi Hirsh Shapira of Munkács (1850–1913) wrote *Darkhei teshuvah* on the laws of slaughter and suitability of various foods.[18] R. Tsevi Hirsh did not finish the work; that task fell to his only son and successor, R. Ḥayim Elazar Shapira (1871–1937), who completed the volume that his father had begun to prepare on laws of menstruation and added a further volume to the series on the laws of ritual baths.[19] R. Ḥayim Elazar—in addition to completing his father's work—published his own commentary on the first section of *Shulḥan 'arukh*, dealing with daily rituals (see figure 2.2), as well as a volume on the laws of tefillin and the laws of circumcision.[20]

Glosses are not all cut of one cloth, and a book's reception history is the result of various factors. R. Ḥayim Elazar's commentaries were part of his gallant attempt to explain Hasidic practice along legal lines.[21] Yet for practical law, existing works of Jewish law held sway. Moreover, his legal writings were eclipsed by his own passionate political activism.

R. Tsevi Hirsh's *Darkhei teshuva* was an attempt to summarize the many rulings that had appeared in the responsa literature. This was a recognized and popular genre, though R. Tsevi Hirsh's effort surpassed those of his predecessors.[22] Indeed, *Darkhei teshuva* was a popular work that was used extensively by rabbis who were charged with overseeing local Jewish law.

R. Wahrman's commentaries sought to understand the base text in light of other legal material, but the author also freely shared his personal experiences and adventures. Thus his discussions are interlaced with irreplaceable pearls about Hasidic life. R. Wahrman was a disciple of the aforementioned R. Levi

Figure 2.2. Title page of R. Ḥayim Elazar Shapira's *Nimukei oraḥ ḥayim*, commentary on *Shulḥan ʿarukh*, orah ḥayim, sections 1–697, printed in 1930 in Turňa nad Bodvou, Czechoslovakia. Source: National Library of Israel.

Yitzḥak of Berdichev and of R. Moshe Leib of Sasów (1745–1807). From 1790, he served in the Jazłowiec rabbinate, and in 1814 he was appointed rabbi of Buczacz, where he served until his death in 1840. R. Wahrman's legal commentaries are printed in standard editions of the *Shulḥan ʿarukh*, though until recently they were not presented in user-friendly typeface.

In his discussion of the Four Species taken on the festival of Sukkot, R. Wahrman related that he specifically sought an *etrog* (citron) from Corfu. At the time, the question of the suitability of Corfu citrons raged. R. Wahrman explained his choice by stating that he was merely following the practice of his teachers, including R. Levi Yitzḥak.[23] This is particularly important testimony, given the forged letter from the Kherson Geniza in which R. Shneur Zalman of Lady allegedly wrote to R. Levi Yitzḥak complaining that his colleague had not sent him one of two citrons that he received from the Land of Israel, as he had done in past years.[24]

Responsa: She'elot u-teshuvot

A responsum is a specific answer to a legal question posed to a jurist. It is limited in scope and application to a particular case, though it may be used as a guiding precedent in future cases. The genre dates back to seventh-century Babylonia and continues to thrive today. Rabbis, judges, codifiers, and other legal writers generally took stock of relevant responsa literature when rendering decisions, writing legal tomes, or giving instructions to their constituents. The responsa literature is the richest source of Jewish law in the late modern period.

Significant collections of responsa by Hasidic masters include *Divrei Yeḥezkel*, by the chief rabbi of Transylvania, R. Yeḥezkel Panet (1783–1845), *Tsemah tsedek*, by R. Menaḥem Mendel Schneersohn of Lubavitch (Lubawicze) (1789–1866), *Divrei ḥayim*, by R. Ḥayim Halberstam of Sanz (Nowy Sącz) (1797–1876), *Avnei nezer*, by R. Avraham Bornstein of Sochaczew (1838–1910), *Minhat Elʿazar*, by the aforementioned R. Ḥayim Elazar Shapira of Munkács, *Divrei yatsiv*, by R. Yekutiel Yehudah Halberstam of Klausenberg (Kolozsvár/Cluj) (1905–1994), and many more. The nature of the genre is such that it often gives voice to realia, as respondents recapitulated detailed scenarios and the practical questions that were posed to them. This style makes the responsa literature an abundant and irreplaceable repository not just of law but also of history, ethnography, culture, and social dynamics.

R. Panet's collection of responsa includes a nonlegal text of extreme import for the history of Hasidism: a letter to the author's father describing his encounter with R. Menaḥem Mendel Turm of Rymanów (1745–1815). This is a rare account of a person who did not grow up in the Hasidic milieu and decided to join the ranks of Hasidism. R. Panet describes the emotional and religious experience of spending time under the tutelage of R. Menaḥem Mendel of Rymanów, recording noteworthy eyewitness testimony.[25]

R. Panet's account is an exception; most of the invaluable historical and cultural material that is preserved in the responsa literature is intertwined with legal discussions. Thus, for instance, R. Panet's collection preserves a legal exchange with R. Tsevi Elimelekh Shapira of Dynów (1783–1841), who was serving at the time in the Munkács rabbinate. The correspondence concerned a bill of divorce executed in Karlsburg (Gyulafehérvár/Alba Iulia) for a Munkács couple. The specifics of the case are not necessary for the present context, but R. Panet's responsum also includes words of sympathy for his beleaguered colleague who was encountering local opposition.[26] This incidental remark—in legal parlance, an *obiter dictum*—may help us understand why R. Tsevi Elimelekh left his Munkács rabbinate after only four years in the post. He then returned to Galicia, where he achieved fame as a Hasidic master.

It is not just *obiter dicta* that provide valuable information; some cases are themselves of interest to scholars of Hasidism. Thus, for instance, from R. Ḥayim Halberstam's responsa we refine our understanding of the development of dynastic succession—a key feature of Hasidism from the nineteenth century through to this day. R. Halberstam was asked whether leadership of a Hasidic community was to be bequeathed to heirs. He suggested that Hasidic leadership was qualitatively different from rabbinic leadership in that it required divinely conferred grace, not just legal proficiency. R. Halberstam therefore ruled that the norms governing inheriting positions of power did not apply to Hasidic leadership.[27]

Despite the wealth and promise of the responsa literature, most collections produced by Hasidic masters are yet to be subject to scholarly analysis.[28]

Legislation: Takkanot and Gezerot

Legal systems require procedures for abrogating or amending law. Such mechanisms are a necessity in order to accommodate change, transition, development, and evolution. In most legal systems, legislation is one of the prime tools for dealing with the vicissitudes of life and contemporary reality. In the Jewish legal system, legislation—*takkanot* and *gezerot*—has essentially disappeared as an effective legal instrument. Notwithstanding the decline, Hasidic masters have made contributions to this field of legal writing.

Some legislation by Hasidic masters addressed the Hasidic community and is more reflective of spiritual leadership than of legal authority. Examples include *Takkanot de-Lozni*, issued by R. Shneur Zalman of Lady around the 1790s in a bid to regulate visits by Hasidim, and rules instituted for Ger Hasidim in the second half of the twentieth century, such as the unwritten guidelines—colloquially known as *Takkunes*—of R. Israel Alter (1895–1977) and his successors regarding sexual conduct.[29]

From a legal perspective, regulations whose impact goes beyond the circle of Hasidic adherents are more significant. Hasidic masters who served in official rabbinic positions had the opportunity to exercise legal authority for the entire community under their jurisdiction. For example, *Takkanot tamkhin de-'orayta* was enacted by R. Tsevi Elimelekh Shapira of Dynów in 1827 or 1828, during his brief stint as rabbi of Munkács. This legislative act strove to provide religious education for all Jewish males in Munkács. To this end the legislation established a society responsible for the execution of the regulations and an elaborate taxation system that was to be applied to members of the society in order to guarantee funding for the program. The regulations also distinctly sought to socialize both students and teachers. Thus the issues emphasized in the ordinances—such as wearing *tsitsit* (fringed garments)—provide a window into the socioreligious challenges that troubled R. Tsevi Elimelekh in the 1820s. Yet *tsitsit* appear in the Bible and in the rabbinic corpus of Jewish law, so "enacting" such a requirement is undoubtedly strange. R. Tsevi Elimelekh was aware that readers might find it absurd that he was "legislating" existing laws. He explained his predicament, pointing out that there were many people who wantonly transgressed, so he felt that he had no choice but to reiterate existing laws.[30] Thus *Takkanot tamkhin de-'orayta* provides a perspective into religious observance in Munkács, Hungary, in the 1820s.[31]

State of Research

Having surveyed the terrain, it is now time to consider what exploration has already been conducted in the field. The answer to this question is painfully simple: very little. This of course begets another question: why have legal texts been ignored by scholars of Hasidism?

Before the academic study of Hasidism had launched in earnest, Gershom Scholem (1887–1982) noted what he termed a "paradox" and a "miraculous thing": a spiritualist revival that nonetheless retained fidelity to Jewish law—that is, "a curious mix of conservatism and innovation."[32] Scholem was not the first scholar to identify this as a puzzle, though he was the most influential. Erich Fromm (1900–1980), in his 1922 doctoral dissertation, discussed the role of Jewish law in the cohesion of three communities: Reform Judaism, Karaism, and Hasidism. Fromm singled out R. Shneur Zalman of Lady as "Der Versuch einer Synthese von Chassidismus und Rabbinismus" (the attempt at a synthesis of Hasidism and Rabbinism).[33] Indeed, R. Shneur Zalman's uniqueness in the annals of nascent Hasidism was a common theme among scholars of Hasidism.[34] From the discussion thus far, it is apparent that the portrayal of R. Shneur Zalman as a lone exception is patently inaccurate; synthesizing between allegiance to Jewish law and the innovative spirit of Hasidism was part of everyday life for many Hasidic leaders, from the early days of the nascent movement right down to contemporary times.[35]

To some extent, identifying the phenomenon as a "paradox" was an assimilation of the eighteenth-century mitnagedic critique of Hasidism.[36] Even if

Hasidic practices could be justified by recourse to the Jewish bookcase, those practices were beyond the pale by dint of the fact that they were not part of regnant tradition. The "paradox," therefore, was predicated on the assumption that an innovative, anomian, and possibly even antinomian religious spirit could not possibly jibe with the strictures of law. This underlying assumption of a spirit/law binary was widely accepted. Alas, the "paradox" was not probed in earnest, and hence the assumption was seldom challenged. The interests of Scholem, his colleagues, and his students lay elsewhere, as they devoted their energies to what would become mainstays of Hasidic scholarship.

In 1940—at around the same time that Scholem described this "paradox"—Aaron Wertheim (1902–1988) submitted his doctoral dissertation, titled "The Halakah in the Hasidic Literature," to the Dropsie College for Hebrew and Cognate Learning, in Philadelphia. Wertheim's dissertation was unknown until 1960, when he published his research in Hebrew. The year 1960—commemorating two centuries since the demise of the Besht—was a heady year for Hasidic scholarship. Yet in the preface to his Hebrew book, Wertheim bemoaned the fact that the legal literature of the Hasidim was still lying untouched, noting how absurd it was that the very system of law that had served as the glue for Jewish communities was being ignored by those who were researching the coalescence of a new form of Jewish community. On the eve of the festival of Shavuot—the eve of the anniversary of the Besht's death—in a succinct review in the Hebrew press, Abraham Meir Habermann (1901–1980) noted that Wertheim "has illuminated Hasidism in an interesting light, that has not yet served as material for extensive and comprehensive research."[37]

Alas, Wertheim's volume received a cool reception in academic circles. Avraham Rubinstein (1912–1993) wrote a scathing critique in which he highlighted three problems with Wertheim's approach. First, Wertheim treated Hasidism as a phenomenon without roots in traditional Jewish mysticism. This resulted in Wertheim mistakenly identifying "innovations," when a nuanced approach would have identified the inflection from existing mystical practice. Second, Rubinstein charged Wertheim with a fanciful image of unified religious observance among Polish Jewry. Third, Rubinstein derided Wertheim's simplistic presentation that did not take stock of different Hasidic masters, schools, regions, or periods. Rubinstein concluded that "the book in general is disappointing."[38]

Rubinstein's critique is well founded, though I believe he adjudged Wertheim hastily. The maladies that Rubinstein pointed out are indeed methodologically problematic, particularly the lack of comparative yardsticks. I would amplify that point by suggesting that research on Hasidic legal texts must take stock of other legal texts, both within the Hasidic milieu and beyond. Nonetheless, Wertheim must be appreciated for recognizing the field and for his initial foray. Wertheim's volume continues to be popular in nonacademic circles—it has been reprinted several times, as well as translated into English.[39] Even in academia—despite

Rubinstein's critique—scholars who approach a topic in the field of law and Hasidism are likely to consult Wertheim as a starting point.[40]

Wertheim was not entirely alone. From the late 1950s through the beginning of the 1970s, Yitzḥak Alfasi (b. 1929) wrote a number of studies in which he discussed sources in Jewish law for Hasidic practice.[41] Alfasi's primary contribution to Hasidic scholarship has been in the form of biographical sketches of Hasidic masters that are enjoyed by a wide readership, though not without critique. His work on Jewish law and Hasidism has not been subject to scholarly review—perhaps an indication of the prevailing belief that this field of research is unlikely to produce significant fruit. It can be said that Rubinstein's critique of Wertheim applies equally to Alfasi.

Wertheim and Alfasi declared similar aims, employed similar methods, and even dealt with some of the same issues. Surprisingly, they did not relate to each other's work. Both scholars began with the assumption that Jewish law was the lynchpin of Jewish life. They then highlighted Hasidic conduct that appeared to contradict codified Jewish law, and identified possible sources in order to correct the misconception that Hasidism was antinomian.

For all the justified critique of their work, it should be said that both scholars correctly identified a lacuna in scholarship. Their virgin efforts were overgeneralized and not sufficiently thorough or nuanced. Their research was bereft of temporal or geographic context. They lacked convincing comparative analysis. But for all their faults, Wertheim and Alfasi recognized that Jewish law has been part of the fabric of Hasidic life and should not be shunted aside.

This is not to say that the field has been neglected entirely. Particular legal issues, specific figures, and select works have been analyzed by scholars. Thus, for instance, the innovation of R. Gershon Ḥanokh Leiner of Radzyń (1839–1891) to reintroduce the blue thread (*tekhelet*) into *tsitsit* has captured attention. In addition, scholars have recently begun to sift through Hasidic homilies for conceptual statements about jurisprudence.[42] Notwithstanding these inroads, much uncharted territory remains. In light of this situation, it is unsurprising that in 2009, historian Moshe Rosman noted that Scholem's "paradox" continued to reverberate.[43]

Thus fuller use of the legal material from the *bet midrash* of Hasidism remains a scholarly desideratum. What might such a mining venture in this unmapped territory look like? The following case study demonstrates one possible vector.

Hasidic Headwear

Distinct garb is one of the most visible ethnographic markers of contemporary Hasidism. The Austro-Hungarian Jewish painter Isidor Kaufmann (1853–1921) famously painted Jews of Eastern Europe in their Shabbat finery. Hasidim continue to be depicted wearing distinctive garments, in particular fur headwear:

shtraymel, *spodek*, and *kolpik*. Yet according to Jewish law there is one Shabbat a year when finery is prohibited. Did Hasidim respect this law and refrain from wearing distinctive fur headdress on that Shabbat?[44]

According to Jewish tradition, there is an annual three-week mourning period commemorating the sweep of tragedies that befell Jews throughout history. This period is divided into stages with progressively increasing mourning strictures. The period culminates with the fast of Tisha be-'av. In general, mourning practices—even during this three-week period—are not observed publicly on Shabbat. What about mourning practices on Shabbat ḥazon, the Shabbat immediately before Tisha be-'av? Following earlier authorities, Remu, in his annotations to *Shulḥan 'arukh*, ruled, "Even on Shabbat ḥazon, one does not change [clothes] to wear Shabbat attire, except for the shirt alone."[45] No other Shabbat finery was to be worn on Shabbat ḥazon. Did Hasidim keep this law and avoid donning *shtraymlekh* on Shabbat ḥazon?

The Hasidic master and legal authority R. Ḥayim Elazar Shapira of Munkács—in his commentary to *Shulḥan 'arukh* and to Remu's annotations (see figure 2.2)—answered this question, telling readers that Hasidim did indeed wear *shtraymlekh* on Shabbat ḥazon:[46]

> [Citation from Remu] Even on *Shabbat ḥazon*, one does not change [clothes] to wear Shabbat attire etc.
>
> [Gloss] And it is questionable because it is like public mourning which is forbidden on Shabbat. And behold see *Bekhor shor* (at the end of *Tevu'ot shor*) to Tractate *Ta'anit* (at *s.v. le-'o[raḥ] ḥ[ayim]*, *siman* 552), regarding what he wrote about the position of the *Magen avraham* (section 552, no. 14), who wrote that if the 9th of *Av* falls on Shabbat or on Sunday a person should not sit at the Third Meal in the company of friends. And the *Tevu'ot shor* questioned this, because if a person is accustomed to this (to sit at the Third Meal with company) it is like public mourning [not to do so], and hence forbidden to exclude the company of friends; see there. If so, how much more so, with regards to Shabbat clothing (*shtraymel*) for someone who is accustomed to [wearing] it on Shabbat and does not remove it on the holy Shabbat and even on Shabbat in the days of his mourning—it should not befall us—everyone is accustomed to go wearing it, because if he will not wear it then it is like making his Shabbat mundane with public mourning. How much more so he should not remove it on *Shabbat ḥazon* (which is far more lenient, because it is mourning over the distant past).
>
> Therefore, the custom of our teachers and our ancestors before us—may their memory be a blessing—and in our generations the Hasidic masters [*tsadikim*] and the Hasidim who have been accustomed to go on *Shabbat ḥazon* with a *shtraymel* like on other holy Shabbats—is good and proper.

And [regarding] that which the medieval authorities—may their memory be a blessing—wrote, as cited by Remu, not to change [to] Shabbat clothes: We must say regarding their custom in their lands, and [regarding] their source from *Or zaru'a* and from *Maharil*, the ancient land of *Ashkenaz*, that they went with a hat (*kapelush*) even on Shabbat. But on Shabbat they just wore the nicer and newer [hat]. And the difference between the clothing of the weekdays and that of Shabbat is not apparent to everyone, at all; just that this one [for Shabbat] is nicer and newer. Therefore, it is not public mourning [to retain the weekday *kapelush*] since it is not so apparent to all. Not so with the *shtraymel*, as mentioned (and see our words above, section 530, no. 3, regarding *ḥol ha-mo'ed*).

And behold I found that which my soul treasures already in the early [authorities]—the brilliant *Radbaz* in [his] responsa (volume 2, section 693): that he protested against this custom that they do not change their clothes on *Shabbat ḥazon* and they wear weekday clothes and it is like public mourning and they make the sacred—mundane. And he wrote that we must say that even the intent of *Or zaru'a* (who the Remu also cited in this matter) was not indicative of the way German Jews acted; these are his cherished words, see there.

And similarly regarding the practices of the Gaon [R. Eliyahu of Vilna, as recorded] in the book *Sha'arei raḥamim* (laws of Shabbat, section 73), that even if 9th of *Av* falls on Shabbat one should not change at all from [wearing] Shabbat clothes; see there, and in *Bi'ur ha-Gra* on [*Shulḥan 'arukh*], *o*[*raḥh*] *ḥ*[*ayim*] on this matter (sub-section 3). And behold we have a further proof from prayer books of the *Ari*, of blessed memory, where they wrote with protest regarding mourners—may the merciful one save us—who do not change their clothing on Shabbat. And how much more so, according to this, on *Shabbat ḥazon* that is mourning for the distant past—certainly one should change [clothing] and wear Shabbat clothing.

We have no comparable visual evidence. Hasidim avoided having their picture taken on Shabbat in general, and it is unlikely that an artist would choose to depict Hasidic subjects specifically on Shabbat ḥazon. To be sure, surviving visual evidence demonstrates that in the late nineteenth and early twentieth centuries such headwear was standard rabbinic attire. At some time in the early twentieth century, *shtraymlekh* and the like became characteristic of Hasidic affiliation, though rabbinic figures and others continued to don furs. It was only at that time that the question became an issue of particularly Hasidic interest. Thus in his legal writing R. Ḥayim Elazar Shapira provides irrefutable evidence of Hasidic practice that is virtually unknown from other sources.[47]

Yet R. Ḥayim Elazar was not interested in recording ethnographic data; he was driven by an entirely different motive. As a Hasidic jurist, he was troubled by the apparent lack of respect for Jewish law by his saintly Hasidic predecessors and by his own Hasidic community. He was interested in explaining how his own interpretive community squared their conduct with codified Jewish law. Indeed, across his writings R. Ḥayim Elazar consistently and creatively sought to demonstrate that Hasidic practice was not brazenly antinomian.[48] The issue was not just a theoretical legal conundrum; it was a matter of personal interest. The matter touched R. Ḥayim Elazar's personal identity. Indeed, one of his disciples recorded that his teacher wore regular Shabbat attire on Shabbat ḥazon without changing one whit.[49]

R. Ḥayim Elazar employed four tools of legal reasoning to make his point: analogy, *argumentum a fortiori*, distinction, and precedent. Understanding R. Ḥayim Elazar's strategy—not just the bottom line—sheds further light on Hasidic history and culture. Let us, therefore, examine the four arguments.

Analogy

R. Ḥayim Elazar argued that the issue at hand was comparable to holding a Shabbat afternoon festive gathering with friends on Shabbat ḥazon, when Tisha be-'av was to be commemorated on Sunday.[50] While some authorities ruled that it was inappropriate, other authorities pointed out that if such a social gathering was a regular Shabbat occurrence, cancelling the gathering on Shabbat ḥazon would constitute forbidden public mourning.[51] R. Ḥayim Elazar extrapolated: a *shtraymel* is worn on each Shabbat; removing it on Shabbat ḥazon would therefore constitute forbidden public mourning.

Argumentum a fortiori

R. Ḥayim Elazar pointed out that people who mourn relatives don Shabbat finery even during the initial seven-day mourning period. According to Jewish law mourning practices recede with time, consequently mourning on Shabbat ḥazon could not be as stringent as mourning the recent death of a close relative, since the tragedies being commemorated occurred way in the past. If full Shabbat attire was worn during the initial seven-day mourning period that commemorates a recent loss, *a fortiori* full Shabbat attire should be worn on Shabbat ḥazon, which commemorates a distant loss.[52] This would include wearing *shtraymlekh*.

Distinction

Two legal arguments were insufficient to trump Remu, whose ruling against changing clothes on Shabbat ḥazon doubtless considered the analogous case and the *argumentum a fortiori*. R. Ḥayim Elazar therefore proceeded to argue that Hasidic headdress was distinguishable from other traditional Jewish headwear.

According to R. Ḥayim Elazar, in medieval Germany and in sixteenth-century Poland, the difference between weekday and Shabbat headwear was barely noticeable. Hence wearing a weekday head covering on Shabbat ḥazon would not be considered public mourning. Thus Remu's ruling against changing headwear would not constitute public mourning. Not so with Hasidim: not wearing *shtraymlekh* would be noticeable and hence tantamount to forbidden public mourning. Remu's ruling, therefore, did not apply to Hasidic *shtraymlekh*.

In addition to distinguishing Hasidic *shtraymlekh* from Remu's *kapelush*, R. Ḥayim Elazar offered a significant implicit argument. Instead of regarding the Hasidic practice as legally questionable, he argued that wearing *shtraymlekh* on Shabbat ḥazon was a display of fidelity to Jewish law, since the practice demonstrated an understanding of the law's rationale.

Precedent

In what appears to be an addendum inserted later, R. Ḥayim Elazar presented a fourth argument, which he opened with a celebratory line: "And behold I found that which my soul treasures"—earlier authorities who stated that on Shabbat ḥazon regular Shabbat finery should be worn. The process of selecting precedents (or using any legal reasoning, for that matter) is subject to judicial discretion, and the present case is a fascinating example of considered selection—and perhaps conscious omission. Thus R. Ḥayim Elazar cited three authorities of different stripes, none of whom was aligned with Hasidism.

First, he cited R. David ibn Zimra (*Radbaz*, c. 1480–1572), a prolific author of responsa, who hailed from Spain and served in the Egyptian rabbinate. Radbaz had been asked why Ashkenazi Jews wore weekday clothes on Shabbat ḥazon. Radbaz was dismissive of the practice, denying that it was widespread and arguing that it was mistaken "because it is against the dignity of the Shabbat, and makes the sacred—mundane."[53]

Second, R. Ḥayim Elazar mentioned R. Eliyahu of Vilna (1720–1797), an unimpeachable authority who had been the figurehead of the opposition to Hasidism. His weekly pre-Shabbat routine included changing all his clothes, and Shabbat ḥazon was reportedly no exception.[54]

Third, he referred to unspecified mystical prayer books, affiliated with the legacy of the great kabbalist R. Yitzḥak Luria (*Ari*), that were highly critical of mourners who did not wear Shabbat finery. This brought R. Ḥayim Elazar back to his *argumentum a fortiori*: if Shabbat attire is appropriate for a mourner who has just suffered a loss, it is certainly appropriate for Shabbat ḥazon, which commemorates ancient loss.

The choice of sources is significant: a medieval jurist, an anti-Hasidic authority, and Jewish mystical tradition. With this battery, R. Ḥayim Elazar argued that there was valid precedent for not removing *shtraymlekh* on Shabbat ḥazon.

Yet it was not just the sources that he chose to cite that are significant. We should also consider the sources he omitted. Four respected jurists who did not identify with Hasidism dealt with the issue of Shabbat finery on Shabbat ḥazon, and R. Ḥayim Elazar did not cite them, perhaps for good reason. Admittedly, we cannot say for certain why R. Ḥayim Elazar chose not to cite these precedents, and an *argumentum ex silentio* is generally a weak claim. Nonetheless, it is worthwhile considering these sources and hypothesizing why R. Ḥayim Elazar did not mention them.

R. Moshe Sofer (*Ḥatam sofer*, 1762–1839), the famed rabbinic figure who inspired Hungarian Orthodoxy, argued against wearing Shabbat attire on Shabbat ḥazon, pointing out that this was exactly how to empathize with the historic tragedies. R. Sofer explained that the Ari's practice of wearing Shabbat finery on Shabbat ḥazon was reserved for people of the Ari's stature who were constantly mourning and therefore did not need to denigrate Shabbat with weekday clothes. Regular people—and R. Sofer included himself in this category—were to properly observe the mourning requirements and wear weekday clothes on Shabbat ḥazon.[55] While R. Sofer was a highly respected figure, R. Ḥayim Elazar could hardly use this precedent, for it undermined his case.

R. Yeḥiel Mikhl ha-levi Epstein (*'Arukh ha-Shulḥan*, 1829–1908) was a rabbi in Nowogródek who authored an impressively comprehensive code of Jewish law. R. Epstein noted that for two or three generations the custom of wearing weekday clothes on Shabbat ḥazon had lapsed, apparently because public mourning was disallowed on Shabbat. Yet R. Epstein understood that this was an insufficient explanation, for Remu had known about the prohibition against public mourning and still ruled against Shabbat attire on Shabbat ḥazon. How then should common practice be understood? Similar to the distinction suggested by R. Ḥayim Elazar, R. Epstein argued that in days of old the poor would wear cheap clothing on Shabbat *and* during the week, while the wealthy would wear expensive clothing during the week *and* on Shabbat. The minor differences between weekday and Shabbat attire led to the norm of avoiding Shabbat clothes on Shabbat ḥazon. In recent times, argued R. Epstein, clothing norms had changed: Shabbat finery was visibly different from weekday clothing, as both the poor and the wealthy wore hats and garments made from noticeably different materials for Shabbat.

R. Epstein, it appears, could have served as a valuable source for R. Ḥayim Elazar. Yet at this point R. Epstein's argument took a turn, as he called for a return to the original law due to current circumstances: "For in this our time, according to the command of the sovereign we have already changed the appearance of our clothing, and Shabbat and weekday both have one appearance, the only difference being between cheap and expensive—certainly it is appropriate to uphold the custom of our forbearers."[56] Once again, this precedent hardly helped R. Ḥayim Elazar's case.

As we recall, R. Ḥayim Elazar cited the testimony regarding R. Eliyahu of Vilna's practice of changing his clothes on Shabbat ḥazon just as on every other week. R. Avraham Danzig (*Ḥayei adam*, 1748–1820), who lived in Vilna and was related to R. Eliyahu, provided further valuable testimony in his compendium of Jewish law. According to R. Danzig, R. Eliyahu's approach was common practice in Vilna: regular Shabbat attire was worn on Shabbat ḥazon, though some people avoided changing one garment presumably in deference to Remu's ruling.[57] Perhaps R. Ḥayim Elazar did not cite this source because Hasidic practice did not insist on preserving a vestige of Remu's ruling.

The omission of R. Ya'akov Israel Emden (1698–1776) from R. Ḥayim Elazar's opinion is perhaps the most fascinating. R. Emden was a fiery rabbinic character and an independent thinker. With a printing press in his own home in Altona, Germany, R. Emden had free rein to publish as he pleased. Inter alia, he printed a prayer book replete with extra information. Regarding Shabbat ḥazon, R. Emden used an *argumentum a fortiori* to state that Shabbat attire should be worn, concluding, "Therefore, there is much to say against the custom of the Ashkenazim who do not change their weekday clothes on Shabbat ḥazon." Furthermore, R. Emden testified that his esteemed father, R. Tsevi Hirsh Ashkenazi (*Ḥakham Tsevi*, d. 1747), had worn Shabbat finery on Shabbat ḥazon. R. Emden added that he, too, followed his father's practice.[58]

Why did R. Ḥayim Elazar not add R. Emden to the battery of sources he presented? The question can be sharpened when we consider that an older contemporary of R. Ḥayim Elazar who had much in common with his counterpart in Subcarpathian Rus' did indeed cite R. Emden. R. Israel Ḥayim Friedmann (1852–1922) served as rabbi of Rahó, Hungary (later Rachov, Czechoslovakia), was affiliated with Hasidism, and wrote on Jewish law. The third volume of Friedmann's work was published in 1911, and regarding Shabbat ḥazon and the Remu's ruling he noted, "Alas, it has become commonplace in our countries, by many who act according to the ways of piety [*be-darkhei ha-ḥasidut*], to wear Shabbat clothes like on other Shabbats."[59] To explain the phenomenon R. Friedmann cited R. Emden (and referred to R. Danzig), thus offering a blanket justification for regular Shabbat attire on Shabbat ḥazon.

R. Friedmann was aware of the argument that not wearing a *shtraymel* constituted public mourning, a claim that had been published in R. Epstein's *'Arukh ha-Shulḥan* and that would be used by R. Ḥayim Elazar. Yet R. Friedmann critiqued this approach, arguing that the public-mourning argument only provided a permit for the most visible items of clothing: a long silk jacket and a *shtraymel*; other garments were not included in the license. R. Emden, however, had provided a solution that went further, dismissing the prohibition against Shabbat clothes in Shabbat ḥazon and granting a comprehensive license. Why did R. Ḥayim Elazar not cite R. Emden?

Let me suggest that citing R. Emden would only have partially served R. Ḥayim Elazar. He would have a source for Hasidic conduct, but the source came at a cost. R. Emden, in his inimitably bold manner, had dismissed Ashkenazi tradition, which included Remu's ruling. Citing R. Emden, therefore, bespoke an audacious approach to Jewish legal tradition. R. Ḥayim Elazar would have won the skirmish but lost the battle: wearing *shtraymlekh* on Shabbat ḥazon would have been justified, but at the cost of taking an impudent approach toward the Remu, one of the pillars of Jewish law.[60]

It may be tempting to dismiss R. Ḥayim Elazar's four-pronged legal analysis as contrived justification for the fact that the Hasidic community spurned Jewish law. Before passing such judgment we would do well to recall that analogy, *argumentum a fortiori*, distinguishing cases, and citing precedents are standard legal fare. Moreover, in Roman law there is a principle that custom is the best interpreter of the law: *optima est legis interpres consuetudo*. This suggests that not only was R. Ḥayim Elazar faithful to his Hasidic heritage, but he was also a bona fide jurist.

R. Ḥayim Elazar's *shtraymel* discussion demonstrates how Hasidic masters who were also legal authorities sought to balance traditional Hasidic practice and the dictates of Jewish law. As rabbi of Munkács, he was vested with communal authority and responsibility for the maintenance of Jewish law. At the same time, he was also the bearer of Hasidic tradition. In the *shtraymel* case, the Hasidic practice appeared to break the law. The rabbi/rebbe of Munkács walked a fine line in a valiant attempt to retain fidelity to both Jewish law and Hasidic tradition. In the process, he provided valuable testimony about Hasidic practice in the early twentieth century.

R. Ḥayim Elazar's discussion indicates the value of legal texts from the Hasidic milieu for students of law and for students of Hasidic history and culture. Indeed, legal writing from the *bet midrash* of Hasidism may be the next scholarly frontier.

SUGGESTED READING

For initial forays, see Aaron Wertheim, *Law and Custom in Hasidism*, trans. S. Himelstein (Hoboken, NJ: Ktav, 1992); Yitzḥak Alfasi, *Ha-ḥasidut: Pirkei tolda u-meḥkar* (Tel Aviv: Zion, 1969), 85–99, 155–162; 184–191, 198–204; Yitzḥak Alfasi, *Meḥkarei ḥasidut* (Tel Aviv: Bnei Brith, 1975), 38–53, 72–91; Yitzḥak Alfasi, *Be-sedei ha-ḥasidut: Meḥkarim, pirkei tolda, havay u-mesoret* (Tel Aviv: Ariel, 1987), 44–59, 81–100, 173–187, 236–243, 335–343, 349–355, 506–512.

For legal theory in Hasidic homilies, see Ariel Evan Mayse, "The Ever-Changing Path: Visions of Legal Diversity in Hasidic Literature," *Conversations: The Journal of the Institute for Jewish Ideas and Ideals* 23 (2015), 84–115; Maoz Kahana and Ariel Evan Mayse, "Hasidic Halakhah: Reappraising the Interface of Spirit and Law," *AJS Review* 42 (2017), 2:375–408.

For legal writings of specific Hasidic masters see the following:

On R. Levi Yitzḥak of Berdichev [Berdyczów] (1740–1809), see Levi Cooper, "Rabbanut, halakha, lamdanut: Hebetim ʿalumim be-toledot ha-rav Levi Yitzḥak mi-Berditchev," in *Rabbi Levi Yitzḥak mi-Berditchev: Historiya, hagut, safrut, ve-nigun*, eds. Z. Mark and R. Horen (Tel Aviv: Miskal, 2017), 62–130.

On R. Shneur Zalman of Lady (c. 1745–1812), in particular his *Shulḥan ʿarukh ha-rav*, see Avinoam Rosenak, "Theory and Praxis in Rabbi Shneur Zalman of Liady: The *Tanya* and *Shulḥan ʿArukh HaRav*," *Jewish Law Association Studies* 22 (2012): 251–282; Moshe Hallamish, "*Shulḥan ʿarukh ha-rav*—bein kabbalah le-halakhah," in *Habad: Historiya, hagut ve-dimuy*, eds. J. Meir and G. Sagiv (Jerusalem: Shazar, 2016), 75–96; Levi Cooper, "Towards a Judicial Biography of Rabbi Shneur Zalman of Liady," *Journal of Law and Religion* 30 (2015), 107–135; Levi Cooper, "Mysteries of the Paratext: Why Did Rabbi Shneur Zalman of Liady Never Publish His Code of Law?" *Diné Israel* 31 (2017), 43–84.

On R. Naḥman of Bracław (1772–1810), see Yitzḥak Englard, "Mistikah u-mishpat: Hirhurim 'al 'Likutei halakhot' mi-beit midrasho shel rav Naḥman mi-Breslov," *Shenaton ha-mishpat ha-'ivri* 6–7 (1979–1980), 29–43; Alon Goshen-Gottstein, "Ha-halakhah be-re'i ha-ḥayim ha-ruḥaniyim: Likutei halakhot le-r. Natan me-Nemirov," in *Masa el ha-halakhah: 'Iyunim bein-tehumiyim ba-'olam ha-ḥok ha-yehudi*, ed. A. Berholz (Tel Aviv: Miskal, 2003), 257–284.

On R. Tsevi Elimelekh Shapira of Dynów (1783–1841), see Levi Cooper, "Legislation for Education: Rabbi Tsevi Elimelekh of Dynów's Regulations for the Support of Torah in Munkács," *Polin* 30 (2017), 43–72.

On R. Ḥayim Halberstam of Nowy Sącz (1797–1876), see Iris Brown (Hoizman), "R. Ḥayim mi-Tsanz: Darkhei pesikato 'al reka' 'olamo ha-ra'ayoni ve-'etgarei zemano" (PhD diss., Bar-Ilan University, 2004).

On R. Ḥayim Elazar Shapira of Munkács (1871–1937), see Levi Cooper, "Ha-'admor mi-Munkatch ha-rav Ḥayim El'azar Shapira: Ha-posek ha-ḥasidi—demut ve-shitah" (PhD diss., Bar-Ilan University, 2011); Levi Cooper, "Neged zirmei ha-mayim ha-zedonim: Ha-'admor mi-Munkatch r. Hayim El'azar Shapira," in *Ha-gedolim*, eds. B. Brown and N. Leon (Jerusalem: Magnes Press, 2017), 259–291.

On R. Yekutiel Yehudah Halberstam of Klausenberg (1905–1994), see Tamir Granot, "Tekumat ha-ḥasidut be-'Erets Yisra'el aḥarei ha-sho'ah: Mishnato ha-ra'ayonit, ha-hilkhatit, ve-ha-ḥevratit shel ha-'admor r. Yekuti'el Yehudah Halbershtam mi-Tsanz-Kloyzenburg" (PhD diss., Bar-Ilan University, 2008).

NOTES

1. Levi Cooper, "Rabbanut, halakhah, lamdanut: Hebetim 'alumim be-toledot ha-rav Levi Yitzḥak mi-Berditchev," in *Rabbi Levi Yitzḥak mi-Berditchev: Historiya, hagut, safrut, ve-nigun*, ed. Z. Mark and R. Horen (Tel Aviv: Miskal, 2017), 62–130.

2. R. Uziel Meisels's works: *Tiferet ha-tsevi* (Żółkiew: G. Letteris, 1803), on the first chapter of tractate *Betsah*; *Kerem shelomoh* (printed together with *Tiferet ha-tsevi*), on Talmudic and legal miscellany; *'Ets ha-da'at tov* (Warsaw: N. Schriftgisser, 1863), on tractate *Ketubot*; *Tiferet 'uziel* (Warsaw: N. Schriftgisser, 1863), Hasidic homilies, including citations from the Besht and Maggid; *Menorah ha-tehora* (Lemberg: U.W. Salat, 1883–1884), commentary on the laws of Shabbat as codified by R. Yosef Karo, *Shulḥan 'arukh*, orah ḥayim, sections 242–343; *'Ets ha-da'at tov* (Lemberg: U.W. Salat, 1886), on tractate *Shabbat*.

3. *Talmud bavli* (Sławuta: Dov Ber ben Israel and Dov Ber ben Pesah, 1801–1806); *Arba'ah turim* (Sławuta: Dov Ber ben Israel and Dov Ber ben Pesah, 1801–1802). R. Shneur Zalman subsequently sold the publications rights; see *Talmud bavli: Berakhot* (Sławuta: Dov Ber ben Israel and Dov Ber ben Pesah, 1808); *Arba'ah turim* (Sławuta: M. Shapira, 1815); *Talmud bavli: Berakhot* (Sławuta: M. Shapira, 1816); Shneur Zalman of Lady, *Igerot kodesh* (Brooklyn, NY: Kehot, 2012), 351–357.

4. Todros ben Tsevi Hirsh of Równe, *Halakhah pesuka* (Turka: Yehoshua Heshel ben Tsevi Hirsh and Shlomo ben Meir, 1765), title verso—commentary on *Shulḥan 'arukh*, yoreh de'ah, sections 1–122. The Maggid's approbation is the ninth and last approbation on the page.

5. Levi Yitzḥak of Berdyczów, *Kedushat Levi* (Sławuta: n.p., 1798), 25b.

6. Meir of Husaków, *Keter torah*, vol. 1 (Meżyrów: Yeḥezkel ben Shevah, 1803); vol. 2 (Żytomierz: n.p., 1806).

7. *Keter torah*, vol. 1, author's introduction. For another example of a Hasidic curriculum that gave prominence to the study of law, see Levi Cooper, "Divide and Learn," *Jewish Educational Leadership* 12 (2013), 1:59–63.

8. *Talmud bavli, Gittin* 6b; *Eruvin* 13b. *Maggid devarav le-ya'akov* (Korzec: Tsevi Hirsh ben Arye Leib and Shmuel ben Yisakhar Ber, 1781), 12.

9. Shneur Zalman of Lady, *Shulḥan 'arukh [ha-rav]* (Szkłów and Kopyś: Y. Yoffe, 1814–1816), 6 vols. Annotated edition by Sh. D. Levin, A. Alashvili, and Y. Wilhelm (Brooklyn, NY: Kehot, 2001–2007). Bilingual edition: *The Shulchan Aruch of Rabbi Shneur Zalman of Liadi*, trans. E. Touger and U. Kaploun (Brooklyn, NY: Kehot, 2002–2014), 8 vols. For details of the editions until 1984, see Yehoshua Mondshine, *Sifrei ha-halakhah shel admor ha-zaken* (Kefar Chabad: Kehot, 1984), 20–185.

10. Levi Cooper, "On Etkes' *Ba'al Ha-Tanya*," *Diné Israel* 29 (2013), 177–189; Levi Cooper, "Towards a Judicial Biography of Rabbi Shneur Zalman of Liady," *Journal of Law and Religion* 30 (2015), 107–135. On the formation of this work, see Levi Cooper, "Mysteries of the Paratext: Why Did Rabbi Shneur Zalman of Liady Never Publish His Code of Law?" *Diné Israel* 31 (2017), 43–84.

11. See Avinoam Rosenak, "Theory and Praxis in Rabbi Shneur Zalman of Liady: The *Tanya* and *Shulḥan 'Arukh HaRav*," *Jewish Law Association Studies* 22 (2012), 251–282.

12. Yitzḥak Aizik Yehudah Yeḥiel Safrin, *Shulḥan ha-tahor* (Tel Aviv: He'asor, 1963–1965). For a bio-bibliography of R. Safrin's works from 1831 to 1853, see Ya'akov Meir, " 'Itsuvah shel lamdanut ḥasidit" (MA thesis, Hebrew University, 2012). Unfortunately, *Shulḥan ha-tahor* was not part of Meir's discussion, though his research deals with legal material found in R. Safrin's earlier writings.

13. Regarding the provenance of the manuscript, see Avraham Aba Zis, "Mavo," in Safrin, *Shulḥan ha-tahor*, 3–4.

14. Safrin, *Shulḥan ha-tahor*, section 1:6 and zer zahav 10.

15. Ibid., section 262:8.

16. See, for instance, regarding the recital of the blessing over wine at a wedding feast: ibid., section 190, zer zahav 1; Yitzḥak Aizik Yehudah Yeḥiel Safrin, *Zohar ḥai* (Lemberg and Przemyśl: J.M. Nik; Hayim Aharon Zupnik and Hayim Knoller, 1875–1881), 4:86b–c; Avraham Aba Zis, *Minhagei Komarno* (Tel Aviv: Zohar, 1965), 31, section 125.

17. *Eshel Avraham* on orah ḥayim, three editions; *Da'at kedoshim* on yoreh de'ah; *'Ezer me-kudash* on even ha-'ezer; *Kesef ha-kadoshim* on ḥoshen mishpat.

18. Tsevi Hirsh Shapira, *Darkhei teshuvah* (Vilna, Munkács, and Szolyva: Romm; Kahane et Fried; Gottleib, 1892–1912), 5 parts in 4 vols., on *Shulḥan 'arukh*, yoreh de'ah, sections 1–182.

19. Tsevi Hirsh Shapira and Ḥayim Elazar Shapira, *Darkhei teshuvah: Nida* (Bratislava-Galanta: S.Z. Neufeld, 1921) on *Shulḥan 'arukh*, yoreh de'ah, sections 183–200. Ḥayim Elazar Shapira, *Darkhei teshuvah: Mikva'ot* (Mukačevo: A.Y. Kalisz, 1934) on *Shulḥan 'arukh*, yoreh de'ah, sections 201–202.

20. Ḥayim Elazar Shapira, *Nimukei oraḥ ḥayim* (Turňa nad Bodvou: Y.Y. Glantz, 1930), on *Shulḥan 'arukh*, orah ḥayim, sections 1–697; Ḥayim Elazar Shapira, *Ot ḥayim ve-shalom* (Berehovo: S.S. Klein, 1921), on *Shulḥan 'arukh*, orah ḥayim, sections 25–45; yoreh de'ah, sections 260–266.

21. Below, I will present a case study that will demonstrate this trend. See also, Levi Cooper and Maoz Kahana, "The Legal Pluralism of an Enclave Society: The Case of Munkatch Hasidism," *Journal of Legal Pluralism and Unofficial Law* 48 (2016), 80–85.

22. Ḥayim Mordekhai Margaliyot, *Sha'arei teshuvah*, printed in *Shulḥan 'arukh*, oraḥ ḥayim (Dubno: Ḥ.M. Margaliyot, 1819–1820); Avraham Tsevi Hirsh Eisenstadt of Białystok, *Pitḥei teshuvah*, printed in *Shulḥan 'arukh*, yoreh de'ah (Vilna: B. Rotenberg, 1836), 2 vols; *Shulḥan 'arukh*, even ha-'ezer (Johannisburg: A. Gonshorowski, [1861]); *Shulḥan 'arukh*, vol. 4: ḥoshen mishpat (Vilna: Romm, 1871); Ya'akov Vilenchyk, *Daltei teshuvah* (Vilna: Y.L. Metz, 1890–1895), 2 vols. The approbations written for R. Tsevi Hirsh's *Darkhei teshuvah* specifically mention Eisenstadt's *Pitḥei teshuva*.

23. Avraham David Wahrman, *Eshel Avraham*, mahadura tinyana, section 648:22. For a full account of where R. Wahrman cites R. Levi Yitzḥak of Berdichev, see Cooper, "Rabbanut, halakhah, lamdanut," 86–88.

24. Shneur Zalman of Lady, *Igerot kodesh*, 472. See Shalom Dovber Schneersohn, *Igerot kodesh* (Brooklyn, NY: Kehot, 1986), 2:925–926. Regarding Corfu citrons, see Aaron Wertheim, *Law and Custom in Hasidism*, trans. S. Himelstein (Hoboken, NJ: Ktav, 1992), 275–279; Yosef Salmon, "Pulmus etrogei Corfu ve–rik'o ha-histori," *AJS Review* 25 (2001–2002), 1–24, Hebrew section.

25. Yeḥezkel Panet, *She'elot u-teshuvot mar'eh Yeḥezk'el* (M.-Sziget: Beit hadefus hameshutefet, 1875), no. 104. Regarding this responsum, see Yosef Salmon, "Igeret ha-kodesh be-mar'eh Yeḥezkel, teshuva 104," *Daat* 68–69 (2010), 277–297.

26. Panet, *Mar'eh Yeḥezk'el*, 44c–45a, no. 79. For an analysis of this responsum, see Levi Cooper, "Polish Hasidism and Hungarian Orthodoxy in a Borderland: The Munkács Rabbinate," *Polin* 31 (2019), 209–211.

27. Ḥayim Halberstam, *She'elot u-teshuvot divrei ḥayim* (Lwów: A.Y. Menkish, 1875), 2, ḥoshen mishpat, no. 32.

28. For research on collections of responsa by hasidic masters, see Iris Brown (Hoizman), "R. Ḥayim mi-Tsanz" (PhD diss., Bar-Ilan University, 2004); Tamir Granot, "Tekumat ha-ḥasidut be-'Erets Yisra'el aḥarei ha-sho'ah: Mishnato ha-ra'ayonit, ha-hilkhatit, ve-ha-ḥevratit shel ha-'admor r. Yekuti'el Yehudah Halbershtam mi-Tsanz-Kloyzenburg" (PhD diss., Bar-Ilan University, 2008); Levi Cooper, "Ha-'admor mi-Munkatch ha-rav Ḥayim El'azar Shapira: Ha-posek ha-ḥasidi—demut ve-shitah" (PhD diss., Bar-Ilan University, 2011).

29. See Shneur Zalman of Lady, *Igerot kodesh*, 35–39, 40; Benjamin Brown, "*Kedushah*: The Sexual Abstinence of Married Men in Gur, Slonim, and Toledot Aharon," *Jewish History* 27 (2013), 477–479, 484–488, 498–512; Nava Wasserman, *Mi-yamai lo karati le-'ishti: Zugiyut ba-ḥasidut Gur* (Sede Boker: Ben-Gurion University, 2015).

30. Tsevi Elimelekh Shapira, *Takanot tamkhin de-'orayta* (Munkács: Blayer & Kohn, 1895), 7b–8a, no. 13.

31. On *Takkanot tamkhin de-'orayta*, see Levi Cooper, "Legislation for Education: Rabbi Tsevi Elimelekh of Dynów's Regulations for the Support of Torah in Munkács," *Polin* 30 (2017), 43–72.

32. Gershom G. Scholem, *Major Trends in Jewish Mysticism* (Jerusalem: Schocken Books, 1941), 345–348.

33. Erich Fromm, "Das jüdische Gesetz: Zur Soziologie des Diaspora-Judentums" (PhD diss., Universität Heidelberg, 1922).

34. See, for instance, Samuel Abba Horodezky, *Leaders of Hassidism*, trans. M. Horodezky-Magasanik (London: Hasefer Agency for Literature, 1928), 61.

35. Regarding contemporary times, see, for example, Levi Cooper, "Bitter Herbs in Hasidic Galicia," *Jewish Studies, an Internet Journal* 12 (2013), 30–40; Levi Cooper, "Ha-meḥadesh be-tuvo be-khol yom: Ma'amad birkhat ha-ḥamah be-ḥatseirot ḥasidiyot," *Daat* 77 (2014), 183–207. In both of these cases, contemporary Hasidic communities define their practice in terms of Jewish law.

36. Mordecai L. Wilensky, "The Hostile Phase," in *Tolerance and Movements of Religious Dissent in Eastern Europe*, ed. B. K. Király (Boulder: East European Quarterly, 1975), 89–113.

37. Abraham Meir Habermann, "Hashpa'at ha-ḥasidut 'al ha-minhag," *Haaretz*, May 31, 1960, 10.

38. Avraham Rubinstein, "Wertheim, A. Halakhot ve-halikhot be-ḥasidut," *Kirjath Sepher* 36 (1960–1961), 281. Gries joined Rubinstein in his critique of Wertheim's book; see Ze'ev Gries, *Sifrut ha-hanhagot* (Jerusalem: Mosad Bialik, 1989), 107 n. 14.

39. Aaron Wertheim, *Halakhot ve-halikhot be-ḥasidut* (Jerusalem: Mosad Harav Kook, 1960; second printing, Jerusalem: Mosad Harav Kook, 1989; additional printing, Jerusalem:

Mosad Harav Kook, 2003); Wertheim, *Law and Custom in Hasidism*, trans. S. Himelstein (Hoboken, NJ: Ktav, 1992). Introductory blurbs to the reprints and translation by Yitzḥak Rafael, Norman Lamm, and Isadore Twersky—a noted academic and Hasidic master—emphasized that the field was still neglected.

40. Indeed, two chapters from Wertheim's book were translated for a collection of academic studies on Hasidism; see Aaron Wertheim, "Traditions and Customs in Hasidism," trans. E. Lederhendler, in *Essential Papers on Hasidism: Origins to Present*, ed. G. D. Hundert (New York: New York University Press, 1991), 363–398.

41. Alfasi's articles were republished in collections of his writings, see Suggested Reading.

42. Ariel Evan Mayse, "The Ever-Changing Path: Visions of Legal Diversity in Hasidic Literature," *Conversations: The Journal of the Institute for Jewish Ideas and Ideals* 23 (2015), 84–115; Maoz Kahana and Ariel Evan Mayse, "Hasidic Halakhah: Reappraising the Interface of Spirit and Law," *AJS Review* 41 (2017), 2:375–408.

43. Moshe Rosman, "Pesak dinah shel ha-historiyografyah ha-yisra'elit 'al ha-ḥasidut," *Zion* 74 (2009), 166, 174.

44. The issue was briefly touched upon by Yitzḥak Alfasi, *Ha-ḥasidut: Pirkei tolda u-meḥkar* (Tel Aviv: Zion, 1969), 89; Alfasi, *Be-sedei ha-ḥasidut: Meḥkarim, pirkei tolda, havay u-mesoret* (Tel Aviv: Ariel, 1987), 177. See also Wertheim, *Law and Custom in Hasidism*, 216. For a broader perspective on the history of Jewish fur headwear, see Levi Cooper, '*Shtrayml*: An Ethnographic Tale of Law and Ritualisation,' *Polin* 33 (2020), forthcoming.

45. Remu, *oraḥ ḥayim*, section 551:1. The shirt exception was due to the fact that it had likely become sullied with sweat. Socks may also be changed for the same reason; see Avraham Danzig, *Ḥayei adam* (Vilna: Menahem Man ben Barukh, 1809), 129:21; *Mishna berura*, 551:6.

46. Ḥayim Elazar Shapira, *Nimukei oraḥ ḥayim* (Turňa nad Bodvou: Y.Y. Glantz, 1930), section 551, no. 2. Translation from the original rabbinic Hebrew; brackets indicate my explanatory additions; parentheses appear in the original text.

47. I say "virtually" unknown because there is another contemporaneous legal source that discusses the issue; see below near note 59. There is also a source that attests to Munkács practice between 1867 and 1879, when R. Ḥayim Sofer (1821–1886) served as a rabbi. According to R. Sofer's son, Munkács residents wore regular Shabbat finery on Shabbat ḥazon (fur headwear is not specifically mentioned). The community rabbi did not publicly protest, but he wore weekday attire and did not leave his home for the duration of the Shabbat. See Ya'akov Shalom Sofer, *Torat ḥayim* (Paks: M. Rosenbaum, 1897–1911), 3:2b second pagination, section 551:4. R. Sofer's course was linked to the opinion of his teacher (but not relative), R. Moshe Sofer; see below near note 55.

48. Using the term *antinomian* with regard to an item of clothing is perhaps too harsh given the Christian and Sabbatean uses of the term; yet in a culture where law is sacred, the slightest deviation may be considered antinomian, even when it is not an attempt to undermine the foundations of the legal system. Shaul Magid termed this "soft antinomianism"; see Shaul Magid, *Hasidism on the Margin: Reconciliation, Antinomianism, and Messianism in Izbica and Radzin Hasidism* (Madison: University of Wisconsin Press, 2003), 215–216.

49. Yeḥiel Mikhl ha-levi Gold, *Darkhei ḥayim ve-shalom* (Munkács: A. Teichman, 1940), section 669.

50. *Tisha be-'av* is commemorated on Sunday if the 9th of Av date falls on Sunday or if the 9th of Av falls on Shabbat and the fast is pushed off until Sunday.

51. Avraham Abele Gombiner, *Magen Avraham*, on *Shulḥan 'arukh*, oraḥ ḥayim, section 552:1. See Alexander Sender Schor, *Bekhor shor*, taanit, commentary to fol. 30a, in idem, *Simlah ḥadashah* (Żółkiew: Aharon and Gershon bnei Ḥayim David, 1733), 116c; Efrayim Zalman Margaliyot, *Yad efrayim*, printed in *Shulḥan 'arukh*, oraḥ ḥayim (Dubno:

Ḥ.M. Margaliyot, 1819–1820), 202a–b and subsequent editions, commenting on *Magen Avraham*, section 552:14. Margaliyot was a descendant of Schor.

52. In Jewish legal parlance an *argumentum a fortiori* is termed *kal va-ḥomer*, roughly meaning "weak and strong" and referring to the two propositions in the argument. R. Ḥayim Elazar did not use the Hebrew term, but he used the term *kol she-ken* (roughly meaning "all the more so") twice and the Aramaic word *de-kil* (for "it is weaker")—terms that indicate an *argumentum a fortiori*.

53. David ibn Zimra, *She'elot u-teshuvot* (Venice, Fürth, Livorno: M. De Zara; et al, 1652–1818), 2:18a, no. 693.

54. Avraham Tsevi Hirsh Katzenellenbogen, *Sha'arei raḥamim* (Vilna: Avraham Yitzḥak and Shalom Yosef Dworzec, 1871), 4b–5a, section 77.

55. Ḥizkiyah Feivel Plaut, *Likutei ḥaver ben ḥayim* (Pressburg, Munkács, Paks, Sziget: P. Blayer; et al, 1878–1893), 2:34b–35a, 3:10b; Ḥayim Sofer, *Tehillim: Sha'arei ḥayim* (Munkács: Blayer & Kohn, 1892), 187b, commentary on Ps. 137:6; Zusman Eliezer Sofer, *Yalkut Eli'ezer 'al tehillim* (Paks: M. Rosenbaum, 1890), 150b, commentary on Ps. 137; Sofer, *Torat ḥayim*, 3:2b second pagination, section 551:4.

56. Yeḥiel Mikhl ha-levi Epstein, *'Arukh ha-shulḥan*, oraḥ ḥayim, section 551:11. In general, R. Epstein was an ardent defender of common practice, making this an exceptional case where he called for a change in practice—albeit a return to the custom of old.

57. Danzig, *Ḥayei adam*, 129:21. It is interesting that R. Eliyahu's position jibed with normative practice in Vilna, since his legal opinions were not necessarily accepted locally.

58. Ya'akov Israel Emden [*Siddur*] (Altona: Y.I. Emden, 1745–1748), 2:68b.

59. Israel Ḥayim Friedmann, *Likutei maharih* (Sziget: M. Blumenfeld and Y.M. David; et al, 1900–1911), 3:51b–52a.

60. Radbaz (above, note 53) also argued against the custom, but he predated Remu and did not belong to the Ashkenazi tradition, meaning that his position would not be considered brazen.

CHAPTER 3

Stories

Uriel Gellman

The Hasidic story is an important dimension of Jewish folklore and modern Jewish literature. Alongside the Hasidic homiletic literature, which holds the main religious and spiritual messages of Hasidism, the Hasidic story presents the most important inner-Hasidic foundation for understanding its social and ethical worldview, and perhaps its history. This literary corpus encompasses hundreds of compilations containing thousands of Hasidic stories, legends, and tales, mainly in Hebrew and, to a lesser degree, in Yiddish, written or printed over the last two centuries. The development of the Hasidic tale as an important genre in the movement's literary production must be studied as part of modern Jewish literature written from the eighteenth through the twenty-first centuries.

As in other areas of the history of Hasidism and its literary development, one can notice how Hasidim tended to reinvent their forms of expression and their channels of public communication. They tended to alter their literature and spiritual message according to exterior challenges and the movement's internal developments. So it is with the Hasidic story as well. Through their immediate surroundings and more distant traditions, Hasidim were well aware of literary genres and styles, and they consciously adopted popular literary forms and means of expression while adjusting style and content to their own social-religious needs. We can see that the literary product in this genre was modified according to historical developments.

Storytelling and Story Writing

As part of the ritualization process that took place in early Hasidism, many extra-religious elements were incorporated into Hasidic religious tradition. Various traditional, formerly esoteric customs and norms were adopted within Hasidic circles as exoteric religious rituals performed by the greater community, while other "new" rituals were invented as part of Hasidic spiritual renewal. These rituals were redefined and integrated into Hasidic customs and became part of the movement's ethos. This ritualization process initiated the sanctification of otherwise neutral routines, including dancing, singing, and preaching, that developed into the essential cultural characteristics of Hasidism. Storytelling, too, ceased to be just a means of entertainment or a way to communicate norms and ideals, but became a central part of the religious sphere and of Hasidic culture as well.

Hasidim started telling stories during the very first appearance of Hasidic groups in the mid-eighteenth century, before the institutionalization of Hasidism into a movement. The Baal Shem Tov and his associates made extensive use of parables and stories in their sermons as a literary tool and as a means of orally disseminating their ideas and theologies. They did so in private conversations as well as in public, official gatherings within these early Hasidic circles. As Hasidism developed into a movement, storytelling was refined in its ritualistic performances and literary narrative sophistication. Distinct styles of stories gradually developed as they became distinctively Hasidic and gained stronger social, theological, and sometimes political meanings.

In his introduction to the very first collection of Hasidic stories, *Shivḥei ha-Besht* (In Praise of the Baal Shem Tov), which was printed first in Hebrew and soon in Yiddish, in 1814 and 1815, the printer cited the following saying attributed to the Besht himself: "When one relates the praises of the tsadikim, it is as if he concentrates on *Ma'aseh Merkavah*"—that is, on the esoteric story of the divine chariot from the prophet Ezekiel.[1] This saying echoes the aforementioned transformation of storytelling into a religious resource in early Hasidism. Like the highest theological discourse, Torah learning, or prayer, so does telling a story, particularly if it is told about a great tsadik, have great spiritual value that surpasses any literary value it may have or any additional social implications it sheds on its listeners.

The following Hasidic story, with which Gershom Scholem chose to end his famous book *Major Trends in Jewish Mysticism*, gives us an insight into the process storytelling went through in the history of Hasidism:

> When the Baal Shem had a difficult task before him, he would go to a certain place in the woods, light a fire and meditate in prayer—and what he had set out to perform was done. When a generation later the "Maggid" of Mezrich [Międzyrzecz] was faced with the same task he would go to the same place in the woods and say: We can no longer light the fire, but we can still speak the prayers—and what he wanted done became reality. Again a generation later Rabbi Moshe Leib of Sassov [Sasów] had to perform this task. And he too went into the woods and said: We can no longer light a fire, nor do we know the secret meditations belonging to the prayer, but we do know the place in

> the woods to which it all belongs—and that must be sufficient; and sufficient it was. But when another generation had passed and Rabbi Israel of Rishin [Rużyn] was called upon to perform the task, he sat down on his golden chair in his castle and said: We cannot light the fire, we cannot speak the prayers, we do not know the place, but we can tell the story of how it was done. And, the story-teller adds, the story which he told had the same effect as the actions of the other three.[2]

Scholem defined this tale as "the very history of Hasidism itself" since it tells the essence of the actual action of storytelling for generations who did not see themselves capable of the great magical and religious deeds of their predecessors.[3]

There are two basic categories of storytelling. First are the hagiographical stories told about famous Hasidic sages, their lives, wisdom, moralities, and miracles. These stories were narrated and delivered in order to set an example of piety for generations of Hasidim and to create a sense of kinship with Hasidism in general or with a specific dynasty within it. There were stories told about so-to-speak "founders" of the movement, and each Hasidic group may have had its own stories devoted to its renowned leaders. These stories may have historical background or might be merely legendary.

The second type of stories was told by the tsadik himself. This category usually contains more allegoric and fantastic elements and is basically a literary alternative to the more widespread homilies spoken by nearly all Hasidic masters.[4] Some Hasidic thinkers were well-known as inspiring storytellers, the most famous of them certainly R. Naḥman of Bratslav (Bracław; 1772–1811), the great-grandson of the Besht and one of the most charismatic Hasidic leaders.[5]

Some of the stories told by the tsadik might consist of very short sayings that hold condensed meanings or that are aimed at hinting to other well-known aspects of his teachings. Other stories can contain a complex narrative or a tangled plot, sometimes delivered over several occasions by the tsadik to his audience. The inventing and performing of a story of such complexity required creativity on the part of the tsadik and depended on his ability to convey the story in a theatrical manner. Both types of stories, those *about* tsadikim and those told *by* tsadikim, were first articulated and then circulated orally in Yiddish—the spoken language of the Jews in Eastern Europe—just as the oral sermon was first formed in this vernacular. Thus, the story bridged over social and cultural gaps within a Hasidic group. The story, more than other means of communication, may be understood throughout the congregation in all its social strata, regardless of the diverse literacy, cultural capital, and religious devotion found among its members.

For these oral stories to be preserved and transcribed, there needed to be an initiative to record them in writing, which obviously did not always exist.

A Very Short History of Hasidic Stories

In the first Hasidic hagiography, *Shivḥei ha-Besht*, we find the following story that deals with the problem of inscribing the mystical teachings of the Besht:

> There was a man who wrote down the torah of the Besht that he heard from him. Once the Besht saw a demon walking and holding a book in his hand. He said to him: "What is the book that you hold in your hand?"
>
> He answered him: "This is the book that you have written."
>
> The Besht then understood that there was a person who was writing down his torah. He gathered all his followers and asked them: "Who among you is writing down my torah?"
>
> The man admitted it and he brought the manuscript to the Besht. The Besht examined it and said: "There is not even a single word here that is mine."[6]

This story clearly seeks to explain to the reader, who did not personally know the Besht, why the Besht had left no written record of his teachings, based, it seems, on the preference for oral instruction over providing written texts. As in analogous traditions surrounding many other religious leaders, including Buddha and Jesus, the absence of writings seems to arise from a rather typical tension between an older, more archaic oral culture and a new attempt at canonizing written traditions. Following this view, the spiritual message of the Baal Shem Tov may not be transcribed whatsoever, and anyone who initiates to deliver his teachings in the form of a written book misses the eminence of his divine wisdoms.

Despite the claim of the story, we know that some of the Besht's disciples, such as R. Ya'akov Yosef of Polnoe (Połonne) and others, did write down the Besht's teachings, perhaps even during his lifetime, although they were only published long after his death. So did the compiler of the first hagiography, in which the prohibition was recorded, put the Besht's life down in writing, forming the Besht's image as the protagonist of Hasidism for future generations. Regardless of the historicity and credibility of this type of legend (which we will discuss later), which for an average Hasid may be a reflection of the Besht's real experience, we may see this story as an attempt at an apologetic, even anachronistic presentation of Hasidic culture as cardinally an oral phenomenon. This specific story clearly tries to explain the relevant absence of any kind of Hasidic literature in the time when the story was written and printed. In this early stage of the formation of Hasidism, there was scarcely any attempt initiated by the tsadikim themselves to reveal their own theology in writing; rather, the vast majority of Hasidic teachings were scribed and distributed by their students or later admirers.

Despite such attempts, stories about early Hasidim, especially the Baal Shem Tov and his circle, began to be written down during the final years of the eighteenth century, and most likely even before that—perhaps even during the Besht's lifetime—but we lack evidence of anything prior to a manuscript written in the 1790s. However, the first printing of a collection of stories did not occur until 1814, with the publication of *Shivḥei ha-Besht* in Kopyś (Kapust), Belarus. The first version of this work, from the 1790s, took the form of a manuscript written by the compiler and transcriber of the originally oral stories, Dov Ber of Linits (Ilińce), who claimed to have personally heard the stories from their firsthand sources. The printed version was intensely edited by Israel Yaffe, a Chabad Hasid, who changed, rearranged, and added to the original text in accordance with his agenda and with the state of the Hasidic movement in the early nineteenth century. The next year, a somewhat differing Yiddish version of the book was published.[7]

In the same year, 1815, a first collection of R. Naḥman of Bratslav's original stories, *Sipurei ma'asiyot*, was also printed. Thus, the first printing of Hasidic stories occurred thirty-five years after the first Hasidic homiletic work was printed (1780) and a total of fifty-five years after the death of the Besht, the protagonist of the first Hasidic hagiography.

For nearly fifty years after the printing of *Shivḥei ha-Besht*, no other Hasidic hagiographies were published. Nevertheless, stories were still being retold and inscribed by Hasidim during that period, but there was no attempt to produce or publish new collections for a wider audience of Hasidim.

Several causes are credited for this long silence involving Hasidic legendary and hagiographic publications: some relate it to the low reputation the legendary genre possessed within Hasidic ethos as popular culture, which prevented later authors from taking part in its dissemination. Others oppose this view and claim that on the contrary, the reception of *Shivḥei ha-Besht* as a sacred Hasidic text was so great that later authors refrained from imitating it. Yet other historians claim that Hasidim were hesitant about printing further hagiographic works after the maskilim mocked *Shivḥei ha-Besht* so strongly. These explanations are not entirely convincing, however, because *Shivḥei ha-Besht* was actually reprinted many times during these years, in Hebrew as well as in Yiddish, and certainly fit Hasidic norms. Nor were restrictions of Austrian or Russian censors responsible for the fifty-year hiatus. Restrictions were not enforced uniformly in all countries, and there were always printing houses that were able to publish Hasidic books. And indeed, Hasidic homiletic works were printed continuously, some of them containing Hasidic tales. Oral and written storytelling continued, even if it did not do so as a separate genre with separate collections of stories. Therefore, the true basis for the half-century-long lack of hagiographic printing remains somewhat unresolved.[8] It can be assumed that there was no single reason for the long respite in the publication of Hasidic stories; rather, there existed a combination of reasons, including more technical reasons, such as the high costs of printing and the growing regulation by the authorities, combined with cultural reasons, such as the fear of internal Jewish criticism, or even some level of indifference by Hasidim themselves as their movement grew larger and assumed an important political position.

An important cultural turn brought about a wave of printing of new collections of Hasidic stories after this long pause. Starting in the mid-1860s, printing of Hasidic hagiography (as well as other genres of Hasidic literature) increased dramatically, enabled perhaps also by a gradual easing of censorship first in Galicia and then in Russia. The most important author-compilers, or "cultural agents," as Zeev Gries called them, who propagated hagiographical works of the Hasidim in this early phase of its development—the later nineteenth century—were Menaḥem Mendel Bodek (1825?–1874), Aharon Walden (1838–1912), and Michael Levi Frumkin-Rodkinson (1845–1905).[9] These authors worked separately but borrowed blatantly from each other. They, and many other less prominent propagators of Hasidic stories, collected material about many figures, Hasidic and pre-Hasidic, which indicates the level of Hasidic institutionalization at this point in its history.

The renewed awakening of the Hasidic tale as a literary genre took place simultaneously with the rise of modern Hebrew and Yiddish literature in Eastern Europe. Hasidic publishers may have sought to create cultural alternatives to modern fiction aimed instead at a traditional audience. The new tales of the tsadikim would compete with modern, mostly secular literature. The Hasidic literary revival was related also to the emergence of Orthodox Jewish historical writing that began midcentury in the wake of the new German Jewish movement of scientific historiography (Wissenschaft des Judentums). Orthodox writers reprinted genealogical literature, chronographic works, and old rabbinical lexicons, while adding new books about rabbinical figures from the eighteenth and nineteenth centuries. The center of this Orthodox-historiography activity was in Galicia, mainly in Żółkiew (Zovkva) and Lwów (Lemberg/Lviv), and later in Warsaw—moving along with the changing centers of the Hebrew press. Such historical work, which straddled the border between traditional rabbinic literature and modern historiography, created the climate for Hasidim to write their own quasi-historical, quasi-legendary stories about their venerable ancestors. The reappearance of Hasidic stories in print was motivated by these external evolutions and served as a countercultural instructive tool within Hasidic society.

Another wave of printing Hasidic stories was conducted at the beginning of the twentieth century, especially during the interwar period. In the printing centers of Poland, many volumes of Hasidic stories were produced, making the Hasidic bookshelf relevant once again for the contemporary Jewish Orthodox reader. The compilers and printers of this phase were the heirs of the nineteenth-century Hasidic cultural agents. They came from different strata of Jewish society; some were well-known rabbis or famous Hasidic figures. Among the most significant author-compilers from this stage was Israel Berger (1855–1919), who served as a rabbi in several communities in Transylvania and later in Bucharest; he published a four-volume series of hagiographic works titled *Zekhut Yisrael*. Similarly, Tsevi Yeḥezkel Mikhelson (1863–1942), who served as rabbi in Płońsk (Central Poland) and then was a member of the rabbinical court in Warsaw, compiled biographies of many tsadikim. His son Avraham Ḥayim Simḥah Bunem Mikhelson did so as well, even more prolifically. Their relative, Yosef Lewinstein (1840–1924), rabbi of Serock, alongside many other less distinguished authors, joined them in producing a wide body of Hasidic knowledge by collecting and printing Hasidic stories and sermons of a number of tsadikim. To be sure, their choices were not necessarily motivated by the "objective" importance of a selected tsadik. In fact, the early twentieth century was an age of inner-Hasidic political competition over prestige and political influence; every dynasty and group strove to position itself as an important successor of the Hasidic tradition. Collections of Hasidic stories praising the holy deeds of the founder of a dynasty were potent instruments in such a conquest for power.[10]

A good example of such a compilation of stories is the aforementioned work by Israel Berger, *Zekhut Yisrael*, which actually consists of a series of books in praise of holy men titled *Eser kedushot*, *Eser orot*, *Eser tsaḥtsaḥot*, and *Eser atarot*. The four parts had apparently been written by 1906, when *Eser kedushot* was first published, but the other volumes had come out by 1910. Each volume contains teachings, stories, letters, and biographical data of about ten different tsadikim. The first volume is dedicated to the specific house of tsadikim to which Berger belonged—the Ziditshov (Żydaczów)-Komarno dynasty, a well-known kabbalistic-oriented Hasidic branch in Galicia. The other volumes contain hagiographies of many other tsadikim, starting with the Maggid of Mezrich and his most prominent disciples and concluding with some lesser known figures whom Berger found important enough to present in his book. Berger attempted to combine historical documents and testimonies with legends and glorifying traditions. His writing style suggests that he was well aware of the new historiographic tendencies in his environment, and that he tried to adopt a modern writing style while framing it in the spirit of inner-Hasidic narrative and traditional hagiography.

But not all the Hasidic story compilers were so skilled and proficient in this task. Many books containing less famous or less well-known Hasidic stories were published by rather mediocre and little-known author-compilers who gathered anything they could recall from Hasidic legends. The growing demand for this type of book in the first half of the twentieth century served chiefly as a countercultural literary body for the Hasidic Orthodox public opposed to secular reading. This resulted in a significant growth in the numbers of these publications, which were not all of high quality; nor did they always carry a deep moral message for the readers. Some less qualified authors, sometimes lacking affiliation with Hasidic doctrine and history, attempted to produce collections that eventually became part of the general body of Hasidic legendary literature and have been recognized as such by the Hasidic community itself, but that lacked much literary quality or credibility.[11]

The real scope of this Hasidic literary body was somewhat unknown until rather recently (for a bibliography of these books, see the end of this chapter). It is clear that there have been ups and downs in the production of story collections in accordance with both cultural contexts and historical events. However, it is now possible to estimate that no fewer than 260 books containing Hasidic stories were printed from 1815 up to the destruction of Eastern European Jewry during the Holocaust. This number includes a relatively wide range of types of compilations and is not limited just to works dedicated entirely to classical Hasidic stories.

Readings into Hasidic Stories

Some Hasidic stories are very specific, condensed, or brief, and yet are able to deliver a precise sharp spiritual or social message. For example, the following famous short story, not found in Hasidic collections, was characterized by Martin Buber as part of the Hasidic oral tradition:

> Near his passing, Rabbi Zusya of Hanipoli said: "If they ask me [in the next world], why wasn't I [like] Moses, I'll know what to answer, but if they ask me why wasn't I [like] Zusya, I will have no answer."[12]

It is obvious that the purpose of such a story was not merely to document a specific event, but primarily to provide a spiritual existential message for a Hasid seeking meaning in his life. The personality of R. Meshulam Zusya of Hanipoli (Annopol) (1718–1800) was chosen because of his image in Hasidic literature as one of the humblest tsadikim of his day.[13]

But there are other varieties of stories. Some have a genuine historical narrative and are designed to portray an inimitable past of the Hasidic movement or to fulfill the reader's curiosity and senses.

Another type of story is the classic hagiographical "praise," designed to glorify and elevate the image of a particular tsadik, to give him an important place in the movement's historical leadership strata or to celebrate his dynasty.

As a rich and heterogeneous literary corpus, which has also altered and evolved over the many phases of its development, Hasidic stories offer a wide range of approaches, interpretations, and readings. The way these stories are read depends, undeniably, on the reader's background and his or her identity. An ordinary Hasid would approach the stories with a mindset quite different from that of the historian, while the latter's perspective would differ from that of the literary scholar, the folklorist, or the bibliographer. Therefore, these stories have often generated discrepancies among their various commentators, who have debated how one ought to approach them, read them, and derive from them anticipated (historical or any other) information about Hasidim and their literature. (For a selection of readings, see the list at the end of the chapter.)

In their anti-Hasidic satires, maskilim mocked Hasidism by manipulating Hasidism's own legendary repertoire and setting it in a ridiculous context, or by presenting fictitious stories with exaggerated meanings that ridiculed tsadikim and their "foolish" followers. By doing so the maskilim demonstrated the great influence these traditions had upon the Jewish mass on the one hand, and used the very same genre to defeat Hasidism by their own capital on the other. The Hasidic story was thus a dominant literary form used in the ideological battlefield between modernists and traditionalists in Eastern Europe.

It was only toward the end of the nineteenth century, and even more so at the beginning of the twentieth century, that Hasidic stories aroused the curiosity of people outside Hasidic circles or other than hostile anti-Hasidic authors. This encounter was part of the rediscovery of Hasidism—often called "neo-Hasidism"—by a group of modern Jewish thinkers, often nationalists, who found in it a model of pure romantic religiosity. By this period the stories and legends told and written by Hasidim had gradually become a legitimate part of the modern Jewish literary canon for non-Hasidic and even non-Jewish readers, and they grew to be widely appreciated by an ever widening spectrum of readers.[14] The reception of neo-Hasidic literature was certainly different from the original, inner-Hasidic reception of the stories. The stories differed from the original religious and moral works designed to define Hasidic society, and they presented an entirely different literary body whose message was more universal, modern, and moral. They were aimed for the modern reader who did not consider himself or herself part of the authentic experience of the story.

From the earliest stages of modern scholarship of Hasidism, scholars disagreed on how to read the legendary sources of Hasidism and how to properly integrate them into the more general understanding of the movement and its ideological-cultural message. Martin Buber, one of the most prominent initiators of neo-Hasidism, was renowned for his refashioning of Hasidic tales and for presenting them to modern readers, first in German and then in modern Hebrew. For him this literary treasure was the most important element for understanding the religious culture of Hasidism, and he saw it as a living tradition that influenced all the Hasidic groups and divisions throughout all periods. So did many other Hebrew and Yiddish novelists, including Yitzhok Leibush Peretz and Shmuel Yosef Agnon, to mention only two of the most prominent, who retold and refashioned Hasidic legends in a modern and most appealing manner. Gershom Scholem, by contrast, as a historian of ideas and mysticism, objected to Buber's view and pointed to homiletic literature, rather than legendary stories, as the fundamental ground for understanding the world of

Hasidism.[15] Still others have presented more complex paths to reading Hasidic stories.

Students of Jewish literature may approach the vast body of Hasidic stories through literary tools that allow them to analyze the stories' symbolic or allegoric meanings. Folklore or ethnographic scholars may derive from the stories valuable information about the culture and traditions of the storytellers and writers of the Hasidic legends. However, one principal approach to Hasidic stories is to read them as historical documents. After all, as mentioned, many of the stories describe (real or fictitious) historical events or present narratives. Therefore, the reader of these stories is naturally tempted to read them as recollections of the historical reality and dramatic events in the history of Hasidism. The historical reading of Hasidic traditions is one issue that has been extensively deliberated in recent scholarship of Hasidism, corresponding to general methodological issues vis-à-vis other Jewish and non-Jewish legendary/hagiographic traditions.

Obviously, among the Hasidim themselves, legends and stories were generally perceived as more reliable and as more trustworthy historical sources than they were by non-Hasidic readers who were not inclined to admire the stories' protagonists. However, many scholarly studies of the history of Hasidism did not adopt sufficiently critical standards in relating to Hasidic legends and drew far-reaching conclusions that contradict other, more reliable historical sources.

The Hasidic story in general is meant mainly to present a moral message, and therefore often includes mythical elements and persuasion to make people think in a certain manner or to adopt particular values. Hence, one ought to regard the Hasidic story as "sacred biography" or "hagiography," and not relate to it simply as a source originally intended to provide a reliable historical narrative nor a realistic reflection of the past. That said, one may still offer a set of methodological tools for retrieving historically reliable data from Hasidic tales.

Scholarly debates over the historicity of Hasidic stories were traditionally held over *Shivḥei ha-Besht* and its historical image of early Hasidism. The issues raised by these debates regarding the first hagiography can be applied to the historical reliability of later collections as well.

Early scholars, starting with Simon Dubnow (1860–1941), tended to treat *Shivḥei ha-Besht* by sifting through its content, disregarding any stories that contained miracles or fantastic tales while accepting other information that seemed more "real" as historical factual material.[16] However, these apparently critical historians, guided by their rational worldview, tended to accept large portions of the book that did not conflict with their own beliefs, with no real source criticism or clear parameters. And so miracles were rejected while "mundane" interventions were assumed to be true, even if they may have violated historical reality. The adherents of this approach actually failed to read *Shivḥei ha-Besht* in its original context, instead imposing modern, skeptical concepts on a cultural trend that saw the supernatural abilities of its heroes as their chief qualities. The authors, publishers, and readers of *Shivḥei ha-Besht* definitely did not see those supernatural events as unrealistic, and precisely the elements that may seem unreasonable to a modern reader were most probably held by many Hasidim as important parts of the book and its cultural message. Hasidim equally tended to sift through *Shivḥei ha-Besht* and admit anything that preserved their own cultural point of view, which was obviously very different from those of the aforementioned historians.

Later historians wished to verify the veracity of tales in *Shivḥei ha-Besht* in light of external sources that may have supported some traditions in the work. Israel Bartal, for example, found external evidence to support the story of the immigration of R. Elazar of Amsterdam to the land of Israel, while Adam Teller pointed out the two wealthy Jewish arrendators called Ickowicz who were also mentioned in a story in *Shivḥei ha-Besht*.[17] However, besides the validation of some realistic background upon which several stories were narrated, these new findings do not actually confirm the truthfulness of the stories themselves or the involvement of the Baal Shem Tov in any way. The external sources do affirm some realistic details known to the compiler, but actually are ineffective in confirming the more specific traditions constructed around the Besht and his associates.

Contemporary scholars differ on the extent to which we can or cannot depend on this collection of stories as a whole or on its specific elements. Moshe Rosman, author of the most important biography of the Besht, holds a very skeptical approach toward *Shivḥei ha-Besht*, regarding its contents as nearly useless in historical terms: "Plausibility, realia, and even historicity are not sufficient criteria, then, for assessing authenticity. . . . Hagiography is primarily concerned with turning the exemplary life into a proof text for a position advocated in the present. *Shivhei Ha-Besht* is no exception."[18] Rosman therefore preferred to contextualize Hasidism in contemporaneous, more reliable, independent documentary sources. Immanuel Etkes, in his likewise important biography of the Besht, opposed the apparent radicalism of Rosman's position and proposed to contextualize the Besht within Jewish mystical traditions.[19] For him *Shivḥei ha-Besht* may hold some reliable historical data that can be extracted cautiously through historical tools despite its obvious disadvantages: "These are, consequently, tales that express and reflect the cultural and social world of the Besht and his associates."[20] Yet other scholars sought to develop a critical apparatus for categorizing Hasidic compilers or books by rating their reliability and credibility. The reliability of authors or works is examined in accordance with the proximity of the specific compiler of the story collection and the subject of the stories themselves, and according to the chain of transmission of the events described in the stories.[21]

Regarding Hasidic stories, we should have in mind two very different categories of historical reality and literary reliability, which should be treated with idiosyncratic tools. On the one hand, there is the factual level of the story narrated: Did it happen? How did it actually accrue? And what parts of it can be regarded as reliable historical information? On the other hand, there are very different inquiries relevant to these texts: How does the story reflect the cultural mentality of the narrator (not of the protagonist of the story!), or, in more contemporary terms, what is the story's representation of the tsadik rather than what we learn about the tsadik himself? In terms used by Rosman in this regard, we may depict the difference between the two historical readings of Hasidic stories as "usability vs. reliability."[22] Needless to say, every historical source has limitations and advantages. Depending on the approach one takes or the information one pursues, the same document may reflect distinctively different data. In approaching any source, we should be asking how it may, and how it may not, be used.

All of this is true not only for Hasidic stories or narratives, but also for the sayings and short religious messages attributed to Hasidic masters. These sayings were often transmitted in the same way in which the stories were transmitted, and occasionally even were delivered side by side in the same collections. Here, too, the reader must examine carefully the attribution of traditions and the nature of the statement attributed to any specific tsadik. Good examples are the aphorisms attributed to the enigmatic tsadik Menaḥem Mendel of Kock (1787–1859). R. Menaḥem Mendel did not deliver sermons or leave any writings. Sayings attributed to him were very concise, at once paradoxical and obscure, transmitted orally by his disciples. However, most of the sayings cannot be reliably attributed to him and have more to do with his later image than with historical reality. Surprisingly, the number of sayings attributed to R. Menaḥem Mendel increased as the years passed following his death, which puts into doubt the authenticity of all his sayings. The credibility and attribution of his teachings turn out to be very problematic, although they are usually very inspiring and attractive.[23]

On the whole, in recent years there has been a steady increase in the study of the Hasidic story and legends as a literary category and as an expression of the popular culture of the storytellers, writers, compilers, printers, and readers of the many varieties of Hasidic literary products. Regardless of their historicity, authenticity, or credibility, they remain a good read and a very important division within modern Jewish literature.

SUGGESTED READING

The most important general studies on Hasidic stories are: Joseph Dan, *Ha-sipur ha-ḥasidi* (Jerusalem: Keter, 1990); Dan, *Ha-novela ha-ḥasidit* (Jerusalem: Mosad Bialik,1966); Gedalyah Nigal, *The Hasidic Tale*, trans. E. Levin (Oxford: The Littman Library of Jewish

Civilization, 2008). Nigal also published a biographical lexicon of compilers of Hasidic stories: *Melaktei ha-sipur ha-ḥasidi* (Jerusalem: Carmel, 1996), as well as several collections of stories (organized according to subject), and annotated editions of original collections of Hasidic stories (especially those from the late nineteenth century)—e.g., *Sipurim ḥasidiyim mi-Lemberg-Lvov* (Jerusalem: Ha-makhon le-ḥeker ha-sifrut ha-ḥasidit, 2005).

The largest collection of R. Naḥaman of Bratslav (Bracław) stories is Zvi Mark, *Kol sipurei rabi Naḥman mi-Bratslav* (Tel Aviv: Yedioth Aḥronot and Mosad Bialik, 2014). An English translation of some of these stories is *Nahman of Bratslav: The Tales*, trans. A. J. Band (New York: Paulist, 1978). On these tales, see also Marianne Schleicher, *Intertextuality in the Tales of Rabbi Nahman of Bratslav: A Close Reading of Sippurey Ma'asiyot* (Leiden: Brill, 2007).

Stories told by tsadikim are treated by Rivka Dvir-Goldberg, *Ha-tsadik ha-ḥasidi ve-armon ha-Livyatan: Iyun be-sipurei ma'asiyot mi-pi tsadikim* (Tel Aviv: Hakibbutz Hameuchad, 2003).

For bibliographical surveys of Hasidic stories, see Yoav Elstein, "Bou litkon: Bibliographia shel ha-sifrut ha-ḥasidit," in *Ma'ase sipur*, ed. A. Lipsker and R. Kushelevsky (Ramat Gan: Bar Ilan University Press, 2006), 99–118; and a more updated list by Ze'ev Kitsis, "Sifrut ha-shevaḥim ha-ḥasidit: Me-reshitah ve-ad le-milḥemet ha-olam ha-sheniyah" (PhD diss., Bar-Ilan University, 2015), 217–310. This work deals especially with the later phase of Hasidic stories, as do Jonatan Meir, *Literary Hasidism: The Life and Works of Michael Levi Rodkinson*, trans. J. G. Amshalem (New York: Syracuse University Press, 2016); Justin Jaron Lewis, *Imagining Holiness: Classic Hasidic Tales in Modern Times* (Montreal: McGill-Queen's University Press, 2009).

An interactive website of Hasidic stories is Zusha: http://www.zusha.org.il/. This collection includes discussions and contemporary interpretations of Hasidic tales.

The first scholarly edition of *Shivḥei ha-Besht* is the English translation by D. Ben-Amos and J. R. Mintz, *In Praise of the Baal Shem Tov* (New York: Rowman and Littlefield, 1984). This edition includes notes and an index of parallel motifs in international folklore. The most useful Hebrew edition is the one by Avraham Rubinstein (Jerusalem: Rubin Mass, 1991). Yehoshua Mondshine published an edition of a newly discovered manuscript version of the book, comparing it to the first printed edition (Jerusalem: Mondshine, 1982). On the editions, see also: Moshe Rosman, "In Praise of the Ba'al Shem Tov: A User's Guide to the Editions of Shivhei haBesht," *Polin* 10 (1997), 183–199. The historicity of this compendium of stories was addressed by Moshe Rosman, "Le-toledotav shel makor histori: Sefer *Shivḥei ha-Besht* ve-arikhato," *Zion* 58 (1993), 175–214.

On the engagement of neo-Hasidic authors in rewriting and popularizing Hasidic stories, see Nicham Ross, *Masoret ahuvah ve-senu'ah: Zehut yehudit modernit ve-ketivah neo-ḥasidit be-fetah ha-me'ah ha-esrim* (Beersheva: Ben Gurion University Press, 2010); Ross, *Margalit temunah ba-hol: Y. L. Peretz ve-ma'asiot ḥasidim* (Jerusalem: The Hebrew University Magnes Press, 2013).

On the Hasidic story in the literary framework of Hasidism, see Zeev Gries, *Sefer, sofer ve-sipur be-reshit ha-ḥasidut* (Tel Aviv: Hakibbutz Hameuchad, 1992). For some new reading into Hasidic stories, see Tsippi Kauffman, "The Hasidic Story: A Call for Narrative Religiosity," *Journal of Jewish Thought and Philosophy* 22 (2014), 101–126; Kauffman, "Two Tsadikim, Two Women in Labor, and One Salvation: Reading Gender in a Hasidic Story," *Jewish Quarterly Review* 101 (2011), 420–438; Zeev Kitsis, *Hamishim kriot be-sipurei ḥasidim* (Tel Aviv: Kinneret Zmora-Bitan Dvir, 2017).

NOTES

1. *In Praise of the Baal Shem Tov: The Earliest Collection of Legends about the Founder of Hasidism*, trans. and ed. D. Ben-Amos and J. R. Mintz (Bloomington and London: Indiana University Press, 1970), The Printer's Preface, p. 1; see also 199.

2. Gershom Scholem, *Major Trends in Jewish Mysticism* (New York: Schocken Books, 1995), 349–350.

3. For more on this, see Levi Cooper, "'But I Will Tell of Their Deeds': Retelling a Hasidic Tale about the Power of Storytelling," *Journal of Jewish Thought and Philosophy* 22 (2014), 127–163.

4. On stories told by the tsadikim, see especially Rivka Dvir-Goldberg, *Ha-tsadik ha-ḥasidi ve-armon ha-Livyatan: Iyun be-sipurei ma'asiyot mi-pi tsadikim* (Tel Aviv: Hakibbutz Hameuchad, 2003).

5. The best collection of R. Naḥman's stories in Hebrew is Zvi Mark, *Kol sipurei al Naḥman mi-Bratslav* (Tel Aviv: Yedioth Aḥronot and Mosad Bialik, 2014).

6. *In Praise of the Baal Shem Tov* (1993), 179.

7. Jonatan Meir, "Ha-mahadurot ha-avudot shel sefer *Shivḥei ha-Besht* be-yidish (1815–1817)," *Kabbalah* 39 (2017), 249–271.

8. For different opinions on this, see Chone Shmeruk, *Sifrut yidish: Perakim le-toledoteha* (Tel Aviv: Mif'alim Universitaim, 1978), 211; Joseph Dan, *Ha-sipur ha-ḥasidi* (Jerusalem:Keter, 1990), 189–195; Yehoshua Mondshine, *Shivḥhei ha-Besht* (Jerusalem: Mondshine, 1982), 52–58; Zeev Gries, "Ha-omnam meitiv ha-sipur ksavo? Makom sifrut ha-shevaḥim be-toledot ha-ḥasidut," *Da'at* 44 (2000), 85–94; Jonatan Meir, *Literary Hasidism: The Life and Works of Michael Levi Rodkinson*, trans. J. G. Amshalem (New York: Syracuse University Press, 2016), chapter 2.

9. On the concept of cultural agents, see Zeev Gries, "The Hasidic Managing Editor as an Agent of Culture," in *Hasidism Reappraised*, ed. A. Rapoport-Albert (London: The Littman Library of Jewish Civilization, 1996), 141–155.

10. For more on this, see Justin Jaron Lewis, *Imagining Holiness: Classic Hasidic Tales in Modern Times* (Montreal: McGill-Queen's University Press, 2009); Ze'ev Kitsi, "Sifrut ha-shevaḥim ha-ḥasidit: Me-reshita ve-ad le-milḥemet ha-olam ha-sheniyah" (PhD diss., Bar-Ilan University, 2015).

11. On this, see Uriel Gellman, "An Authors' Guide: Authorship of Hasidic Compendium," *Zutot* 9 (2013), 85–96.

12. Martin Buber, *Or ha-ganuz* (Jerusalem: Schocken, 1968), 231. Translation and brackets after David Biale et al., *Hasidism: A New History* (Princeton, NJ: Princeton University Press, 2018), 145.

13. Tsippi Kauffman, "Hasidic Performance: Establishing a Religious (Non)Identity in the Tales about Rabbi Zusha of Annopol," *Journal of Religion* 95 (2015), 51–71.

14. Nicham Ross, *Masoret ahuvah ve-senu'ah: Zehut yehudit modernit ve-ketivah neo-ḥasidit be-fetah ha-me'ah ha-esrim* (Beersheva: Ben Gurion University Press, 2010).

15. On the Buber-Scholem polemic regarding Hasidic stories, see Gershom Scholem, *Ha-shelav ha-aharon: Meḥkarei ha-ḥasidut shel Gershom Scholem*, ed. D. Assaf and E. Liebes (Jerusalem: Am Oved Publishers, the Hebrew University Magnes Press, 2008), 325–355, including a bibliographical essay on this topic; Karl Erich Grözinger, "The Buber-Scholem Controversy about Hasidic Tale and Hasidism: Is There a Solution?" in *Gershom Scholem's "Major Trends in Jewish Mysticism" 50 Years After*, ed. P. Schäfer and J. Dan (Tübingen: Mohr Siebeck, 1993), 327–336; Steven Katz, *Post-Holocaust Dialogues* (New York: New York University Press, 1983), 52–93.

16. Simon Dubnow, "The Beginnings: The Ba'al Shem Tov [Besht] and the Center in Podolia," in *Essential Papers on Hasidism: Origins to Present*, ed. G. D. Hundert (New York: New York University Press, 1991), 25–57; Israel Zinberg, *A History of Jewish Literature*, trans. and ed. B. Martin (Cleveland, OH: Press of Case Western Reserve University, 1976), 9:27–61.

17. Israel Bartal, "Aliyat r. Ele'azar me-Amsterdam le-erets Yisra'el bi-shenat [1740]," in *Galut ba-'arets*, ed. I. Bartal (Jerusalem: Hasifria Hatziyonit, 1994), 23–40; Adam Teller, "Masoret Slutsk al reshit darko shel ha-Besht," in *Meḥkerei ḥasidut*, ed. I. Etkes et al.

(Jerusalem: Mosad Bialik, 1999), 15–38. See also Yaakov Barnai, "Some Clarifications on the Land of Israel Stories of 'In Praise of the Baal Shem Tov,'" *Revue des etudes juives* 146 (1987), 367–380.

18. See Moshe Rosman, *Founder of Hasidism: A Quest for the Historical Baal Shem Tov* (Oxford: The Littman Library of Jewish Civilization, 2013), 153. See also Rosman, *Stories That Changed the History: The Unique Career of Shivḥei ha-Besht* (New York: Syracuse University Press, 2007).

19. Immanuel Etkes, *The Besht: Magician, Mystic, and Leader*, trans. S. Sternberg (Waltham, MA: Brandeis University Press, 2005). See also Etkes, "The Historical Besht: Reconstruction or Deconstruction?" *Polin* 12 (1999), 298–306.

20. Etkes, *The Besht*, 248.

21. See Glenn Dynner, "The Hasidic Tale as a Historical Source: Historiography and Methodology," *Religion Compass* 3–4 (2009), 655–675.

22. Moshe Rosman, "Hebrew Sources on the Baal Shem Tov: Usability vs. Reliability," *Jewish History* 27 (2013), 153–169.

23. The teachings attributed to the Rebbe of Kock are analyzed for their authenticity by Yaakov Levinger, "Imrot otentiyot shel ha-rabi me-Kotsk," *Tarbiz* 55 (1986), 109–135; Levinger, "Torato shel ha-rabi me-Kotsk le-or ha-imrot ha-meyuḥasot lo al yedei nekhdo R. Shmuel me-Sokhachev," *Tarbiz* 55 (1986), 413–431.

CHAPTER 4

Mitnagedim

Uriel Gellman

It is hard to imagine scholarship on the history of early Hasidism without considering the large textual body written by its opponents—the mitnagedim. As with many other historical events, one can learn a lot about Hasidism not only through studying its own writings, which present an inner perspective, but also through taking note of external observational descriptions by its opponents or from other outside spectators. Since we lack much of this external perspective from the early stages of Hasidism, mitnagedic sources are crucial for our understanding of its formation as a movement. These texts were written mostly during the last three decades of the eighteenth century, and they provide, in fact, the broadest and richest description of the nascent Hasidic movement, from a very critical, yet original, perspective. Contrary to later portrayals of Hasidism originating from governmental officials or anti-Hasidic maskilim, we deal here with sources written by the traditional rabbinic elite of East European Jewry who were in contest with Hasidism, alongside some communal authorities.

Historical Background

The first groups of Hasidim in Podolia and Volhynia did not draw special attention or attract significant opposition from within Jewish society. The small circles of Hasidim associated with the Baal Shem Tov and his disciples were an integral part of the Jewish cultural elite strata of their time. They were perhaps another one of the groups of what is commonly referred to as "old-style Hasidim" that existed in East European communities. It was only after Hasidism went through the first stages of becoming a movement and began spreading geographically and demographically that it attracted special interest or opposition.[1] The spread of Hasidic cells into Jewish Lithuanian cultural regions was also one of the main causes of organized disapproval of Hasidism.

The most prominent opponent of Hasidism was R. Eliyahu ben Shlomo Zalman, the Gaon of Vilna (1720–1797). He held no formal office in his town but was considered to be one of the most renowned rabbinic scholars of his time and was also an "old-style" ascetic pietist.[2] During the winter of 1771–1772, rumors reached the Gaon about a new sect of Hasidim who exhibited extraordinary patterns of behavior. The accusations claimed that the Hasidim were involved in immodest behavior while praying, scorned rabbinic scholars, and held a heretical interpretation of a passage in the Zohar. Prominent Hasidic leaders in White Russia tried to persuade the Gaon of their innocence, but after refusing to meet with them he eventually declared that Hasidim were heretics and should be persecuted. The Gaon's vigorous objection to Hasidism in some sense represented a quarrel within elite rabbinic circles. It can be understood as part of a cultural dispute over the true nature of religious piety, and over the genuine, essential definition of the term *ḥasid* ("pious") to denote an ascetic religious figure.

Immediately after Passover 1772, the Vilna Jewish Council (*kahal*) began to gather testimonies against Hasidim who had established themselves in the town. Local Hasidim were excommunicated and their separatist prayer houses prohibited. The Vilna opponents to Hasidim tried to convince other communities in Lithuania and beyond to join their verdict. They sent out letters to some of the most important communities, but only a handful, mostly in the Lithuanian domain and fewer in Galicia, joined the ban or took any active stance toward persecuting the Hasidic presence in their vicinities.[3]

The battle against Hasidism was executed by the tool of letters of excommunication forbidding the establishment of Hasidic prayer houses, ordering the public burning of Hasidic literature (first in manuscript form, and then from 1780 in print as well), encouraging the humiliation of Hasidic leaders, and banning contact with them or their followers.

The strength of the hostility toward Hasidism—indeed, rabbis' outrage—was essentially caused by the Hasidic claim of supremacy of prayer over Torah study and by Hasidic disrespect for Torah scholars. Mitnagedim opposed the Hasidic popularization of Jewish mysticism and the opening of kabbalistic practice for the masses. Generally speaking, the antagonism was based on the outward behavioral dimensions of Hasidic experience and not so much on more ideological or theological Hasidic values. The Gaon apparently had more to say about Hasidic false interpretations of kabbalistic doctrine and some new ideas they were spreading that seemed radical and heretical to him, but we have only vague hints in his own writings against Hasidism on the nature of this sort of criticism. The new rituals and innovative social structures invented by the Hasidim were the main cause for the dramatic public dispute. Finally, opposition to Hasidism had great socioeconomic and political dimensions. The elaborate claims of Hasidic tsadikim were threatening to the rabbinical leadership of the Jewish community. Hasidic separatism, which was most evident in the establishment of local prayer houses, challenged traditional authority and presented an economic problem for *kahal* leadership.[4] The separate kosher meat slaughtering held by Hasidim had a spiritual dimension but was attacked especially for its dramatic drain of the communal treasury income from taxes related to the kosher meat supply and the separatism it caused within communities.[5]

Both the Gaon, from a somewhat more theological stance, and the *kahal* authorities, from a socioeconomic-political side, were motivated to crush the emerging movement through a series of very harsh decrees—especially the widespread use of the ban of excommunication (*ḥerem*), the most powerful weapon in the rabbis' arsenal. The last quarter of the eighteenth century witnessed several waves of hostility toward Hasidism in accordance with the pace of Hasidic expansion and its institutionalization. It was the printing of Hasidic homilies and conduct literature, starting from the 1780s, in addition to the founding of new courts and other institutions, that instigated hostility time and again. In the later stages of this era of contention, the mitnagedim sought any means useful to extinguish the "new sect" that was still attracting followers and gaining ever more power, including involving the new Russian officials in this inner Jewish dispute.

However, by the beginning of the nineteenth century, this harsh ideological and social conflict reached an important crossroad, and the organized active opposition to Hasidism faded. There were several grounds for the decline of organized opposition to Hasidism in the early nineteenth century. The most important were the passing away of the Gaon, the most authoritative figure behind the struggle against the Hasidim, in 1797, and the de facto legal recognition by the Russian authorities of Hasidic separatism in 1804.[6] There were several severe outbreaks of anti-Hasidic persecution in the early years of the nineteenth century, but they were quite sporadic. Starting in the second decade of the nineteenth century, Hasidism faced a very different ideological challenge in the form of Jewish Enlightenment in Eastern Europe.

Although these historical events are at times considered to be some of the most dramatic political disputes that initiated the fragmentation of Jewish culture in the modern era, it is important to grasp their accurate proportions. We should realize that dramatic as they may have been, most East European Jews had nothing to do with the Hasidic-mitnagedic conflicts and did not have to choose a side or identify with one of the rival camps. Most Jewish communities were indifferent to this nuanced conflict taking place as an ideological dispute within the small segment of the rabbinical elite. We should assume that, contrary to some conventional accounts, Jewish society in the late eighteenth century was not split between these rival camps, though the very dramatic events apparently had a great influence on the ideological and cultural evolutions in Jewish society of the nineteenth century and up to our day. At the same time, the most important outcome of the Hasidic-mitnagedic controversy was that it brought the Hasidim themselves to reflect on their self-determination as a defined socio-religious entity. The mitnagedim placed a mirror before Hasidic separatism and by doing so incited Hasidim to define themselves as a new religious group, in some way egging on the emergence of Hasidism as a movement.[7] Throughout a very long historical process, and as the result of the emergence of Jewish conservatism, ultra-Orthodox Jewish society today is divided between Hasidim and the so called Lithuanians, after the region where anti-Hasidic activity originated—but this was hardly the case during the early phase of the dispute, when this schismatic social split remained relatively insignificant.

A Bibliographical Survey

The mitnagedic campaign against Hasidism in the late eighteenth century is relatively well documented. The various sources provide a general outline of the events and details of some of the most important aspects of the cultural dispute. These include a variety of genres: public announcements, letters, chronicles, rabbinic verdicts, halakhic literature, official *kahal* documents, governmental materials, testimonial protocols, and more. Some of these documents were published over the course of the events themselves, others were discovered and published much later, and several are still awaiting their publication or are considered to be lost. The majority of existing documents were collected and published in Hebrew in two volumes by Mordecai Wilensky in 1970.[8] This very beneficial publication includes detailed introductions and a large collection of annotated texts.

The initial phase of the organized campaign against Hasidism was documented in the first published anti-Hasidic polemical treatise: *Zemir aritsim veharbot tsurim*, printed in Nowy Oleksiniec (Aleksnits), following the events of the summer of 1772. This now extremely rare pamphlet incorporates a detailed account of the events, partially written by the anonymous compiler himself (apparently a professional scribe from Brody). It includes a number of documents originating from Vilna and several additional Jewish communal boards scorning the Hasidim.[9] Additional documents survived from the first breakout of the dispute and from the next waves of the public debate during the years 1781 to 1797.[10] The remainder of Wilensky's first volume contains a variety of documents from the three waves of persecution that occurred from 1772 to 1797. These include official bans on Hasidim, descriptions of public debates with some Hasidic leaders, accounts of local disputes in some communities, and so on.

There are very few traces of Hasidic literary response to the events throughout the entire period of mitnagedic criticism. Generally speaking, the Hasidic tactical decision was not to respond directly to mitnagedic accusations but to continue developing and increasing their influence as if nothing had happened. Valuable information was preserved in the letters of R. Shneur Zalman of Lady, the founder of Chabad Hasidism in Belarus, who provided an internal Hasidic perspective of the events in the many letters he wrote to his followers, encouraging them in the face of attacks by their opponents.[11] Additional information can be found regarding the two imprisonments of R. Shneur Zalman by Russian authorities following a report by the mitnagedim. The investigations of the Hasidic leader have left many archival documents that illuminate the relationship between Hasidim and Russian governmental officials, up to Tsar Alexander himself.[12]

Wilensky's second volume of collected documents primarily contains the writings of two of the later literary opponents to Hasidism: David of Maków (d. 1814) and Israel Löbel of Słuck (dates unknown). David of Maków published his *Zemir aritsim* in Warsaw in 1798, giving a detailed description of the corruption of contemporary Hasidism as he regarded it. Briefer parts of his polemic, including his late will, appear in Wilensky's volume as well. The lengthiest polemic ascribed to David of Maków is *Shever poshi'm* (occasionally referred to by other names), published much later from manuscripts, and it contains documents from earlier stages of the battle against Hasidism alongside more detailed historical descriptions of the new Hasidic "sect." These texts provide rare depictions of great historical value of some of the early Hasidic courts and leaders, shedding light on this otherwise nearly unknown stage of Hasidic development. The attribution of some of these texts to David of Maków is in question, but they were no doubt recorded by those in the circles closest to this vehement preacher.[13] Israel Löbel's writings include *Sefer vikuaḥ* (Warsaw, 1798)—an imaginary debate between a Hasid and a mitnaged, from which we can learn about their different opinions at this stage of the controversy. Löbel's significance is more for his stance as a literary bridge between mitnagedic polemics and the later maskilic (Jewish Enlightenment) literary attacks on Hasidism. Israel Löbel published a pamphlet in German (Frankfurt/Oder, 1799), which later maskilim and early professional historians found informative about the Hasidic movement and which was very useful for their own battles against Hasidism.[14]

It is rare to find any severe anti-Hasidic polemics from the nineteenth century (obviously except for the numerous anti-Hasidic writings by maskilim). Very few texts were written by active individual rabbinic opponents of Hasidism in this latter period, when maskilim had already become the most articulate opponents of Hasidism. Several tracts were preserved by Galician maskilim, such as Josef Perl of Tarnopol, which were probably written by late mitnagedim (or early maskilim holding traditional worldviews).[15] Additionally, we may find sporadic polemics written by individual rabbinic figures who persistently wished to maintain ideological separatism from Hasidism, even once it was clear that this sort of attack was basically futile since Hasidism was thriving within Jewish communities.[16] Nonetheless, some later ideological or theological debates between Hasidim and other non-Hasidic authors lack harsh attacks or any attempt to eradicate Hasidism as a legitimate socioreligious entity among East European Jewry. The most famous of these works is *Nefesh ha-Ḥayim* (Vilna, 1824), written by the most prominent disciple of the Gaon, R. Ḥayim of Volozhin (Wołożyn). In clear contrast to earlier anti-Hasidic bans and literary polemics, and opposed to his admired teacher's approach, he acknowledged that the Hasidim had become invincible and were actually not heretics, but he still considered Hasidic religious values and ritual practices wrong and even dangerous for traditional Jewish society.[17] R. Ḥayim presented a dialectic ideological approach, based on kabbalistic traditions, that sought to maintain a traditional religious framework on the one hand, while applying alternative ideals against Hasidic doctrine on the other.

This more intellectual argumentative approach contributed to the downplay of hostility between Hasidim and their opponents and marked a new phase when the rival camps certainly did not agree in religious or ideological terms, but were actually able basically to coexist on an ordinary communal level despite the great social and religious discrepancies between them.[18] Harsh ideological attacks were replaced by a socially oriented struggle. Clashes between Hasidim and mitnagedim extended beyond the religious elitist discourse, with both sides attempting to seize positions of power and influence on the communal level. Both parties tried to take over official positions in the community, such as the rabbinate, by limiting the steps of the other side and issuing regulations that strengthened their own control and influence among local inhabitants.

Contextual Reading of the Mitnagedic Polemics

Eighteenth-century Hasidim rarely ever referred to their own environment or institutional structures, nor did they document their life stories or special events. Moreover, Hasidim did not leave any chronological descriptions of the birth or the development of their own movement. Most of the Hasidic leadership were inactive in literary affairs, while the few Hasidim who did occasionally leave traces in writing tended to ignore reality altogether. Thus, outside observer's testimonial descriptions have great historical value for understanding early Hasidism.[19]

Mitnagedic polemic literature is thus one of our primary sources for any historical evaluation of early Hasidism, and not only of its conflicts with other groups in Jewish society. By positioning themselves as the most outspoken antagonists of early Hasidism, these opponents might be the greatest vital preservers of its historical magnitude. As a matter of fact, if we had had no anti-Hasidic polemics, or if we had for any reason ignored them as historically valuable tracts, we would have missed information not only about the cultural conflict itself but also about several early Hasidic courts, as well as Hasidic geographical and demographical dimensions. Even the organizational structure of Hasidism would have been unclear. We would have been left predominantly with Hasidim's inner ideological self-perspective, which presents only one side of the story of its turning into a mass movement and does so anachronistically. Equally, the very same literature sheds light on the formation of the identity of rabbinic elite in Lithuania, cultivated in this period also through its opposition to Hasidism.[20]

The text presented below incorporates some of the most essential claims against Hasidism as well as a narration of the outbreak of the dispute and a general overview of Hasidism's historical image. Since it is an official declaration written in a polemical style, it is important for us to read it cautiously from a complex contextual perspective in order to obtain some preliminary historical information. In what follows I will demonstrate how the mitnagedic polemical text can be used not only to reconstruct their anti-Hasidic opinions of opponents, but—even more importantly—to analyze basic facts about the early stage of Hasidic expansion, its organizational features, modes of operation, and more.

A letter from the Vilna kahal *to the Brody* kahal, *May 11, 1772. This is an official petition announcing the dangers of Hasidism and encouraging Brody representatives to join the ban against Hasidim. The Brody* kahal *was one of the few communities to declare* ḥerem *against Hasidism, on June 20, 1772:*

> A copy of the essence of a fervent epistle written in the holy city of Vilna, may God protect it, written on Monday, 8 Iyar 5532 [1772] from a certain famous and respectable person.
>
> After inquiring as to your health, I feel it necessary, by the way, without having been asked to do so, though who am I to offer any comment, yet, my stomach was growling and nothing would satisfy from announcing publicly the atrocity that has transpired among the Jewish community. While the elders of our community took upon themselves to mend the breach in the Jewish people, which was broken due to our countless sins—that which has been breached is greater than [the poles supporting] the fence that [still] stands, the poles being the study of Torah and the worship of God. For our souls were aggrieved by what our ears have heard about those who sanctify and purify themselves.[21] Those who are profane have made themselves pure, wearing a hairy mantle in order to deceive, and calling themselves Hasidim and God's holiest, and their tongues speak with cunning. Designated black ones and found white ones, clay apples in golden showpieces, ardent lips and evil heart, covering wine that is the venom of the asps under their clothing, burning with the heat of anger, in which every heart will melt and every knee will buckle, from the sound that will be heard in our land and country of the abolishment of the study of Torah and worship of God. Here have been and here were [once] white vases [now] full of ashes, soil of the city of iniquity. For seven

abominations are in their hearts to hunt pure souls and they abolish Torah study from the people and they strip from their necks the yoke of Torah as well as from the necks of those most gifted youth who would sit in the first row of the court of the king; Who are the kings? The Torah scholars. Who read, study, and go to the study house early in the morning and leave it late in the night. For it is not study that is the most important but deed. Because these Torah scholars would follow the path of the holy ones about whom none has ever heard anything of disgrace. And since these "gentiles" have come into being they have taken the yoke from their necks and are always walking and meeting two by two, like [heretic] meets its like [heretic], and they parade around in their iniquity, by telling them every day: it is a shame to spend one's life in the study of the Torah; instead [better to spend it] on worship, which is prayer. And God forbid to be sad, but always be joyful and laughing. For they say sadness abolishes the Oneness of God. And God forbid to be sorry for any sin you have committed in the past, for if you will be sorry you will reach sadness. And always they would delay their prayer at least two hours at least until after the time of *Kriyat Shema* and after the time of prayer. And they waste their days in the smoke that flows from their mouths.[22] And neither this nor that have they achieved for they abandoned their Torah study and so too their prayer is a disgrace. For they say God forbid to intend the meaning of the words of the prayers, and should you [do that]—[it] is an alien thought. From them hang rings of rage like those of unclean Temple offerings. And they teach their children to behave like jesters during their prayer for they are a treacherous breed and they do somersaults in front of the holy ark as if thrown over by strangers and gentiles, their heads down, their feet up in the air. Has such turmoil ever before been seen or heard of? And their law is different from [that of] the Jewish people and they do not obey the law of the king, who is the Almighty, and they make to gather themselves into bunches who abandon the customs of the ancestors and they breached the border that our ancestors defined in their prayers.[23] And everyone runs from the sound of their voice from the noise of their prayer and the city is rent asunder by the uproar. And they halt in the middle of the prayer, and they humiliate the students of the holy scripture, and are always engaged in laughter and merrymaking. All this is just the tip of their behavior.

And some dirty rumors have been heard about them, which you can't even write about in public because of the enormous abomination that happened among the Jews, which is unbelievable if it wouldn't be repeated from mouth to ear. And so far their tracks are not known for they are full of deceit and their explanations of their behavior are defective. And their smooth-tongued sayings penetrate the hearts of everyone; and thus far the essence of their nature was not clear and all their deeds have been committed in darkness. But because of our many sins over the past last year our little lambs were stolen from the shepherds. How in our many sins a couple of hundred of our still suckling babes died. For this we girded our loins to ascertain and to proclaim who is responsible for this evil. And we took note of their evil inclinations and we toiled until we found the pure blood among their wings [that they were responsible]; Lo and evil we beheld, the abolishing of Torah study and worship and other ugly deeds that cannot be put to paper because of the desecration of the Lord. And with God's mercy over the remnants of the Jewish people their sin has been revealed from heaven. The stones of the wall will cry out [Proverbs 16:26] what is on his lips is like a scorching fire, boils multiply on them all, a concealed impurity erupts through the slit of the snake, for they are listening to the voice of magicians who wrote their books and their teachings. They are wise to do bad and they have nothing good. And we must be concerned that their springs, a dirty and corrupted source, won't spread all over, for deliverance ceased and every vision was blocked by those going down roundabout paths. Until we rose up, our large and great city, the holy community of Vilna, may God protect it, and our communal elders who girded their loins and clothed themselves with the zeal of God. And with the participation of the honorable and learned rabbi head of the rabbinical court,[24] and with the participation of two groups of rabbinical court judges who are serving our community, and at their head, the jewel of our crown, our teacher and rabbi, Lamp of Israel, the right pillar, the mighty hammer, the true *Gaon*, the divine kabbalist whose name is known everywhere, the honor of his glory and of his fame fill the world illuminated by his honor, our master Rabbi Eliyahu, righteous and humble, to push them out and to pursue them with all necessary means. And they removed the jewel in their crown, none other than our Rabbi Ḥayim who was a preacher in our community, and they fired him from his glorious position, and as he is one of the elite, so he should be twice beaten, as he deserves for his deed. And one more thing, our elders of the community did and they burned the thorns of the Lord's vineyard, and burned their religious books which are different from all other Jewish books. And they burned them at the entrance to the community synagogue, by the stocks, before the start of the Sabbath. And their leaders are a stock sprouting poison weed and wormwood; he is the seducer, he is the agitator who added further sins to the crime among us, when it became known to all through a very reliable testimony that he committed an ugly and evil deed just like the disgraceful deeds of the heretics and his mouth emits evilness. He emits evil, Iser is his name, villain is his name, his fame before was known among the Jews as a false prophet, and he acquired his fame as the names of the highest leaders of their evil sects, such as Mendel of Minsk.[25] And also about this Mendel we saw many testimonies about ugly actions which are forbidden among the Jewish people. . . . And that same Issur [lit. thing that is forbidden, = Iser] who added sin to the above mentioned crime was imprisoned and was publicly

> lashed with a whip of anger in front of the entire community. In order that all the evil people will learn not to do such infamous deeds as happened in front of our eyes. And the Almighty shall make the crooked straight, follow the tracks of the holy sheep that are in the land, the pillars of the world, the Torah and the worship which is prayer, to add another fence to the fence so that they won't return anymore to their folly.
>
> And we issued a great ban in all the synagogues as a warning to one and all God forbid that they will not leave the community and will not establish their own separate sects. And we also wrote to every community and to all the elders and leaders of the Jewish communities so that the Jews should be ready to avenge themselves on the enemies of God to make a fence and a safeguard, to rebuild the ruined breaches and put out the flame, for God forbid, this evil family will continue the Lord's wrath against the Jewish people, and the righteous man perishes and no one reflects, etc. And with this, Be well.[26]

The language and style of this text, as with most mitnagedic literature, are essentially rabbinic. It uses biblical and Talmudic terminology, as was common in the intellectual Jewish elite of that time. This is not universal, though. There are a few anti-Hasidic texts written in the vernacular, Yiddish, the spoken language accessible to the masses, such as oral testimonies recorded by anti-Hasidic campaigners.[27]

Like many other Jewish polemical texts of the early modern era, anti-Hasidic literature is sometimes difficult to understand. Its authors use extravagant language that holds ambiguous meanings and allusive hints. It is sometimes difficult even for Hebrew speakers to comprehend the full meaning of some of these flamboyant texts composed of numerous pieces of verses and sayings of the sages. Contemporary polemics were usually presented in an ambiguous argumentative style as part of a persuasive tactic to garner public opinion. It is therefore important to restore the dialectal resources of these texts in order to grasp the meaning of their linguistic suggestive references. This approach to the polemics was presented by Wilensky in his annotated texts, which are now accessible to Hebrew readers.

Once this is done and the document is legible, one can review the text by cross-reading it in comparison to other sources covering the same events, if such are available. This comparative method may assist the reader to dismantle the text, thus enabling the vital distinction between polemical rhetoric and truly important historical content. In what follows I will briefly present four such insights one might receive from this short passage: into internal Jewish politics, modes of operation of emergent Hasidism, early Hasidic rituals, and patterns of anti-Hasidic persecution.

First, an aspect that can be observed in the document is the dynamics of internal Jewish politics of the period. Our text emphasizes the centrality of Vilna and the Vilna elders in the initial decision making to defeat Hasidism, in taking measures against local Hasidim, and in obtaining allies for their prosecuting Hasidim throughout the entire region. The authority to act forcefully against a group within the Jewish community derived from the importance of this central community but also from the authority of the Gaon positioned within it. Vilna was calling upon Brody, the largest Jewish community in the Polish-Lithuanian Commonwealth and the seat of the famous *kloyz* (an exclusive studying society), to join its initiative against Hasidism, which it actually did several weeks later.[28] The authoritative ability of this body to enforce its ideological or religious views on the Jewish community in Poland is noteworthy. So are the limitations of this power, which had eventually enabled committed Hasidim to establish themselves as a fully legitimate entity regardless of harsh political opposition.

Second, equally interesting is the insight provided by the analyzed text into Hasidic activities and modes of dissemination of Hasidic ideology. Since one of the straightforward accusations raised by the mitnagedim involved pointing to what they regarded as the hypocrisy of Hasidic lore, they tended to go into detailed descriptions of Hasidic reality. We notice the very fact that these people actually named themselves "Hasidim" as early as 1772, even before the group had crystallized or had been categorized as the new Hasidism. In other polemical texts they are occasionally referred to as "Karliners," after the court founded by one of the Maggid's disciples, R. Aharon Perlow, in Karolin near Pińsk, a title that reflects the diffusional nature of Hasidic cells and the decentralized structure of Hasidic leadership from its very beginning.[29]

The Vilna mitnagedim recognized the successful attempts by Hasidim to attract adherents, especially young, talented Talmudic scholars, to their courts. They attributed this to the success of emissaries who orally spread the word of the new religious group to great distances. This was accomplished by modifying the traditional hierarchies of religious values, like favoring ecstatic prayer over the more intellectual Torah study, and the denunciation of the traditional scholarly elite. The continuous atmosphere of debauchery at Hasidic gatherings enchanted young people drawn to the new "sect." The term *sect* was used here clearly to delegitimize the gatherings' function in an attempt to push the Hasidim outside the bosom of Judaism.

One of the most important elements of Hasidic presence was the establishment of separate prayer halls, where Hasidim could pray and act according to their religious norms and spiritual desires. Calling out this separatism was quite a common accusation raised by the movement's opponents; in fact, separatism was a key reason for the successful spread of Hasidism in Eastern Europe.[30]

Mitnagedic sources tell us also about the literary products of the early Hasidic movement. Though Hasidism is known as a religious phenomenon whose values were transferred mainly in oral form, these sources reveal the earliest attempts to write down Hasidic teachings. For instance, despite the fact that the first Hasidic book was printed in 1780,[31] we learn from the anti-Hasidic polemics that Hasidim did actually put some of their ideas in writing and that these manuscripts circulated among Hasidim before any were composed as books or printed. In the text cited above, the concern over the spread of Hasidic writings among Jews of the region was raised explicitly, and testimony was even given about the burning of Hasidic writings collected from local Hasidim in Vilna in a public ceremony by the entrance to the synagogue. Since few of these earliest writings have survived, the mitnagedic testimony is evidence of their existence and popularity.[32] We can see how Hasidim actually utilized the writings as propaganda, but with all the hostility of the mitnagedim toward these writings, Hasidism was spread more via oral dissemination and less by the rather esoteric early theological fragments.

Third, the passage above, as is true of many other texts by the mitnagedim, allows for a unique insight into early Hasidic rituals, one not available in any other sources. The success of Hasidism in widening its audiences in the last decades of the eighteenth century is attributed to, among other things, its adoption of kabbalistic rituals and innovative religious practices.[33] In fact, from reading our sources carefully, we can see that these rituals were among the most essential reasons for declaring battle against Hasidism. Here again, anti-Hasidic polemics offer acquaintance with some otherwise unknown Hasidic religious practices in this period. For example, the Hasidic practice of ritual bathing, beyond the frequency required by Jewish law, was borrowed from earlier kabbalistic traditions.[34]

From these texts we may even get some idea of how Hasidim looked or acted. They report the adoption—at least among the Hasidic leadership—of the kabbalistic custom of wearing white garments on the Shabbat and on Jewish high holy days. The joyful atmosphere within Hasidic circles, alongside the avoidance of any feelings of grief in their religious practice, was a noticeable behavioral feature of Hasidism that irritated the mitnagedim.

The mitnagedic text reveals that the most essential elements of Hasidic separatism were their distinctive customs of prayer. Hasidic prayer differed in its liturgical style, its ecstatic passion, and its body and vocal gestures. Their most blunt practice was the performance of summersaults during prayers, which in the eyes of the mitnagedim was anarchic and antinomian. Conflicting with the traditional way of Jewish prayer, these features of Hasidic prayer pushed the Hasidim to establish separate prayer houses that antagonized *kahal* authorities. Hasidim violated the time frame set in Jewish law for prayer because they were preoccupied with bodily cleansing and spiritual preparation for the worship of

God. This accusation was actually the only one raised by the opponents, who claimed it violated legal norms and was well documented and widespread among Hasidim. Some other claims of antinomian behavior are somewhat exaggerated and perhaps were no more than polemical tactics.

Finally, the excerpt provides a rich picture of actions undertaken by the rabbinic opposition against the Hasidim and of the patterns of persecuting them. From this official correspondence one can learn a great deal about the course of events. This document illustrates the attempt made in Vilna as a joint effort by the local rabbinic strata alongside the lay leadership. The *kahal* may have operated under the religious authority of the Gaon, but it also made use of local autonomous judicial institutions, and even collected convicting evidence through formal networks.

Local Hasidim were the first to suffer from the persecutions. Such was the case of the local preacher (Maggid) Ḥayim in Vilna, who was removed from his stand. Other Hasidim in the community were persecuted and sentenced by the *kahal* to severe punishment, including imprisonment and lashing. Hasidic writings were collected from individuals and burnt in front of the entire community at the entrance to the central communal synagogue. The most vehement stance against Hasidism was the announcement of a formal ban against any separatism, private initiatives, or public Hasidic ceremonies. These were the initial steps taken against Hasidim as presented in the very first published text of the breakout of the conflict against Hasidism.

From this rather basic reading into only one excerpt, one may realize the great potential in obtaining valuable historical information from the wide textual corpus of mitnagedic polemics. Accordingly, scholars of Hasidism have made extensive use of these texts since the beginning of modern scholarship, by Simon Dubnow and his contemporaries, and even in earlier descriptions of Hasidism.[35] Dubnow himself based a large portion of his path-breaking history of Hasidism on these texts, to an extent that he turned the Hasidic-mitnagedic episode into its most dramatic and longest section.[36] The aforementioned publication by Wilensky facilitated access to these texts and initialized many more studies in the field of early Hasidism based on them, sometimes reevaluating earlier conventions. For instance, studies on early Hasidic courts,[37] the image of some early Hasidic masters and of the Gaon,[38] and some very important perceptions derived from the polemical text were used to introduce a more balanced and comprehensive narrative of early Hasidism in general.[39] Nonetheless, despite this valuable harvest, there is still more work to be done in this field: some historical disputes on the events themselves have not yet been solved; some of the well-known texts still need to be thoroughly examined and their authorship recognized; some texts that are still in manuscript need to be published; and finally there is still more material in archives and libraries awaiting discovery to reveal the full story of the ideological struggle between Hasidim and their opponents.

SUGGESTED READING

For the best collection of annotated primary sources on the dispute between Hasidim and mitnagedim, see Mordecai Wilensky, *Ḥasidim u-mitnagedim*, 2 vols., 2nd ed. (Jerusalem: Mosad Bialik, 1990 [1970]). In his introductions to the various texts, Wilensky provides descriptions of the historical events narrated in the texts as well as important bibliographical information. A systematic account of the events may be found in Simon Dubnow, *Toledot ha-ḥasidut* (Tel Aviv: Dvir, 1930); Mordecai Wilensky, "Hasidic-Mitnaggedic Polemics in the Jewish Communities of Eastern Europe: The Hostile Phase," in *Essential Papers on Hasidism*, ed. G. D. Hundert (New York: New York University Press, 1991), 244–271. A more recent and comprehensive reflection on the dispute is Immanuel Etkes, *The Gaon of Vilna: The Man and His Image*, trans. J. M. Green (Berkeley: University of California Press, 2002). A different approach was taken by Yehoshua Mondshine, "Ha-GRA ve-ḥelko be-milḥamta shel Vilna ba-ḥasidim," in *Tsadik ve-'edah: Hebetim histori'im ve-ḥevrati'im be-ḥeker ha-ḥasidut*, ed. D. Assaf (Jerusalem: The Zalman Shazar Center, 2001), 297–331. An important study of the social-religious situation in Vilna is Israel Klausner, *Vilna bi-tekufat ha-Gaon* (Jerusalem: Rubin Mass, 1942). Putting the Hasidic-mitnagedic dispute into more accurate proportions was done by Ada Rapoport-Albert, "Hasidism after 1772: Structural Continuity and Change," in *Hasidism Reappraised*, ed. A. Rapoport-Albert (London: The Littman Library of Jewish Civilization, 1996), 76–140. The ideology of the mitnagedim is presented widely in Allan Nadler, *The Faith of the Mithnagdim: Rabbinic Responses to Hasidic Rapture* (Baltimore: The Johns Hopkins University Press, 1997). For studies on the local tension between rival groups, see, for example, Mordechai Nadav, *The Jews of Pinsk, 1506–1880*, ed. and trans. M. Rosman (Stanford: Stanford University Press, 2009), 294–312; Isaiah Kuperstein, "Inquiry at Polaniec: A Case Study of a Hassidic Controversy in 18th Century Galicia," *Bar-Ilan Annual* 24–25 (1989), 25–39. For involvement of Hasidic leadership, see Immanuel Etkes, *Rabbi Shneur Zalman of Liady: The Origins of Chabad Hasidism*, trans. J. M. Green (Waltham: Brandeis University Press, 2015), chaps. 6–7. Later polemics are published in Uriel Gellman, *Sefer ḥasidim: ḥibur ganuz bi-genuta shel ha-ḥasidut* (Jerusalem: The Zalman Shazar Center, 2007); Allan Nadler, "Meir ben Elijah of Vilna's 'Milhamoth Adonai': A Late Anti-Hasidic Polemic," *Journal of Jewish Thought and Philosophy* 1 (1992), 247–280.

NOTES

1. On the debate regarding opposition to Hasidism up to 1772, see Gershom Scholem, "Shetei ha-eduyot ha-rishonot al ḥavurot ha-ḥasidim veha-Besht," in Scholem, *Ha-shelav ha-aḥaron*, ed. D. Assaf and E. Liebes (Jerusalem: Am Oved Publishers, the Hebrew University Magnes Press, 2008), 64–81, and in the bibliographical survey by David Assaf, idem, 82–90, 102–105.

2. Immanuel Etkes, *The Gaon of Vilna: The Man and His Image* (Berkeley: University of California Press, 2002), 73–96. For essential reading on the events of the opposition to Hasidism from 1772 to 1815, see Mordecai Wilensky, "Hasidic-Mitnaggedic Polemics in the Jewish Communities of Eastern Europe: The Hostile Phase," in *Essential Papers on Hasidism: Origins to Present*, ed. G. D. Hundert (New York: New York University Press, 1991), 244–271.

3. For an alternative narrative of these events, claiming that the communal authorities, and not the Gaon, initiated the battle against Hasidism from a political rather than an ideological or theological motivation, see Yehoshua Mondshein, "Ha-GRA ve-ḥelko bemilḥamta shel Vilna ba-ḥasidim," in *Tsadik ve-'edah: Hebetim histori'im ve-ḥevrati'im be-ḥeker ha-ḥasidut*, ed. D. Assaf (Jerusalem: The Zalman Shazar Center, 2001), 297–331.

4. Glenn Dynner, "The Hasidic Conquest of Small-Town Central Poland, 1754–1818," *Polin* 17 (2004), 51–81.

5. Chone Shmeruk, "Mashma'uta ha-ḥevratit shel ha-sheḥitah ha-ḥasidit," in Shmeruk, *Ha-kria'ah le-navi*, ed. I. Bartal (Jerusalem: The Zalman Shazar Center, 1999), 33–63; Shaul Stampfer, *Families, Rabbis and Education* (Oxford: The Littman Library of Jewish Civilization, 2010), 342–355.

6. "If in any particular location a dispute of factions should arise, and the division should reach the state that one division of sects should occur, and the rift between them should be so deep as to prevent the one from sharing its prayer-house with the other, then one of the sects should be allowed to build its own prayer-house and to select its own rabbis, so long as there remains only one *kahal* in each locality"—translation after Shmuel Ettinger, "Hasidism and the Kahal in Eastern Europe," in *Hasidism Reappraised*, ed. A. Rapoport-Albert (London: The Littman Library of Jewish Civilization, 1996), 73.

7. The traditional view of the historical outcome of the Hasidic-mitnagedic dispute can be seen in Simon Dubnow, *Toledot ha-ḥasidut* (Tel Aviv: Dvir, 1931), who devoted approximately one-third of his book to opposition to Hasidism. The more updated narrative is A. Rapoport-Albert, "Hasidism after 1772: Structural Continuity and Change," in *Hasidism Reappraised*, 76–140; David Biale et al., *Hasidism: A New History* (Princeton, NJ: Princeton University Press, 2018), 85–98.

8. Mordecai Wilensky, *Ḥasidim u-mitnagedim: Le-toledot ha-pulmus she-beinehem 1772–1815*, 2nd ed. (Jerusalem: Mosad Bialik, 1990 [1970]).

9. Wilensky, *Ḥasidim u-mitnagedim*, 1:36–69.

10. Ibid., 1:70–210.

11. Ibid., 1:296–313; *Igerot Kodesh* ed. S. D. Levin (Brooklyn, NY: Kehot, 2012).

12. Wilensky, *Ḥasidim u-mitnagedim*, 1: 230–295; Yehoshua Mondshine, *Ha-ma'asar ha-rishon* (Jerusalem: Knizhniki, 2012).

13. Mordecai Wilensky, "The Polemic of Rabbi David of Makow against Hasidism," *Proceedings of the American Academy for Jewish Research* 25 (1956), 137–156.

14. See Rachel Manekin, "A Jewish Lithuanian Preacher in the Context of Religious Enlightenment: The Case of Israel Löbel," *Jewish Culture and History* 13 (2012), 134–152.

15. See Uriel Gellman, *Sefer ḥasidim: ḥibur ganuz bi-genuta shel ha-ḥasidut* (Jerusalem: The Zalman Shazar Center, 2007).

16. For example, Allan Nadler, "Meir ben Elijah of Vilna's 'Milhamoth Adonai': A Late Anti-Hasidic Polemic," *Journal of Jewish Thought and Philosophy* 1 (1992), 247–280.

17. Etkes, *The Gaon of Vilna*, 151–209; Norman Lamm, "The Phase of Dialogue and Reconciliation," in *Tolerance and Movements of Religious Dissent in Eastern Europe*, ed. B. K. Király (Boulder, CO: East European Quarterly, 1975), 115–129.

18. See Allan Nadler, *The Faith of the Mithnagdim: Rabbinic Responses to Hasidic Rapture* (Baltimore: Johns Hopkins University Press, 1997).

19. This surely does not mean that Hasidim never developed historical narratives or self-insights into the processes of their movement's development, but these are usually later reflections that cannot always be regarded as historically trustworthy. See Ada Rapoport-Albert, *Hasidic Studies: Essays in History and Gender* (London: The Littman Library of Jewish Civilization, 2018), 199–266.

20. See Uriel Gellman, "Ha-'elitah ha-lamdanit be-Yahadut Lita: Demutah ve-tadmitah," in *Toledot Yehudei Russia*, vol. 2, ed. I. Luria (Jerusalem: The Zalman Shazar Center, 2012), 113–123.

21. Hinting to the Hasidic custom of frequent immersion in the mikveh.

22. Smoking has become a hallmark of Hasidim, whether as a means for spiritual atmosphere or as a cleansing of the body before prayer.

23. The separation of Hasidim from the community and the establishment of separate Hasidic minyanim.

24. R. Shmuel ben Avigdor, rabbi of Vilna between 1750–1791.

25. R. Menaḥem Mendel (1730–1788), a disciple of the Maggid of Mezrich, functioned as a tsadik first in Minsk and then moved to Witebsk.

26. This is the first document in *Zemir aritsim ve-harbot tsurim*. See Wilensky, *Ḥasidim u-mitnagedim*, 1:37–44, trans. Sharon Assaf.

27. See, for example, Wilensky, *Ḥasidim u-mitnagedim*, 1:44–49, 78–83, 102–105; 2:91–92, 138–41.

28. Ibid., 1:44–49.

29. For the use of the term *Karliner*, see ibid., 1:64–65, 204–205, 275–76. The crystallization of the terms *Hasid*, *Hasidism*, *tsadik*, and the like was a lengthy process that reflects the maturation of Hasidism as a full-fledged movement by the closing of the eighteenth century.

30. Marcin Wodziński, *Hasidism: Key Questions* (New York and Oxford: Oxford University Press, 2018), 1–42; Shaul Stampfer, "How and Why Did Hasidism Spread?" *Jewish History* 26 (2013), 201–219.

31. See chapter 1.

32. Zeev Gries, *Sefer, sofer ve-sipur be-reshit ha-ḥasidut: Min ha-Besht ve-ad Menaḥem Mendel mi-Kotsk* (Tel Aviv: Hakibbutz Hameuchad, 1992), 17–21.

33. The most extensive (yet rather outdated) study on Hasidic rituals is Aaron Wertheim, *Law and Custom in Hasidism*, trans. Sh. Himelstein (Hoboken, NJ: Ktav, 1992).

34. Tsippi Kauffman, "Mikve Yisra'el: Tevilah be-reshit ha-ḥasidut," *Tarbiz* 80 (2012), 409–425.

35. See, for example, *Shalom al Yisra'el* (Zhytomyr, 1868–1870) by the Russian maskil Eliezer Zweifel (1815–1888), who presented a positive evaluation of Hasidism. See, too, one of the harshest late critics of Hasidism, Ephraim Deinard, who also published some unknown polemics that were preserved in manuscript form, for example, *Miflagot be-Yisra'el* (New York, 1899); *Zemir aritsim* (Newark, 1899); *Herev hadah* (Kearny, 1904).

36. See note 6.

37. Immanuel Etkes, "The Early Hasidic 'Court,'" in *Text and Context: Essays in Modern Jewish History and Historiography in Honor of Ismar Schorch*, ed. E. Lederhendler and J. Werthimer (New York: Jewish Theological Seminary, 2005), 157–187. Haviva Pedaya, "Le-hitpatḥuto shel ha-degem ha-ḥevrati-dati-kalkali be-ḥasidut: Ha-pidyon, ha-ḥavurah veha-aliyah la-regel," in *Tsadik ve-'edah*, 343–397, deals with the financial and social aspects of early courts based mostly on anti-Hasidic polemics.

38. See Wolf Ze'ev Rabinowitsch, *Lithuanian Hasidism from Its Beginnings to the Present Day* (London: Vallentine, Mitchell, 1970); Etkes, *The Gaon of Vilna*, 96–150.

39. Rapoport-Albert, "Hasidism after 1772."

CHAPTER 5

Maskilim

Marcin Wodziński

Without a doubt, relations between Hasidism and the Haskalah are one of the best-known aspects of the interaction between nineteenth-century ideological options among East European Jews. They are also the subject of the strongly mythologized division into two opposing and warring camps and the source of an extensive body of literature. This chapter's task will be to investigate what one can learn about Hasidism from the maskilic and postmaskilic writings, and not only about the perception of the Hasidim by their ideological opponents, but also about real forms of life, interactions, and beliefs of the Hasidic community. Ultimately, the goal of the chapter is not so much to probe how much truth there is in the widespread conviction of the centrality of the war between the Haskalah and Hasidism, but rather how one can overcome these and other notional limitations in use of the maskilic literature in research of Hasidism. In other words, how one can use highly biased, partisan, and polemical literature by the maskilim not only for the study of the maskilic attitudes toward Hasidism but also for the study of Hasidism itself?

Views

The main accusations that the maskilim leveled against Hasidism can be divided into social, economic, political, cultural, and above all religious ones. Following Menaḥem Mendel Lefin, Eastern European maskilim defined Judaism as a religion that was developing along two tracks. The rationalist current had been represented by, inter alia, Moses the lawgiver, by Moses Maimonides, and now by Moses Mendelssohn and the Haskalah. The other current was the irrational, mystical tradition rooted in magical thinking. In the past it had been represented by kabbalah, and Hasidism was indeed meant to be its current incarnation. This fundamental distinction between the two traditions was Eastern European

Haskalah's basic category of self-definition, and the simplest explanation of its ideological hostility toward Hasidism. As the incarnation of religious obscurantism, it represented everything that was alien to the Haskalah, and in fact alien to pure Judaism. Beginning with Mendel Lefin and Josef Perl right up to the twentieth-century postmaskilic press, the leaders of Hasidism were depicted as shady shamans or kabbalistic Dalai Lamas—in the rationalist language of the day the personification of the crudest kind of religious obscurantism.

The most important type of social criticism was the accusations of separatism and of Hasidism's alleged antisocial features. The Hasidim were accused of retaining differences in Jewish dress, language, and customs, but above all of anti-Christian prejudice, double standards of morality, and xenophobia. It was held that the Hasidim were destroying Jewish religious tradition and were extending the concept of idolatry (*'akum*) to Christians, and that they were deploying all the most immoral behavior against them. "All their actions are filled with immorality, intolerance, and disdain for everything that a Hasid is not. They teach often and quite shamelessly that idolaters can be deceived and officials bribed."[1] This is not just inherently immoral, but is also a basic obstacle on the path to the Jews' social and cultural integration into the surrounding Christian societies. The Hasidim's separatism was thus perceived as a feature precisely contrary to the program of the maskilim, who believed that isolating oneself from the Christian population would reduce the chance for current and future Jewish generations to solve the basic social problems associated with a failure to adapt to changing conditions in the outside world. Furthermore, the maskilim were convinced that the hostility shown toward Christians by Jews would lead to Christian hostility toward the Jews, which would make the Jewish population's position even worse. In their view, Hasidic separatism was the quintessence of the negative and harmful tendencies in Judaism.

The Haskalah, with its absolute principle of political legalism, also looked suspiciously at Hasidism's attitude toward non-Jewish authorities. The most rabid opponents of the Hasidim wrote reports criticizing them for a lack of respect for authorities and also for revolutionary tendencies. But the key category in the sociopolitical criticism was the controversy over the leadership of the Jewish community, personified for the Hasidim in the person and role of the tsadik. Apart from the individual attributes of specific tsadikim, the maskilim rejected the principle of leadership based on religious charisma as completely irrational and unmerited. They believed instead that political representation should rest in the hands of those who were the best educated, who had the best political contacts, and who above all best understood the challenges of the modern world; thus, in their hands. Criticism of the principle of leadership resting in the hands of the tsadikim was also nourished by anticlericalism, which had become rooted in general Enlightenment concepts of the rationalization and secularization of the sociopolitical structure, and in a general suspicion of the spiritual hierarchy. The influence of David Hume's and Voltaire's concepts of the natural history of religion was visible in the writings of the Galician maskilim, especially Josef Perl and Yehudah Leib Mieses. In line with these views, basic and natural human feelings of fear before the forces of nature were used by perverse priests for taking control of the masses and for exploiting them. All spiritual hierarchies were thus the result of historical deception and were nourished by the people's naivete. According to this logic the tsadikim were the representatives of this deceitful class of priests. Leaving political authority over the Jewish people in their hands not only would be immoral but would above all maintain the prevailing catastrophic state of affairs and would make reform impossible.

Finally, the broadest category of sociocultural criticism included accusations against the Hasidim of a whole series of crimes against Jewish culture. Among them were cultivating a bastardized version of German (Yiddish) and an aversion to grammatically accurate Hebrew. Similarly reprehensible was an aversion to modern, secular science, which, in the opinion of the maskilim, was essential to dragging the Jewish people out of a state of civilizational backwardness. But the most important accusations focused on the most fundamental issues of supposed Hasidic obscurantism, which we can see to mean the argument around the bourgeois ethos and lifestyle, which Hasidism in fact rejected and the maskilim saw to be the only real ones. Perez Smolenskin, a maskilic Hebrew writer, saw in this a Hasidic revolution against hierarchy and social order: "When a Hasid sees a rich, honorable, wise, and educated man he stifles his feelings of awe by saying that he will negate him in his mind, and having once done so, he no longer respects him, but rather disdains him and regards himself to be superior."[2] In this same tone of indignation toward Hasidism for the violence done toward bourgeois decorum, he attacked their habit of smoking tobacco to ward off constipation, which they supposedly took to be an obstacle on their road to achieving *unio mystica*. Numerous maskilic descriptions of alleged Hasidic abuse of alcohol and accompanying licentiousness belonged to this same category. As Yitzḥak Ber Lewinsohn complained, "And I hear great noise from those drinking alcohol, dancing in herds and singling loudly, who bring new customs to our town."[3] In a great many such accusations, the shame that their "progressive" coreligionists felt toward the Hasidim showed through.

However, before reaching any further conclusions about the attitudes of the Haskalah toward Hasidism and the negative image of the latter by the former, we need to note that the negative image just described should not be taken as the only or even the dominant one. Above all, maskilic anti-Hasidic rhetoric did not in the least have to be, and often was not, about the Hasidim. In fact, the delegitimizing language of the battle with Hasidism was often used as a universal polemical language, often without any real link to Hasidism.

More important still was the fact that throughout the whole of the nineteenth century, there were those maskilim who consciously rejected the dominant anti-Hasidic discourse and actively opposed it. For example, one of the most valuable postmaskilic sources was an article on Hasidism by Daniel Neufeld. Unlike prevailing authors on the subject of Hasidism, Neufeld pays very little attention to the movement's beginnings and ignores its basic ideas. Instead he provides first-rate ethnographic material. Although the article is not free of the accusations typical of Haskalah writing, especially against the Besht and unnamed "backward" Galician tsadikim, he draws attention to Hasidism's positive aspects, including its folk nature.[4] This is perhaps the first testimony to the fascination with folk Hasidism in secular Jewish circles of Eastern Europe. Somewhat better-known pro-Hasidic texts from the camp of the Haskalah were written by Jakub Tugendhold, Jacob Samuel Bik, and, the best known of them, Eliezer Zweifel, a Russian maskil, who penned the tract *Shalom al Yisrael* (Peace upon Israel, 1868). Especially in many of the writings by Jakub Tugendhold, one can find references to Hasidism, information on individual tsadikim, critical yet well-balanced and positive descriptions of various aspects of the Hasidic movement, and more. Also, in the writings of many other maskilim, such as Isaac Mieses, Solomon Judah Rapoport, and Moses Berlin, one can find a lot of fascinating material on Hasidism.[5]

To conclude, a bipolar, absolute division of the world into the Haskalah and Hasidism is convenient for a simple, intuitive way of seeing and describing reality, but it very rarely describes accurately the real divisions. The persuasive power of such a perspective is oftentimes the result of exaggerating the significance of voices that are radical, thus the loudest and yet at the same time marginal, while ignoring the statements of milder, subtler, often dominant, but ambiguous ones that are thus harder to interpret. Furthermore, a conviction of the eternal and inevitable conflict between Hasidism and the Haskalah not only treats this conflict as absolute, while also ignoring other forms of interaction, but also positions it as the principal division in the Ashkenazi world from the end of the eighteenth century up to the Holocaust. However, such an assumption is at least controversial, giving pride of place as it does to an ideological approach to modernizing processes—one of the many ideological categories dividing the nineteenth-century world—while at the same time ignoring other categories of division, such as those of culture, geography, economy, or class. The use of the maskilic literature should take all those caveats into account before drawing any conclusions from these fascinating yet difficult sources.

Writings

It is no wonder that the maskilic writers, for whom Hasidism was such an important and dangerous phenomenon, left an extremely voluminous library of sources on the subject of Hasidism. Some of them will be discussed further in this book—for example, in chapter 9, on the press, the vast majority of which represented the ideology of the Haskalah. Maskilic texts will be also discussed in the chapters on ego-documents (chapter 6) and archival collections (chapter 8). In this chapter, we are primarily interested in the genres that are not discussed elsewhere in the book: belles-lettres (satires, dramas, poems, novels, etc.), philosophical and political treaties, memorandums, conduct literature, apologetic and polemical writings, catechisms, textbooks, and other forms of maskilic textual production.

It was Mendel Lefin who made a definitive mark on the development of anti-Hasidic Haskalah literature and injected it with an Enlightenment predilection for satire as the most effective type of didactic literature, as well as with a conviction of the need to fight Hasidism precisely with the aid of satirical literature.[6] It seems that it was precisely his convictions that affected later writers of the Galician and indirectly the Russian Haskalah, in which satirical texts represented the largest and most visible body of anti-Hasidic literature. The most interesting and best known among them was a story titled *Megale temirin* (The Revealer of Secrets), by Josef Perl (1773–1839), a wealthy merchant and maskilic activist from Tarnopol, Galicia. Published in 1819 under the pseudonym Ovadia ben Petahia, this epistolary novel is a collection of alleged Hasidic letters, which the writer supposedly obtained as the result of his magical ability to transport himself instantaneously and become invisible. Extending over 151 letters, the story describes the efforts of Hasidim who learn about the existence of a certain anti-Hasidic book that appears to be none other than Perl's own *Über das Wesen der Sekte Chassidim*. Enraged by their discovery, they attempt at all costs to obtain and destroy it. The Hebrew that Perl puts in the mouths of his fabricated Hasidim is deliberately fractured, thus adding another level of anti-Hasidic satire. While pretending to be a Hasidic work, the book sharply criticizes Hasidic beliefs, customs, and ethical double standards by parodying actual Hasidic texts, in particular *Shivḥei ha-Besht* and the tales of R. Naḥman of Bratslav. *Megale temirin* is widely acknowledged to be the first Hebrew novel, and its influence on the subsequent development of Hebrew writing was considerable. Haskalah writers in the nineteenth century frequently referred to it, and two decades later Perl himself published a continuation of the novel titled *Boḥen tsadik*.

Other well-known examples of anti-Hasidic satirical texts were *Divrei tsadikim* (The Words of the Just, 1830), by Perl and Yitzḥak Ber Lewinsohn, and Yehudah Leib Mieses's *Sefer kinat ha-'emet* (The Book of Zealousness for Truth, 1828), a dialogue between Maimonides and R. Solomon of Chełm, a rabbi and an early maskil, who both attack belief in demons, amulets, witchcraft, and miracle workers.[7] Yitzḥak Erter, a close friend of Yehudah Leib Mieses, left a number of anti-Hasidic satires in Yiddish, mostly ridiculing rabbinical elite and Hasidic leaders. A less-known but very interesting work in this vein is Ephraim Fischel Fischelsohn's drama *Teyator fun khsidim* (The Theatre of the Hasidim), a disputation between the enlightened hero Leib Filozof and a group of Hasidim of Bełz, another important instance of using Yiddish, not Hebrew, for anti-Hasidic criticism. The discussion takes place in a Hasidic study hall (*bet midrash*) where Leib is studying traditional Hebrew texts by Maimonides. Enlightened but faithful to religion and tradition, he calls on typical Haskalah arguments against Hasidism, proves its irrationality, and points to the parasitical lifestyle of the tsadikim. The debate ends in the maskil's triumph, and the yeshiva students who are watching vote for Leib and attack the Hasidim as "beggars and frightful rogues."[8]

Possibly the most important Yiddish text of the late maskilic criticism of Hasidism was the pseudo-autobiography of Yitzḥak Yoel Linetsky (1839–1915), entitled *Dos poylishe yingl* (The Polish Lad, 1867–1869). The book, initially published in installments, became an instant best seller and was one of the most popular Jewish literary works in the nineteenth century, splendidly parodying Hasidic society's life and customs.[9]

After Linetsky, the anti-Hasidic motives did not die out. They, in fact, appeared quite regularly in the writings of the late- and postmaskilic Hebrew writers, such as Peretz Smolenskin (1842–1885), Abraham Mapu (1808–1867), Shalom Abramowich (1835–1917), better known as Mendele Mokher Sforim, and Ruben Asher Braudes (1850–1902).[10] Toward the end of the nineteenth century, Yiddish prose inherited the Hasidic motives from the postmaskilic Hebrew writers.

Possibly the most characteristic feature of this vast body of maskilic texts on Hasidism is that, unlike other sources discussed in this book, they are literary ones. This allows for using the tools of literary analysis far more effectively in researching the maskilic sources than any of the other types of sources on Hasidism mentioned above. This includes analyzing genres, literary conventions, literary strategies, stylistic features, poetics, features of the sociology of literature, and how these texts actually functioned socially, among other methods of study. At the same time, it needs to be noted that many of the historical studies of Hasidism that do use maskilic literary texts attempt to treat them in a somewhat reductive way as an accurate reflection of the historical realities, even if at times biased and hyperbolic. I propose seeing this limitation of the scholarly literature as an invitation for a more nuanced, methodologically sophisticated revisiting of apparently well-known sources and research questions.

Yet, as was mentioned before, belles-lettres was not the only form of maskilic writings on Hasidism. Quite the contrary. In fact, the other, nonliterary writings constitute the vast majority of the textual output of the Haskalah in Eastern Europe, so they provide as much information on the Hasidic movement as the belles-lettres, or more. For example, in 1816, Josef Perl wrote a lengthy anti-Hasidic political tract in German, *Über das Wesen der Sekte Chassidim* (On the Nature of the Hasidic Sect), perhaps the most important anti-Hasidic work of the Haskalah. The tract was addressed to the Austrian civil authorities and the Christian reader, and it was meant to explain Hasidism in a way that was systematic yet accessible to the uninitiated reader. After explaining the movement's name, Perl discusses the history of its formation and presents its main principles, which he reduces to slavish obedience toward the tsadikim and to the search for *devekut*, the state of spiritual ecstasy that he trivializes as an alcoholic stupor. Every Hasidic group, he explains, must have its leader, called *Rebbe*, who does not have to come from the family of the Besht nor even be a descendant of the tsadik, although descent from a family of tsadikim greatly helps in such a career. A great many benefits accrue from being a tsadik: the wealthiest families want to ally themselves with him, the tsadik leads a lavish lifestyle, he is showered with gifts, he rides round the district collecting tribute. The whole country is divided into spheres of influence, and each tsadik fights to increase his turf, leading to numerous quarrels between Hasidic groups. Perl presents the Hasidim as economically indolent and the tsadikim as frauds living off the simple folk. In addition, all the Hasidim plot against non-Hasidim, the state, and Christians generally, whom they recognize not as human but as idolaters whom one can cheat, rob, deceive, and bribe.

The image of Hasidism that Perl created was so shocking that the authorities did not agree to publish the tract for fear that it might lead to social unrest. Still, *Über das Wesen der Sekte Chassidim* circulated widely in manuscript form and eventually turned out to be perhaps the most important source of information on Hasidism for Christian circles and liberal Jews in Central Europe in the first half of the nineteenth century.

Naturally, Perl's tract is only one example of the vast corpus of maskilic writings on Hasidism. In addition to the numerous texts devoted solely or largely to the issue of Hasidism, such as Perl's, there were many more writings that mentioned Hasidism only in passing, or referred to it obliquely, or provided only a chapter or a section or just a hint on Hasidism. Together, they create a vast library of maskilic texts on Hasidism. The main problem has always been how to use them.

Historiography

From the very beginning of Hasidic historiography, maskilic writings were one of the important sources for research into this movement, indeed often a prime source. Especially in the early phase of Jewish historiography, in the nineteenth and early twentieth centuries, historians relied to an enormous extent on maskilic writings as one of the two basic sources (alongside pieces by mitnagedim) of knowledge about Hasidism. The first professional history of Jewish sects, written in the 1820s by Marcus Jost and partly describing Hasidism, is based above all on information from the writings of Josef Perl, as well as from the work of the Prague maskil Peter Beer. For Heinrich Graetz, Perl was also a basic source of information on Hasidism, as was Salomon Maimon's well-known autobiography.

Likewise, Simon Dubnow, who declared himself to be far more critical of the veracity of maskilic writings, liberally referred to them, often unconsciously borrowing not just facts but also interpretative frameworks. Thus from Dubnow comes the tradition of ambivalent, inconsistent approach to the maskilic literature. One the one hand it warns against the bias in maskilic sources, and even criticizes the whole Jewish Enlightenment, which is rooted in the nationalist antiliberal discourse. But at the same time its overarching concept of the history of Hasidism is rooted in even deeper maskilic narrative models, starting with the definition of Hasidism as a sect, by way of the myth of the Hasidic conquest of Eastern Europe, the conviction of Hasidism's Sabbatean roots, up to the image of Hasidism as a movement of Jewish poverty.[11] The last of these stereotypes is a good illustration of how Dubnow's writings are intertwined with maskilic narrative models. Although the image of Hasidism as a movement of poverty is not confirmed historically in any of the quantitative sources known to Dubnow, and is even highly dubious in light of most narrative sources he used, it represents one of the axioms on which he built a whole picture of early Hasidism. Although subsequent research has produced a large corpus of primary and analytical material throwing this stereotype into question, the image of Hasidic poverty has remained in principle a widely accepted truism to the present day.

Thus, despite awareness of their bias and natural limitations, criticism of sources of maskilic origins by Dubnow and his followers was rather lenient and impressionistic, more along the lines of common sense and probability, and thus is an unreliable tool for source analysis. A preferable approach would have forced an examination of many of the interpretative frameworks within these source materials.

However, at the end of the day it is hard to heap any real condemnation on this uncritical approach to studying maskilic source materials, for it needs to be remembered that despite all its limitations this source is in many regards exceptional and exceptionally valuable. For most of the nineteenth century, the maskilim were the group most interested in describing Hasidism, even if their descriptions were never meant to be objective. Thanks to this interest, maskilic writings provide us with uniquely valuable information on Hasidism in its various forms and permit us to look into areas where the historian has no other access. One could say that for Hasidism in the nineteenth century, maskilic sources are what mitnagedic sources are for Hasidism in the eighteenth century.

Somewhat schematically, scholarly use of the Hasidic material in Eastern European maskilic texts can be summarized as falling into three main categories.

The first one, about which we have already warned, is the unconscious acceptance of maskilic interpretative clichés, whether in relation to the whole of Hasidism or just to certain aspects of it. As the distinguished historian of Eastern European Jewry Israel Bartal has shown, the interpretative clichés emerging from maskilic writings are dangerous, because they are exceptionally widespread and to this day remain unquestioningly accepted by many.[12] According to Bartal the five most widespread cognitive clichés are: (1) a conviction of Hasidism's mass and popular character; (2) a conviction of its unproductive nature rooted in Hasidic theological concepts; (3) a conviction that Hasidism weakened traditional Jewish self-governance in Eastern Europe; (4) a conviction of the insurmountable barrier between the intentions of Eastern European governments and Hasidic aims; (5) a similar conviction of the eternal and insurmountable hostility between the world of Hasidism and the Haskalah. As Bartal points out, all these ideas are not fully supported in the source materials and were introduced into the everyday historical consciousness precisely by maskilic discourse. Likewise, the conviction of the early Hasidim's Sabbatean connections was raised by a great many classical scholars of the movement, from Gershom Sholem to Isaiah Tishby by way of Joseph Weiss, but was never, however, even confirmed.

The second category is the troubling and extremely risky use of maskilic texts as sources for knowledge on the Hasidic world at the micro level of individual, everyday events. Of course, a great many maskilic texts tend to notice only a certain type of event, mainly episodes that show the Hasidim in a bad light; they also often present these events in a crooked mirror. Careful examination of a source allows us, however, to use these materials in a productive way, especially since they often describe facts not noted in other sources. Press articles in particular (see chapter 9) are a mine of information on tsadikim and their journeys, community conflicts, local battles over rabbis, ritual slaughterers, and so on. However, literature—especially memoirs—sometimes contains exceptionally valuable information, too. For instance, the memoirs of Yekhezkel Kotik provide a detailed description of a "conversion" to Hasidism and its accompanying motivations, home interactions, and the operations of a Hasidic group in the field of economic activity.[13] The memoirs of the maskil Avraham Ber Gottlober, a generation older, contain a great many unknown facts on Hasidic life, such as details of a tsadik's dress, motivations for choosing one tsadik over another, family matters, and especially details undermining the maskilic stereotypes, for instance a tale on the availability of modern maskilic education in the home of a zealous Hasid, or the fluidity of the boundaries between the supporters of these two worldviews.[14] Likewise, the encyclopedia entry on Hasidism already mentioned, written by Daniel Neufeld in 1862, described unknown facets of Hasidic customs, rituals, and convictions on the basis of the author's ethnographical observations. A great many maskilic texts contain elements of ethnographical description before the advent of regular ethnographical research into Hasidism at the end of the nineteenth century.

Finally, the third category of information on Hasidim in maskilic texts is the actual maskilic image of Hasidism itself, hence the maskilim's attitude toward the Hasidic movement. Although this is not a description per se of Hasidism and does not provide information on the Hasidic movement itself, it is hard to claim that this is not an important element in the history of Hasidism as widely understood, and of the social changes that it wrought. Thus this image has been the subject of many studies, some of which have become classics. Perhaps the most important of these works is Raphael Mahler's *Hasidism and the Jewish Enlightenment*, which, on the basis of a diverse corpus of source materials, including numerous maskilic writings, has reconstructed the image of Polish and Galician Hasidism as well as the Haskalah's attitude toward it. Mahler's work shaped for the next few decades the image of Hasidism and the Haskalah in the historiographical writings, and to this day it remains strikingly influential, even though many aspects of his work have been radically challenged over the last twenty years.[15]

Case Study

One of the interesting examples of the way in which maskilic writings provide us with information on Hasidism, how they formed interpretative frameworks, and how they were used by the historiography of the movement could be the short chapter written by the Polish maskil Jacques Calmanson at the time of the debate over the so-called Jewish Question during the Great Sejm in the final years of the Polish-Lithuanian Commonwealth (1788–1792).

As far as we are aware, Jacques Calmanson (1722–1811) was one of the earliest advocates of the Haskalah to speak out on the Hasidic question. Originating from Hrubieszów, Calmanson received a broad education, studied medicine in Germany and France, knew French, German, and Polish in addition to the Jewish languages, and traveled on a number of occasions around Germany, France, Turkey, and Russia. He settled in Warsaw and was for many years King Stanisław August Poniatowski's doctor. He was also active in public life, drafting a memorial on changes to the Jewish taxation system, translating Hebrew and Yiddish texts on plans for the reform of the Jews, and more. After retirement, he spent the rest of his life in Warsaw, as a resident of one of the Catholic monasteries.[16]

Calmanson did not leave behind a rich written heritage. His one known text, *Essai sur l'état actuel des Juifs de Pologne* (Essay on the Current State of the Polish Jews and Their Betterment), is a treatise on the project to reform Polish Jews. Its Polish translation, in which Calmanson expanded on the original text, was published in 1797, several years after the Great Sejm, for which it had been originally drafted.

The first chapter of Calmanson's work is devoted to religion. The chapter is divided into five paragraphs, which discuss in order the general principles of the Jewish religion, as well as the Karaite, Hasidic, and Frankist "sects," and the ban.

The short paragraph on Hasidism is entitled "Concerning the Sect Named the Choside, or Zealots, the Bigots," and it reads as follows:

> The sect, known in greater detail to Polish Jews only, emerged no more than twenty years ago. Międzybóż, a town in Podolia, is its cradle. It owes its nature to a rabbi steeped in fanaticism, who, taking advantage of the gullibility of those people who have always been immersed in a lack of learning, who have always craved novelty and been astonished by anything that resembles a miracle, was so adept that he was considered a prophet among them. He claimed that he had the power to cure all diseases through kabbalah. This particular novelty initially resulted in great adulation. The common people, attracted by one mere nothing and simultaneously repelled by another, eagerly ran to the fanatic's mud hut to regain their health, and although they could find only fault under his roof, the number of his followers nevertheless grew considerably.
>
> The sect, which endures even now, rejects any teachings of law; it treats a lack of learning as a matter of pride; the very lack of learning of which its supporters were earlier accused was seen as a fault and a vice and today it is made a virtue of, seen as beautiful, or at least suited to sloth; it knows only one teaching, that of kabbalah, but in this it has neither reason nor restraint. It recommends a contemplative life as the only life for which man has been made; in public it conceals personal gain with all manner of neglect, but clandestinely it does not have sympathy with such a belief. All their property is held in common and nearly always administered by their elders, of whom they think very highly and whom they even venerate with the title *the unerring*, which is more for show than for respectability's sake. Moreover, this kabbalistic skill, the profoundness and benefits of which their elders praise to the skies, and the secrets of which they conceal from the crowd carefully and prudently for their own gain, with a view not only to preserving the relentless tyrannical power which they have over minds, which is the sole rule and basis of their standing, but also with a view to asserting some right to the property of incoming adherents; I state that this same kabbalistic skill is an unfathomed mystery to them themselves. These two circumstances force one to wonder at how skillfully they abuse the injudicious ardor of the misguided simple folk. But, on the other hand, one should pity their lack of enlightenment, the good but misguided faith of these uneducated, gullible souls who believe that they are serving God with this insane fanaticism, whereas, in fact, all their pains are, as if it were, victim to the eccentricity of a number of fictitious zealots, in whose persons they have, and will have, strenuously prevailing despots if the authorities do not contrive any effective means of eradicating this spreading pestilence.
>
> It should undoubtedly be expected that the authorities will undertake immediate and effective measures to put a check on the further spread of such

> a dangerous sect in terms of its theories, and even more dangerous in its effects; a sect that is spreading with greater enthusiasm than its vapid beginnings could have foreseen and that has already infected almost all synagogues with its devastating poison. Why should not the country in which this reptile breeds, and not only Jews, fear its ferocity if there is no resolute dam to the attacks of folly of these dazzled zealots? Their fanaticism is all the more menacing for the fact that they, in good faith bordering on error, envisage themselves as fighting under the banner of religion; while they make it one of their priorities to concern themselves with the establishing and spreading of their dogmas, which are as ungodly as they are terrible.[17]

Since Heinrich Graetz published the French version of Calmanson's text as an appendix to his monumental *History of the Jews*, it has been used as an example of the vehement criticism of Hasidism among the first East European maskilim, thus providing evidence of the early origins of this conflict.[18] However, this thesis appears to be founded on a misunderstanding of the fundamental meaning of the work, even if only because the author made a clear distinction between an evil, swindling leadership and the good, but naive, adherents of "the new sect." Calmanson seems, if anything, to have pitied rather than despised the Hasidim. Equally ambiguous is the author's attitude to the Hasidim's interest in kabbalah. Calmanson wrote that even the tsadikim were unfamiliar with kabbalistic learning, but he did not condemn this fascination with antirationalistic kabbalistic studies; rather, he spoke of it with a certain amount of respect.

The introduction of these qualifications does not, of course, mean that Calmanson's picture of Hasidism was necessarily positive; on the contrary, Hasidism was consistently criticized in his work. But the misinterpretation of his supposedly aggressive anti-Hasidic attitudes comes from a superficial reading of this criticism, in which a two-page paragraph about Hasidism has been taken out of the context of the seventy-page work. In reality, Calmanson presented Hasidism more as a curiosity than as a real social threat. While he warned of the potential danger to the country of the fanatical nature of the movement and of its rapid growth, this is all fairly mild in comparison with the charges leveled at traditional Jewish institutions—in particular, at the whole of the "religious aristocracy." This is consistently referred to in the treatise as the greatest plague and the cruelest exploiter of the Jewish people. Hasidism, therefore, was only one of the elements of Jewish social life to be criticized. It was not viewed as the most dangerous, and it remained very much in the shadow of the most powerful enemy—the *kahal* and the rabbinical elite.

In addition, an accurate understanding of Calmanson's accusations against Hasidism requires us to compare them with his depiction of other "sects," to which he devoted a large portion of his book. According to Calmanson, the Jewish sects that existed in the Polish-Lithuanian Commonwealth constituted the best evidence of the decline of the Jewish community since they represented deviations from pure Mosaic principles. He wrote about three such "sects," ranking them in order of significance and degree of fanaticism. He began with a relatively amicable description of the Karaites, followed by a critical depiction of Hasidism and a scathing criticism of the Frankist movement. A short paragraph on the Karaites described them as simple people, uneducated but honest. The section on Frankism is four times as long as the paragraph about Hasidism, comprising half of the chapter on the Jewish religion. In it, Calmanson declared that "this sect is quite numerous, especially in Warsaw,"[19] whereas he wrote of Hasidism only that "it is spreading with greater enthusiasm than its vapid beginnings could have foreseen." The author consistently described Frankism as the most dangerous eruption of religious fanaticism and the most powerful example of the errors to which antirationalist religious views were liable to lead. Calmanson strongly emphasized the sect's economic base, the greed of Jacob Frank, and his swindling and exploitation of the members of the sect—his criticism here is similar to but stronger than his criticism of Hasidism. His belief that the Frankist sect was more numerous and more dangerous than Hasidism was no doubt the result of the existence of a powerful Frankist community in Warsaw; this is why Calmanson came to estimate such a low figure for the adherents of Hasidism, and it also casts light on how we should interpret his anti-Hasidic criticism. In reality in 1759 the total number of Frankist converts stood at fewer than two thousand.[20] In Calmanson's opinion, the Hasidim were less numerous and less fanatical than the Frankist sect.

Some conclusions may be also drawn from Calmanson's lack of familiarity with his subject matter. Unlike other parts of his book, the paragraph devoted to Hasidism is lacking in detail and full of errors. The only information concerning the doctrine of the Hasidim relates to their alleged glorification of indolence and of kabbalah. This leads us to believe that the author knew little about them and that his knowledge was, in any case, second- or thirdhand. This is not to be taken as evidence that there were no Hasidim in Warsaw or that such information was unobtainable; we know that there were Hasidic groups in Warsaw at the time, just as there were in other towns in central Poland.[21] In addition, Calmanson must have personally known Shmul Zbitkower, one of the patrons of the Hasidim, because they mixed in the same royal circles. It must therefore be presumed that Hasidism was simply not a major topic of conversation in Warsaw's Haskalah circles and that the level of interest in the Hasidim and knowledge of their fellowship (albeit incorrect) was simply proportional to society's perception of their significance. If this is correct, we may conclude that the first generation of Polish maskilim viewed Hasidism as a fairly insignificant curiosity, rather than as a threat to Jewish society in Poland.

It might come as a surprise, then, that Calmanson's arguments, so ill-informed and so marginally interested in Hasidism, became one of the foundational stones of the maskilic criticism of the Hasidim. Of all the anti-Hasidic and generally anticlerical rhetoric, the motif that appears to be at the center of Calmanson's critique of Hasidism is the fraudulent economic behavior of the Hasidic leaders. The motive of economic gain by the tsadikim had appeared even earlier in the writings of the mitnagedim, but it was Calmanson who first made it a major feature in the description of Hasidism and extrapolated from it a strongly defined division between swindling exploiters and the good, but deceived, masses. This view was eminently relevant to the basic thesis of the treatise on the exploitation of the simple masses by the Jewish aristocracy. Thus, according to Calmanson, Hasidism was simply another embodiment of the general Jewish conflict between the religious-financial elite and the common people.

Significantly, criticism of the economic structures of Hasidism and of financial exploitation by the tsadikim soon became one of the most regular threads of maskilic criticism of the Hasidim.[22] The maskilim accused the tsadikim of consciously preying on their followers' naivete in order to fleece them of money. The collection of offerings (*pidyonot*) and taxes (*ma'amadot*) by the tsadikim led, in the opinion of the maskilim, to the impoverishment of the whole Jewish population, especially Hasidic families, in which a hungry wife and ragged children awaited the return of their profligate father, who squandered their hard-earned money at the tsadik's court. Even worse, the boundless faith in the tsadik made the Hasidim economically submissive, leading to indolence and failure to take up gainful employment. This stood in stark contrast to the Haskalah program of refashioning the Jewish economy in Eastern Europe along modern, productive lines.

The view of Hasidism as economically demotivating and Hasidim as economically underprivileged became a common wisdom. Without any serious evidence, historians from Dubnow to Mahler and contemporary scholars maintained that the Hasidim were on average poorer than non-Hasidim, that their families suffered poverty, and that the Hasidim were economically inactive. When the evidence suggested the contrary, it was dismissed as nonrepresentative. In an influential study by Raphael Mahler, the sole evidence to support his claim that Hasidism was the movement of "poor, unemployed people" consisted of anti-Hasidic writings by the maskilim.[23] In effect, even though a number of scholars, from Israel Halpern and Yeshayahu Shachar to Moshe Rosman and Glenn Dynner, attempted to challenge or qualify this image, the myth of Hasidic poverty has remained one of the dominant stereotypes about Hasidism, present in both popular and academic writings.[24] It is informative to see its origins in the ill-informed and clearly partisan treatise by an early maskilic writer.

It is also informative to understand that this image of Hasidism, as presented in one short paragraph of the treatise by Jacques Calmanson, was far from unanimously negative. In fact, the author was aware of the positive characteristics of Hasidism, did not consider it especially harmful, and did not put too much emphasis on combating the Hasidic movement. Like many other maskilim, Calmanson was critical of some Hasidic features but appreciative of others. He differentiated between corrupted leadership and ill-informed but essentially good-meaning masses. He criticized the social activities of the Hasidim but expressed a certain degree of understanding for their interest in kabbalah. Most importantly, his treatise was not intended to be and should not be read as the vehicle of the anti-Hasidic war of the Haskalah. Such a reading might be useful for the bipolar, dichotomous view of the past realities, but it obscures our understanding of the real attitudes of Calmanson toward Hasidism, and of the relations between the East European Haskalah and Hasidism more generally. It also hinders our understanding of what Hasidism of the time really was.

SUGGESTED READING

A good introduction to the issue of the impact of maskilic writings on the historiography of Hasidism is the short article by Israel Bartal, "The Imprint of Haskalah Literature on the Historiography of Hasidism," in *Hasidism Reappraised*, ed. A. Rapoport-Albert (London: The Littman Library of Jewish Civilization, 1996), 367–375. A broad survey of the maskilic literature with the focus on anti-Hasidic polemics is Israel Zinberg, *A History of Jewish Literature*, trans. B. Martin, vol. 9: *Hasidism and Enlightenment* (Cincinnati and New York: Hebrew Union College Press, Ktav Publishing House, 1972–1978). See also Shmuel Werses, *Megamot ve-tsurot be-sifrut ha-haskalah* (Jerusalem: Magnes Press, 1990); idem, *Hakitsah ami'. Sifrut ha-haskala be-'idan ha-modernizatsyah* (Jerusalem: Magnes Press, 2001); Shmuel Feiner, *Haskalah and History: The Emergence of a Modern Jewish Historical Consciousness* (Oxford and Portland: The Littman Library of Jewish Civilization, 2002), esp. 91–115, 306–317; Marcin Wodziński, *Haskalah and Hasidism in the Kingdom of Poland: A History of Conflict* (Oxford and Portland: The Littman Library of Jewish Civilization, 2005).

The most well-researched anti-Hasidic text by a maskil is Josef Perl's *Megale temirin*. The recent critical edition has been published as Josef Perl, *Megale temirin*, ed. J. Meir, 2 vols. (Jerusalem: Mosad Bialik, 2013); the edition is accompanied by an extensive monograph by Jonatan Meir, *Hasidut medumah* (Jerusalem: Mosad Bialik, 2013). The novel has also been published in the English translation as *Joseph Perl's Revealer of Secrets: The First Hebrew Novel*, ed. and trans. D. Taylor (Boulder, CO: WestviewPress, 1997). Another important anti-Hasidic text by Josef Perl is *Über das Wesen der Sekte Chassidim*, ed. A. Rubinstein (Jerusalem: The Israel Academy of Sciences and Humanities, 1977). Of the secondary literature focusing on Perl's anti-Hasidic writings and activities, see Raphael Mahler, *Hasidism and the Jewish Enlightenment: Their Confrontation in Galicia and Poland in the First Half of the Nineteenth Century*, trans. E. Orenstein, A. Klein, J. Machlowitz Klein (Philadelphia: Jewish Publication Society, 1985), 121–168. For other important studies on Perl, including his attitudes toward Hasidism, see Shmuel Werses, *Ginzei Yosef Perl*, ed. J. Meir (Tel Aviv: Bet Sholem Aleikhem, Merkaz Zalman Shazar, Universitat Tel Aviv, 2012), and Jeremy Dauber, *Antonio's Devils: Writers of the Jewish Enlightenment and the Birth of Modern Hebrew and Yiddish Literature* (Stanford: Stanford University Press, 2004), 209–310.

Late maskilic and postmaskilic Hebrew literature on Hasidism has been studied mainly by David Patterson. See *The Hebrew Novel in Czarist Russia: A Portrait of Jewish Life in the Nineteenth Century*, 2nd ed. (Lanham, MD: Rowman & Littlefield Publishers, 1999), and idem, *A Phoenix in Fetters: Studies in Nineteenth and Early Twentieth Century Hebrew Fiction* (Savage, MD: Rowman & Littlefield Publishers, 1988), 51–92. On the late-nineteenth-century representations of the Hasidim in liberal Jewish writings, historiography, and ethnography in Poland, see, again, Wodziński, *Haskalah and Hasidism*, chapters 6–8.

On the maskilim who took conciliatory views of Hasidism, see Shmuel Werses on Samuel Bik, "Ben shenei 'olamot: Ya'akov Shemu'el Bik ben haskalah le-ḥasidut; 'iyun meḥudash," *Gal-Ed* 9 (1986), 27–76. On Jakub Tugendhold, see Marcin Wodziński, "Jakub Tugendhold and the First Maskilic Defence of Hasidism," *Gal-Ed* 18 (2001), 13–41. Eliezer Zweifel has gained the most attention; see Shmuel Feiner, *Milḥemet tarbut: Tenu'at ha-haskalah ha-yehudit ba-me'ah ha-19* (Jerusalem: Zalman Shazar Center, 2010), 150–180, and Gloria Wiederkehr-Pollack, *Eliezer Zweifel and the Intellectual Defence of Hasidism* (Hoboken, NJ: Ktav, 1995).

NOTES

1. Josef Perl, *Über das Wesen der Sekte Chassidim*, ed. A. Rubinstein (Jerusalem: The Israel Academy of Sciences and Humanities, 1977), 141–142.

2. In David Patterson, *A Phoenix in Fetters: Studies in Nineteenth and Early Twentieth Century Hebrew Fiction* (Savage, MD: Rowman & Littlefield Publishers, 1988), 67.

3. Yitzḥak Ber Lewinsohn, *Yalkut ribal* (Warsaw, 1878), 72.

4. Daniel Neufeld, "Chassyd," in *Encyklopedia Powszechna* (Warsaw: Orgelbrandt, 1861–1862), 5:169–77. More on the issue in Marcin Wodziński, *Haskalah and Hasidism in the Kingdom of Poland: A History of Conflict* (Oxford and Portland: The Littman Library of Jewish Civilization, 2005), 184–193.

5. For more on these, see David Biale et al., *Hasidism: A New History* (Princeton, NJ: Princeton University Press, 2017), 477–501.

6. On Lefin, see Nancy B. Sinkoff, *Out of the Shtetl: Making Jews Modern in the Polish Borderlands* (Providence, RI: Brown Judaic Studies, 2004).

7. On Mieses and his rabidly anti-Hasidic writings, see Yehuda Friedlander, "Hasidism as the Image of Demonism: The Satiric Writings of Juda Leib Mieses," in *From Ancient Israel to Modern Judaism: Intellect in Quest of Understanding. Essays in Honor of Marvin Fox*, ed. J. Neusner, E. S. Frerichs, and N. M. Sarna (Atlanta: Scholars Press, 1989), 3:159–177.

8. [Efraim Fishl Fischelsohn], "Teyator fun khsidim," *Historishe Shriftn fun YIVO* 1 (1929), 645–694. For the introduction, see Khaim Borodianski, "Araynfir-shtudie tsum *Teyator fun khsidim*," *Historishe Shriftn fun YIVO* 1 (1929), 627–644.

9. Isaac Joel Linetsky, *The Polish Lad*, trans. M. Spiegel (Philadelphia: Jewish Publication Society, 1975).

10. See a good overview of these publications in David Patterson, *The Hebrew Novel in Czarist Russia: A Portrait of Jewish Life in the Nineteenth Century*, 2nd ed. (Lanham, MD: Rowman & Littlefield Publishers, 1999), and idem, *A Phoenix in Fetters*, 51–92.

11. For the criticism of these views, see Marcin Wodziński, *Hasidism: Key Questions* (New York: Oxford University Press, 2018), xxi–xxxi.

12. Israel Bartal, "The Imprint of Haskalah Literature on the Historiography of Hasidism," in *Hasidism Reappraised*, ed. A. Rapoport-Albert (London: The Littman Library of Jewish Civilization, 1996), 367–375.

13. Yekhezkel Kotik, *A Journey to a Nineteenth-Century Shtetl: The Memoirs of Yekhezkel Kotik*, ed. D. Assaf, trans. M. Birnstein (Detroit: Wayne State University Press, 2002). Second volume: *Na' ve-nad: Zikhronotav shel Yeḥezkel Kotik, ḥelek sheni*, trans. D. Assaf (Tel Aviv: Universitat Tel Aviv, Bet Sholem Aleikhem, 2005).

14. Avraham-Ber Gottlober, *Zikhronot u-masa'ot* (Jerusalem: Mosad Bialik, 1976), 1:57–58, 80, 110, 118, 128–129.

15. See Raphael Mahler, *Hasidism and the Jewish Enlightenment: Their Confrontation in Galicia and Poland in the First Half of the Nineteenth Century*, trans. E. Orenstein, A. Klein, J. Machlowitz Klein (Philadelphia: Jewish Publication Society, 1985). For the criticism of Mahler, see especially Rachel Manekin, "Hasidism and the Habsburg Empire 1788–1867," *Jewish History* 27 (2013), 2–4:271–297.

16. For a short bio and a discussion of his views on Hasidism, see Wodziński, *Haskalah and Hasidism*, 27–31.

17. Jacques Calmanson, *Uwagi nad niniejszym stanem Żydów polskich i ich wydoskonaleniem* (Warsaw: [s.n.], 1797), 18–19. Translation after Wodziński, *Haskalah and Hasidism*, 259–260.

18. See, e.g., Heinrich Graetz, *Geschichte der Juden von den ältesten Zeiten bis auf die Gegenwart* (Leipzig: O. Leiner, 1876), 11:71, 218–219, 595–596.

19. Calmanson, *Uwagi nad niniejszym stanem Żydów*, 20.

20. See Jan Doktór, "Warszawscy frankiści," *Kwartalnik Historii Żydów* (2001), 2:194–209.

21. See Emanuel Ringelblum, "Khsides un haskole in Varshe in 18-tn yorhundert," *YIVO-Bletter* 13 (1938), 124–132; Tsevi M. Rabinowicz, *Ben Pshisḥa le-Lublin: Ishim ve-shitot be-ḥasidut Polin* (Jerusalem: Ksharim, 1997), 21–100.

22. See more on this in Israel Bartal, "Le'an halakh tseror ha-kesef? Ha-bikoret ha-maskilit al hebeteha ha-kalkaliyim shel ha-ḥasidut," in *Dat ve-kalkalah—yaḥase gomelin*, ed. M. Ben-Sasson (Jerusalem: Zalman Shazar Center, 1995) 375–385.

23. Mahler, *Hasidism and the Jewish Enlightenment*, 8.

24. More on this in Wodziński, *Hasidism: Key Questions*, 201–240.

CHAPTER 6

Ego-Documents

Marcin Wodziński

Autobiographical writing, from St. Augustine's confessions to the diaries of Anne Frank and Emanuel Ringelblum, are among the most avidly read and studied literary texts and historical sources. The variety of types and literary traditions represented in autobiographical documents does, however, create some serious problems for describing, categorizing, and understanding them, and thus for using them in historical research. The concept of the ego-document, which we shall be using in this chapter, is of great help in grasping these extremely varied types. It encompasses every form of autobiographical literature: autobiography *sensu stricto*, memoirs, journals, diaries, as well as travelogues, letters, official testimonies, and wills. It was introduced into academic discourse in the 1950s by the Dutch scholar Jacob Presser, whose aim was to capture these disparate texts' common nature and thus to point to the similar relationship between the writer and the work's subject. Hence—and of great interest to historians—we can explore the specific relationship within an ego-document between the narrative and the nontextual "historical truth." In the French literary scholar Philippe Lejeune's well-known phrase, this latter element is an "autobiographical pact"; in other words, "the autobiographical genre is a contractual genre" whose nature rests on an agreement between the author and the reader as to the truth of information presented in the autobiography.[1] Thanks to this agreement, the reference point for an ego-document is the text not as literature but as reflection of nontextual reality.

As we know, this does not mean that autobiographies do not contain mistakes, inaccuracies, and even fabrications and conscious fiction. Standard history textbooks warn against overreliance on autobiographical sources. Current thinking is that memoirs need to be approached with great care, as their details can well be warped by memory if they are written after the passage of time. Furthermore, as critics of autobiographies point out, every text is by its very nature self-serving—its overriding intention is not to present "things as they really were," but to present the author in terms of his own narrative strategy, often to justify his own past actions, to present himself in a better light than do other accounts, or to win the reader's subjective allegiance.[2] An almost forensic examination of autobiographical narratives, in which numerous scholars track errors and exaggerations on the author's part, have become the norm when dealing with autobiography. This suspicion is indeed justified, but it is also naïve because it assumes that other types of sources—including archival sources so beloved of traditional historians—are cognitively safer, less burdened by an author's personal perspective, or simply more objective. As we know, this is a fundamentally false premise, since there is no such thing as an objective source, and each one must be subjected to the same thorough analysis. Ostensible objectivity is in fact the worst trap. To some extent ego-documents are cognitively safer, since their nontextual objectives and authorial intent are clear and relatively easy to define, often laid out *expressis verbis*; thus, examination of the source is more likely to uncover the correct key to unlocking its twists and turns. The fundamental premise of the autobiographical pact therefore creates the possibility of using ego-documents as exceptionally valuable historical sources, opening perspectives into areas of the past that traditional sources have found difficult to access and that did not hold much interest for researchers, and which modern historiography places at the center of academic research. By this we mean the whole of historiography in an anthropological sense: social history, history of mentality, history of daily life, and so on.

Contemporary historians regularly and lavishly use ego-documents as historical sources. Many fundamental works of microhistory that have shown the way for historiography over the last half century have been based almost entirely on a deep reading of ego-documents. Among works of this type it is worth mentioning perhaps the best-known book of microhistory: Carlo Ginzburg's analysis of the life of the sixteenth-century miller and heretic Menocchio. Also significant is the exemplary analysis of three early modern women's memoirs by Natalie Zemon Davis.[3] Thus the significance of ego-documents as historical sources is today self-evident.

Ego-Documents, the Jews, Hasidism

The oldest known ego-documents, such as Julius Caesar's *Commentaries on the Gallic Wars*, go back to antiquity, yet many scholars consider autobiography to be a modern form, deriving either from a Renaissance tradition, or, like Philippe Lejeune, from the eighteenth-century tradition of Jean-Jacques Rousseau and his *Confessions*. The correlation of this chronology with Jewish memoir writing is not obvious. One of the most eminent twentieth-century scholars of autobiography, Charles Gusdorf, maintained that autobiographical literature is inextricably linked with Christian tradition and that its founder was St. Augustine with his *Confessions* of the end of the fourth century C.E. Yet the *Vita* of Josephus—a Jewish historian writing in Greek in the first century C.E.—is considered to be the oldest Jewish memoir. The traditions of Jewish autobiographical writing were also represented by family scrolls, as well as by the Renaissance memoirs of Italian Jews. In many respects the memoir of Glückel of Hameln (1646–1724), composed by a German Jewish woman in Yiddish at the turn of the seventeenth and eighteenth centuries, was an exceptional document.

Jewish memoirs, including by East European Jews, began to appear with somewhat more frequency only toward the end of the eighteenth century. The classic work of the time, Salomon Maimon's *Lebensgeschichte*, published in 1791 and 1792, was in fact inspired by a text by Rousseau and to a certain extent confirms the form's modern roots. In addition to Maimon, the representatives of this earliest period were the merchants and diarists Dov Ber Birkenthal of Bolechów in Galicia and Moshe Wassercug from Wielkopolska.

The real explosion of the form's popularity came in the nineteenth century and is represented first by the Hebrew memoirs of maskilim, then by German, Russian, and, to a lesser extent, Polish memoirs of post-Haskalah writers, and finally, starting at the end of the nineteenth century, by a growing tide of Yiddish memoirs of ever more varied ideological, class, and regional origins. At this time, too, a growing number of ego-documents by women appeared. The ideological backdrop to the greatest number of these memoirs by far was the confrontation with modernity and a sense of the growing speed with which the East European Jews' traditional way of life was disappearing.[4]

Hasidic content appears in the earliest memoirs by East European Jews. The best known is the memoir by Salomon Maimon (1754–1800), mentioned above, in which the writer described his visit to the court of the famous tsadik R. Dov Ber, the Maggid of Mezrich (Międzyrzecz). For Maimon, unlike for the mitnagedim, Hasidism did have some positive features since it criticized the ascetic extremism of traditional Judaism as well as the degeneration of the rabbinical tradition into barren legalism. Yet that is where its positive side ended. In Maimon's view, the creator of the new movement, Rabbi Joel (sic!) Balschem, was a quack and a charlatan, who, by means of "cabalistic hocus-pocus," had gained the common herd's approval.[5] When Maimon visited the Maggid's court, he was initially impressed but eventually came to the conclusion that Dov Ber himself was a fraud and his practices as a tsadik a mere pack of tricks. This narrative displaying ambivalence toward Hasidism became a model for a large segment of later maskilic writing.

Interesting mentions of Hasidism appeared, too, in the memoirs of Dov Ber Birkenthal of Bolechów, written at the turn of the eighteenth and nineteenth centuries, although the subject is only touched on marginally. In many respects, however, in terms of both the Jewish tradition of memoir writing and Hasidic writing, the memoirs of R. Natan Sternharz of Nemirov (Niemirów), the closest pupil and then successor of tsadik R. Naḥman of Bratslav (Bracław), were exceptional. The principal subject of this work, written around 1835, was his "conversion" to Hasidism and his intimate friendship with the tsadik, as well as spiritual longing for him and the continuation of his work after his death. Other ego-documents from around this time that treated the subject of Hasidism were almost without exception maskilic accounts, in which a dark image of Hasidism represents a typical reference point for youthful experiences and a counterpoint to the moment of "enlightenment," or choosing the path to Haskalah, the Jewish Enlightenment. Among the best-known accounts of this type are the autobiographical writings of Avraham Ber Gottlober (1811–1899), who included in his memoirs fascinating ethnographic descriptions of Hasidic customs, vitriolic little philippics against Hasidic superstitions, and very personal tales of his own divorce and banishment from the house when his father-in-law discovered that he was reading "seditious" maskilic books.[6]

During the second half of the nineteenth century, numerous memoirs of ex-Hasidim describing traces of their former life in the world of tradition continued in the same vein. An important stage in this development was the Yiddish pseudo-autobiography of Yitzḥak Yoel Linetsky (1839–1915), titled *Dos Poylishe Yingl* (The Polish Lad, 1867–1869), an anti-Hasidic satire that was partly based on the author's real story.[7] The book became one of the most popular Jewish literary works in the nineteenth century.

Many other memoirs of the second half of the nineteenth century were written in German, Russian, or Polish. A less well-known yet perfect model of the form is the German "memoirs of a former Hasid," by Josef Ehrlich of Brody.[8] Orphaned as a baby, Josef was given to the local shoemaker to be raised. Josef describes local customs, his own fanaticism, and his devotion to the tsadik of Bełz. Everything changes when the local progressive Jewish school places a large order for shoes with Josef's foster father on condition that he send his adopted son to the school. The shoemaker agrees, which opens up Josef's path to education, initially in Brody, and then in Vienna, where he eventually becomes a prominent journalist. The story is typical of many other memoirs of the time, such as the well-known Russian autobiography of Grigorii Bogrov (1825–1885), which invariably focus on the clash between Hasidic obscurantism and modern education, as well as on the one-way path from backwardness to enlightenment.[9]

It was only toward the end of the nineteenth century that a trend of memoir writing that dealt with the world of Jewish tradition, including Hasidism, appeared and treated the topic much less critically. The trend included a conspicuous stream of nostalgic publications, thanks to which the image of the Hasidic movement was drastically revised. Many of these texts were inspired by neo-Hasidism—an unorthodox current of often nostalgic interest in Hasidic culture that appeared at the turn of the nineteenth and twentieth centuries as a

Jewish version of fin-de-siècle enthusiasm for folk culture and peasantry. This does not mean that Hasidism's image became immediately and unambiguously positive. Rather more typical were the memoirs of Yekhezkel Kotik (1847–1921), perhaps the most important Jewish memoirs of the era. Having abandoned Hasidism in his youth, Kotik was critical of the movement, but he wrote with admiration of many of its attributes. Joseph Margoshes and Yitzḥok Even, although they had abandoned Hasidism, still retained positive feelings for it, and their excellent knowledge of Hasidic culture afforded them a splendid insight into the subtleties of that world.[10] The crisis of integrationist ideology and acculturation also turned a great many memoirists of the day to question the validity of the path of progress, and thus to a more positive view of the world of tradition, including Hasidism. For Pauline Wengeroff (1833–1916), who came from a Lithuanian non-Hasidic family, the movement remained a marginal subject, although in the clash between Hasidism and progress, it was rather the latter that became her nemesis.[11]

This last example points to the next great change that took place at this time: a growing number of memoirs were being written by women, thanks to which we see a radically new perspective on Hasidism. At the start of the twentieth century, Malka Shapiro (1895–1971), coming from the family of the tsadik of Kuznits (Kozienice), wrote a personal account of her time growing up.[12] Not much later came the memoir of a simple woman from a Hasidic family, Hinde Bergner (1870–1942), as well as one from Puah Rakovsky (1865–1955), an heir of the anti-Hasidic tradition who was also a Zionist activist.[13] Dozens of similar accounts followed. World War II and the Holocaust led to a further democratization of Jewish memoir writing; hence one also sees an increase in the scale of autobiographical texts on Hasidic subjects. These include camp memoirs, memorial books, testimonies of Holocaust survivors, and monumental memoirs, such as the work of Yekhiel Yeshaia Trunk (1887–1961), descendant of a well-known Hasidic family and a journalist between the wars, who right after World War II published seven volumes of semiautobiographical writings about prewar Poland.[14]

Over time—and representing perhaps the final stage in the development of the subject of Hasidism in memoir writing—a growing number of memoirs were written by representatives of the world of Hasidism who remained within that world, or close to it; today this often takes the form of digital ego-documents. We shall return to that theme shortly.

Typology

Typologically speaking, we can divide autobiographical texts in which Hasidic elements appear into three basic categories. First are ego-documents written by external observers, such as the aforementioned Pauline Wengeroff, who, encountering Hasidim and Hasidism at some stage in their life, react to the movement's observed differences and glaringly obvious features. Although many of their observations are stereotypical—for instance, the commonplace confrontation between Hasidim and Litvaks—the great virtue of these works lies in their sensitivity to the differences encountered, and thus to those aspects of Hasidic customs that are often invisible to people steeped in the culture. At the same time, descriptions made by more or less random external observers are often striking in their naïveté, as the writers confuse relevant elements with peripheral ones, often misunderstanding them. The relatively smallest—although especially interesting—segment of this category of memoirs is non-Jewish accounts. They have the advantage of a "fresh eye," precisely because of the writers' exceptionally weak knowledge of Hasidism, and often because of their lack of preconceived ideas and images. These accounts might contain especially valuable information, some purely factual, and they might deal with Hasidic customs, beliefs, and practices. A good example of such an account in nineteenth-century German literature is from Leopold Sacher-Masoch (1836–1895), the son of Lwów's chief of police and a well-known writer. In 1857 he paid a visit to the tsadik of Sadagura and wrote an interesting semiautobiographical account filled with mystical, oriental, and erotic fascination.[15] A somewhat less known example comes from the memoirs of Franciszek Karpiński (1741–1825), a Polish sentimentalist poet, who recalled an encounter with Lithuanian Hasidim around 1800 or 1801 in the town of Nieśwież.[16] We can assume that the "rabbi," whom Karpiński described as giving a general explication of the Hasidic attitude toward mourning a father's death, is identical with R. Ya'akov Aryeh of Neskhiz (Niesuchojeże) (d. 1837), whose father, Mordekhai of Neskhiz, died in 1800, shortly before the meeting of Karpiński and R. Ya'akov Aryeh.

The typological second category—perhaps the most common—comprises memoirs written by former Hasidim, often people who are hostile, ambivalent, or excessively critical about the world they abandoned. The virtues of these accounts are their excellent knowledge of the Hasidic world and the authors' desires to describe the world's obvious features, but also—perhaps especially—its dark sides. Of course, this is also a weakness, for the resulting accounts often become overtly polemical, losing both their objectivity and some of their value as historical sources. Nevertheless, the memoirs of former Hasidim—whether overtly anti-Hasidic, such as those of the aforementioned Salomon Maimon and Avraham Ber Gottlober, or critical and nostalgic, such as Kotik's account—are today the most frequently used and often uncritically quoted descriptions of Hasidism. Unaware that Maimon's intention was not to present Hasidism as faithfully as possible, but to confirm the credibility of his own path from the world of Jewish, traditional Lithuania to the salons of Enlightenment Berlin, many treat his prescriptions as objective historical testimony. Despite this caveat, this group's memoirs—including the narratives of Yitzḥok Even and Joseph Margoshes, and of Ita Kalish (1903–1994), of the famous dynasty of tsadikim of

Vorke (Warka)—remain an exceptionally valuable source for the history of Hasidism.[17]

The third category is the memoirs of Hasidim, written from an insider's perspective and often with apologetic intention. Unfortunately, this category is relatively the smallest. The Jewish mystical tradition, unlike, for instance, Christian traditions, has not developed a genre of memoirs or spiritual diaries, which is perhaps the result of suspicion of a genre that places the author at the center of the narrative. In the case of Hasidism, the source of this antipathy might also have been an identification of autobiographical categories with the modern impulse for uninhibited expression of one's own personality and, more generally, with hostilely treated modernity. An exception particularly worthy of note is the spiritual memoir of R. Yitzḥak Aizik Yehudah Yeḥiel Safrin of Komarno (1806–1874), which depicts episodes and mystical experiences from this important tsadik's life.[18] The previously mentioned text by R. Natan Sternharz of Nemirov belongs to the same small set of Hasidic memoirs. The few surviving ego-documents written by followers of Hasidism describing their own experiences of contacts with a tsadik include reminiscences of tsadik R. Simḥah Bunim of Przysucha (1765–1827), written by his secretary Shmuel of Sieniawa, or the stories about R. Ḥayim Halberstam of Nowy Sącz (1797/9–1876) (Sanz), written by his attendant Rafael Tsimetbaum.[19] These texts fall within the broad definition of ego-document, but they cannot be recognized as classical autobiography given that the center of the narrative is not the author-*cum*-narrator but the tsadik who is being depicted.

The very interesting "memoir" by R. Yosef Yitzḥak Schneersohn (1880–1950), the sixth tsadik of the Chabad-Lubavitch dynasty, illustrates a quite different phenomenon. It is an apologetic attempt to devise a tradition, to create Hasidic historical literature that would present an alternative image of the history of Hasidism for secular historians. Written under the name of R. Yosef Yitzḥak Schneersohn, the memoir consciously violates the autobiographical pact and thus has been widely challenged over its veracity and historical value.[20] This criticism is, however, the result of a poorly formulated research question: the memoir is indeed a valuable historical source, not for the history of the tsadik and his family, but rather for the history of the autocreation of a historical image and historical consciousness of twentieth-century Chabad-Lubavitch Hasidism.

An interesting addition to this last, valuable, but also relatively small category of memoirs written by actual Hasidim is accounts created by those "on the cusp of two worlds": people whom it is difficult to acknowledge as Hasidim in the full meaning of the word, but who never truly left the Hasidic world. Good examples are the hybrid memoirs written by Kaja Finkler on the basis of interviews carried out with her mother Golda Finkler, a descendant of famous Hasidic dynasties of Lublin and Modrzyce (Dęblin).[21] Of course, as with all other sources, the accounts of this group require a close examination of sources, and an analysis of the context of the account's inception, the narrative strategy, and the author's twists and turns. Still, as historical sources they are valuable since they complement the narratives occupying an unambiguous position in the ideological dispute between Hasidim and their opponents.

An interesting and at the same time dramatic example of a text on the border of these categories is the confessions of tsadik R. Yitzḥak Naḥum Twersky of Shpikov (Szpików) (1888–1942), who admittedly had not abandoned the world of Hasidism but who wrote an exceptionally sharp critique of it. The liminal status of this text, written by a hostile insider, allowed David Assaf to produce an analysis of an individual struggling with the social roles imposed upon Hasidic leaders, and of the conflict between the antimodernist ethos of the Hasidic community and the challenges of the modern world. Even though Assaf notes that "as an historical document, its [the confession's'] value for the study of Hasidism and its history is limited, even problematic," his exemplary analysis exposes the ways in which the crisis of the Hasidic world in the late nineteenth and early twentieth centuries, its conflict with modernity, and a deepening sense of loss affected Hasidic leaders. Assaf's text, together with an annotated English translation of the actual confessions, continues to be an exceptional study of Hasidism based entirely on ego-documents.[22]

In addition to the three categories we have enumerated, there is another "borderline" set of texts that touch on elements of Hasidism: memorial books of Jewish communities. A collection of some eight hundred volumes produced for the most part after 1945, these describe Jewish life in hundreds of towns and villages of Eastern Europe before the Holocaust, as recalled by their former Jewish inhabitants (for the literature on memorial books, see the suggested reading list below). The memorial books comprise dozens of different types of texts, of which only a part are ego-documents. To complicate matters, the documents are written in different languages, mainly Hebrew and Yiddish, but sometimes Hungarian, Romanian, Polish, English, or Spanish. This factor makes analyses difficult. Nonetheless, the memory books are an unusually valuable source, including of autobiographical texts, for two basic reasons. First, more than eight hundred extensive volumes and 350,000 pages of text provide an enormous body of work that allows for the use of analytical tools exceeding individual literary analysis. Comparative studies, quantitative linguistic analysis, and mapping are all possible, given that the corpus of the memorial books is both extensive and a relatively homogenous source. Second, the thousands of authors of reminiscences in the memory books are almost ideal "anonymous authors." Even if we do know their first and last names, they are people unknown to history (understood as the actions of great people), and everything that we do know about them comes precisely from their reminiscences. Perhaps each of these writers felt his or her life to be in some way unique. No matter the motive behind the writings, these memoirs, by virtue of their numbers and repetitiveness, provide us with a priceless large-scale description of the everyday life of thousands of ordinary people in the small towns of Eastern Europe, including their religious life, their involvement in Hasidism, their ways of articulating Hasidic identity at the local level, their forms of devotion expressed far from a Hasidic court, the physical layout of the Hasidic houses of prayer they attended, their relations with non-Hasidim, and many other subjects that the historiography of Hasidism would be unable to study with the aid of conventional sources.

A good example might consist of an analysis of the daily life of thousands of Hasidim and the deep social structures of Hasidism during World War I, as well as of the dramatic changes that the world was then undergoing. Thanks to the accounts written down in the memory books, we are able to reconstruct the dynamics of Hasidic migrations, the catastrophes of the Hasidic courts, the dramatic process of urbanization of the Hasidic leadership, and the no less dramatic results of this process for Hasidic devotion, as well as a great many other profound social processes. It would have been impossible to obtain this information without the large-scale analysis of hundreds of memorial books.[23]

What Should We Study?

The works mentioned that study the psychology of the Hasidic leadership and its crisis on the basis of the confessions of the tsadik of Shpikov, or Hasidism during World War I on the basis of memorial books, are of course merely individual examples of much broader possibilities inherent in these types of sources. As I have written, memoirs afford access to aspects of the Hasidic world that have traditionally been beyond the reach of scholars, at the same time opening up new methodologies and approaches, subjects on the fringes of the Hasidic world, the rank-and-file followers as much as their leaders, the ethos and form of daily life as much as the ideology.

One subject that has lately been studied intensively is the place of women in Hasidism, both historically and today. As I have written elsewhere in more detail, while we know a great deal about exceptional female leaders and the place of women in the Hasidic worldview, few historical sources shed light on the nature of the association with Hasidism of women belonging to rank-and-file Hasidic households, or on the degree to which this association may have found expression in their everyday domestic lives.[24] The only sources that do throw some light on this phenomenon are ego-documents. Yekhezkel Kotik, for example, describes the relationship between his parents, Moshe and Sarah Kotik, who were both from anti-Hasidic families. As was often the case, soon after his wedding, the young Moshe Kotik ran away from his wife to the court of the tsadik and decided to become a Hasid. His father, Aron Leyzer Kotik, shunned Moshe, but Sarah reacted quite differently: she was completely indifferent to her husband's spiritual life, as was Moshe to hers.[25] Similar accounts of husbands whose wives were indifferent to their Hasidic beliefs appear in many other memoirs from this period, including those of Pauline Wengeroff and of the writer Israel Joshua Singer (1893–1944), brother of Isaac Bashevis Singer.[26] In another example, Michel Berciński, a Hasid from Pińsk, married his son into a well-known anti-Hasidic family, while his daughter wed a maskil and graduate of the mitnagedic Volozhin (Wołożyn) yeshiva, Yitzḥak Meir Shaykevich (1849–1905).[27] The poet Eliakum Zunser (1836–1913), another maskil, was matched with the daughter of a wealthy Hasid, who was so pleased with the match that immediately after the wedding he took Zunser to the court of R. Shlomo Ḥayim of Koidanov (Kojdanów) to show the tsadik the "treasure" he had acquired for his daughter.[28] Clearly, the non-Hasidic identity of Zunser did not trouble his Hasidic father-in-law.

To the extent that any conclusions may be drawn from the available memoirs, marriages between the children of Hasidim and non-Hasidim, including those holding anti-Hasidic views, occurred relatively often and did not carry any "mixed-marriage" stigma; the unions were, after all, arranged by the families with complete agreement on both sides, and the question of belonging or not belonging to a Hasidic movement did not affect relations between them.[29] The ego-documents thus prove that there was no trace of Hasidic endogamy, an important indicator of the nature of this religious movement.

This evidence allows also for conclusions of a more general nature. For a woman to marry or to be born to a Hasid did not imply that she had thereby acquired Hasidic affiliation. Nor did such association have to dominate her own or the family's religious practice, or have a significant impact on the quality of the relationship between a husband and a wife. No act of "conversion" to Hasidism or declaration of identification or sympathy with its values and practices was required of women from non-Hasidic households who married Hasidim. Affiliation with Hasidism was entirely the concern of male members of the family. Fathers naturally transmitted it to their sons,[30] but they did not expect their own affiliation to extend to mothers, sisters, daughters, or wives.

The memoirist sources are thus of critical importance for understanding some of the most important characteristics of the Hasidic movement and its wider social ramifications within and outside of Hasidism.

R. Leib Rakowski versus Hasidim: The Case Study

What is possibly most fascinating is that the autobiographical material does not need to be read in isolation. In fact, more often than not, ego-documents allow for a dream of every seasoned historian: triangulation of historical evidence, verification and falsification of primary sources vis-à-vis other historical evidence, and simply a greater degree of historical nuance.

The aforementioned Puah Rakovsky, well-known feminist, Zionist activist, and author of an influential memoir,[31] was descended from R. Azriel Aryeh Leib Rakowski (Plotsker) (1822–1893), a mitnaged from a prominent rabbinic family.

In 1853, Rakowski was appointed rabbi of Stawiska (Central Poland), and in 1863 he was made rabbi of the provincial capital of Płock, also Central Poland.[32] There, Rakowski was active in multiple community projects, such as building a hospital and establishing scholarship funds.[33] According to local tradition, he was also responsible for changes in the community's educational system, supplementing the traditional Jewish curriculum with elements of secular knowledge, which led to opposition from the local Hasidic community.

Two additional elements likely played a role in this opposition. First, Rakowski replaced R. Eleazar ha-kohen Leipziger (1791–1881), an important Hasidic leader. R. Eleazar ha-kohen was suspected of multiple abuses, and after three years of conflict with the local community he was suspended from his position as the rabbi of Płock, which antagonized the local Hasidic community.[34] Second, Rakowski's letters were printed in the maskilic magazine *Ha-magid*. Although the correspondence was neutral and informative, the very fact that it was published in a German newspaper (printed in Lyck/Ełk) and connected to the Haskalah was read as a sign of Enlightenment sympathies. R. Rakowski's stay in Płock met with strong Hasidic opposition from the outset. These attacks on his position ultimately led him to depart for Łomża in 1867.[35] That same year, he moved back to Płock, where he remained until 1880, when he was offered a rabbinic position in Mariampol in Suwałki Province, a much smaller community, but devoid of any Hasidic influence.[36]

All those events find expression in archival documents, Hebrew press, rabbinical literature, and, most of all, in the ego-documents. Without reading them together in light of the memoir we cannot understand the real nature of the social ferment around his person. Puah Rakovsky, his granddaughter, wrote several stories about conflicts with Hasidim in Stawiska and Płock based on traditions recounted by her family members. The stories play a significant role in her memoir, testifying to the prominent function of this tradition in the identity of the Rakovsky family. First, Puah describes an episode that took place in Stawiska:

> My grandfather Leybele Plotzker was a great *Misnagid*. He detested the *Hasidim*, who therefore gave him horrible troubles. For example, in Stavisk, where Zeyde [grandfather] had been the rabbi as a young man, they had on one Friday put nails with their points sticking up into his bath. By chance, one of Zeyde's children happened to be sick in the house, so he didn't leave home to go to the bath house that day. When the water was later poured out, the nails were found in the bottom of the tub. After that episode, Zeyde left for Plock, where, too, there was a large community of Hasidim. There was constantly an open battle between the Misnagdim, who were the rabbi's adherents, and the Hasidim, who turned out to be clear-cut opponents of his.[37]

The next episode memorialized in Puah's diaries concerns Płock. According to her, the Hasidim hated her grandfather because of his frankness, artlessness, and uncompromising criticism of everything that did not meet his approval. These traits caused criticism to be heaped on him, as can be seen from the following:

> It happened one Yom Kippur before *Ne'ila*, the closing prayer. Grandfather was delivering his sermon. . . . All of a sudden, in the middle of the sermon, he noticed on the *Bima* a Gentile woman holding a child. She approached the rabbi and asked him for food *for his child*. Grandfather controlled himself and said very calmly to the woman: "If this is my child, then you know where I live. Come to me at home." And with the same inner calm, and with his previous fervor, he finished his sermon.
>
> Later, they said in town that the Gentile woman was really a disguised man who was frightened of the rabbi's majestic bearing. Subsequently, the man gave my grandfather the names of the Hasidim who had sent this person to "negotiate." Years later, my grandfather's adherents claimed that all the people involved came to a bitter end. Zeyde didn't want to stay in such a town any longer. Right after the fast, he left. But his adherents pursued him, unhitched the horse, hitched him to the carriage, and brought the rabbi back with a big parade. After that incident, Zeyde didn't stay long in Plock.[38]

The incident quoted above is corroborated by sources other than stories within the Rakowski family. First, the "bitter end" of the rabbi's detractors might be connected to an epidemic in 1867, which swept through Płock right after Rakowski's departure for Łomża. Correspondence written by Yehudah Ya'akov Meizler and sent to the maskilic weekly *Ha-magid* indicates that the epidemic's sudden appearance was interpreted by local inhabitants as punishment for the harassment of R. Rakowski at the hands of the Hasidim (*ba'alei kat mit-ḥasdim*). This interpretation led Jews from Płock to travel to Łomża to beg for Rakowski's return to Płock.[39] This might not exactly correspond to "bringing the rabbi back with a big parade," but there clearly is a prototype of the family tradition transmitted by Puah.

There is yet more. Archival sources allow us to supplement our knowledge about the 1867 conflict in Płock even further. According to a report of the Płock Jewish community board, in 1867 Rakowski took part in a wedding ceremony arranged by a certain Samuel Segał.[40] At the party, a group of Hasidim extinguished the lights and tried to beat up Rakowski. They failed, however, as the non-Hasidic guests stood up for the rabbi. Three days later, local Hasidim posted placards that protested the rabbi in the synagogue, which were then torn off by the rabbi-supporting community representatives. At midnight, unidentified perpetrators used pieces of brick to break four panes in the rabbi's windows. Though the perpetrators were never caught, Rakowski suspected that the damage had been done by the "Hasidim living in house No. 254 at Chorowitzes."[41]

Finally, on the night of April 10, unknown perpetrators spread out sixteen copies of lampoons in the synagogue, *bet midrash*, and various other spots in the town. The placards were torn off at four A.M. by a synagogue attendant, one copy having been delivered to the rabbi. The rabbi came to the conclusion that the lampoon had been written by a Hasidic bookbinder whose name we do not know.[42] Rakowski asked the municipality to form an investigatory committee comprised of non-Hasidic bookbinders who would compare the suspect's fonts with those of the lampoon. Fortunately, one of the lampoons has survived. By examining its text we can see the nature of the accusations made by the Hasidim (see figure 6.1).[43]

THE APOSTATE LEIBEL, MAY HIS NAME AND MEMORY BE ERASED

Leibel sins	He violates decrees
Violates prohibitions	Commits sins
Eats what is proscribed	May he be met with hardship
Prohibitions which are rebellious	His bones [ought to] be crushed
Leibel is a dog	And eyes gouged
Become blind!	May it atone
very soon	

Here, Płock, is the city in which Leibel Rakowski, may his name and memory be erased and may the name of the wicked rot, was buried.

He converted near Augustów

And married a non-Jew near Łomża

Leibel the Litvak, excommunicated and ostracized (according to a short count).

From the lampoon we understand that Hasidim were accusing Rakowski of being in a relationship with a non-Jewish woman, as testified in Puah Rakovsky's memoirs. They even claim that he converted to Christianity, was baptized near Augustów, and formalized his relationship with the woman by getting married near Łomża. The lampoon thus confirms that the family story described by Puah Rakovsky about Hasidic accusations of Rakowski's romance with a Christian woman did happen. It seems that the event reported in the memoir was in fact an attempt to stage and validate the same accusations as were made in the lampoon.

The memoir and other supplementary sources are unique in that they complement our knowledge of the dynamics of the conflict in Płock, revealing forms of social confrontation at the communal level and the political struggle between Hasidim and their opponents. The lampoon reveals a fairly typical phase of

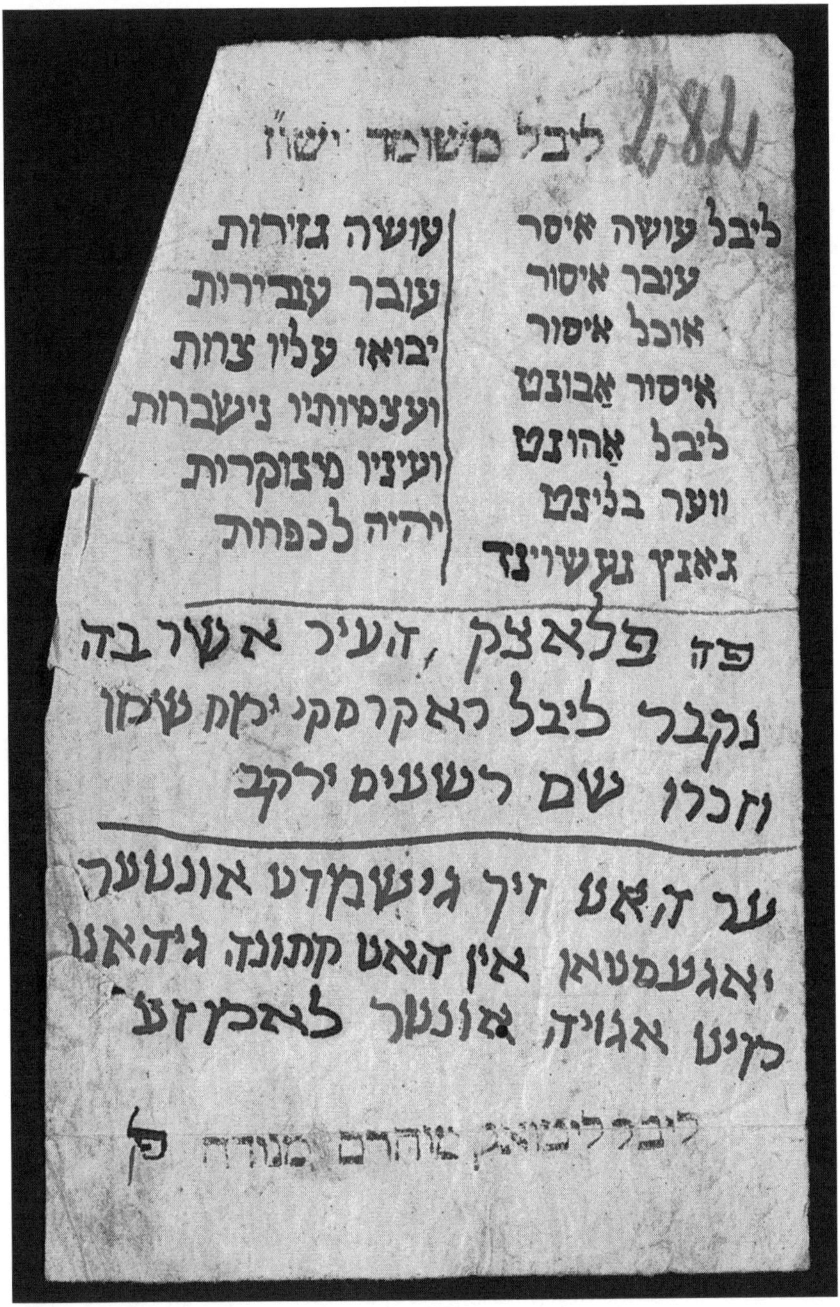
ליבל משומד ישו"ז

ליבל עושה איסר
עובר איסור
אוכל איסור
איסור אבונט
ליבל אהונט
ווער בליצט
גאנץ געשוינד

עושה גזירות
עובר עבירות
יבואו עליו צרות
ועצמותיו נישברות
ועיניו מצוקרות
יהיה לכפרות

פה פלאצק, העיר אשר בה
נקבר ליבל ראקרסקי ימח שמו
וזכרו שם רשעים ירקב

ער האט זיך גישמדט אונטער

Figure 6.1. Hasidic lampoon against the mitnagedic rabbi of Płock, R. Leib Rakowski, 1867. Source: The State Archives in Płock, collection: Akta miasta Płocka, call no. 569, folio 282.

communal conflict, in which the escalation of the means led to the conflict itself becoming independent of its origins and overshadowing the original objectives set by both sides of the confrontation, turning into an escalation of violence, whether verbal or physical. Without the memoir we would miss out on the details of the confrontation, and nor would we know about the social memory of those skirmishes. As we see in the memoir, verbal aggression often was accompanied by or led to physical aggression. In this case, there was an attempt to beat up Rakowski at the wedding, break his windows, bruise him in the baths, and finally shame him in front of the whole community.

To understand what really happened in Płock of 1867, it is necessary to read the memoir and the lampoon together. The lampoon specifies neither the conflict's causes nor the real reasons for the Hasidic opposition to Rakowski. Nor does it attempt to persuade a course of action against Rakowski. Its primary function is to injure the rabbi and his followers by ridiculing him in the eyes of his supporters and the wider public, thereby serving as an act of symbolic violence that would give a sense of superiority to the Hasidim and discharge negative emotions. It was nothing but pure aggression. The importance of the document, thus, is not that we learn the nature of the real objections of the Hasidim to Rakowski, but rather that it gives flash to the family tradition, as recorded in the memoir, and shows the dynamics of the conflict between him and his Hasidic opponents, of which we learn primarily from the memoir. Together with the memoir, the lampoon and other archival and press materials create a rich picture of the social conflict between the Hasidim and their opponents in nineteenth-century Eastern Europe.

Conclusion

Ego-documents, as the above examples have shown, open up almost limitless possibilities for historical analysis, including the history and culture of Hasidism. Most obvious are the lines of inquiry that focus on autobiographies as accounts of a writer's specific thought process and treat them as a work of literature. The example of Puah Rakovsky's memoir proves, however, that ego-documents, especially when we can compare them with other types of sources, can also be useful in more traditional historical research focused on factual reconstruction. In chapter 13, we will demonstrate how they can be used in quantitative and spatial research and in other forms of the digital humanities.

We should not be surprised that different ego-documents and different ways of using them exist, given the great number of such surviving documents of the last 250 years—the lifetime of Hasidism. The introduction of conscious, critical analysis of ego-documents into the toolbox of current historiography has led to the formulation of new questions and to the development of effective new methods, of which microhistory is the best example. We should expect that better use of ego-documents in the study of Hasidism will open up the field to even more new questions and new methods that at present are less well represented in research into Hasidism. This can be expected especially in the area of history of the mentality and social history understood as the history of the broad structures of thousands of followers of the movement, or the history of religion understood as the history of lived experience, that is, everywhere history is interested in individual experiences and their recordings.

Besides, ego-documents often quite simply make wonderful, fascinating reading.

SUGGESTED READING

The literature on ego-documents and autobiographical literature is immense. For the most general introduction to the topic, with a focus on the multiple relationships between autobiographical literature and historical narrative, see Jeremy D. Popkin, *History, Historians, and Autobiography* (Chicago: University of Chicago Press, 2005); Rudolf Dekker, ed., *Ego-documents and History: Autobiographical Writing in Its Social Context since the Middle Ages* (Hilversum: Verloren, 2002). Sidonie Smith and Julia Watson, *Reading Autobiography: A Guide for Interpreting Life Narratives*, 2nd ed. (Minneapolis: University of Minnesota Press, 2010), is a general introduction to the reading of ego-documents. See also the classic introduction to the genre of autobiography in Philippe Lejeune, *On Autobiography*, ed. P. J. Eakin, trans. K. Leary (Minneapolis: University of Minnesota Press, 1989 [1975]).

For the history of Jewish autobiographical writings, see, first of all, Marcus Moseley, *Being for Myself Alone: Origins of Jewish Autobiography* (Stanford, CA: Stanford University Press, 2005) and Michael Stanislawski, *Autobiographical Jews: Essays in Jewish Self-Fashioning* (Vancouver: University of Washington Press, 2004). While the former seems far more thorough and comprehensive, the latter is more insightful.

Jewish autobiographies, including Hasidic ones, lack the wealth of research tools, bibliographies, anthologies, and critical editions that would ease the access to this vast corpus of sources. Of the few bibliographies that might prove helpful, one should list Yekhezkel Lifschutz, *Bibliografye fun amerikaner un kanader yidishe zikhroynes un oytobiografies af yidish hebreish un english* (New York: YIVO Institute for Jewish Research, 1970). This excellent catalogue of Jewish autobiographies in the New World gives brief descriptions of several hundred such memoirs in Yiddish, Hebrew, and English, including the authors' religious context, not infrequently relevant to their Hasidic origins. Of anthologies, one should start with the standard Leo W. Schwarz, ed., *Memoirs of My People: Jewish Self-Portraits from the 11th to the 20th Centuries* (New York: Schocken Books, 1963), a section of which contains excerpts from memoirs on the Hasidic experience. See also Monika Richarz, ed., *Jewish Life in Germany: Memoirs from Three Centuries* (Bloomington: Indiana University Press, 1991) and Albert Lichtblau, ed., *Als hätten wir dazugehört: Österreichisch-jüdische Lebensgeschichten aus der Habsburgmonarchie* (Vienna: Böhlau, 1999).

For a general introduction to the topic of memorial books as a source for historical research, see Monika Adamczyk-Garbowska, Adam Kopciowski, and Andrzej Trzciński, "Księgi pamięci jako źródło wiedzy o historii, kulturze i Zagładzie polskich Żydów," in *Tam był kiedyś mój dom . . . Księgi pamięci gmin żydowskich*, ed. M. Adamczyk-Garbowska, A. Kopciowski, and A. Trzciński (Lublin: Wydawnictwo Uniwersytetu Marii Curie Skłodowskiej, 2009), 11–86; also see Abraham Wein, "Memorial Books as a Source for Research into the History of Jewish Communities in Europe," *Yad Vashem Studies* 9 (1973), 255–272; Jack Kugelmass and Jonathan Boyarin, "Introduction," in *From a Ruined Garden: The Memorial Books of Polish Jewry*, 2nd ed., J. Kugelmass and J. Boyarin

(Bloomington: Indiana University Press, 1993), 1–48. The newest bibliography of the memorial books is to be found in Adam Kopciowski, ed., *Jewish Memorial Books: A Bibliography* (Lublin, 2008). Most memorial books are available online at the website of the New York Public Library, Dorot Jewish Division (https://www.nypl.org/collections/nypl-recommendations/guides/yizkorbooks).

It is impossible to list all, or even most, important ego-documents that hold Hasidic-related content. For several dozen representative titles, see the notes to this chapter. For others, see the bibliographies above. Useful collections of Hasidic-related ego-documents can be found in Hasidic periodicals of semiacademic character, especially *Hekhal ha-Besht* and *Kerem Chabad*, in which a number of memoirs related to Hasidism have been published or reprinted. For some classic memoirs, see also *Reshumot* (1918–1930). Likewise, it is worthwhile to check autobiographies sent in to YIVO in the interwar period for Hasidic content: Jeffrey Shandler, ed., *Awakening Lives: Autobiographies of Jewish Youth in Poland before the Holocaust* (New Haven, CT: Yale University Press, 2002); Ido Bassok, ed., *Alilot ne'urim: Otobiografyot shel benei no'ar Yehudim mi-Polin ben shetei milḥamot ha-olam* (Tel Aviv: Merkaz Zalman Shazar, Universitat Tel Aviv, 2011); Alina Cała, ed., *Ostatnie pokolenie: Autobiografia polskiej młodzieży żydowskiej okresu międzywojennego ze zbiorów YIVO Institute for Jewish Research w Nowym Jorku* (Warsaw: Sic!, 2003).

NOTES

1. Philippe Lejeune, *On Autobiography*, ed. P. J. Eakin, trans. K. Leary (Minneapolis: University of Minnesota Press, 1989), 19. For the most general introduction to the nature of the autobiographical literature and its relationship with historical writing, see the bibliography at the end of this chapter.

2. See, e.g., Anthony Brundage, *Going to the Sources: A Guide to Historical Research and Writing* (Hoboken, NJ: John Wiley and Sons Inc., 2018), 19–20; John Tosh with Sean Lang, *The Pursuit of History: Aims, Methods and New Directions in the Study of Modern History*, 4th ed. (Harlow: Longman, 2006 [1984]), 64–65.

3. Carlo Ginzburg, *The Cheese and the Worms: The Cosmos of a Sixteenth-Century Miller* (London: Routlege, 1976); Natalie Zemon Davis, *Women on the Margins: Three Seventeenth-Century Lives* (Cambridge, MA: Harvard University Press, 1995).

4. For an introduction to the history of Jewish autobiography, see the bibliography at the end of the chapter. See also a very useful introduction to the history of the East European Jewish memoirs in Marcus Moseley, "Autobiography and Memoir," in *The YIVO Encyclopedia of Jews in Eastern Europe*, ed. G. D. Hundert (New Haven, CT: Yale University Press, 2008), 1:89–95; available also online: http://www.yivoencyclopedia.org/article.aspx/Autobiography_and_Memoir (accessed December 21, 2018).

5. Solomon Maimon, *The Autobiography*, trans. J. Clark Murray (London: Horovitz Publishing Co., 1954), 179.

6. Avraham Ber Gottlober, *Zikhronot u-masa'ot*, 2 vols. (Jerusalem: Mosad Bialik, 1976).

7. Isaac Joel Linetsky, *The Polish Lad*, trans. M. Spiegel (Philadelphia: Jewish Publication Society, 1975).

8. Josef R. Ehrlich, *Der Weg Meines Lebens: Erinnerungen eines ehemaligen Chassiden* (Vienna: L. Kosner, 1874).

9. Grigorii Bogrow, *Memoiren eines Juden*, trans. M. Ascharin (Petersburg: A. E. Landau, 1880).

10. Yekhezkel Kotik, *A Journey to a Nineteenth-Century Shtetl: The Memoirs of Yekhezkel Kotik*, ed. D. Assaf, trans. M. Birnstein (Detroit: Wayne State University Press, 2002); Yitzḥok Even, *Funem rebens hoyf* (New York: I. Even, 1922); Joseph Margoshes, *A World Apart: A Memoir of Jewish Life in Nineteenth Century Galicia*, trans. R. Margolis and I. Robinson (Boston: Academic Studies Press, 2008).

11. Pauline Wengeroff, *Rememberings: The World of a Russian-Jewish Woman in the Nineteenth Century*, ed. B. D. Cooperman, trans. H. Wenkart (Bethesda: University Press of Maryland, 2000). New full translation in Wengeroff, *Memoirs of a Grandmother: Scenes from the Cultural History of the Jews of Russia in the Nineteenth Century*, 2 vols., trans. S. Magnus (Stanford, CA: Stanford University Press, 2010–2014).

12. Malka Shapiro, *The Rebbe's Daughter: Memoir of a Hasidic Childhood*, trans. N. Polen (Philadelphia: Jewish Publication Society, 2002).

13. Hinde Bergner, *On Long Winter Nights . . . : Memoirs of a Jewish Family in a Galician Township (1870–1900)*, trans. J. D. Cammy (Cambridge, MA: Harvard University Press, 2005); Puah Rakovsky, *My Life as a Radical Jewish Woman: Memoirs of a Zionist Feminist in Poland*, ed. P. E. Hyman, trans. B. Harshav and P. E. Hyman (Bloomington and Indianapolis: Indiana University Press, 2002).

14. Yekhiel Yeshaia Trunk, *Poyln: Zikhroynes un bilder*, 7 vols. (New York: Ferlag Medem Klub, 1944–1953).

15. See Larry Wolff, *The Idea of Galicia: History and Fantasy in Habsburg Political Culture* (Stanford, CA: Stanford University Press, 2010), 209.

16. Franciszek Karpiński, *Pamiętniki* (Warsaw: Drukarnia Granowskiego i Sikorskiego, 1898), 154. It is possible that Karpiński meant in fact Niesuchojeże [Neskhiz].

17. Ita Kalish, *A rabishe haym in amolikn Poyln* (Tel Aviv: I.L. Peretz Publishing House, 1966); full Hebrew version in Kalish, *Etmoli* (Tel Aviv: Kibutz Meuhad, 1970); partial English translation in Kalish, "Life in a Hassidic Court in Russian Poland toward the End of the 19th Century," *YIVO Annual of Jewish Social Science* 13 (1965), 264–278.

18. *Jewish Mystical Autobiographies*, preface M. Idel (New York: Paulist Press, 1999).

19. Shmuel of Sieniawa, *Ramatayim tsofim* (Warsaw: Walden and Kalinberg, 1881); Rafael ha-levi Tsimetbaum, *Sefer kol ha-katuv le-ḥayim; bo nikhlal sefer Darkhei ḥayim . . . maran rabenu Ḥayim Halberstam . . .* (Jerusalem: Z. Moshkovitz, 1962).

20. Joseph I. Schneersohn, *Lubavitcher Rabbi's Memoirs*, 2 vols., 3rd ed. (Brooklyn, NY: Otzar Hachasidim, 1956). On the phenomenon, see Ada Rapoport-Albert, "Hagiography with Footnotes: Edifying Tales and the Writing of History in Hasidism," in *Essays in Jewish Historiography*, ed. A. Rapoport-Albert (Middletown, CT: Wesleyan University Press, 1988), 119–159.

21. Kaja Finkler, Golda Finkler, *Lives Lived and Lost: East European History before, during, and after World War II as Experienced by an Anthropologist and Her Mother* (Boston: Academic Studies Press, 2012).

22. David Assaf, *Untold Tales of the Hasidim: Crisis and Discontent in the History of Hasidism*, trans. D. Ordan (Hanover, NH, and London: Brandeis University Press, 2010), 206–235.

23. See Marcin Wodziński, "War and Religion, or, How the First World War Changed Hasidism," *Jewish Quarterly Review* 106 (2016), 3:283–312.

24. See Marcin Wodziński, "Women and Hasidism: A 'Non-Sectarian' Perspective," *Jewish History* 27 (2013), 399–434.

25. See Kotik, *A Journey to a Nineteenth-Century Shtetl*, 187, 251–258.

26. Wengeroff, *Rememberings*, 154–156, 164; Israel Joshua Singer, *Of a World That Is No More: A Tender Memoir*, trans. J. Singer (New York: Vanguard Press, 1970), 17, 29–36.

27. See Miriam Shomer Zunser, *Yesterday: A Memoir of a Russian Jewish Family* (New York: Stackpole Sons, 1939), 98–99.

28. Eliakum Zunser, *Tsunzer's biografye geshriben fun ihm alayn* (New York: Zunser Jubilee Committee, 1905), 31.

29. This is corroborated by many other memoirs, e.g., Isaac Leib Peretz, *My Memoirs*, trans. F. Goldberg (New York: Citadel Press, 1964), 132–133; Anis D. Pordes and Irek Grin, *Ich miasto. Wspomnienia Izraelczyków, przedwojennych mieszkańców Krakowa*

(Warsaw: Prószyński i S-ka, 2004), 32–35, 78–80, 114; Aliza Greenblat, *Baym fentster fun a lebn* (New York: Farlag Aliza, 1966), 20.

30. See Kotik, *A Journey to a Nineteenth-Century Shtetl*, 188–189.

31. See English translation in Rakovsky, *My Life as a Radical Jewish Woman*.

32. Archiwum Główne Akt Dawnych w Warszawie, collection: Centralne Władze Wyznaniowe call no. 1667, pp. 723–725.

33. See "Plotsk," *Ha-magid*, 9 June 1869 (no. 22), 30.

34. Archiwum Główne Akt Dawnych w Warszawie, collection: Centralne Władze Wyznaniowe call no. 1667, pp. 181–260, 586–701. On Eleazar ha-kohen, see Shlomo Grynszpan, "Rabanim: Kovets masot al rabanei Plotsk," in *Plotsk: Toledot kehilah atikat-yomin be-Polin*, ed. E. Eisenberg (Tel Aviv: Plotsker Landslayt Farayn in Argentine, 1967), 102–104.

35. Yehudah Ya'akov Meizler, "Plotsk" (correspondence), *Ha-magid*, 28 August 1867 (no. 34), 10.

36. "Plotsk," in *Pinkas ha-kehilot Polin*, vol. 4 (Jerusalem: Yad Vashem, 1989), 358–372; Grynszpan, "Rabanim," 104–106.

37. Rakovsky, *My Life as a Radical Jewish Woman*, 32.

38. Ibid.

39. Meizler, "Plotsk," 10.

40. Archiwum Państwowe w Płocku, collection: Akta miasta Płocka call no. 569, p. 271.

41. Ibid.

42. Ibid., 280–281.

43. Ibid., 282–283. The lampoon and some other documents related to the investigation are reprinted in *Hasidism in the Kingdom of Poland, 1815–1867: Historical Sources in the Polish State Archives* (Kraków and Budapest: Austeria Publishing House, Institute for the History of the Polish Jewry, Tel Aviv University, 2011), 482–486.

CHAPTER 7

Folk Narratives

Galit Hasan-Rokem and Shaul Magid

Hasidism has been amply studied by social and cultural historians as well as theologians, phenomenologists, and historians of religious thought.[1] There are numerous collections of narratives attributed to leaders of the movement or told by the followers on their charismatic leaders, and they have been dominant in shaping the image of the Hasidim outside their traditional communities. Much work has also been devoted to reactions to Hasidism by its detractors (known as mitnagedim) in the rabbinic elite.[2] But what about the majority of Jews who populated the Pale of Settlement, the Austro-Hungarian Empire, and Poland, where Hasidism flourished?

This chapter is an attempt to investigate the ways in which Hasidim were viewed by Jewish people in everyday life by eliciting such views from Jewish folk narratives that represent and construct cultural memories of the lives of Jews in Eastern Europe before the Shoah. Folk narratives are told by individuals who draw on the collective tradition of their group, in this case East European, Yiddish-speaking Jews. By basing our analysis on these personally transmitted, collectively anchored traditions, we suggest a methodological innovation to the study of Hasidism that opens a window to an expressive layer of culture that has been until now relatively unrecognized and understudied in comparison to the tales of the Hasidim themselves. The latter have gained much attention and have been widely published by philosophers (Martin Buber), novelists (Y. L. Peretz, Sh. Agnon), and scholars (Joseph Dan and others).

Folk narratives from the oral tradition have been collected by folklore scholars among the Jews of Eastern Europe.[3] Many of them are still in manuscripts in various archives, and some have been published in collections and anthologies.[4] An outstanding collection, edited and annotated by Beatrice Silverman Weinreich, includes a significant number of tales reflecting popular views and images regarding Hasidim and Hasidism.[5] Silverman Weinreich makes some important observations about the presence of Hasidim and Hasidism in folk narratives both from the inside perspective: "For over two hundred years a rich oral storytelling tradition flourished in Hasidic courts"[6] and from an outsider view: "From anti-Hasidic camps come tales that poke fun at the so-called miracle workers. Both the traditionalist anti-Hasidic misnagdim as well as the modern enlightened maskilim scoffed at the supernatural powers attributed to the Hasidic rebbes. Amusing as such tales might be, the collectors of Yiddish oral legends tended to concentrate more on the Hasidic than the anti-Hasidic tales."[7]

Our sample of narratives stems from the Israel Folktale Archives (IFA) at the University of Haifa, named after its founder, Dov Noy.[8] Because the collecting of tales for this archive began in 1955, in the case of East European Jews the stories reflect the memory of pre-Shoah life in Europe, mainly in Poland, Russia, and other East and Central European countries, while at the same time addressing the cultural and political realities of the present and the situation of the narrators and their audiences.[9] Consequently, most of the texts referred to were narrated in Hebrew or translated from Yiddish to Hebrew in the process of their recording. This was also the standard practice for Hasidic literature, which consisted largely of oral discourses in Yiddish that were later transcribed into a Hebrew that often preserved the Yiddish linguistic flavor and syntax.[10]

Hasidic Ideas in Folk Narratives

Folk narratives are characterized by a rich interaction of materials from the lived reality and experience, with elements of creative imagination and fantasy. The tales that lean more toward the lived reality and experience, have been termed by scholars *legends*, and they are usually rich in real-life details, including supernatural beliefs and magical practices. In many cases, they also refer to figures known from history who play prominent roles in these imaginative narratives. The tales that include more imaginary and fantastic contents are called folktales (or fairy tales) and are characterized by the presence of the traditional motifs of transformation, enchantment, and otherworldly behavior as well as by stock figures associated with such phenomena. Folklorists maintain that while these narratives are not "historical" in the strict sense of depicting a past reality, they capture the imaginative force and often also the lived reality of many of those who occupy a status below the elite class of rabbinic scholars whose own work largely ignores them. The boundaries between these two major folk narrative genres are porous and unstable, so that any distinguishing categorization between them should move along a scale rather than present a dichotomy. The following is the tale of a poor rabbi in pursuit of matzo before Passover:

> Rabbi Yeḥiel Hazanowitz was much liked by the inhabitants of the town of Mogielnica. Jews as well as gentiles all honored him and approached him with

enquiries regarding the laws of Torah and the laws of edification. Everyone also knew that Rabbi Yeḥiel had been a rich man, but was impoverished because his gentile neighbor burnt his flour mill. The town tried to support him, lent money to him, but everything was in vain. The Jews of his town said that the gentile had "cut his fortune."

In his plight Rabbi Yeḥiel left his town and settled in another town far away. As he was in dire condition he made public that he was accepting children for tutoring in both sacred and secular studies. And Rabbi Yeḥiel did not remember the saying "School-teaching (*melamedut*) could be a prosperous business unless it was in the hands of teachers (*melamedim*)."

There was severe poverty in Rabbi Yeḥiel's home. And especially in the month of Adar (the month of the merry holiday of Purim when it is said: "As Adar enters there is much merriment"), his home was very sad. Moreover, Passover was approaching, and he didn't have any money, and the walls [of his home] were shining with green mold. And how will he have means to whitewash them? And from where will he get the means for shoes and clothes? And above all—wherefrom will he have means to buy matzo for Passover?

Having no choice, he went to the father of one of his students, a rich man, told him all his troubles, and asked for a little money, an installment payment for the son's studies, so that he could buy matzo for Passover.

"I cannot give you money," said the rich man (*gevir*), "but I promise that you'll have matzo for Passover . . . don't worry! Every Jew is sure to have matzo for Passover."

All Rabbi Yeḥiel's pleas did not succeed in moving the rich man. Rabbi Yeḥiel returned home with a broken heart, expecting a miracle.

Passover Eve arrived. "What shall we do," asked Rabbi Yeḥiel's wife? "Will we, heaven forbid, remain without matzo for Passover?" "Rest calm, my dear, with God's help everything will be in the best order. The rich man will certainly send matzo, he almost promised," and when he had said so, he fell down like a log, fainting on the floor.

His wife began to scream: "Help! Jews, help!" and Jews, neighbors as well as those passing by, were scared, entered Rabbi Yeḥiel's home and alerted a doctor, who brought remedies.

When Rabbi Yeḥiel regained consciousness he also had matzo for Passover. Because ultimately Jews are merciful, descending from the merciful.[11]

Whereas this tale does not single out any specific Hasidic group or leader (R. Yeḥiel appears to be a fictional character, or at least not a rabbi known in wider circles), the story line is predicated on a kind of evident trust in the goodness of humans. It maintains the idea that God answers prayers yet works in mysterious ways, and that when all seems lost, salvation is near. This sentiment lies at the foundation of folk pietism that draws from Hasidic spirituality. It testifies to the values of "belief" (*emunah*) and "trust" (*bitaḥon*), which are highly valued in the teachings of Hasidic rabbis to their audiences.[12]

The genre of this tale is obviously related to legends, and consequently its basis in lived reality is emphasized by the mention of the place of origin of the rabbi, the town of Mogielnica in Central Poland, although his new town of domicile, in which the events narrated in the story unfold, is not mentioned.[13] Although not easily identifiable as a famous rabbi by his name, the appellation may encode a reference to a known R. Ḥayim Meir Yeḥiel of Mogielnica (whose last name, however, was Shapiro). It is not uncommon in folk narratives like these to borrow the names of well-known or even lesser-known rabbis and places, as a means of authenticating, or at least bringing to life, the tale in the eyes of its readers. In some cases, as here, the inexact reference enables the legend to contain an element of historical validity while maintaining enough anonymity to add imaginary coloring to the story.

The Eve of Passover is a classical time for miracles in Jewish folk narratives. Perhaps this is because Passover is a holiday associated with the miracle of the Ten Plagues, the redemption from Egypt, and the Parting of the Red (Reed) Sea. While Hanukkah and Purim also celebrate miracles that saved Jews from likely destruction, Passover represents the quintessence of God miraculously saving the Jews.

Moreover, the association of Passover with a sumptuous, full-night meal, the Seder—from antiquity modeled on the Greek *symposion*—also makes the occasion a time of direst need for those who do not have access to the funds required for such a meal. A specific mitzvah called "matzo money" (*ma'ot hitim* or *qimha de-fisha*) is codified in Jewish legal sources. Since the consumption of matzo is the central biblical commandment of Passover ("you shall eat matzot seven days"—Exodus 13:6–7) the community takes upon itself to focus its charity in this season on providing resources for those who cannot afford to purchase matzo. Not being able to afford matzo on Passover is a sign of utter destitution in the Jewish tradition; a community without the resources or the generosity to provide it becomes stigmatized. In addition, the traditional reading of the Seder, the Haggadah, more or less opens with a text inviting all (specifically the poor) to partake in the meal to commemorate the "bread of poverty" (Aramaic: *lahma 'aniya*; Hebrew: *lehem 'oni*) that the Israelites were able to take with them from Egypt, and the prescriptive custom of "flour for Passover" (*qimha de-fisha*) is a marker of a conscious reflection on the existence of people who are too poor to feast accordingly without the intervention of solidarity, generosity, and also miracles.

The plot structure of our story aligns it with the Jewish tradition of miracle tales. The gender division, in which the wife expresses uncertainty and the husband represents trust and belief, is already extant in the series of tales recounting miracles that befell one of the first men characterized as Hasid in Rabbinic literature, Rabbi Hanina ben Dosa (BT Ta'anit 24b–25a).[14] The happy ending of the tale characteristically links together the trustful individual, the keeping up of the tradition of Passover, divine Providence, and the solidarity of the Jewish community, encompassing both rich and poor. It also raises the question of why the rich man simply didn't provide for the rabbi's needs beforehand. It is as if the rich man served as a proxy for God, who was testing the rabbi's faith. Here we can see that even apparent lack of empathy on the part of the rich man can serve as a link in a chain that will ultimately show the power of God. The rich man, who in the beginning of the story embodies a kind of miserly villain, turns out to be the carrier of a divine plan. The tale thus functions on two parallel planes: the plane of social criticism and the plane of belief in Providence.

It is perhaps unnecessary to point out that the folk narrative here functions as a powerful expression of wishful thinking rather than as a realistic representation of lived experience. Whereas the values reinforced by the legend may have strengthened their keeping among the narrators and their audiences, it is also important to mention that the reality may have been less ideal. The violent caesura placing the past projected in the tale onto the other side of the cataclysm of the Shoah also adds to the reverential idealization of the life of the past.

In addition, the tale embodies the very sudden nature of the Passover miracle (the Torah describes Israelite redemption as happening "suddenly"—*b'hipazon*—in the Deuteronomic retelling of the Exodus narrative, Deuteronomy 16:3; cf. Isaiah 52:12). Just as the Jews have all but given up hope, and at the very last instance are saved from destruction, so too R. Yeḥiel. At the moment in which he expresses faith in the impossible ("Rest calm, my dear, with God's help everything will be in best order. The rich man will certainly send matzo, he almost promised"), R. Yehiel loses consciousness. It is this very life-threatening state that results in his personal salvation, reflected in his having matzo for Passover. The episode is akin with narrative traditions describing an entrance into the realm of death before a miraculous resurrection. This element of revival is typical of spring festivals in general and of the Christian Easter in particular. The folk narrative is in a way a retelling of the Exodus story in the life of one man of faith. The Passover Haggadah states that everyone must see themselves as if they are the ones going out of Egypt. This tale is the story of one hapless rabbi's embodiment of that liturgical flourish.

The narrator of the tale, Zvi Moshe Haimowitz, told the tale from memory, a common practice in Hasidic storytelling. He was a devoted collector of folk narratives who contributed 310 items to the archives. He himself was born in Mogielnica in the year 1900; his father, whose name significantly was Yeḥiel, the name of our protagonist, perished of hunger in the ghetto that the Nazi Germans erected in the town; his mother, Bat Sheva neé Guttman, daughter of R. Zvi Moshe Guttman from Mogielnica, died in Auschwitz. The father was the son of a rich man who owned a large farm and flour mill in Mogielnica. The father was also, according to his son, a learned man. This defies the idea that Hasidism was necessarily linked to a lesser appreciation of learning. These details are interestingly echoed in the tale, not uncommon in folk narratives of the legend genre.

The narrator himself, Haimowitz, was politically active in Jewish socialist circles in Mogielnica and in the city council, until his 1931 migration to Palestine, where he continued his political activity in addition to serving in the military and being an agricultural pioneer in a collective settlement called a *moshav*. For many years he was the director of a labor union (*Histadrut*) home for the elderly, where he had the opportunity to record many folk narratives, especially from immigrants from Iraq.

The tale above bears witness to the constancy of the Hasidic tradition from the teller's childhood even after all the life changes that occurred to him. This is not uncommon among modernized Jews who left the world of their traditional childhood yet carried with them an emotional and often romanticized memory of a fantastical world that modernity had largely transformed with reason and science. Folk narratives such as these often serve to add a different perspective, an altered orientation, specifically to the skeptical world that Zvi Moshe Haimowitz inhabited. This is a frequent phenomenon in modern literature, apparent in works of Yiddish and Hebrew authors such as Yitzhok L. Peretz, Sholem (Rabinovich) Aleichem, Micha Y. Berdyczewski, S. Y. Agnon, and Isaac Bashevis Singer.[15]

Our analysis demonstrates how the folk narrative interweaves personal moments of the storyteller's life with characters such as the rich grandfather who owned a flour mill and the father who died of hunger, and with elements of collective tradition such as food symbolism and miracles especially connected to Passover. The narrative transmits the values of belief and trust in God and humans, as emphasized in Hasidic teachings. Ḥaimowitz's father's fate—who may have indeed fainted before his untimely death (at least in his son's imagination)—now resounds in that of the protagonist's, in a miracle. In this sense, the folk narrative enables its teller to relive personal history, in this case tragic history, by revising tragedy through a fantastical lens of redemption. The narrated R. Yeḥiel Hazanowitz, standing for the father Yeḥiel Haimowitz, gets to eat his matzo on Passover and tell the story of Israel's redemption through the revisionary lens of his son's imagination. The real Yeḥiel Haimowitz suffered the tragic fate of not being redeemed, becoming a victim of the most horrific evil committed by humans.

Folk Narratives as a Contact Zone

Based on this reading, the Hasidic narrative provides a means of symbolically revising the past, and thereby again envisioning the future in a modern world.

It is thus interesting to look at another tale in which Hasidism is exhibited in a different, perhaps less idealizing or romanticizing mode.

Yitzḥak Yam-Suf (Isaac, the Sea of Reeds)

On one of the Shabbats between Purim and Passover, the rabbi visited his few Hasidim in a town populated almost solely by mitnagedim. At the time of *shlos-sudes* [the third meal of the Shabbat that begins in late afternoon] he recited *divrei-Torah* [words of learning] with great devotion (*devekut*) and repeated a number of times to his Hasidim, that every Jew may experience and feel the miracle of the Opening [literally "tearing"] of the Sea of Reeds, if he only wants, and fortunate is he who receives this grace.

The *Rebbe's* words penetrated the heart of Yitzḥak the teacher of children (*melamed*) and he thought about them repeatedly and often. Yitzḥak "from his shoulders and upward was taller than any of the people,"[16] the tallest man in town, but as he was tall he was also modest, lower than "the hyssop on the wall"[17] and he had a good heart. He loved his few students with all his soul, all of them sons of poor people, since the rich people (*ba'alei batim*) from the mitnagedim boycotted his *ḥeder* [the elementary educational institution for Jewish boys] as they were saying that instead of the Torah of Moses he was teaching his students the Torah of the Hasidim. And indeed, from his hut Hasidic melodies poured out from the morning until the evening, since he maintained that it was good to study with a *niggun* [wordless melody]. Among them were tunes of happiness and joy, and tunes full of sadness, and the students swallowed the *parasha* of the *ḥumash* [weekly portion of the Torah] or the section of the Talmud, as they memorized their Torah while singing.

And lo, the day of the Festival of the Exodus approached, the air was filled with spring fragrances, and the holiday tunes flowed out of Yitzḥak the *melamed's ḥeder*. That year, after he had heard the rabbi's word about the "opening of the sea," Yitzḥak the *melamed* frequently sang with his students the verses "When Israel went out of Egypt,"[18] and the tune was like a march, as if the students were accompanying those leaving Egypt walking after Moses, and when they reached the verses "The sea saw it and fled, Jordan was driven back"[19] the tune gushed forth as a waterfall, and the voices of the children were mixed with the voices of those who were baking the matzos in the hamlet [Hebrew: *'ayara*; Yiddish: *shtetl*].

Close to the holiday a rumor spread in the town that Yitzḥak the *melamed* would tear open the Sea of Reeds [also known as the Red Sea]—and the town started to boil. Some laughed with a big mouth and others judged it as blasphemy (*hillul ha-kodesh*). And so the sanctified eve of the holiday arrived, and many in the hamlet hurried to finish the *Seder*, hastily sang the *Had Gadya* [the last song in the Ashkenazi Haggadah] and ran over to Yitzḥak the *melamed's* cabin.

The *melamed* was seated at the table like a king with his wife and his five children, reading the Haggadah in great joy, tune follows tune, and all the Hasidim fill the room following them in their reciting. When midnight arrived the tall Yitzḥak rose with his eldest son and they brought into the house a trough filled with water, Yitzḥak shouldered a bag with *shmure matze* [matzo made with extra care for its lack of contact with water and fermenting substances], standing in line with his wife and children, and when he arrived at the verse "Speak unto the children of Israel that they go forward"[20]—the *melamed* entered into the water-filled trough, after him his wife and children, and after them the Hasidim, and they sing loudly "The sea saw it and fled,"[21] when the mitnagedim who were flocking outside burst into the house and called out to the *melamed*: Yitzḥak Yam Suf (Sea of Reeds), Yitzḥak Yam Suf. . . .

When the *rebbe* heard what had happened on the Seder night at the home of Yitzḥak the *melamed* and the surge of the mitnagedim, he said about them: "eyes have they, but they see not,"[22] because if they would have merited they would have seen the six hundred thousand leaving Egypt rejoicing in their redemption. . . .

But from that day onward the people in the hamlet called the *melamed* "Yitzḥak Yam Suf" [Yitzḥak Sea of Reeds] and his name haunted him.[23]

In this tale the point of view of the narrator is somewhat more distanced than in the tale discussed above. The population of the little town, not identified by name, is predominantly non-Hasidic, even anti-Hasidic, outspoken mitnagedim. This defines the social status of the protagonist, Yitzḥak the *melamed*, as almost an outcast. The *melamed* or teacher of children was considered to be a lowly, albeit an important, profession in traditional Jewish society. The Baal Shem Tov was said to be a *melamed*. There are other instances in Hasidic lore where the *melamed* is really a righteous man (*tsadik*) who conceals his identity from the rest of the community by teaching young children.[24]

A point of similarity with the earlier tale is seen in the contrast between the *melamed*'s poverty and the expectation to celebrate the Passover Seder with abundance and joy. The connection between teaching small children and poverty is once more reinforced, emphasized here by the unwillingness of the townspeople to let their children be influenced by Hasidism. It was quite common in non-Hasidic communities that men from Hasidic groups would be hired as school teachers for young boys. And they would secretly teach the children Hasidic works. One example is that of R. Joseph Soloveitchik (1903–1993). Although he was from a staunchly anti-Hasidic family, his father hired a private tutor from the Lubavitch group to teach his young son Torah; this *melamed* indeed taught him *Tanya*, the classic text of Lubavitch Hasidism.[25]

In the present tale, however, the poverty of the *melamed* remains secondary, and his real struggle is with his ideological opponents, the mitnagedim. The happy ending thus goes beyond a mere satisfaction of the need to eat—the miraculous matzos of the tale of R. Yeḥiel—albeit matzos are present in the sack that Yitzḥak carries on his back.

The tale suggests an actual *imitatio Mosis*, Yitzḥak the *melamed* leading his family like Moses led the Israelites. The ritual described in the tale is partly performed in many Jewish ethnic groups, especially in those formerly from Muslim countries, to this day. The part they perform is the procession with bags of unleavened bread on the shoulders, without, however, the concrete presence of a body of water. Some Hasidim—for example, the Karlin-Stolin Hasidim in Jerusalem—all meet in the synagogue at midnight on the seventh day of Passover (the day the sea split), pour water all over the floor, and dance on the water singing the Song of the Sea (Exodus 15:1–21).

While the plot focusing on Yitzḥak proceeds as a relatively realistic narrative, two points unsettle the realism. The first is the *Rebbe*, whose devotion (*devekut*) inspired Yitzḥak to fulfill in a concrete fashion the identification of each Jew who celebrated the Exodus, with the generation that left Egypt. The *Rebbe*'s appearance in the final section of the tale, where he reflects on a secondhand report of the events, introduces a mystical dimension that indicates that only believers may have seen the miracle, the actual appearance of the ancients. This connects to the custom of *ushpizin*, or inviting the ancients to the Sukkah on the holiday of Sukkot. Hasidim took this tradition very seriously and claimed that in a state of true *devekut*, one can see the ancients rejoicing with them in festivities.

But the last word belongs to the community and to the power of collective naming to haunt an individual through his life. The miracle of the Seder night did not erase the social reality of being a Hasidic minority in a non-Hasidic community, a situation in which one could experience derision and continuing poverty. Hasidim have a practice that they share with many other communities—for example, Native Americans and the Hakitiya-speaking Jews of Tétouan in Spanish Morocco—of assigning names to people based on their actions. For example, Moshele Ganav (Moshe the Thief) and Yossele ha-Kamzan (Yossele the Miser) are characters in Hasidic stories told by Shlomo Carlebach. The practice helps to distinguish people in a community where many people share the same name. In this story we have Yitzḥak Yam Suf.

Although the biographies of the narrators and the collectors of IFA reflect the subjective perspectives of the formulators of the biographies, they may still provide important information that illuminates and deepens the understanding of the tale.

The town where the narrator, David Cohen, was born in 1894, a small Belarusian/Lithuanian town in the vicinity of Nowogródek (Novardok) in the Grodno region, can be viewed as a characteristic contact zone for Hasidic culture to meet with mitnagedim. It was famous for its Litvak yeshiva, led by an early master of the Musar movement, R. Yosef Yuzel Hurvitz of Novardok (1847–1919).[26] But it also had a yeshiva for the Hasidim of the group of Słonim. The tale reflects such a contact zone in an area where Hasidim were not necessarily a majority among local Jews. David Cohen's grandfather (also!) had a mill, according to Cohen a watermill, so it probably was on a river (the Niemen River flows in this region), and he was a wealthy man. He thus easily found *yeshive bokhers* (young yeshiva students) to marry his three daughters, and the father of the narrator, Avraham Eliezer, was a student at the great Volozhin (Wołożyn) yeshiva that was founded by the disciple of the Gaon of Vilna, R. Ḥayim of Volozhin (1749–1821).[27] Although the yeshiva was of Litvak character, the narrator states that his father was very interested in mysticism and in messianic expectations. He combined the role of pulpit rabbi in a very small town with active kabbalistic practice. After a failed attempt to bring the Messiah, Avraham Eliezer had to move to another town, taking a lower position as a *dayan* (the *dayan* was solely responsible for legal matters, while the rabbi was the overall spiritual leader of the community). David himself was the fourth and youngest child who at the age of eleven or twelve left home to escape the severe discipline of his father. He wandered around in Ukraine, making his living as a *maggid*, a profession whose work he describes as follows: "telling legends and bringing the audience to tears." *Maggidim* would often travel from town to town, charging money to tell stories of wonder to the townspeople, conveying news from other regions as well. He stayed at the home of his uncle, who was a head of the yeshiva in Proskurow (today's Khemelnetsky, Ukraine). His aunt wanted to enlist him as a caretaker for her children, so he escaped again and arrived at a very little village where the Jews made him their children's *melamed*.

His autobiographical narrative in the archival file says that he became politically involved and even met Ber Borokhov (1881–1917), an important Jewish socialist Zionist. At a later stage, his grandfather wanted him to return to work at his watermill, to which he consented after the grandfather promised to let him socialize freely with the Christian workers. He was, however, attracted by the head of the Novardok yeshiva, R. Yosef Yuzel Hurvitz, to attend the yeshiva, which he did for a while, but then he opted for the more joyful lifestyle found at the Słonim Hasidic yeshiva. Cohen's seesaw movement between Hasidism and Litvak yeshivot did not end there. From another period, when he was at the Volozhin yeshiva, he emerged as a Zionist and was expelled from the yeshiva. He settled for a while in Vilna and was active as a journalist and writer in Yiddish and Hebrew, including composing a treatise on Hasidism in Belarus. During most of World War I, though, David Cohen was at the Novardok yeshiva. After the war he settled in Vilna and was active in socialist Zionist groups and as a journalist for *Di yiddishe shtime*, where he published columns and printed legendary narratives while also working for a Hebrew weekly. In 1923 he first visited Palestine and emigrated there with his wife and son in 1924. Under the guidance of the Zionist activist Berl Katznelson, he became a leader for working youth, using tales and legends as an educational tool, publishing Hasidic legends in a biweekly publication that he cofounded, and telling stories in oral performances. Volumes of his tales were published and became very popular.

Both the Hasidic and the folk literary aspects of the tale are richly informed by many interpretive keys supplied by the detailed autobiography that David Cohen submitted to the Israel Folktale Archives. His account reports travels around vast areas of Eastern Europe that were populated by Jews before the Shoah, as he spent long periods in Nowogródek, Vilna, and Proskurow before making the trip to Palestine. Moreover, the stories about his youth blatantly contradict the idea of a hermetic separation between the worlds of the Hasidim and the mitnagedim, and we hear about his move numerous times between the Litvak yeshiva and the yeshiva of the Słonim Hasidim. On the contrary, the interface between the mitnagedim and Hasidim seems to be the most vibrant but also the most urgent and unsettling contact zone in Cohen's intellectual and emotional growth. This interface also provides the internal tensions of the tale: the Hasidic *Rebbe*'s teaching inspiring Yitzḥak's ritual performance finally approved by the *Rebbe*'s affirmation of the miracle on one hand, and the mitnagedim townspeople's refusal to let Yitzḥak teach their children, their curiosity to see his idiosyncratic ritual, and their persistent use of his nickname "Yitzḥak Sea-of-Reeds." The nickname may, however, be seen as growing to become a name of honor and sanctity, of Hasidism. In a way, Yitzḥak starts out as a teacher of children, looked down upon by the townspeople, but he ends up as a Hasid, a pious man who has fully embodied the spirit of the festival. This is a common trope in Hasidic tales. In this case, however, it is the conclusion of a tale told *about* Hasidim rather than *by* Hasidim.

The tale is marked by an unusually rich application of quotations from sources, as well as Hebrew and Yiddish terms. The mode of narration reflects a scheme that has been suggested in scholarship: in the phases of the cultural adaptation in the performance of Jewish folk narratives in Israel, the first stage is in the language of the country of origin and the last stage is all in Hebrew, with a minimum of cultural associations taken from the old language and country; in the interim stage the narrators intersperse their verbal performance with many cultural associations from the diaspora, including words in the language of yore, such as Yiddish in this case.[28] But Cohen also displays another mode of cultural literacy in his knowledge of classical Hebrew sources, the Bible, the prayer book, and the Haggadah. Still in Europe, Cohen had developed his literary talent both in Yiddish and in Hebrew; tales of various genres, especially legends of Hasidim, are his specialty. The tale is well rehearsed, belongs to a rich repertoire, and was published by Dov Noy in 1959 in the newspaper for new immigrants in "easy Hebrew," *Ha-omer.*

This tale moves from the wholesome register of the total Hasidic trust in God's (and humans') grace and mercifulness of the first tale, to a more socially colored register that acts out both the tensions between Hasidim and mitnagedim and the lively discursive and social interface between them. It manages to depict both the self-image of the imaginative and artistic Hasid who excelled in teaching by song and staging the Exodus, and the criticism of the non-Hasidic environment against the Hasid's unrealistic approach to the world.

Narrative of a Tune

The third story is sparse in words but replete with meaning. Its form parallels its message, as it conveys the importance of nonverbal communication in the world of Hasidism and the vital role of that mode of expression, the *nign* (or niggun), the melody unaccompanied by words, sung by the *Rebbe* and more widely transmitted by his Hasidim. These Hasidic melodies were often in tune with the various kinds of music that were popular in whatever environment the particular Hasidic group or "court" resided; as such, they were a marker of the interaction of the Hasidim, like other Jews, with their non-Jewish neighbors.[29] Freed from the linguistic and theological particularity of verbal religious expression, the musical creativity of the Hasidim indeed opened their world to other groups to a greater extent than any other ritual or symbolical expression they practiced.[30]

IFA 1199 was recorded by Zvi Sofer from his memory, as is the case of many East European Jewish folk narratives in the Israel Folktale Archives. Unlike most other Jewish immigrant communities represented in IFA, who arrived in Israel often in considerably organized modes and retained the structures of their traditional communities by settling together in neighborhoods (e.g., Iraqis in Ramat-Gan) or largely ethnically monolithic development towns or *moshavim* (e.g., Yemenites in Rosh ha-Ayin), most of the Jews of Eastern Europe arrived after the Shoah, when their communities and families had been crushed and the traditional storytelling community had lost its functionality. Hasidic communities and rabbis have been famously making great efforts to reconstruct the broken dynasties and their flocks. This is especially true about the Hasidic group from which this tale stems, Chabad.[31] Lithuanian/Belarusian Chabad developed largely outside the orbit of other Hasidic groups that were centered in Poland, Hungary, Ukraine, and Galicia; as a result, they produced an internal body of literature and a very specific musical tradition. By the end of World War I, Chabad resettled in Poland and then in the United States and Israel, becoming a worldwide movement focused on internal proselytizing (*kiruv rekhokim*) and providing religious services for far-flung Jewish communities.[32] Today they are arguably the most well-known Hasidic group among non-Hasidic Jews.[33]

Chabad Hasidic piety is centered on the notion of "contemplation" (*hitbonenut*), a focus of the mind on the unity of the divine in the world.[34] It developed a highly intellectualized mystical theology whose primary goal was mindful connection to the divine through thought. The state of contemplation is often accompanied by the musical niggun, or wordless melody, sung as a group or individually at times of prayer, festive meals, and Torah-teaching gatherings (known in Chabad's Yiddish nomenclature as *farbrengin*). Niggunim serve a central function in Hasidic communities, including Chabad, and the niggun is a distinctive mark of Hasidism in comparison to other Jewish groups.[35]

In Hasidism, the niggun is not only a table song or liturgical accompaniment, as it is in many non-Hasidic circles. Rather, it is a vehicle for achieving *devekut*, proximity to God.[36]

> *The Power of Nign*
>
> The *Rebbe* of Liady [the founding *Rebbe* of Chabad] felt that among those listening to his words was one old man who did not understand them. He summoned him and told him: "It seems to me that my *droshe* (sermon) is not clear to you. Listen to this melody"—and he began to sing without words, and in that melody one could hear the words of Torah and the belief in the one God, the longings for the *Shekhina* and the love of the Creator.
>
> "Now I understand what you want to teach me," said the old man. "I feel in my heart a great longing, I want to be one (*lehidabek*) with God and unite with Him."
>
> The niggun of the Rebbe said everything to the old man, although it didn't have one single word.[37]

The notion that thoughts can be communicated through melody is not uncommon in Hasidism. The story illustrates the way in which discursive teaching and song provide two intertwined methods of communicating Torah. One wonders whether this notion of metalingual communication gestures toward mystical theories of revelation where God reveals God's will without the articulation of words.[38] The story also indicates the populism of Hasidism, showing that a complex Torah discourse can be digested in the form of a wordless melody by one who is open to hearing its message. The purpose of Torah in Hasidism is to experience a closeness to God. This can be accomplished through study, prayer, and melody. This tale illustrates how two models of proximity to God overlap and can substitute one for the other. In this sense the tale may be a polemic against the mitnagedim's focus on study as categorically superior to other forms of divine worship.[39]

Zvi Sofer's biography at the IFA supplies fewer materials to support a cultural contextual analysis than the reported biographies of the two other narrators. It is possibly his slightly more outsider perspective as a folklore scholar that has lead him to record from his memory a tale on the emblematic element of music rather than a more material practice-oriented episode.

The third tale from IFA that we have discussed in this chapter adds a voice that identifies with Hasidic piety in perhaps its most specific mode, music. Together with the tale of the miracle of the Passover Matzos with its critical overtones rooted in the narrator's loss of his father in the Shoah, and the tale of Yitzḥak "Sea of Reeds" demonstrating the porosity between Hasidic and non-Hasidic worlds of life and discourse, the IFA tales reflect a complex and multivocal image of Hasidism and Hasids as articulated among East European Jews after Shoah.

SUGGESTED READING

This chapter takes a folkloristic approach to a series of stories about the Hasidim. The literature on general folklore is, of course, voluminous, and Jewish folklore studies constitute an important topic of Jewish studies in general. The work on Hasidic folklore or the study of Hasidism from a folkloristic perspective is minimal. Most of the work on Hasidic folklore extends from the study of Jewish folklore and of East European Jewish life. Below are some examples.

Bar-Itzhak, Haya, *Jewish Poland: Legends of Origin: Ethnopoetics and Legendary Chronicles* (Detroit: Wane State University Press, 2001). A scholarly monograph on the legends of Polish Jews, narrating their history from its beginning to the sad end. Sources include printed, written, and archived oral records. Comparative Polish texts and scholarship are included.

Bar-Itzhak, Haya, *Pioneers of Jewish Ethnography and Folkloristics in Eastern Europe*, trans. L. Schramm (Ljubljana: Scientific Research Centre of the Slovenian Academy of Sciences and Arts, 2010). Some important early contributions of East European folklore scholars, translated, introduced, and contextualized by scholars of East European Jewish folk narratives and of the history of Jewish folklore in Eastern Europe.

Ben-Amos, Dan and Dov Noy (eds.) *Folktales of the Jews: Tales from Eastern Europe*. (Philadelphia: Jewish Publication Society, 2007). Seventy-one East European Jewish folk narratives from the collections of the Israel Folktale Archive at the University of Haifa, recorded from oral performances, edited, annotated, with extensive historical and cultural commentaries, including indexing by international folk tale types and motifs and comparisons to Jewish tales as well as tales from other cultures.

Gottesman, Itzik Nakhmen, *Defining the Yiddish Nation: The Jewish Folklorists of Poland* (Detroit: Wayne State University Press, 2003). An analysis of the development of Yiddish folklore and its role in the creation of Yiddish nationalism in Poland between the two World Wars, focusing on three important folklore circles in Poland: the Warsaw group led by Noyekh Prilutski, the S. Ansky Vilne Jewish Historic-Ethnographic Society, and the Ethnographic Commission of the YIVO Institute in Vilna.

Gross, Naftoli, *Maaselekh un mesholim* (New York: Forverts, 1955). A Yiddish collection of tales by an important collector and literary scholar.

Hasan-Rokem, Galit, "The Birth of Scholarship out of the Spirit of Oral Tradition: Folk Narrative Publications and National Identity in Modern Israel," *Fabula* 39 (1998), 277–290. Essay describing Dov Noy's pioneering endeavor in establishing the Israel Folktale Archives and its publishing projects in the context of the emergence of Israeli national identity and ideology.

Schwarzbaum, Haim, *Studies in Jewish and World Folklore* (Berlin: Walter de Gruyter, 1968). A comprehensive comparative study and annotation of Naftoli Gross's collection of tales.

Silverman-Weinreich, Beatrice, ed., *Yiddish Folktales*, trans. L. Wolf (New York: Penguin/Random House, 1988). A collection of Yiddish folk narratives of various genres in English translation, based largely on the YIVO collections created in the 1920s and 1930s, annotated with information about the collectors and the narrators, as well as the cultural context of the narratives.

Yassif, Eli, *The Hebrew Folktale: History, Genre, Meaning* (Bloomington: Indiana University Press, 1999). An ambitious, comprehensive history of Hebrew folk narratives from biblical texts to contemporary Israeli oral tales of all genres. The author addresses questions of literary and historical character and provides extensive scholarly references.

NOTES

1. Gershon D. Hundert, *Essential Papers on Hasidism: Origins to Present* (New York New York University Press, 1991).

2. Mordechai Wilensky, *Ḥasidim u-mitnagedim*, 2 vols. (Jerusalem: Mosad Bialik, 1970); Alan Nadler, *The Faith of the Mithnagdim* (Baltimore: Johns Hopkins University Press, 1997); David Assaf, *Untold Tales of the Hasidim: Crisis and Discontent in the History of Hasidism* (Waltham, MA: Brandeis University Press, 2010). See also chapter 4.

3. Itzik Nakhmen Gottesman, *Defining the Yiddish Nation: The Jewish Folklorists of Poland* (Detroit: Wayne State University Press, 2003).

4. Naftoli Gross, *Maaselekh un mesholim* (New York: Forverts, 1955). For comparative notes for this collection, see Haim Schwarzbaum, *Studies in Jewish and World Folklore* (Berlin: Walter de Gruyter, 1968). For Hasidim and Hasidism, see especially introductory notes, p. 23 ff; for particular tales on these themes, see p. 304, no. 335; p. 304, no. 335; p. 307, no. 348. Among the seventy-one East European Jewish folk narratives from IFA, Israel Folktale Archive at the University of Haifa, in Dan Ben-Amos and Dov Noy, eds., *Folktales of the Jews*, vol. 2: *Tales from Eastern Europe. Edited with a Commentary* (Philadelphia: Jewish Publication Society, 2007), nine tales address the Hasidic milieu (nos. 8–16, pp. 58–122); tales nos. 11 and 15 reveal an outsider perspective.

5. Beatrice Silverman-Weinreich, ed., *Yiddish Folktales*, trans. L. Wolf (New York: Penguin/Random House, 1988), e.g., tale 67 on p. 195; tales 107–138, pp. 265–311. The editor comments on the sources of her tales, the YIVO archives, on p. 404, n.12.: "the great repository of East European Ashkenazic culture, of which American Jewry is the heir. The YIVO Archives and Library represent the single largest and most comprehensive collection of materials on East European Jewish civilization in the world." See also the website of the organization: https://www.yivo.org/archives-library.

6. Silverman-Weinreich, *Yiddish Folktales*, 260.

7. Silverman-Weinreich, *Yiddish Folktales*, 262. See also the insights of Yiddish folk humor collector Alter Druyanow on the dynamics of Yiddish and Hebrew in tales of Hasidim and on them, Haya Bar-Itzhak, *Pioneers of Jewish Ethnography and Folkloristics in Eastern Europe* (Ljubljana: Scientific Research Centre of the Slovenian Academy of Sciences and Arts, 2010), 128.

8. The authors thank Haya Milo, the administrative director of IFA, without whose kind assistance in providing copies of the texts and the contextual details about them we could not have written this chapter, and Professor Dina Stein, the academic head of IFA, who kindly read the manuscript and commented on it.

9. Galit Hasan-Rokem, "The Birth of Scholarship out of the Spirit of Oral Tradition: Folk Narrative Publications and National Identity in Modern Israel," *Fabula* 39 (1998), 277–290.

10. See chapter 1 in the present volume.

11. IFA 248 "Matzos for Passover," recorded by Zvi Moshe Haimowitz, born in Poland, from his own memory. The archival recording was closely translated by the authors of the chapter. The words in parentheses are part of the text, and when italicized they are

transcriptions of the text's original Hebrew. Our additions to the text of the tales appear in square brackets.

12. Yoets Kim Kadish Rakatz, *Siaḥ sarfei kodesh* (Łódź: Masora, 1928–1931) 3:17–23. See Arthur Green, *Tormented Master: A Life of Rabbi Nahman of Bratslav* (Woodstock: Jewish Lights Publishing, 1992), 285–337; Joseph Weiss, "Mystical Hasidism and Hasidism of Faith: A Typological Analysis," in *God's Voice from the Void: Old and New Studies in Bratslav Hasidism*, ed. S. Magid (Albany: State University of New York Press, 2002), 277–286.

13. Gedaliah Nigal, "New Light on the Hasidic Tale," in *Hasidism Reappraised*, ed. A. Rapoport-Albert (London: The Littman Library of Jewish Civilization, 1996), 345–353.

14. Shmuel Safrai, "Hassidic Teaching in Mishnaic Literature," *Journal of Jewish Studies* XVI (1956),15–33; Geza Vermes, "Hanina Ben Dosa," *Journal of Jewish Studies* XXIII (1972), 28–50; XXIV (1973), 51–64; Baruch M. Bokser, "Wonder-Working and the Rabbinic Tradition: the Case of Hanina ben Dosa," *Jewish Studies Journal* 16 (1985), 49–92; Galit Hasan-Rokem, "Did the Rabbis Recognize the Category of Folk Narrative?" *European Journal of Jewish Studies* 3 (2009), 1:19–55.

15. David Roskies, *A Bridge of Longing: The Lost Art of Yiddish Storytelling* (Cambridge: Harvard University Press, 1998).

16. The description of Saul in I Sam. 9:2.

17. See I Kings 4:33 (Hebrew Bible I Kings 5:13); BT Mo'ed Qatan 25b.

18. Ps. 114:1, KJV. Included in the Haggadah read on Passover Eve.

19. Ps. 114:3, KJV; cf. the recent note.

20. Ex. 14:15.

21. Ps. 114:3

22. Ps. 115:5; see also Jer. 5:21.

23. "Itzhak, 'Sea of Reeds," IFA 1708, was told by David Cohen, born in 1894 in a small Belarusian/Lithuanian town in the vicinity of Nowogródek (Novardok) in the Grodno region; from his memory.

24. This idea of the hidden tsadik has roots in the Zohar, where we find the mystical circle meeting an unremarkable Old Man gathering sheaves who begins to reveal to them the secrets of the universe. See Pinhas Giller, *Reading the Zohar* (New York: Oxford University Press, 2000), 35–68.

25. See also Yekhezkel Kotik, *A Journey to a Nineteenth-Century Shtetl: The Memoirs of Yekhezkel Kotik*, ed. D. Assaf, trans. M. Birnstein (Detroit: Wayne State University, 2002).

26. Chaim Grade, *The Yeshiva* (New York: Menorah, 1977).

27. Immanuel Etkes, *The Gaon of Vilna: The Man and His Image* (Berkeley: University of California Press, 2002); Eliyahu Stern, *Genius: Elijah of Vilna and the Making of Modern Judaism* (New Haven, CT: Yale University Press, 2014); Shaul Stampfer, *Lithuanian Yeshivas of the Nineteenth Century* (London and Portland: The Littman Library of Jewish Civilization, 2014).

28. "Three stages of narration can be distinguished in the acculturation process in Israel: a) The ethnic narration, in which the original language is preserved; b) the transition stage narration, in which the language has been changed to Hebrew, but the cultural associations, including terminology, names, rhymes, proverbs are preserved in the original language; c) the acculturized narration, in which the narration is in Hebrew and all ethnic cultural associations are explained, or, in the case if proverbs, either translated or replaced by a Hebrew proverb, often a Biblical or Rabbinic passage." Galit Hasan-Rokem, *Proverbs in Israeli Folk Narratives: A Structural Semantic Analysis. Folklore Fellows Communications* 232 (Helsinki: Academia Scientiarum Fennica, 1982), 14.

29. Peninnah Schram, "The Nigun in a Hasidic Story," available online: http://hasidicstories.com/Articles/Background_and_Sources/nigun_intro.html.

30. For more on this, see chapter 11.

31. Immanuel Etkes, *Rabbi Shneur Zalman of Liady: The Origins of Chabad Hasidism*, trans. J. M. Green (Dartmouth, NH: University Press of New England, 2015).

32. Susan Fishkoff, *The Rebbe's Army: Inside the World of Chabad-Lubavitch* (New York: Schocken Books, 2005).

33. Jan Feldman, *Lubavitchers as Citizens* (Ithaca, NY: Cornell University Press, 2003); Maya Balakirsky Katz, *The Visual Culture of Chabad* (Cambridge: Cambridge University Press, 2014).

34. Naftali Lowenthal, *Communicating the Infinite* (Chicago: University of Chicago Press, 1990); Lowenthal, "Habad Approaches to Contemplative Prayer," in *Hasidism Reappraised*, ed. A. Rapoport-Albert, 288–300; Rachel Elior, *The Paradoxical Ascent to God* (Albany: State University of New York Press, 1993).

35. Ellen Koskoff, *Music in Lubavitcher Life* (Champaign-Urbana: University of Illinois Press, 2000); Yaakov Mazor, "The Power of Niggun in Hasidism and Its Role in Religious and Communal Experience," *Yuval: Studies of the Jewish Music Research Centre* 7 (2002), 23–53; Naftali Loewenthal, "Spirituality, Melody, and Modernity in Habad Hasidism," in *Proceedings of the First International Conference in Jewish Music* (London: City University Department of Music, 1997); Abraham Z. Idelson, "Ha-Negina ha-hasidit," *Sefer Hashanah: The American Jewish Yearbook* (1931), 77–78; Zalman Schachter-Shalomi, "Niggun!: Soul in Song," in his volume *Davening: A Guide to Meaningful Jewish Prayer* (Woodstock, VT: Jewish Lights Publishing, 2012), 38–57.

36. In 2004 Israeli musicologist Yaakov Mazor produced a CD set entitled *The Hasidic Niggun as Sung by the Hasidim*, complete with an extensive booklet on the histories of the melodies recorded. The collection includes extensive field recordings Mazor made while traveling to many Hasidic communities in Israel and the Diaspora.

37. IFA 1199, recorded by Zvi Sofer from memory. The narrator recorded seven folk narratives for the Israel Folktale Archive in the late 1950s and the early 1960s. In 1965 his dissertation, titled *Das Urteil des Schemjaka*, and addressing a tale type on absurd judgments (international tale type AT 1534; Antti Aarne and Stith Thompson, *The Types of the Folktale: A Classification and Bibliography. Folklore Fellows Communications* 184 (Helsinki: Academia Scientiarum Fennica, 1973), 439) was approved at Georg-August Universität in Göttingen. In 1979 he published a Jewish cookbook in German, and in 1981 a catalogue of his collection of Jewish ritual textiles and texts was published by the Museum of the German town of Hameln.

The tale analyzed here may be, however weakly, correlated to the genre of wit (the German *Schwank*), also at the focus of Sofer's abovementioned dissertation.

38. See, for example, in Shaul Magid, "The Word of God That Is No Word at All," in *Imagining the Jewish God*, ed. K. Koltun-Fromm and L. Kaplan (Landham, MD: Lexington Books, 2016), 163–178.

39. See Nadler, *The Faith of the Mithnagdim*.

CHAPTER 8

Archives

Yohanan Petrovsky-Shtern

In 1978, Moshe Rosman, a Chicago-born scholar who is now a distinguished professor of history in Israel, was working in the Polish archives on his book-length project on Jews and landlords in early modern Poland.[1] A historian with profound socioeconomic intuition, Rosman sought to create a "thick description" of the relations between Polish magnates and the Jews residing on their latifundia. One of the best depositories for this kind of research was the Czartoryski Archive in Kraków, a pompous building in the historical center of the city housing thousands of archival documents from the wealthy and influential Czartoryski family of Polish landlords. Polish archivists offered Rosman what any archive in an Eastern-bloc country would offer at that time: a handwritten inventory that was unsearchable and unindexed, and some general finding aids to what was stockpiled in boxes on the four floors of the archive. Rosman was lucky: he found hundreds of documents of various types, illuminating what he subsequently called the "marriage of convenience" between the Jews and the magnates.

While his future monograph on Jews and magnates was slowly taking shape, one particular thought captured Rosman's imagination. The Czartoryskis possessed dozens of private towns, among them Międzybóż (Medzhybizh, Ukraine), now a village-type settlement around the ruins of the bygone magnate's fortress and castle. According to Hasidic legend, the Besht, considered to be the founder of Hasidism, resided in Międzybóż and was buried there. With the exception of a private letter known as the *Igeret ha-kodesh* (Holy Epistle), presumably written sometime between 1747 and 1752 and ascribed to the Besht, and a tombstone in Międzybóż with the name of the Besht on it, there were practically no documents either corroborating or refuting his presence in that private town of the Czartoryskis. The legends compiled in a hagiographic source, therefore, hardly seemed reliable.[2] Who was Israel ben Eliezer as the town dweller, the person of his time and place? Was he really a popular leader who allegedly initiated a Hasidic revolution against the ossified power of the *kahal*, a charismatic individual with dozens of disciples? What were his relations with the local and provincial Jewish authorities? And where to look for answers? So far, skeptical historians and believing adherents of Hasidism have had to make due with orally transmitted legends and published hagiographical sources. Was it at all possible to find the historical Besht in the archival dungeons?

This question was highly relevant, since Rosman was working precisely in the archive where tens of thousands of sources from the Czartoryski private towns had been stockpiled. Finding the Besht was tantamount to finding a needle in a haystack, yet Rosman decided to place an order for several boxes of communal tax records from Międzybóż, covering the period from the 1730s, before the Baal Shem Tov had allegedly settled in the town, through the 1770s, after he presumably had passed away and was buried there. Intuition did not betray the researcher; he found tax records that repeatedly mentioned the Besht and did so in the most revealing manner. It turned out that the Besht had joined a small group of Jewish kabbalists that preceded him in Międzybóż, and that the *kahal* had hired him as a kabbalist-in-residence and supported him financially. There were no traces of the supposed downfall of the local economy—which, as previous historians have claimed, triggered the rise of the Hasidic movement. In fact, there is no evidence in the documented relations between the communal administration and the Besht of a revolutionary upsurge or clash between the two. Eventually, Rosman published a new book based on his archival findings. For the last twenty years his study of the initial stages of the rising Hasidic movement remains unsurpassed.[3]

Rosman's younger colleague, Adam Teller, was also working on early modern Poland–Lithuania, focusing on relations between Jews and magnates, primarily on the estates of the Radziwiłł magnate family. Like the Czartoryskis, the Radziwiłłs were exceptionally numerous, influential, and wealthy. They boasted ownership of dozens of private towns across the breadth and width of what is today Poland, Lithuania, and Belarus. Teller's project covered a variety of aspects of Jewish life in prepartition Poland–Lithuania and apparently had nothing to do with the Besht or with Hasidism. But Teller told me in an oral conversation that he always kept the multiple literary reflections of this subject matter in mind. Among them was a story about the Besht meeting a wealthy Jewish leaseholder, who was well connected to the influential Polish magnate families. The Besht was invited to bless the new house of this Jew, who resided in Słuck—but on his own volition the Besht also prophesized the leaseholder's death in twelve years. The prophecy provoked the wrath of the Słuck tycoon; the Besht had to escape.[4]

Teller knew that one does not go to an archive to find the paper trail of a particular person or a distinct episode, unless this individual is outstanding and distinguished by a *personalia* archival collection. This was not the case of the

Słuck Jewish leaseholder or of the Besht. Still, the reconstruction of the encounter between the Besht and this influential Jewish nouveau riche seemed difficult yet perhaps possible. Working in the Radziwiłłs' collections in three countries, Teller came across one Ickowicz, an exceptionally well-connected Jew from Słuck, who was purchasing and leasing multiple and expensive properties on the Radziwiłłs' estates. Ickowicz was a prominent person mentioned in dozens of legal, financial, and epistolary documents from several archival depositories. Among these documents, Teller came across a *pinkas*, Ickowicz's personal ledger, in which he meticulously recorded his real estate deals. Around 1733, Ickowicz apparently started to note down his deals, and in 1745, he was arrested for his sleazy mediating between Frederick the Great, the king of Prussia, and the Radziwiłłs, the kings' debtors. Before his arrest, Ickowicz had gained notoriety as an extremely active and not particularly scrupulous leaseholder who appointed his relatives as communal rabbis and settled deals between the highest nobleman in the Germanic lands and Poland–Lithuania.

Piecing together the complex and complicated documentary story of Ickowicz and the story taken from *Shivḥei ha-Besht*, Teller was able to reconstruct the important context of the early years of the Besht's career as a *ba'al shem*, practical kabbalist. Teller proved that the Besht was regarded as an influential practical kabbalist with significant clout, whom clients such as Ickowicz invited to sanctify a new house situated hundreds of miles from where the Besht was active. Also, Teller managed to provide a more accurate dating of Israel ben Eliezer's birthday (1699, not 1700) by balancing evidence from the hagiographic source and external archival documents. From the perspective of source criticism, Teller showed that *Shivḥei ha-Besht* might contain some corrupted details as a hagiography published half a century after the death of the Besht, but its general picture was quite accurate.[5]

Institutional Secrets

Archival adventures such as those of Rosman and Teller have significantly reshaped our understanding of the Hasidic movement and helped locate the legendary founding fathers of Hasidism in a nuanced historical context. Yet working with the archival sources is not an easy task. Some archives (for example, the Central Archives for the History of the Jewish People in Jerusalem, CAHJP) are user-friendly; there is free access to thousands of microfilms from all over Central and Eastern Europe, with the option to print the specific frames one needs and to order copies of entire microfilm rolls. For more than a quarter of a century, Benyamin Lukin, an insightful historian and an archivist at the CAHJP, has amassed hundreds of microfilmed archival documents, among them dozens related directly to the history of Hasidism from the least-visited Belarusian, Ukrainian, Polish, and Lithuanian archives.[6]

However, most archives in Eastern Europe are very different. Catalogues are exceptionally cumbersome, copying is restricted, and access to documents is critically limited. One must order the archival guides first, especially if they are published, preferably before traveling to the corresponding archival depository in Eastern Europe. One should keep in mind that the multivolume printed guides for archives such as the Russian Historical Archive in St. Petersburg (Rossiiskii gosudarstvennyi istoricheskii arkhiv, RGIA) or the Central Archives of Historical Records in Warsaw (Archiwum Główne Akt Dawnych, AGAD) contain general surveys and rather superficial inventories of the available collections of documents.[7] One must choose specific collections where documents related to Hasidim might be found, and then one can order more detailed inventories of these specific collections. Only then, with these second-level inventories in hand, is one able to request concrete files with documents, the titles of which might have little or no reference to Hasidic-related content. Recently, such quests have become somewhat easier due to several archival inventories produced within the framework of Project Judaica, administered by the Jewish Theological Seminary of America. These include thoroughly indexed search aids of Jewish documents in the archives of St. Petersburg, Moscow, Kiev, and central and southern Ukraine.[8] Marcin Wodziński, the leading Polish scholar of the Hasidic movement, painstakingly brought together a wealth of indispensable sources from the Polish archives in a neatly edited five-hundred-page volume.[9]

In order to find new sources related to individual Hasidic masters or a distinct Hasidic group, one needs the special skills of a historian familiar with the institutional, social, and political developments of the region. If one underestimates these developments, one would undermine the ability to accomplish one's quest successfully. Working on the first hundred years of Hasidism, one should keep in mind that the Aleksandrów, Bełz, Boian, Bobowa, Czarnobyl, Ger (Góra Kalwaria), Karolin, Lubavitch, Makarów, Talne, Vizhnitz (Vijniţa/Vyzhnytsia), and other Hasidic dynasties all emerged in their namesake shtetlekh, took their names from these shtetlekh (which in many cases were privately owned Polish towns), and were inseparably connected to the history of these towns and their complex interactions with Russian authorities, Polish noblemen, Jewish elites, Christian clergy, and Belarusian, Polish, and Ukrainian peasants. Rosman had to be an expert in the history of Polish private towns in order to realize that one needed the archive in Kraków to locate the Besht in Międzybóż, and not the Międzybóż (Medzhybizh) documents at the Ukrainian regional archives such as Zhytomyr and Vinnitsa, let alone the Central Historical Archive in Kiev (Tsentral'nyi derzhavnyi istorychnyi arkhiv Ukrainy, TsDIAU), where one would have logically started. Intuition also helps—not only a clear understanding for what a specific file contains, but also what it might reveal.

As a personal example, working at a regional archive in Kyiv (Kiev before 1991), I came across a three-hundred-page file entitled "The 1848 Data on the

Quantity of the Male and Female Jewish Population."[10] As a rule, files with such titles contain dozens of pages of tables meticulously prepared by regional clerks—and dozens of them were available at the same archive and in the published nineteenth-century governmental sources. One never knows what the dullest collection of data might contain; I decided to order the file. Among other socioeconomic descriptions, I found detailed information on the relations between one Ganski and the Twersky Hasidic family. The former was a Polish landlord and the owner of the town of Hornostajpol (Yid.: Hornosteypl). The latter were the founders of the Hornosteypl group in Hasidism (a branch of the Chernobyl dynasty descending from Menaḥem Naḥum of Czarnobyl). The socioeconomic data in the document that initially promised little turned out to be revealing: it proved a direct connection between the establishment of the tsadik's court in the town, the growth of the local Jewish population, and the rise of the local market economy—ultimately a mutually beneficial alliance between the Jewish Hasidic elite and the town owner.

Working through archival inventories, one must consider other, much less obvious, obstacles. In many archives in Poland, Moldova, and in most countries of the FSU (former Soviet Union), there is a quantitative restriction: one can order a maximum of five files daily. It does not matter if the file contains a two-page-long document or hundred-page ones; what matters is the number of files. A historian striving to create a full description of a Hasidic group (for example, early Chabad-Lubavitch or Ger Hasidim) or of a Hasidic master such as R. Shalom Rokeaḥ of Bełz or R. David Twersky of Skwira, would need months to identify, order, and digest the critical mass of primary documents. Therefore, the better one knows how the archive is organized internally, the better one's chances of working through a significant number of sources. Most archives reflect the institutional structure of the state or empire in which the archive was formed at the time when it was formed. To work with eighteenth- or nineteenth-century Polish documents, one has to know how pre- and postpartition Poland functioned institutionally, what specific subdivisions of the state dealt with issues related to Jews, how the institutional structure changed during the time of the Napoleonic invasion through Congress Poland, how the influential Senator Nowosilcow (Nikolai Nikolaevich Novosiltsev, the right hand of the Polish viceroy) ran and ruled the country with his own chancellery, and on what principles the Jewish Committee in Warsaw operated. The same is true of the Russian Empire, the USSR, and the successor independent states such as Ukraine, Belarus, and Lithuania. Governmental institutions change their names, their geographical subdivisions (for instance, a *województwo* in Poland or a *gubernia* in the Russian Empire), and their borders. Towns from one district (for example, Berdyczów [Rus.: Berdichev, Ukr.: Berdychiv, Yid.: Barditchov], so important in the development of late eighteenth-century Hasidism) might appear in three different institutional and geographical subordinations over just thirty years in the first half of the nineteenth century. An historian of the Hasidic movement will be better off when he or she is in full command of the political and cultural history of the entire region. Otherwise, one would be placing Hasidic leaders in a vacuum, losing the sense of their embeddedness in local economies, their spiritual influence, and their interaction with the local Catholic, Eastern Orthodox, or secular leadership.[11] And more practically, one would be unable to find the relevant sources.

The search aids, inventories, and catalogues reveal just the tip of the iceberg of what is really available in the archival depositories. Yet it is important to work with these guides first, before figuring out where one would like to start. The eighteenth-century documents on the denunciations against Hasidic leaders written to Emperor Pavel I in the wake of the Polish partitions can be found at the Russian National Archive of Old Documents (Rossiiskii gosudarstvennyi arkhiv drevnikh aktov, RGADA) in Moscow. Papers on the arrests and interrogations of R. Shneur Zalman of Lady, the founder of the Chabad movement, can be found at the Russian National Historical Archive (Rossiiskii gosudarstvennyi istoricheskii arkhiv, RGIA) in St. Petersburg, and documents from the archive of R. Yosef Yitzḥak Schneersohn ended up in the Special Archive (Osobyi arkhiv) in Moscow, the holdings of which Russian Federation authorities redistributed among other Moscow-based archives to avoid restitution claims.[12] Multiple documents reflecting the social aspects of the Hasidic movement in the southwestern regions of the Russian Empire in the nineteenth century can be found at the Central National Historical Archive of Ukraine (Tsentral'nyi derzhavnyi istorychnyi arkhiv Ukrainy, TsDIAU) and at the National Archive of the Kyiv Region (Derzhavnyi arkhiv kyivs'koi oblasti, DAKO), both in Kyiv. These and other archival sources are indispensable for anyone seeking to inscribe the Hasidic movement into the complex history of the Jewish people in Eastern Europe, to elucidate *why* Hasidism as a social movement of religious enthusiasm was exclusively an East European phenomenon, and to understand *how* its development depended on and was shaped by the external and internal aspects of Jewish life in the Russian Empire and Congress Poland. One more skill is required, in addition to an in-depth knowledge of general East European sociopolitical and institutional history: languages. The archival catalogues are routinely written in Ukrainian, Lithuanian, or Polish, and the contents of the documents described are in Russian.

Facilitators of Success

Historical imagination is a no less crucial skill. Without it, one would be searching for documents on R. David of Talne (the Tolner *Rebbe*) in Talne or Skwira, and documents on Elimelekh of Lizhensk (Leżajsk) in Leżajsk or nearby Rzeszów or Jarosław. One must consider a number of alternatives: Who was the owner of the town? Where did this or that Hasidic master live? What kind of institutions dealt with the Jews in that area? To whom were those institutions and their governmental clerks subordinate, and to whom did they report their findings? One must keep in mind that the most interesting contextual materials are oblique in character. Brainstorming possibilities of where to find something might take months, but the rewards will exceed expectations. There are many more documents on the Hasidic movement that one can still hunt for. We need to reconstruct the historical R. Levi Yitzḥak of Berdichev (Berdyczów), R. Aharon of Karolin (Rus.: Karlin), and R. Naḥman of Bratslav (Bracław), as well as the Hasidic masters arrested by the NKVD, such as R. Levi Yitzḥak Schneersohn of Dnepropetrovsk (Ekaterinoslav), those murdered in the concentration camps and ghettos, such as Kalonymos Kalman Shapira of Piaseczno (the "Esh Kodesh"), and those ransomed from the Nazis, such as R. Aharon Rokeaḥ of Bełz (the "Wonder Rabbi").

Many primary sources, some microfilmed, some not, await researchers in the existing libraries and collections. Two depositories must be singled out: first, the Department of Manuscripts and the Institute for Microfilmed Manuscripts at the Jerusalem National Library. Amassed over more than half a century, this formidable collection has dozens of underexplored manuscripts (in the original and on microfilm) by seventeenth- and eighteenth-century East European mystics, many of them anonymous, who formed the expanded circle of practical kabbalists of which the Besht was a part. Identifying these manuscripts and connecting them to the pre-Beshtian pietistic Hasidim and to the rising Hasidic movement still remains a high-priority scholarly desideratum. In addition, some well-known manuscripts also await reconsideration. For example, working at this collection, Gershon Hundert, scholar of early modern Poland–Lithuania, explored the unpublished *Divre binah* manuscript of Dov Ber Birkenthal (1723–1805), the preface to which, so far neglected by scholars, contains multiple critical remarks regarding the early Hasidic movement.[13]

Hundert's discovery was particularly significant since there is little external information on the early stages of the movement, with the exception of Salomon Maimon's *Autobiography*, in which Maimon described his travels to the court of Dov Ber of Mezrich early in the 1770s,[14] and later the invectives and excommunications by the mitnagedim against the rising Hasidim, assembled by Mordekhai Wilensky in a formidable two-volume collection.[15] Although Birkenthal's caustic assertions against Hasidim were predictably biased, some of his remarks remain of high value. A wealthy merchant and communal leader from Galicia with strong enlightened proclivities, Birkenthal linked the rising phenomenon of Hasidism to the appearance of kabbalistic works in East European houses of study and to the proliferation of the *ba'alei shem* and their kab-

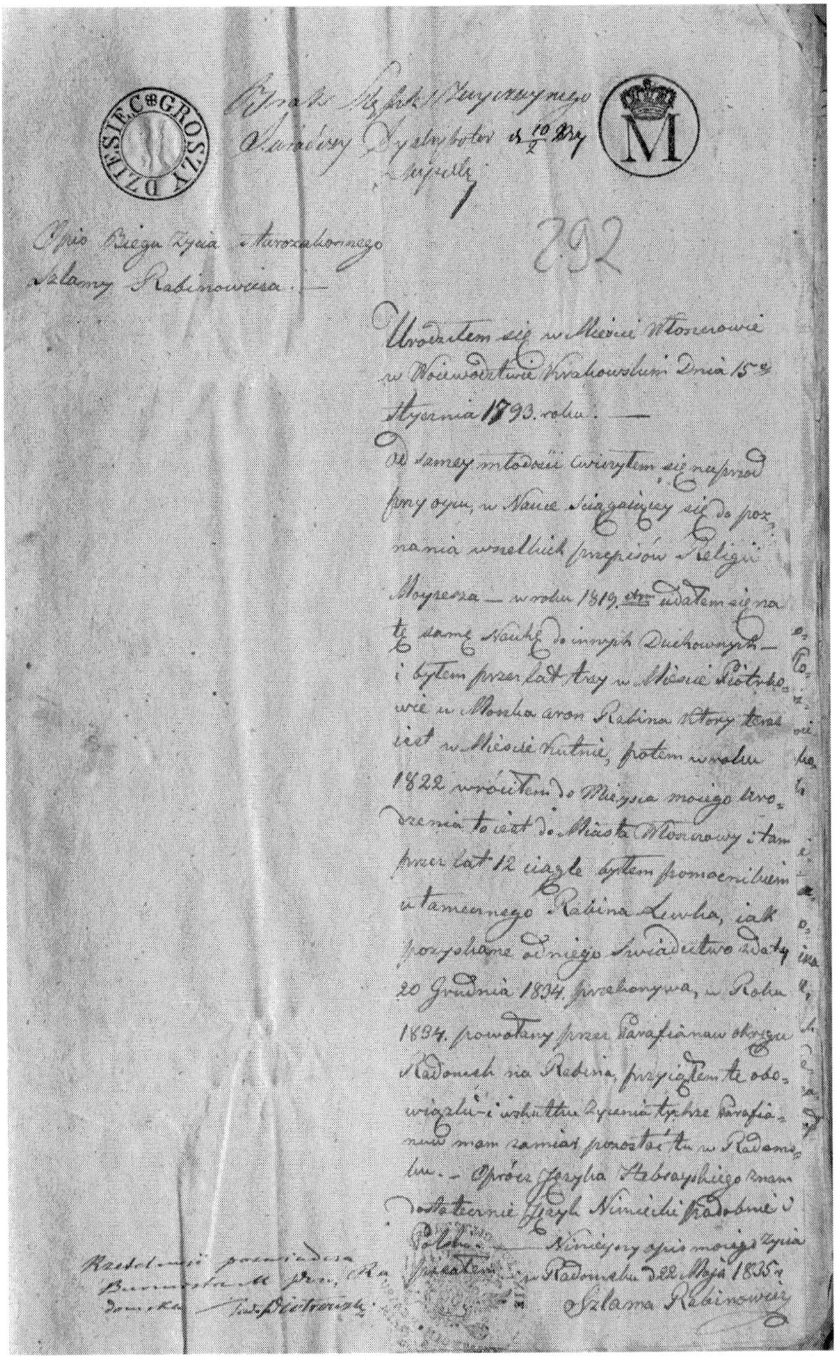

DZIESIEC GROSZY

Opis Biegu Życia Starozakonnego Szlamy Rabinowicza. —

292

Urodziłem się w Mieście Włoszczowie w Województwie Krakowskim Dnia 15go Stycznia 1793 roku. —

Od samey młodości ćwiczyłem się naprzód przy oycu, w Nauce ściągaiącey się do poznania wszelkich przepisów Religii Moyżesza — w roku 1819 [illegible] udałem się na tę samę Naukę do innych Duchownych — i byłem przez lat trzy w Mieście Piotrkowie u Monka aron Rabina który teraz iest w Mieście Kutnie, potem w roku 1822 wróciłem do Miasta mojego urodzenia to iest do Miasta Włoszczowy i tam przez lat 12 ciągle byłem pomocnikiem u tamecznego Rabina Lewka, iak [illegible] od niego Świadectwo z daty 20 Grudnia 1834 [illegible], w Roku 1834 powołany przez Parafianów okręgu Radomsk na Rabina, przyiąłem te obowiązki i skutkiem życzenia tychże Parafianów mam zamiar pozostać tu w Radomsku. — Oprócz Języka Hebrayskiego znam dostatecznie Język Niemiecki [illegible] i Polski — Niniejszy opis mojego życia pisałem w Radomsku d. 22 Maja 1835 r.

Szlama Rabinowicz

Figure 8.1. Official curriculum vitae of R. Shlomo Rabinowicz of Radomsko (1801–1866), written by himself. Source: Central Archives of Historical Records in Warsaw, collection: Komisja Województwa Kaliskiego, call no. 710, p. 292.

balistic books and amulets. His viewpoint is that of a moderate and conservative Talmudic scholar, critical of a broader contemporary mystical fashion, the spread of which proves that Hasidic ideas fell on fertile ground.

Another rich and underexplored depository is the Chabad-Lubavitch Library at 770 Eastern Parkway in Brooklyn, New York, with its formidable collection of Hasidic manuscripts, including the original writings of the leaders of the Schneersohn dynasty. Yehoshua Mondshine, a prolific and meticulous scholar, bibliographer, and researcher, as well as a Chabad rabbi, published a previously unknown manuscript of *Shivḥei ha-Besht* from the Brooklyn library, including in his edition a neat comparison of this source with existing editions and spelling out the differences between them.[16] Some of the voluminous writings of the Lubavitch tsadikim, including correspondence, rabbinic responsa, book endorsements, communal documents, excerpts from diaries, and legal and exegetical *novellae*, are included in the multivolume history of Chabad (in Poland, Lithuania, tsarist Russia, the Soviet Union, the land of Israel, and the United States) and in several important printed collections of Chabad sources edited by Shalom Dover Levin, chief librarian at the Chabad-Lubavitch headquarters.[17] Like Levin, several leading scholars representing various branches of the Hasidic movement who are also in charge of the archives or/and library of this branch have edited various periodicals that have published, with brief commentaries, some invaluable Hasidic documents, mostly from inaccessible private collections. These documents include the signatures of the Hasidic masters in communal registers (*pinkasim*), private correspondence, responsa, travel passes, spiritual wills, governmental documents, personal documents of the Hasidic *Rebbes*, and marginal notes containing legal and theological *novellae* that the Hasidic masters left in their books and that are of great value for the representatives of the movement, if not for Judaic learning in general. Among other editions of this type, one should consult, for this purpose, *Kovets Bet Aharon ve-Yisrael*, a periodical issued by the Karlin-Stolin Hasidim in Jerusalem.

Deciphering the Documents

Since Hasidim lived among other Jews and evolved into a full-fledged social movement within the larger Jewish community, the most revealing archival documents for the study of Hasidism reflect Jewish communal life in general and the role of Hasidim in particular. Among the underexplored documents of a more general character are the *pinkasim* or record books of the Jewish *kehilot* (communities) and *ḥavurot*—brotherhoods, confraternities, voluntary institutions, and professional guilds, all of which were not necessarily and not entirely Hasidic. These documents require excellent knowledge of rabbinical Hebrew, basic Yiddish, and Judaic liturgy, as well as profound paleographical skills. The

Jewish Theological Seminary of America has more than 140 such manuscripts, the Russian Museum of Ethnography in St. Petersburg about four (one explicitly Hasidic), the Russian National Library in Moscow about fifteen, and the Vernadsky Library of the National Academy of Sciences of Ukraine in Kyiv about one hundred. Some of them are originals; others are copies by experts in Jewish ethnography and paleography from the first quarter of the twentieth century. Copied by Yeḥiel Ravrebe, the 1755 society statute that the *mohalim* of Bar included in their record book gives some basic rules characteristic of any professional Jewish guild. The status stipulated the even distribution of commissions for circumcising Jewish baby boys, established the price for fulfilling the circumcision, threatened anyone who violated the rules of the society with excommunication, and prescribed the obligatory learning of Judaic traditional texts. The following year's addition to the statute also had several revealing details, one of which prescribed that society members assemble at the bed of a dying member of the community and read the *Book of Zohar* out loud next to him.[18]

This one line in an archival (in this case, a manuscript collection) document is difficult to overestimate. Scholars of Jewish mysticism have extensively debated the ways in which Hasidim brought Kabbalah to the masses, but little was known about how it really happened. This brief entry in the statute of the mid-eighteenth-century Podolian Jewish confraternity of specialists in circumcision gives an unexpected answer. The *Zohar*, the thirteenth-century kabbalistic compendium, was associated with pietistic learning traditions and with the elitist club of kabbalists, the *kloyz*. The book was written in Aramaic and was comprehensible only to educated members of the Jewish community. Multiple rabbinic regulations (*takkanot*), especially after the seventeenth-century Sabbatean controversy, repeatedly introduced restrictions regarding the study of the *Zohar*, namely stating that the book contained the essential esoteric understanding of the Torah, was designated for dedicated mystics, and had been kept away from ordinary Jews.

What the *mohalim* of Bar were prescribing to their members represented a radical change in the established handling of the *Zohar*. If the *Zohar* entailed mystical powers, then the kabbalists should use this book to help the agonizing Jewish body release its immortal Jewish soul. The previously restricted and elitist book was now brought to the public and read out loud so that everybody present—the dying person of either gender, family members, women and children gathered in the room—was exposed to it. On the other hand, it was not so much the esoteric book itself that was the change (printed editions of the *Zohar* already circulated in the Polish-Lithuanian Commonwealth in the late sixteenth century) but rather its new role in the Jewish community. From then on, even illiterate Jews in the Jewish community of Bar, not only ordinary ones, would become familiar with the *Zohar* as a major source of healing and comfort. The kabbalistic book gained the power of a new liturgical text and became part of a special ritual to bring together representatives of the Jewish pietistic elites and ordinary Jews. Just one paragraph in a communal source shed brand-new light on the transformation of the elitist and pietistic Hasidim into much more communal-oriented Hasidim.[19] Of course, we do not know whether this practice was immediately implemented throughout the Podolia and Volhynia provinces in the 1750s to 1770s; nor do we know how many people actually became adherents of the rising new movement.

The question of whom we call Hasidim and how we mark their numbers from the first fifty years of the rise of the movement opens up a crucial aspect of archival work: how one interprets the sources one finds. The depositories of the Central Archive of Historical Records in Warsaw contain the correspondence of Polish bureaucrats from the early nineteenth century, complaints of Jews from a number of Polish towns where Hasidim seem to have suppressed the traditional Jewish leadership, requests of leaders of Hasidic groups to the authorities for the establishment of a new prayer house, and statistics of the Jewish population assembled by local clerks. Glenn Dynner and Marcin Wodziński drew their material from almost the same pool of archival sources and almost the same figures in order to measure the magnitude of the spread of Hasidim in Poland in the late eighteenth and early nineteenth centuries. Both scholars questioned the famous adage of the founders of East European Jewish historiography, who claimed that in the last quarter of the eighteenth century, Hasidism captured the territories of Russia, Lithuania, and Poland. Both presented their vision of how to read the sources, how to consider people usually circumvented by statisticians (most importantly, women), and how cautiously to dismiss the biases of groups presenting either purposefully boosted figures (missionaries, Hasidim, enlightened thinkers) or underestimated figures (Polish bureaucrats). Amazingly, the two scholars presented fundamentally opposing views: Dynner argued that Hasidim represented a significant part, up to one-third (more than 30 percent), of the Jewish population in Congress Poland, whereas Wodziński maintained that the numbers were small, probably about 10 percent.[20] These conclusions highlight that one must keep in mind that archival sources, even the most trustworthy, are man-made, reflecting the agenda of those who produce them and serving a certain purpose that might not be the most obvious one. Archival sources should therefore be cautiously balanced with other types of evidence.

Back to the Sławuta Affair

Some Hasidic documents—or documents with strong Hasidic underpinnings—may illuminate the most dramatic moments in Jewish history in general, as well as its intersection with Russian and Polish history, particularly in the era of the state-sponsored Enlightenment (under the rule of Alexander I, Nicholas I, and Alexander II). However, such documents need to be carefully contextualized and inscribed into a broader background. This context gives the document its general sense; the document modifies the meaning of the events and eventually contributes to a reassessment of the context. This dialectical interaction of the archival document with the general context may be explained by the following example. Two Sławuta dwellers, Mordko (Mordekhai) and Beila Shapiro, sent a petition to Count Dmitrii Bibikov (1782–1870), the general governor of Kiev, Volhynia, and Podolia Provinces:

> Forty-nine years have passed since our father, Sławuta third-guild merchant Moshko, son of Pinkhas Shapiro, established in the town of Sławuta a printing press, which he brought to perfection through his persevering work and significant expenditures, involving all the family members in its operation. The printing press began to operate in 1790, based on a privilege provided by the Lieutenant General Count Hieronim Sanguszko under the Polish king Stanisław August, then ruler of all the Western Polish provinces. After which, with the return of these provinces to Russia in 1801, the Volhynia province administration approved the right to publish books with a preliminary endorsement of them by the Riga censorship committee, and finally, in most recent times, namely on December 20, 1829, our father received a corresponding privilege on his printing press from [Pavel Ivanovich] Averin, the former Volhynia civil governor. Our father assiduously followed the rules of censorship, despite all the newly introduced changes. He published books with great diligence such as one can expect only from a loyal son of the fatherland. Ultimately, when our father reached seventy-five, he passed the management of the printing press on to his son and our brother, Shmuel Aba Shapiro, and this was for the benefit of the entire family, since the will of the old man came true when he saw his son justifying the trust of his parent and the goals of the government.
>
> It seemed that peaceful old age was secured for our father; but what happened? Fate suddenly struck him like a thunderbolt. He found himself at the edge of the precipice and suddenly lost his tranquility, patrimony, freedom, and children, and even more painful—his honor, which became marred in the eyes of the government. In a word, he, poor creature, lost everything that was for him dear and holy!
>
> Your Excellency, you, as the chief authority, are well aware of an accident which occurred in the town of Sławuta—the suicide of the Jew Protagain, found hanged in the hallway of a prayer house.
>
> People who did not wish our father, Shapiro, well, took advantage of this accident, interpreting it in a dishonest way, baselessly libeling the Jews who allegedly murdered this Protagain, basing their slander on a false interpretation

of a statement in the book of Jewish law published with the censor's approbation. They managed to draw the attention of the central administration and the autocrat.

According to the highest order, Prince Vasilchikov, the adjunct of His Majesty the Emperor, was sent to investigate this case, and as our brothers Shapiro, Pinkhas and Aba, were found implicated in this case, they were arrested and the printing press sealed (as it becomes clear from the attached governmental copy of Your Excellency's no. 180 resolution) until the resolution of the case is made and our brothers found guiltless.

Because of this, we have not finished printing many books already approved by censorship, many of the first-time published books have been released and distributed among subscribers, while others were stopped. Two paper manufactures producing paper exclusively for book printing and leased by the printing-press from a landlord, have now caused a considerable loss, since the paper is stockpiled in large quantities, which costs considerable sums of money. In addition due to the disruption of the printing-press operation, the paper loses its value, while the contractors demand the payment of the agreed sums. Commerce is down, credits are disrupted, the sums of money owed to us are not forthcoming as no books are delivered. In a word, ruin is reigning and our entire family is bereft of daily bread. This is a living example of human fate!

The main reason to shut down our printing press was the report of Your Excellency's [representative] Count Guriev, which alleged that it had been publishing forbidden Jewish books. Apparently, this report was the result exclusively of a number of books from our printing press provided by [Ya'akov] Lips, as it becomes clear from the resolution of the Ministry of the Interior no. 9,518 a copy of which Your Excellency will find attached.

Your Excellency! Could you imagine how fate mercilessly threw us into calamity! How could one have suspected our printing press of anything illegal before requesting all the endorsements of the censorship committee for the mentioned books? We are firm in our belief that if the documents had been requested from us, we, without doubt, would not only have been able to prove with the available documents that all the published books had been endorsed by the censors, but also that the censorship committee had rightly allowed these books to be printed. We would have stated that, 1) the translated books provided by Count Vasilchikov and Lips had really been approved and published before the 1826 statute, that they were approved and published according to the 1804 statute [on censorship], which in its paragraph no. 21 states that "if a suspected place [in a book] has a double meaning, it is plausible to interpret it in a positive sense for its author, rather than persecute it." Based on this, the censorship committee approved these books. Another proof is that, 2) in the report to His Majesty the Emperor, the Minister of the People's Education argued that, as far as the new June 19, 1826, statute is concerned, the censorship based on the 1804 statute was insufficient as it did not prevent the harm to enlightenment caused by bad books! Therefore, any contradictory statements in the books approved on the basis of the 1804 statute should not be considered as proof that these books had been wrongly approved for publication, and furthermore, as time goes by the same allegedly suspicious books have been again approved according to the new 1826 statute, which excluded many statements [now reclassified as suspicious].

We suffer for no reason and find ourselves in a horrible situation. We are convinced that our brothers acted legally. We yearn for justice, which must sooner or later triumph over slander. We expect that our printing press and our brothers will regain the freedom they deserve. Yet cruel fate seems to take from us even this last hope regarding our printing press.

After the Highest resolution ordered the closure of all Jewish printing presses except two, one in Vilna and one in Kiev, for the sake of better control over them, some people decided to exploit the troubles of their brethren and eradicate our hope for the resolution of our case and for a merciful return of our printing press to Kiev. Those people declared their intent to establish a printing press and request a privilege, which in the case that it is granted, would bring our downfall to a final ruin.

Only one hope remains for us—the protection of Your Excellency. We beseech you, look with mercy at our troubling situation! Be so kind as to give orders so that all the above circumstances and the attached documents (privilege no. 36,255; documents of the Vilna Censorship Committee, Nowogród Wołyński [Rus.: Novograd-Volynskii] city council no. 422, also Zasław Land court no. 1822), proving our diligent and legitimate book-print production of a quality that supersedes all other books prints, be forwarded to the corresponding authority.

Your Excellency, be our protector, do not allow other Jews to establish a printing press in Kiev! Take into consideration the rights given to our father, the magnitude of our industry and the long-term management of 17 printing-machines and 700 puds [c. 25,000 pounds] of type, let alone other necessities, and also the unnecessary suffering of our brothers, and in general, the entire ruin of our family—we should have the advantage of transferring our printing press to Kiev.[21]

Mordekhai and Beila Shapiro were brother and sister of the famous Hasidic family in Sławuta, children of Moshe Shapiro (the founder of the largest Jewish printing press in Ukraine), and grandchildren of R. Pinḥas of Korets from the intimate circle of the Maggid of Mezrich and the Besht. They hired a scribe, Hersh Ber Feinberg of Zasław (today Iziaslav), to put their petition on paper. The document contains some well-known names of leading Polish rulers and Russian administrators and several illustrious Jewish names. It discusses book production, paper manufacturing, the book-printing industry, economic competition, a case of suicide, and governmental regulations regarding censorship and Jewish books.

The petition is meticulously composed—precisely because it presents the problem from a predominantly socioeconomic standpoint and carefully neutralizes any ideological and religious underpinnings. The rhetoric of the document is fascinating. The Shapiros emphasize idiosyncratic Russian values: the legacy of their forefathers (sanctity of the printing press); the legitimacy of their business from the viewpoint of the Polish and the Russian regimes; their family character; the loyalty to Russia of the printing-press owners and their respect for state laws; the high profitability of their business for the state; and the general usefulness of their enterprise, for which they use a Russian word meaning both "education" and "enlightenment." All of that should have fallen on the receptive ears of the enlightened Russian bureaucrats who knew well that Nicholas I's administrators were trying to enforce enlightened reforms on the Jews.

It is as important to reconstruct what the document says as what it leaves out. This particular petition is remarkably reticent about the 1836 religious accusation against the entire Hasidic press and Hasidic book print, which triggered the ban of the Jewish presses.[22] It does not even mention the accusation against the Shapiro family of having purportedly published books with explicit anti-Christian and obscurantist messages. And it passes over the persecution of the Hasidic printers responsible for publishing books of Kabbalah in the entire Volhynia and Podolia areas, although this was an event of significant magnitude: some twenty presses fell victim. The petition does not contain a single word about any Hasidim and does not even hint at any role of Hasidism in this case. The rhetoric of the petition does not obfuscate what actually is at stake.

Contextualizing the Document

The 1836 calamity known as the Sławuta Case was the focus of Saul Ginsburg, a younger contemporary of Simon Dubnow and a wonderful historian in his own right. Ginsburg described in great detail how an anti-Judaic-minded Russian envoy with the help of some local Jewish informers (such as Ya'akov Lips, mentioned in the petition) managed to transform the family drama of Sławuta typesetter Lazar Protagain, known for his domestic violence, drunkenness, and depression, into a Hasidic war against the rationally inclined critics of Kabbalah and mysticism. A suicidal drunkard was turned into a martyr of the Enlightenment, and his bosses, the Shapiros, into murderous fanatics. It all revolved around books on Kabbalah and Hasidism, printed in disproportionately large quantities in the Jewish printing presses of Ukraine, such as the one in Sławuta. These mystical books that celebrated the insights of the Hasidic masters, the acts of the wonderworking kabbalists, the secret meanings of Judaic liturgy—together with their printers—the regime found guilty. Those responsible for the production of mystical books—together with the books—violated what was called at that time the "enlightened intentions" of the government and should bear responsibility. What the censors drawing from the 1804 censorship statute had allowed, and the censors using the 1826 statute had confirmed, was now strictly forbidden. The career-seeking informers who used the governmental rhetoric of Enlightenment to push their agenda wrote one denunciation after another to the bureaucrats in Kiev and St. Petersburg, seeking to curb the spread of Hasidism by disrupting Hasidic book-publishing activity. As a result of their denunciations and governmental investigation, the owners of the Sławuta press were arrested, accused of murder, lashed, and exiled indefinitely outside the Pale of Settlement.

By the same token, the books were penalized too. Misinformed by unscrupulous bureaucrats, Nicholas subsequently ordered all the Jewish printing presses shut down for allegedly publishing books circumventing censorship. The only two printing presses allowed to operate were in Vilna and in Kiev. The people who contributed to the downfall of the Shapiros sought to secure a governmental endorsement for the establishment of a printing press in Kiev. However, since at that time Kiev was excluded from the Pale of Jewish Settlement, and the Shapiros managed to convince the government that they knew the market, had a paper-manufacturing industry, and boasted experience in a business nobody else knew how to operate, the second printing press was instead established in Zhitomir, and the privilege to operate it was granted to the Shapiros. The price was high: certain highly popular works on Hasidism and Kabbalah disappeared from their inventory.

The petition of the Shapiros marks the end of the era of dozens of free Jewish printing presses in the Tsarist Empire—and opens a new one, with just two competing presses in Zhitomir and Vilna under much stricter government supervision. It shows how the elitist Jews of formidable Hasidic pedigree used the rhetoric of the Russian administration in order to regain control of the highly lucrative enterprise. The petition does not explain the significance of the controversy but indirectly throws light on an intense ideological battle between Hasidic entrepreneurs fostering the spread of the Hasidic movement and those who sought to suppress the movement and who accused Hasidim of spreading antirational, hence anti-Enlightenment, fanaticism. The Shapiros appealed to the authorities using the same language of profitability, loyalty, rationalism, and legalism. Hasidim—alleged obscurantists and fanatics—were in fact mastering how to survive in new ideological circumstances and how to manipulate the new political vocabulary.

For a scholar of Hasidism, finding such a document as the *Sandakim* Confraternity of Bar or the petition of the Shapiros is tantamount to finding a precious gem. But this gem sits loose without a setting. Building the context and honing the skill of contextualization create the setting, which eventually gives meaning (or shape) to the archival gem. Only within the contextual setting can one prove the distinct nature of an archival document and divulge its unique meaning. Therefore, the archival quest for Hasidic documents should start with a thorough study of the history, geography, languages, and cultures of the people among whom the Hasidim dwelled.

SUGGESTED READING

Online Archival Aids, Databases, and Electronic Catalogues

http://baza.archiwa.gov.pl/sezam/index.php—the best available general database of Polish archival sources (in Polish only).

http://www.archives.gov.ua/Publicat/Guidebooks/—list of references to the online version of the Ukrainian archival guides (only basic info on archival holdings; in Ukrainian only).

http://web.nli.org.il/sites/nlis/en/manuscript—Ktiv digitalized collection of the Hebrew National Library manuscripts (brief descriptions in Hebrew and English).

http://cahjp.nli.org.il/—a searchable guide to the documentary collections at the Central Archives for the History of Jewish People in Jerusalem (with brief references in English).

Published and Indexed Archival Guides on the Most Important FSU Holdings Containing Documents on East European Jewish History

Ivanov, Aleksandr, Mark Kupovetskii, and Aleksandr Lokshin, *Dokumenty po istorii i kul'ture evreev v arkhivakh Sankt-Peterburga: Putevoditel'* (St. Petersburg: Mir, 2011).

Kupovetskii, Mark, et al., *Dokumenty po istorii i kul'ture evreev v arkhivakh Moskvy: Putevoditel'* (Moscow and New York: Rossiiskii Gosudarstvennyi Gumanitarnyi Universitet, 1997).

Melamed, Efim, ed., *Dokumenty po istorii i kul'ture evreev v regional'nykh arkhivakh Ukrainy: Putevoditel'. Volynskaia, Zhitomirskaia, Rovenskaia, Cherkasskaia oblasti* (Moscow: Rossiiskii Gosudarstvennyi Gumanitarnyi Universitet, 2009).

Melamed, Efim, and Mark Kupovetskii, ed., *Dokumenty po istorii i kul'ture evreev v arkhivakh Kieva: Putevoditel'* (Moscow/New York: Jewish Theological Seminary of America, Russian State Univeristies for the Humanities, State Committee on Archives of Ukraine, 2006).

Melamed, Efim, and Dmitrii Eliashevich, *Arkhivnaia iudaika Rossii, Ukrainy i Belorussii: Materialy dlia ukazatelia literatury* (St. Petersburg: Peterburgskii universitet iudaiki, 2001).

Woszczyński, Bolesław, and Violetta Urbaniak, eds., *Źródła archiwalne do dziejów Żydów w Polsce* (Warsaw: DiG, 2001).

Published Collections of Documents on the History of the Hasidic Movement in Russia and Poland

Wilensky, Mordekhai, *Ḥasidim u-mitnagedim: Toldot ha-pulmus she-benehem*, 2 vols. (Jerusalem: Mosad Bialik, 1970).

Wodziński, Marcin, ed., *Źródła do dziejów chasydyzmu w Królestwie Polskim, 1815–1867, w zasobach polskich archiwów państwowych = Hasidism in the Kingdom of Poland, 1815–1867: Historical Sources in the Polish State Archives* (Kraków: Wydawnictwo Austeria, Institute for the History of Polish Jewry and Israel-Poland Relations, Tel Aviv University, 2011).

Published Collections of Sources on Specific Episodes of Hasidic History

Deich, Genrikh, *Tsarskoe pravitel'stvo i khasidskoe dvizhenie v Rossii: Arkhivnye dokumenty* (New Jersey: G. Deich, 1994).
Karlinsky, Nahum, *Histoṛyah she-ke-neged: "Igrot ha-hasidim me-Erets-Yisrael": Ha-ṭeḳsṭ veha-ḳonṭeḳsṭ* (Jerusalem: Mosad Ben-Zvi, 1998).
Kovets igra de-ve hilula: leket igrot kodesh mi-kitve yad rabo (Bnei Brak: Mekhon Ginze Bet Tchernobyl, 1996).
Mandelbaum, Raphael, *From the Wellsprings of Alexander: Insight and Inspirations Based on the Writing of Rebbes of the Alexander Dynasty* (Lakewood, NJ: Machon Sofrim, 2013).
Margolin, Ron Pinḥas, *Hafnamat ḥayei ha-dat veha-maḥshavah be-doroteha ha-rishonim shel ha-ḥasidut: Mekoroteha u-vesiseha ha-episṭemologiyim* (Jerusalem: Magnes Press, 1999).
Schneersohn, Joseph Isaac, *The Debate in Minsk: From the Diary of Rabbi Yosef Yitschak of Lubavitch* (New York: Kehot, 2016).
Schneersohn, Shalom Dov Baer, *Igrot kodesh me-et Moharshav* (Brooklyn: Kehot, 1982–2012).

NOTES

1. The results of his research were summarized in Moshe J. Rosman, *The Lords' Jews: Magnate-Jewish Relations in the Polish-Lithuanian Commonwealth during the Eighteenth Century* (Cambridge: Harvard University Press for Harvard Ukrainian Research Institute, 1990).

2. *Shivḥei ha-Besht. In Praise of the Baal Shem Tov. The Earliest Collection of Legends about the Founder of Hasidism*, trans. and ed. D. Ben-Amos and J. R. Minz (Bloomington and London: Indiana University Press, 1970).

3. New edition with a substantial preface summarizing the polemical debates around this book, Moshe Rosman, *Founder of Hasidism: A Quest for the Historical Baal Shem Tov* (Oxford: Littman Library of Jewish Civilization, 2013), xxxv–lvii. Rosman's contribution was discussed and celebrated at the panel "Moshe Rosman's *Founder of Hasidism*: A Decade Later," organized by Glenn Dynner and me at the 38th Annual Conference of the Association of Jewish Studies, December 17–19, 2006, San Diego, CA.

4. *Shivḥei ha-Besht*, 211, 215, 216.

5. See Adam Teller, "Masoret Słuck al reshit darko shel ha-Besht," in *Meḥkarei ḥasidut*, ed. I. Etkes, D. Assaf, and J. Dan (Jerusalem: National and University Library, 1999), 15–38. His findings reinforced some of the key points made by Rosman. See also the discussion of Teller's findings in Emmanuel Etkes, *The Besht: Magician, Mystic, and Leader* (Waltham, MA: Brandeis University Press, 2004), 221–223.

6. See Benyamin Lukin, "The Creation of a Documentary Collection on the History of Russian Jewry at the Central Archives for the History of the Jewish People," *Slavic and East European Information Resources* 4 (2003), 2–3:17–36; Lukin, "Documents on the Emigration of Russian Jews via Galicia, 1881–82, in the Central Archives for the History of the Jewish People in Jerusalem," *Gal-Ed* 21 (2007), 101–117; Lukin, "Israeli Archives with Material on Russian Jewish History: The Central Archives for the History of the Jewish People," *Jews in Eastern Europe* 1 (1996), 29:65–81.

7. A. R. Sokolov and D. I. Raskin, eds., *Rossiiskii gosudarstvennyi istoricheskii arkhiv: Putevoditel v 4-kh tt.* (St. Petersburg: Statis, 2000–2008); Jadwiga Karwasińska, ed., *Archiwum Główne w Warszawie: Przewodnik po zespołach* (Warsaw: Państwowe Wydawnyctwo Naukowe, 1975); Franciszka Ramotowska, ed., *Archiwum Główne Akt Dawnych w Warszawie. Przewodnik po zasobie*, vol, 2: *Epoka porozbiorowa* (Warsaw: DiG, 1988).

8. For the list of bibliographic references, see the suggested reading list for this chapter.

9. Marcin Wodziński, ed., *Żrodła do dziejów chasydyzmu w Królestwie Polskim, 1815–1867, w zasobach polskich archiwów państwowych* (Kraków: Austeria, 2011).

10. Derzhavni arkhiv Kyivs'koi oblasty, fond 1, opys 336, sprava 4051 ("Svedenia o kolichestve muzhskogo i zhenskogo evreiskogo naselenia," 1848).

11. For the critique of such works, see my "*Hasidei de'ar'a* and *hasidei de-kokhvaya*': Two Trends in Modern Jewish Historiography," *AJS Review* 32 (2008) 1:141–167.

12. See David E. Fishman, Mark Kupovetskii, Vladimir Kuzelenkov, ed., *Nazi-Looted Jewish Archives in Moscow: A Guide to Jewish Historical and Cultural Collections in the Russian State Military Archive* (Scranton, PA: University of Scranton Press, 2010).

13. Gershon David Hundert, "The Introduction to *Divre binah* by Dov Ber of Bolechów: An Unexamined Source for the History of Jews in the Lwów Region in the Second Half of the Eighteenth Century," *AJS Review* 33 (2009), 2:225–269.

14. Solomon Maimon, *Autobiography*, trans. J. Clark Murray (Chicago: University of Illinois Press, 2001); on the accuracy of Maimon's recollections, see David Assaf, "Torato ha-Magid r. Dov-Ber mi-Mezrich be-zikhronot Shlomo Maimon," *Zion* 71 (2006) 1:99–101.

15. Mordekhai Wilensky, *Ḥasidim umitnagedim: Toldot ha-pulmus she-benehem*, 2 vols. (Jerusalem: Mossad Byalik, 1970).

16. Yehoshua Mondshine, *Shivḥei ha-Besht: Faksimil mi-ktav-ha-yad ha-yeḥidi ha-noda' lanu* (Jerusalem: Y. Mondshain, 1982).

17. Shalom Dover Levin, ed., *Mi-bet ha-genazim: Mikhtavim, mismakhim u-khetubot, temunot ve-tsiyurim, tefilin, megilot va-ḥafatsim, sefarim nedirim ve-khitvei yad mi-bet ha-genazim asher be-Sifryat Agudat ḥasidei ḥabad* (Brooklyn, NY: Sifriyat Agudat Hasidei Habad, 2009); Levin, ed., *Kovets kaf menaḥem-av shishim shanah: Leket mikhtavim me-arkhiyono shel Leṿi Yitzḥak Schneersohn* (Brooklyn, NY: Kehot, 2004).

18. The Vernadsky National Library of Ukraine, Orientalia Department, *Pinkasim* collection, font 321, opys 1, dielo 3 [op. 4]: [*Pinkas shel ḥevrat mohalim*], Bar (Podolia, 1755–1775) [Copyist: Yeḥiel Ravrebe], l. 2. On the copyist, an excellent Judaica specialist, paleographer, and historian shot by the NKVD (*Narodnyi komissariat vnutrennikh del*, the People's Commissariat of Internal Affairs, the USSR secret service in the 1930), see Abraham Greenbaum, "Yehiel Ravrebe, Jewish Poet and Scholar," *Jews and the Jewish Topics in the Soviet Union and Eastern Europe* 17 (1992), 27–36.

19. For more on that issue, see Yohanan Petrovsky-Shtern, "Hasidism, *Havurot* and the Jewish Street," *Jewish Social Studies* 10 (2004), 2:20–54.

20. See Glenn Dynner, "The Hasidic Conquest of Small-Town Central Poland, 1754–1818," *Polin* 17 (2004), 51–81, and Marcin Wodziński, *Haskalah and Hasidism in the Kingdom of Poland: A History of Conflict* (Oxford: Oxford: Littman Library of Jewish Civilization, 2005), 94–115, especially n62 on p. 97. The debate about statistics and the demography of Hasidim turned into a major conversation about the usage of the sources; see Marcin Wodziński, "How Many *Hasidim* Were There in Congress Poland? On the Demographics of the Hasidic Movement in Poland during the First Half of the Nineteenth Century," *Gal-Ed* 19 (2004), 13–49; Glenn Dynner, "How Many 'Hasidim' Were There Really in Congress Poland? A Response to Marcin Wodziński," *Gal-Ed* 20 (2006), 91–104; Marcin Wodziński, "How Should We Count 'Hasidim' in Congress Poland? A Reply to Glenn Dynner," ibid., 105–120. For a summary of the debate, see my "*Hasidei de'ar'a* and *Hasidei dekokhvaya*': Two Trends in Modern Jewish Historiography," *AJS Review* 32 (2008), 1:157–159, and Antony

Polonsky, *Jews in Poland and Russia* (Oxford: Littman Library of Jewish Civilization, 2010), 2:296–297.

21. Central Archives for the History of the Jewish People in Jerusalem (CAHJP), HM8925.3 (Central National Historical Archive of Ukraine [TsDIAU], font 442, opusk 1, sprava 2349, "Po prosheniiam evreiskikh kuptsov i obshch[estvennykh] deiatelei ob otkrytii evreiskoi tipografii v Kieve," 1836), ark. 82b–86.

22. Saul Ginsburg, *The Drama of Slavuta*, trans. from the Yiddish by E. Prombaum (Lanham: University Press of America, 1991); for the most recent treatment of the ban, see my *The Golden Age Shtetl: A New History of Jewish Life in East Europe* (Princeton, NY: Princeton University Press, 2015), 329–339; for the heretofore neglected circumstances leading to the 1836 ban, see my "Haim Vital, Founders of Other Faiths, and the Censors of Nicholas I," in *Mutant Biographies, Hostile or Appropriative*, ed. E. Nissan (Turnhout: Brepols, 2019), forthcoming.

CHAPTER 9

Press

David Assaf

The Jewish press printed in the Russian Empire and Congress Poland from the 1860s to World War I is a comprehensive and important corpus of primary source material for the history of Hasidism and its followers. This is especially true of newspapers published in Hebrew, and to a lesser extent of those written in Yiddish, Polish, German, and Russian. As for Hasidism in the interwar period, the material embedded in the hundreds of Jewish newspapers published in Poland (mainly in Yiddish), Palestine (in Hebrew), and the United States (in Yiddish and English) is invaluable. The history of Hasidism after the Holocaust and after the establishment of the State of Israel is also covered extensively in newspapers and other mass-communication media. This veritable treasure trove has been neglected and underutilized, mainly due to a lack of efficient indices and search keys, as well as inconvenient accessibility to the newspapers themselves.

What Can We Find in the Press about Hasidism?

The Hebrew newspapers published in the second half of the nineteenth century originally appeared as weeklies or biweeklies, and only from 1886 did some of them adopt a daily format. The five most important newspapers (listed in order of appearance) were as follows:

1. *Ha-magid* (1856–1903), published in Lyck, Prussia (today Ełk, Poland), and later in Berlin, Kraków, and Vienna[1]
2. *Ha-melits* (1860–1904), first published in Odessa, and from 1871 in Saint Petersburg[2]
3. *Ha-tsefirah* (1862, 1874–1931), published in Warsaw, with a short period of publication in Berlin[3]

4. *Ha-levanon* (1863–1886), first published in Jerusalem, and then in Paris, Mainz, and London[4]
5. *Ha-yom* (1886–1888), the first Hebrew-language daily, published in St. Petersburg.[5]

Although *Ha-yom* (Today) was published for only two years, the competition it generated among readers was the impetus for *Ha-melits* and *Ha-tsefirah* to change their respective formats to daily newspapers in 1886.

Modern newspapers in Yiddish also played an important role. Especially significant in terms of sources for the history of Hasidism was *Kol mevaser*, published in Odessa from 1862 to 1873, first as an addition to *Ha-melits* and later as an independent newspaper.[6] Another important weekly in Yiddish was *Yidishes folks-blat*, published from 1881 to 1890.[7] *Der fraynd* (The Friend), the first daily newspaper in Yiddish, began to appear in 1903, first in St. Petersburg and later in Warsaw. Published until 1913, it heralded the appearance of the two large daily newspapers that were published in Warsaw in the interwar period: *Haynt* (Today; 1906–1939) and *Der moment* (1910–1939). In the United States, the most prominent newspaper was the *Forverts* (The Forward), which began publication in New York in 1897 and continued to appear as a daily newspaper until 1983.

In addition to the large newspapers that appeared on a daily, weekly, or biweekly basis, there were also important local Hebrew weekly journals, among them *Ha-carmel*, published from 1860 to 1880 in Vilna, Lithuania (in 1870 it switched to a monthly focused more on scholarly articles), and *Ivri anokhi* (Jewish Am I), which was published from 1865 to 1890 in Lwów (Lviv/Lemberg) and Brody, Eastern Galicia. To complete the picture we should also mention the many monthly, quarterly, and annual Hebrew publications that appeared during the nineteenth century and that were devoted mainly to editorial, literary, and scholarly articles, but which also contained important material on Hasidism. The most prominent of these was the monthly *Ha-shaḥar* (The Dawn), published in Vienna from 1868 to 1885 under the editorship of Peretz Smolenskin, and which featured stories, poetry, and anti-Hasidic satires, as well as editorials that dealt with Hasidism, usually from a negative and critical perspective.

These newspapers and journals, in both Hebrew and Yiddish, all of which have been digitized and scanned and are easily accessible via the Internet (see below), contain valuable and as yet untapped information about Hasidism and its world.[8]

Over time, these newspapers, which initially for the most part expressed an enlightened perspective and naturally contributed to the shaping of this outlook, turned into a much broader cultural phenomenon, able to encompass many different and even competing viewpoints.[9] The newspapers, with their multiple voices and opinions, were disseminated and read by millions of Jews, not only in Eastern Europe but also in Jewish communities across the globe, from the Ottoman Empire in the east to the United States in the west. In this way, newspapers not only succeeded in connecting Jews spread throughout the Jewish diaspora but paradoxically were also a unifying factor in a new virtual community. They provided an open arena for public discourse, and within their framework diverse and even contradictory voices were heard with regard to numerous questions on Jews' agendas.[10]

The prevailing assumption that these newspapers (with the exception of *Halevanon*, which was identified with Orthodox circles) were maskilic and therefore promoted an anti-Hasidic agenda does not do justice to the complexity, diversity, or dynamic development of attitudes toward Hasidism, among both maskilic circles and the newspapers themselves. A systematic review of the perception and reflection of Hasidism on the pages of these newspapers shows the diversity of opinion among the maskilic community and its multiple voices. One could read the opinions of prominent leaders and spokespersons of the Haskalah movement regarding Hasidism in stories, polemics, and satires that appeared in an array of printed forums, but for rank-and-file maskilim, those who were not destined for fame, newspapers were often the only outlet open to them to express their views. Furthermore, because of its continuous chronological nature, the newspaper format reflects developments in the maskilic outlook in general and regarding Hasidism in particular, and enables one to point to a variety of views about Hasidism, from the negative and mocking, through indifference and empathy, and even to expressions of nostalgia and admiration. A survey of these sources offers a more balanced picture of the complex relationship between maskilim and Hasidim than we derive from the traditional sources.[11]

The most prominent example of this is the newspaper *Ha-melits* and its founder and editor Alexander Zederbaum, who was known by his pen name *Erez* (cedar, a Hebrew translation of his surname). Born in Zamość, Poland, Zederbaum (1816–1893) was intimately familiar with Hasidism and acquainted with some of its contemporary tsadikim,[12] and therefore over decades he showed a special interest in the movement and its adherents. Even though he rejected Hasidism and its way of life, he understood its centrality in Jewish life and viewed it as a legitimate movement whose leaders allegedly collaborated in the vision of religious and spiritual renewal, which his newspaper promoted. Thanks to him, *Ha-melits* became the most important forum for articles and news items about Hasidism. These reports were often accompanied by Zederbaum's personal, generally critical, and polemical—but in many instances also moderate and sometimes even sympathetic—remarks that stemmed from his wish to "repair" Hasidism and his hope to integrate Hasidim into modern Jewish society.[13]

Although most of the material about Hasidism found in the Jewish press relates to Eastern Europe, a significant portion also involves the history of Hasidism in other places where Hasidim had moved, mainly Palestine but also Western Europe.[14] The *ḥalukah* arrangements—money collected among Jewish communities in the diaspora to support members of the Jewish settlement in Palestine, including Hasidim—were constantly criticized in the Jewish press.[15] However, alongside the sharp criticism, much can also be gleaned about Hasidic settlement in the Holy Land, especially in the "four holy cities" (Jerusalem, Safed, Tiberias, and Hebron).[16]

Hasidism and its world were reflected in the press within a variety of journalistic and literary genres; the space devoted to the subject varied as well—from a few lines to longer serialized articles published in installments. The main genres can be classified as follows:

1. Editorials/Op-Eds: articles, reportages, or essays about Hasidism, pro and con, especially regarding current events on the public agenda
2. News reporting (*korespondentsyes*): frequent reporting about current affairs, both significant and marginal, involving tsadikim or Hasidim that transpired in various communities in the Russian Pale of Settlement or in Poland. This information was for the most part sent to the newspapers by readers living in those communities who wished to see their names in the press
3. Translations: news items about Hasidim published in newspapers in various languages (mainly Russian, but also in Polish, German, and English). These items were translated, shortened, and printed in the Hebrew press, usually with additional notes by the writer or editor[17]
4. Literature: satires, humorous stories, poetry, and short fiction depicting Hasidic daily life[18]
5. Original historical documents (e.g., letters written by tsadikim or polemic documents)[19]
6. Obituaries of tsadikim, including their dates of death, descriptions of their funerals, and eulogies.[20]

Unexpected sources about Hasidism can be found also in the "*petit letters*" sections of the newspapers. The back pages of the newspapers were usually devoted to commercial advertisements and to announcements by the newspaper's editor (usually printed in smaller font). Included were detailed lists of contributions collected in various communities in support of Zionist projects or for Jewish workers in Palestine. These are important sources of information about Hasidic groups (*minyanim*) and study houses (*batei midrash*) that took part in Zionist activities.[21] More surprising are the advertisements placed by tsadikim, or by their relatives or descendants, offering their services as insurance agents. Items like these have no parallel in other sources and are of great importance for understanding the economic state of the families of tsadikim and their relations with their followers at the end of the nineteenth century.[22]

The Importance of Newspapers in the Research of Hasidism

In recent years, the focus of research on Hasidism has shifted to what is called "late Hasidism": Hasidism of the nineteenth and twentieth centuries. This field was neglected by the founders of the study of Hasidism and their successors, who showed a clear bias against it and concentrated on the study of early Hasidism: from the eighteenth century until 1815. Notwithstanding the developments made in researching late Hasidism,[23] there is still a "black hole" with regard to Hasidism in the late nineteenth and early twentieth centuries, especially from the 1880s through World War I.[24] Despite the demographic growth of Hasidism at that time and its presence in practically every corner of Jewish Eastern Europe, the state of research and knowledge of this period remains scant and leans heavily on internal Hasidic sources that have not been critically vetted. The sources on the history of Hasidism within the Jewish press are not "new" in the ordinary sense of the word; they have been there all the time, but are buried among thousands of pages of relatively inaccessible newspapers. In fact, very few scholars have made use of these newspapers, and even then the use has been random and unsystematic. Therefore, the study of Hasidism as reflected in the press offers an abundance of new and varied sources that remain virtually untapped.

Moreover, the study of Hasidism up to the last generation focused on sources and documents written by the elite—that is, by tsadikim and their eminent disciples on one hand, and by non-Jewish government clerks on the other. Hence, the history of Hasidism was generally written as a history of tsadikim, while rank-and file Hasidim were rarely, if at all, mentioned.[25] The Jewish press offers an array of sources for the historical and cultural study of Hasidic daily life and a grassroots history that official documents and literary sources lack.

It should also be remembered that the Jewish press began publication in the 1860s, and in those same years the first Hasidic stories were published after more than a half-century hiatus.[26] Critical attitudes toward Hasidism as reflected in the press contribute to a more balanced view of the contemporaneous Hasidic-hagiographic "renaissance" and explain the background of the growth of the Hasidic tale as a "kosher" literary alternative, which was competing with secular newspapers for the leisure time of the contemporary Jewish reader.

News Reporting

The main body of knowledge hidden in the daily and weekly newspapers—in terms of size, scope, and importance—is the actual reporting of news by correspondents. Thousands of reports—known as *korespondentsyes*—were sent to editors of the newspapers from various communities in the Jewish world, mainly from Eastern Europe and Palestine. They were written by nonprofessional journalists or sometimes by experienced authors who were amateur correspondents, equivalent to what today would be called "field reporters." These news reports, which usually presented reliable firsthand accounts based on seeing or hearing events, greatly enrich our picture of Hasidism. Although the reports were often written from a negative, critical perspective, sometimes even displaying a disparaging and mocking point of view, they still contain valuable information. They reflect the daily life of Hasidic communities in diverse locations; relations between different circles of Hasidim in the locality and between them as a whole and other groups in the community; communal quarrels and tensions in light of the Hasidim's activities; special events, such as weddings or funerals of the tsadikim; visits of tsadikim and their entourage to a town, and visits of the tsadikim's emissaries or fundraisers; activities of charlatans pretending to be tsadikim; reports that mock or criticize Hasidim for their customs and behavior—and much more.

This information expands the traditional research that focused on tsadikim and their courts to include Hasidim who lived on the Hasidic periphery. Most Hasidim resided in small communities that were far away from the large Hasidic centers, and these reports, even the many that were negative and critical, can tell us much about the lives of the Hasidim, their social and economic structures, and their relationship with the distant "court." In addition, the accumulated information about the Hasidic presence in various towns enables a more accurate and richer understanding of Hasidic geography and the limits of Hasidic expansion in general, and of certain groups in particular—including data about Hasidism outside the borders of Eastern Europe—and the demographic, social, and economic profile of Hasidim in various communities. These reports are therefore a rich source for the study of Hasidism from "below."

Here is a typical example of a report sent in 1894 from the community of Białynicze (Mohylew province), home to 130 Jewish families. The report describes all aspects of the Jewish community, including the religious situation:

> In this town there are three prayer houses for Jews, one for the mitnagedim and two for the Hasidim, who are the majority in number. But when I say Hasidim and mitnagedim let the reader not be mistaken in thinking that there is a great difference in spirit between the Hasidim of B.[iałynicze] and its mitnagedim. The *Tanya* and *Likutei Torah* and all the other books of this type will not be seen or found anywhere in this town. There is not a single householder who would have the faintest idea about Hasidic ways or its spiritual profile, and even the lone rabbi in the town, who is considered to belong to the Hasidic faction, will not study any Hasidic books, and his entire Hasidic conduct is limited to his praying in the study house in the Hasidic rite . . . and in his sermons we have heard nothing of Hasidic hints or secrets, even though many of the listeners think they are hearing real Hasidic teaching.[27]

Here we have a report about a small town in Belarus, which, naturally, is comprised of Hasidim and mitnagedim. Though the Mohylew province is known to be under the influence of Chabad, the author testifies that there is no real significance to the Hasidic affiliation of those who identify themselves as "Hasidim," and not one among them has the slightest understanding of the Hasidic teachings. In fact, there is no difference between them and the others called "mitnagedim," beyond how each group defines itself. Even the Hasidic rabbi is not a Hasid, and his Hasidic identity consists of the fact that he prays in a Hasidic prayer house.

Unlike historiographic writing (which summarizes events based on an abundance of sources that are critically examined over time), or literary and artistic writing (that is meticulous in its aesthetics), newspapers, and news reporting in particular, reflect the rapid pulse of a community's daily life. Their importance as a historic source relies on their nature as real-time writing that responds immediately to events as they were seen or experienced by the authors.

Material appearing in newspapers, and especially in news reports, did not usually stand on its own. Articles and news items often aroused responses, discussions, and denials, making it possible to identify clusters of connected items that were printed over a period of time. This aspect necessitates refraining from drawing conclusions based on a single item, mainly of a sensationalist nature, which might be categorically denied in a subsequent issue or issues of a newspaper.[28]

Here is a typical example of the problematic nature of such news items and the methodological difficulties they can cause for the historian. In December 1886, *Ha-magid* reprinted an item that had appeared in the Yiddish weekly *Drohobyczer zeitung*, about an incident that supposedly occurred at the Sadagura Hasidic court after the death of the former tsadik, Avraham Ya'akov Friedman (who had died three years earlier). According to the report, the tsadik's estate included a gold chair that had been in his use and was valued at approximately 120,000 florins. Forty-nine of Sadagura's eminent Hasidim had decided that the successor to the tsadik was to be his youngest son, Israel, and in exchange he was to pay his older brother half the value of the chair.[29] The existence of such a chair was subsequently denied by one of the newspaper's subscribers, an intimate of the Sadagura court, who wrote to the editor of *Ha-magid*, in response to the first item, that "there is no gold chair and the whole thing is a lie." The editor, who published the denial, also thought it prudent to add: "For the motto of *Ha-magid* is 'the truth and the peace [*ha-emet ve-ha-shalom*],' without taking any side, we therefore saw as our duty to publish these things . . . and if we are mistaken . . . we are not to blame, for we did not publish this fact out of our imagination, but from the *Drohobyczer zeitung*, which is closer in proximity to where the event transpired."[30] Clearly, had a denial not reached the newspaper, written by someone familiar with the editor, this fake news would have been considered factual. Notwithstanding, the report about the quarrel between the two sons of the deceased tsadik, Yitzḥak of Boian (the elder) and Israel of Sadagura (the younger), is true.[31]

Another example is a collection of items reporting the scandal surrounding the divorce of the *Rebbe* of Trisk's son and the *Rebbe* of Stolin's daughter, who married in 1890 and separated eight years later. Out of respect for those involved, efforts were made to conceal the matter and have it handled in secrecy by a rabbinical court. Yet it was leaked to the press. The information was published in a cluster of reports, enabling the reconstruction of this sensational and embarrassing affair.[32] Were it not for the publication in the press, all that would have been known about the case would have been a vague halakhic response published without context by the renowned Galician Rabbi Shalom Mordechai Schwadron. Beyond the importance of the story as a source for the history of the specific Hasidic dynasties involved, this is an example of investigative journalism exposing to the sunlight embarrassing episodes that Hasidim would have liked to have kept hidden or obscured so as not to air their "dirty laundry" in public.

These clusters point to the need to relate to the complete corpus of the Jewish press as part of a poly-system comprising many and diverse sources of information. From this perspective, the knowledge accumulated in the newspapers regarding Hasidism may also shed light on other obscure sources (such as historical documents, and printed rabbinic, Hasidic, or maskilic sources) that can be verified or disproved, just as these other sources might enrich our understanding of the information buried among the pages of the Jewish press.[33]

Despite the importance of news reports as sources, studying and interpreting them also involves methodological matters to determine authenticity and reliability, which necessitates caution and critical thinking on the part of the researcher. Beyond the fact that the editorial writing in these newspapers generally (but not always) reflects a negative attitude toward Hasidism, in the news reports, even though the writers pretended to provide an accurate and objective report, one finds open hostility, exaggerations, personal vendettas, and, as we have mentioned, denials of earlier reports.

Still, despite the bias and judgment, these reports also contain important and factual information that cannot be found in other sources. We can draw a lot of information and conclusions from this data, such as verification or refutation of dates in the lives and activities of tsadikim; social, economic, and statistical profiles of certain Hasidic groups in various communities; interrelationships between Hasidic groups, and between them and communal institutions on one hand and the tsadik in his court on the other hand; relations between Hasidim and non-Hasidim, non-Jews, and the authorities; and more about daily life, customs, folklore, popular folk beliefs, rituals, magic, and so on.[34]

Here is an example of an article that was published in *Ha-magid* in 1881, written by the journalist and author Gershom Bader, describing his travels across

Galicia, Bukovina, and Romania. In his report about Śniatyń in Eastern Galicia, he wrote about the town's quarrelsome nature. "A day doesn't go by without the flames of war burning among our people." And what is, in his view, the reason for this? The splintering of the many Hasidic groups in the town, which he lists by name:

> If you were to ask me why there is more controversy there than in the other towns? I would answer: The town of Śniatyń has ten different kinds of Hasidim: 1. Vizhnitz (Vijnița) Hasidim; 2. Sadagura Hasidim; 3. Chortkov (Czortków) Hasidim; 4. Husiatyn Hasidim; 5. Kosów Hasidim; 6. Zabłotów Hasidim; 7. Nadwórna; 8. Zhidatchov (Żydaczów); 9. Ułaszkowce; 10. Radowce Hasidim. Besides the householders (that is how we call those who do not travel to the tsadikim, though they will also not speak badly of them, as do the Hasidim who are loyal to another tsadik) . . . all these different cults, ten in number, different as a woman is from her friend, in their customs and conduct, in their prayers and beliefs, and each one will fanatically hate the other. Each cult wishes to rule over its opponent . . . according to the wish of their own tsadik and his adherents.[35]

Even if we were to ignore the judgmental tone of the author, who blames the Hasidim for all the strife in the town, this sample is still a credible source about the presence of certain Hasidic groups in one typical town in Galicia.

As the main channel for the dissemination of information about events in remote communities, the correspondents in the field contributed significantly toward shaping the image of Hasidism among readers. This point is especially important in the study of the historiography of Hasidism, since the press had a decisive effect on the views of the intellectual elite in general, and of the first generation of historians of Hasidism in particular. Some of these writers, including Yehudah Leib Levin (Yehalel), Micha Yosef Berdyczewski, and Shmuel Abba Horodezky, even published articles and reports about Hasidism in the newspapers.[36] Therefore, the press enables us to trace the development of the public discourse about Hasidism, from its maskilic sources through its expression in modern Jewish studies.[37]

Limitations and Possibilities

Use of these press resources for the purposes of research is limited, first and foremost, because of the problem of accessibility to the newspapers themselves, the state of their large crumbling pages, and the fact that numerous volumes are not available on the library shelves for leafing through. No less problematic is the matter of searching, indexing, and regulating the information. New search tools and possibilities are now available to scholars wishing to use the Jewish press for the purposes of research, including on the topic of Hasidism.

1. *Historical Jewish Press* (JPress). This digitization project is sponsored by Tel Aviv University and the National Library of Israel. More than three hundred newspapers have been scanned so far, including all the important newspapers published in Eastern Europe and Palestine in the nineteenth century. The scans are high quality, and it is possible to flip through the pages of the newspapers and to conduct searches using key words. Keep in mind that the results of a search will be partial due to the original poor quality of the print, which does not allow for an exact search of old font styles, and also due to the many variations in the spelling of names of people and places. The site is accessible for free at: web.nli.org.il/sites/JPress/English/Pages/default.aspx.
2. *Yiddish Press Index*. This bibliographic database is sponsored by the Yiddish Department of the Hebrew University of Jerusalem in cooperation with the National Library of Israel. Eight hundred newspapers and periodicals in Yiddish have been indexed, and it is possible to retrieve information according to the names of authors, subjects, and titles. The disadvantage of this project is that it indexes only signed articles, with special attention to literature, but not news items or names mentioned in the articles. The index includes all the Yiddish newspapers published in tsarist Russia, the two important dailies published in Poland up until the Holocaust (*Haynt* and *Moment*), and many literary periodicals. However, users are unable to see the newspapers, just the index results. The site is accessible for free at: yiddish-periodicals.huji.ac.il/#IntroEng.
3. *New Sources for the Research of Hasidism: The Hebrew Press in Eastern Europe*. This is an ongoing research project, conducted at Tel Aviv University since 2014, with the support of the Israel Science Foundation. Its aim is to identify and index all the material related to Hasidism from the Jewish press of the nineteenth century. The index includes names of people, places, Hasidic courts, books, and other subjects related to Hasidism, with an emphasis on daily life (such as rituals, magic, prayer, and marriage). Each entry includes a scan of the relevant section in the newspaper with a short description. So far, approximately one thousand clippings have been indexed. The site is accessible for free at tau-primo.hosted.exlibrisgroup.com/primo-explore/collectionDiscovery?vid=TAU&collectionId=81264597260004146.

SUGGESTED READING

A number of general introductory studies tell the history of the Jewish press. Much information on various aspects of the Jewish press are found in the more than fifty volumes of *Kesher*, a scholarly journal devoted to the history of all kinds of Jewish and Hebrew media and press. *Kesher* is published by the Andrea and Charles Bronfman Institute for the Study of Jewish Press and Communications at Tel Aviv University. On the eighteenth-nineteenth-century Hebrew press in general and on each newspaper separately, see Menucha Gilboa, *Leksikon ha-itonut ha-ivrit ba-me'ot ha-shmone-esreh veha-tesha-esreh*

(Jerusalem: Mosad Bialik, 1992). On the Hebrew press as a source about daily life in the Russian Pale of Settlement, see Dror Segev, "Tafkida ha-ḥevrati shel ha-itonut ha-ivrit ba-imperya ha-rusit be-tekufat Aleksander ha-shlishi (1881–1894)" (PhD diss., Tel Aviv University, 2015). On the Russian Jewish press, see Yehudah Slutsky's two volumes, *Ha-itonut ha-yehudit-rusit ba-me'ah ha-tesha-esreh* (Jerusalem: Mosad Bialik, 1970) and *Ha-itonut ha-yehudit-rusit ba-me'ah ha-esrim (1900–1918)* (Tel Aviv: Tel Aviv University, 1978). On the Hebrew press in nineteenth-century Palestine, see G. Kresel, *Toledot ha-itonut ha-ivrit be-Erets Yisrael* (Jerusalem: Hasifriya hatsiyonit, 1964); Galia Yardeni, *Ha-itonut ha-ivrit be-Erets Yisrael ba-shanim 1863–1904* (Tel Aviv: Hakibbutz hameuchad, 1969). On the Orthodox and *ḥaredi* press, see Menaḥem Keren-Kratz, "Ḥomot shel hafradah: Neturey Karta ve-itonehem be-tekufat kum ha-medinah," *Kesher* 50 (2017), 71–88. On the emergence of the modern Yiddish newspapers, see Chone Shmeruk, "Sifrut Yiddish ve-reshita shel ha-itonut ha-modernit be-Yiddish," in Shmeruk, *Sifrut Yiddish: Perakim le-toledoteha* (Tel Aviv: Tel Aviv University, 1978), 261–293. On the role of women in the Yiddish press until World War I, see Nurit Orchan, *Yots'ot me-arba amot: Nashim kotvot ba-itonut be-yidish ba-imperyah ha-rusit* (Jerusalem: Zalman Shazar Center, 2013). On the Jewish press between the wars, with a special attention to Eastern Europe, see Yehuda Gothelf, ed., *Itonut Yehudit she-haytah* (Tel Aviv: Ha'igud haolami shel itona'im yehudim, 1973). On the Hebrew press between the wars, see Shmuel Werses, "Ha-itonut ha-ivrit ve-kor'eha be-Polin ben shetei milḥamot olam," in *Ben shetei milḥamot olam: Perakim me-ḥayei ha-tarbut shel Yehudei Polin li-leshonotehem*, ed. Ch. Shmeruk and Sh. Werses (Jerusalem: Magnes Press, 1997), 73–95. For the Yiddish press, see Nathan Cohen, *Sefer, sofer ve-iton: Merkaz ha-tarbut ha-Yehudit be-Varsha, 1918–1942* (Jerusalem: Magnes Press, 2003).

The secondary literature on the Hasidic content in the press is much less available. For topical bibliographies containing a wealth of press materials related to the history of Hasidism, see David Assaf, *Braslav: Biblyografyah mu'eret* (Jerusalem: Zalman Shazar Center, 2000); Assaf, "Parashat Bernyu me-Leova u-maḥloket Tsanz–Sadigora: biblyografyah mu'eret," *Jerusalem Studies in Jewish Thought* 23 (2011), 2:407–481 (esp. 420–428). On Hasidic content in the Polish-Jewish press of the nineteenth century, see Marcin Wodziński, *Haskalah and Hasidism in the Kingdom of Poland: A History of Conflict*, trans. S. Cozens (Oxford: The Littman Library of Jewish Civilization, 2005), 180–248. On the image of Chabad in the maskilic writings, including the Hebrew press, see Jonatan Meir, "Dimuya shel ḥabad be-sifrut ha-haskalah: Kabalah, reformah ve-natsrut," in Jonatan Meir and Gadi Sagiv, eds., *Ḥabad: Historia, hagut, ve-dimuy* (Jerusalem: Zalman Shazar Center, 2017), 183–200.

NOTES

This chapter is part of the project "New Sources for the Research of Hasidism: The Hebrew Press in Eastern Europe" and was supported by the Israel Science Foundation (grant no. 471/14). I am grateful to Dr. Dror Segev for overseeing this project.

1. On this newspaper, see Menucha Gilboa, *Leksikon ha-itonut ha-ivrit ba-me'ot ha-shmone-esreh veha-tesha-esreh* (Jerusalem: Mosad Bialik, 1992), 117–135.

2. On this newspaper, see Alexander Orbach, *New Voices of Russian Jewry: A Study of the Russian Jewish Press of Odessa in the Era of the Great Reforms, 1860–1871* (Leiden: Brill, 1980); Gilboa, *Leksikon ha-itonut*, 137–157. We still do not possess any comprehensive study on this important newspaper.

3. On this newspaper, see Gilboa, *Leksikon ha-itonut*, 167–181; Oren Sofer, *Eyn lefalpel! Iton Ha-tsefirah veha-modernizatsyah shel ha-siaḥ ha-ḥevrati ha-politi* (Jerusalem: Mosad Bialik, 2007).

4. On this newspaper, see Gilboa, *Leksikon ha-itonut*, 186–195; Roni Beer-Marx, *Al ḥomot ha-niyar: Iton Ha-levanon veha-ortodoksyah* (Jerusalem: Zalman Shazar Center, 2017).

5. On this newspaper, see Gilboa, *Leksikon ha-itonut*, 320–324; David Tal, *Yehuda Leib Kantor: Haluts ha-yomon ha-ivri—biografyah* (Tel Aviv: Hakibbutz hameuchad, 2011).

6. The famous anti-Hasidic satire *Dos poylishe yingl*, by Yitzḥak Yoel Linetsky, was published first in *Kol mevaser* (1867; in installments) and contributed to the newspaper's popularity. On this newspaper, see Shmuel Werses, "Kol ha-ishah ba-shavu'on be-Yiddish 'Kol mevaser,'" in Werses, *"Hakitsah ami": Sifrut ha-haskalah be-idan ha-modernizatsyah* (Jerusalem: Magnes Press, 2001), 321–350; Avraham Novershtern, "*Kol mevaser*," Historical Jewish Press website, accessed December 31, 2018, web.nli.org.il/sites/JPress/English/Pages/Kol-Mevaser.aspx.

7. On this newspaper, edited by Alexander Zederbaum, the editor of *Ha-melits*, see Nurit Orchan, *Yots'ot me-arba amot: Nashim kotvot ba-itonut be-yidish ba-Imperyah ha-rusit* (Jerusalem: Zalman Shazar Center, 2013).

8. Attempts at a systematic collection of sources on the history of Hasidism that were printed in the press may be found in two of my bibliographic annotated projects; see the suggested reading for this chapter.

9. An example for the complexity is the changes in the views toward Hasidism in *Ha-tsefirah* during the 1870s; see Marcin Wodziński, *Haskalah and Hasidism in the Kingdom of Poland: A History of Conflict* (Oxford: The Littman Library of Jewish Civilization, 2005), 170–176.

10. Israel Bartal, "'Mevaser u-Modi'a le-ish yehudi': Ha-itonut ha-yehudit ke-afik shel ḥidush," in Bartal, *Letaken am: Ne'orut u-le'umiyut be-mizraḥ Eropa* (Jerusalem: Mosad Bialik, 2013), 315–325.

11. See David Assaf, "Son'im—sipur a'havah? Hitpatḥuyot be-meḥkar yaḥasey ha-gomlin ben ha-ḥasidut veha-haskalah," in *Ha-haskalah li-gevaneha: Iyunim ḥadashim be-toeledot ha-haskalah uve-sifrutah*, ed. S. Feiner and I. Bartal (Jerusalem: Magnes Press, 2005), 183–200.

12. According to his testimony, he personally knew Rabbi Yehudah Leib Eger of Lublin, and therefore wrote a eulogy filled with unusual praise. See Alexander Zederbaum, "Zekher tsadik livrakha," *Ha-melits*, February 13, 1888, 266–268. See also his testimony about a meeting in Odessa with an unnamed tsadik, who asked to hear about the aims of the newspaper: Zederbaum, *Ha-melits*, March 5, 1886, 227–228.

13. See, for example, *Ha-melits*, June 13, 1867, 163.

14. For example, a report about the visit of a tsadik in London in 1895, which began with the words: "Who would tell us that here too, in the city of London, Hasidism will spread its fortress and tsadikim and holy men will come to deceive masses of people, to the shame of our people in general and Russian Jews in particular." *Ha-melits*, February 10, 1895, 3 (translation mine). The report refers to Alter Noaḥ ha-Kohen of Drohobycz, an unusual self-appointed tsadik who eventually found his way to Palestine; see *Ha-melits*, February 24, 1895, 1; David Assaf, *Derekh ha-malkhut: Rabi Yisrael mi-Ruzhin u-mekomo be-toledot ha- ḥasidut* (Jerusalem: Zalman Shazar Center, 1997), 131–132. Also, the travels of Moshe Twersky, the heretical grandson of the tsadik Yoḥanan of Rachmistrivka (Rotmistrzówka), to Berlin, London, and Paris, are documented in the press; see David Assaf, *Ne'eḥaz ba-sevakh: Pirkei mashber u-mevukhah be-toledot ha-ḥasidut* (Jerusalem: Zalman Shazar Center, 2006), 331–332 n55; Gadi Sagiv, *Ha-shoshelet: Bet Chernobyl u-mekomo be-toledot ha-ḥasidut* (Jerusalem: Zalman Shazar Center, 2014), 377.

15. For example, the series of articles by Alexander Zederbaum on the flaws of the *ḥalukah* money and about the Hasidic *kollelim* in the Holy Land, in which a great deal of information was published, including letters and documents. See *Ha-melits*, November 14 and 21, 1870, and December 5, 12, and 19, 1870, pp. 320, 327–329, 343–344, 352–353, 358–359.

16. For example, the book by Menaḥem Mendel Eilboim, *Erets ha-tsevi* (Vienna, 1883; reprinted Jerusalem: Yad Izhak Ben Zvi, 1982), based on a series of critical articles originally published in the monthly *Ha-shaḥar*, includes a firsthand description of Hasidic life in Safed. For an example of an effective use of the press for the understanding of the nineteenth-century Hasidic community of Safed, see Rivka Embon, "Ha-Rav Shmuel Heler

(1803–1884) u-mekomo ba-kehilah ha-Yehudit bi-Tsefat" (PhD diss., Tel Aviv University, 2016). On the Hebrew press in nineteenth-century Palestine, see above in suggested reading.

17. For example, a report taken from the Russian newspaper *Golos* about a visit of the tsadik Yitzḥak of Skwira in Winnica: *Ha-melits*, June 29, 1880, 228. Translation from English of an article by Laurence Oliphant about his visit in Sadagura: *Ha-tsefirah*, November 13, 1883, 330. Translation of a report that was published in a Russian journal in Odessa about the tsadik Ḥayim Menaḥem of Zinków; apparently, a rumor spread among his Hasidim that he was pregnant! He was taken to Kamieniec Podolski for medical treatment, where it was found that he had intestinal parasites: *Ha-melits*, April 13, 1885, 388.

18. For example, the humorous story "Shimshon ha-gibor," by Menaḥem Mendel Dolitzky, which describes a tsadik who has taken ill and is prescribed to drink goat's milk. His attendant travels to the nearby town to procure it, but a prankster there replaces his ewe with a billy goat; this goes back and forth until the tsadik dies: *Ha-melits*, April 9 and 16, 1883, 391–394, 423–424. Sholem Aleichem used this folk motif with no connection to Hasidism in his well-known story "Der Farkishufter shnayder," which was first published in 1900.

19. For example, when the tsadik Dov Ber of Leova (Bessarabia) defected from the Hasidic camp, he choose to publish his open letter in the newspaper *Ha-magid*, February 24, 1869, 10. His announcement of remorse was also first published in the newspaper: *Ha-magid*, July 14, 1869, addition, 36. Newspapers followed this scandalous affair and the internal Hasidic controversy that stemmed from it, and depicted it in detail in many genres: authentic documents, news reporting, articles, satires, and polemical writings. See David Assaf, *Hetsits ve-nifgah: Anatomyah shel maḥloket ḥasidit* (Tel Aviv: University of Haifa Press, 2012).

20. For example, the death of the tsadik Barukh Shapira of Czyżewo: *Ha-magid*, August 15, 1877, September 12, 1877, pp. 294, 328; the death of Yehudah Leib Eger of Lublin: *Ha-tsefirah*, February 9, 1888, p. 3; the death and funeral of Elimelekh Shapira of Grodzisk Mazowiecki: *Ha-tsefirah*, April 3 and 21, 1892, pp. 280–281, 320; eulogy of Ya'akov Yitzḥak of Makarów: *Ha-tsefirah*, July 4, 5, 10, and 11, 1893, pp. 564, 568, 584, 589.

21. For example, on Lubawicze Hasidim in Uzlyany (Minsk province) and Hasidic prayer houses of Makarów and Turzysk [Trisk] in Miropol: *Ha-melits*, October 13, 1898, 7; Hasidic study houses in Kobryń, among them Karlin, Słonim, Janów: *Ha-melits*, February 12, 1899, 7; Hasidic prayer houses in Kowel, among them Karlin, Lubawicze, and Turzysk: *Ha-melits*, January 22, 1901, 4; the study house of Lubawicze in Shchedrin: *Ha-melits*, December 22, 1902, 4.

22. See David Assaf, "Ha-tsadikim ve-iskei ha-bitu'aḥ: Perek lo yadu'a be-toledot ha-kalkalah ha- ḥasidit," in *Pinkas le-vet Yisrael: Festchrift for Israel Bartal*, ed. G. D. Hundert, J. Meir, D. Shumsky (Zalman Shazar Center; forthcoming).

23. For the most comprehensive and up-to-date discussion of "Late Hasidism," see David Biale et al., *Hasidism: A New History* (Princeton, NJ: Princeton University Press, 2017).

24. See David Assaf and Gadi Sagiv, "Hasidism in Tsarist Russia: Historical and Social Aspects," *Jewish History* 27 (2013), 241–269; Marcin Wodziński, "War and Religion, or How the First World War Changed Hasidism," *Jewish Quarterly Review* 106 (2016), 283–312.

25. For a sample for conducting such research on the rank and file, see Marcin Wodziński, "Space and Spirit: On Boundaries, Hierarchies and Leadership in Hasidism," *Journal of Historical Geography* 53 (2016), 63–74.

26. On the nature, history, and various genres of the Hasidic tale, see Zeev Kitsis, "Sifrut ha-shevaḥim ha-ḥasidit me-reshitah ve-ad le-milḥemet ha-'olam ha-sheniyah: Tekufot, kanonizatsyah ve-tahalikhei gibush" (PhD diss., Bar-Ilan University, 2015).

27. *Ha-melits*, July 5, 1894, 2. Translation mine.

28. For example, a report from Irkuck in Siberia claimed that the Hasidim murdered the local butcher: *Ha-melits*, August 20, 1872, 42–43. Nine months later, this story was denied after it became clear that the Hasidim had no connection to the murder: *Ha-melits*, May 13,

1873, 107–109. A murder case was reported to have occurred in the prayer house of Aleksandrów Hasidim in Radom: *Ha-melits*, March 17, 1896, 3–4; that story also was denied within a short period of time: *Ha-melits*, April 7, 1896, 3–4.

29. *Ha-magid*, December 2, 1886, 379. This report ended with a witty line against Hasidism, which was not well received by a reader; see *Ha-magid*, January 6, 1887, 7.

30. *Ha-magid*, January 31, 1887, 14. Translation mine.

31. Assaf, *Derekh ha-malkhut*, 456–457.

32. See *Ha-melits*, February 14, 1899, 4 (noteworthy, the writer mentioned that "this disgraceful case" was already published in the Russian press); *Ha-tsefirah*, March 1, 1899, 170–171; April 19, 1900, 336; *Ha-melits*, July 3, 1900, 1; July 9, 1900, 1; July 12, 1900, 1.

33. See, for example, the extensive information about the persecutions of Bratslav Hasidim during the 1860s, which completes and verifies printed sources. See David Assaf, *Untold Tales of the Hasidim: Crisis and Discontent in the History of Hasidism* (Waltham, MA : Brandeis University Press, 2010), 120–153.

34. For the use of information from the newspapers to reconstruct Hasidic rituals, see Gadi Sagiv, "Hasidism and Cemetery Inauguration Ceremonies: Authority, Magic, and Performance of Charismatic Leadership," *The Jewish Quarterly Review* 103 (2013), 328–351.

35. Gershom Bader, *Ha-magid*, January 19, 1881, 20–21. Translation mine.

36. For example, Palmoni Ha-Hevrony (Yehalel) on Minsk: *Ha-melits*, September 14, 1865, October 19, 1865, pp. 528–529, 574–576; Micha Yosef Berdyczewski on Dubova: *Ha-tsefirah*, February 23, 1888, 3; Shmuel Abba Horodezky on Berdyczów: *Ha-tsefirah*, April 14, 1896, 354.

37. See Israel Bartal, "Mi-bavu'a me'uvetet le-uvdah historit: Sifrut ha-haskalah u-meḥkar tenu'at ha-ḥasidut," in Bartal, *Letaken am*, 107–122.

CHAPTER 10

Iconography

Maya Balakirsky Katz

The "visual turn" arrived belatedly to the field of Jewish studies, where the subjects of study have long been celebrated as "the people of the book" and their culture as a "logocentric" one.[1] When scholars did turn to Jewish art, they focused on ceremonial objects that they interpreted as the fulfillment of textual commandments or the beautification of prescribed ritual.[2] In the 1950s and 1960s, the work of archeologist Erwin Goodenough challenged the notion of a unilateral directionality between the Word of God and social action. Modernists have found this analytic lens especially relevant because of the functional relationship between the Jewish entry into modernity and the Jewish embrace of the arts.[3] Scholars Barbara Kirshenblatt-Gimblett and Jonathan Karp have even wondered "whether the 'modern Jewish experience' has in some sense been a pointedly artistic one."[4] This radical reorientation opened new throughways, but, unfortunately, these inquiries have overwhelmingly focused on the narrative of acculturation, secularization, and nationalization in urbanized Jewish centers such as Berlin, Warsaw, Vilna, Vienna, and New York. In comparison, we know little about the role that visual culture played in the *religious* experience, the resistance to Westernized liberalism, and the bulwarking of in-group identity, especially in more provincial centers in Eastern Europe.

One of the richest areas for the study of the cross-pollination between Jewish artistic and religious practices is Hasidism, which embraced oral, visual, and material expressions of religion. The scholarly systemization of Hasidic primary sources, famously wrestled over by Martin Buber and Gershom Scholem, mirrors the struggles that gave birth to the movement in the late eighteenth century in response to the spiritual and social lacuna resulting from a hypertextualized rabbinical culture.[5] In fact, few early Hasidic leaders wrote scholarly books because the medium was associated with an arrogant rabbinic culture.[6] Yet, the legitimizing force of literary sources grew so influential in the interwar years that

Hasidic leader R. Yosef Yitzḥak Schneersohn (1880–1950) falsified documents that he claimed belonged to the so-called Kherson Genizah (a repository for discarded sacred texts) to retroactively create authoritative source material for early Hasidism.[7] The notion that religious claims required the validation of textual sources, partially introjected by the Hasidic world, resulted in a neglect of the core legacy of Hasidic material sources and visual practices. It is only in the last two decades that the more bulky materials that visualize Hasidism have passed into the purview of Jewish-studies discourse.[8]

The methodological models for conceptualizing religious material culture are ever evolving, but existing scholarship has predominantly focused on Hasidic visuality through two general focuses: the study of "things" and the religious implications of the sensory apparatus that I call "thinging." In general, scholars use "things" to study Hasidim (people) and "thinging" to study Hasidism (theology). It goes without saying that Hasidic visual culture requires an integrated approach between "things" and "thinging"—especially when one conflicts with the other as it so often does—but I have decided to maintain this distinction because the existing heuristic structures clarify both the advances and limitations of the field today.

First *Things* First: The Object-Centered Approach

Hasidic movements have produced a rich visual culture in the service of religious life, much of which revolved around the tsadik's court (*hoif*), an institution shaped by the adoption of the dynastic model of leadership in the late eighteenth century, when itinerant miracle workers settled down into permanent residences.[9] Hasidic courts were architecturally varied, but whether in the "palaces" that wealthier groups in Bukovina and southwestern Ukraine acquired for their *wunder-rebbes* or in the modest wood buildings that most *Rebbes* occupied across Poland and Belarus, Hasidic courts collected monies to commission lighting fixtures, carpets, and tables.[10]

Any contextual study of the *Rebbe's* court must take into consideration its institutional mission, which was directed toward the master-disciple relationship. The division of internal space and all the "things" within the court strove to emplace the spiritual master and to optimize the space for the *Rebbe's* interaction with his Hasidim.[11] At court, the *Rebbe* accepted donations (*pidyon hanefesh*) and handwritten supplications (*kvitlekh*), administered blessings in face-to-face meetings (*yehidus*), held and returned blessed coins (*shmire*) to supplicants, held public meals (*tish*), and distributed food from his own plate (*shirayim*). In turn, Hasidim emulated the *Rebbe's* preference for melodies, costume, and ritual, even in seemingly irreligious objects, such as the *Rebbe's* pipe (*lyulke*) and snuffbox (*tabak-pushke*), as acts of fealty and imported his teachings at court into their own communities. Upon leaving court, followers could purchase or commission ceremonial objects (as early as the 1830s) and photographs (beginning in the 1890s) of the external façade of the court as mementos of the *wunder-rebbe* who resided inside the court and whose portrait was generally unavailable.

In order to develop and nurture the master-disciple relationship, the court shaped its institutional character on two main fronts. On the one hand, the *Rebbe's* court and its material life elbowed into the established Jewish institutions that tended to emphasize communal prayer and Torah study as the principal paths toward spirituality. At the same time, the development of this new institutional structure necessitated the individuation of each *Rebbe's* court from all other Hasidic courts. Therefore, it is as important to understand differences between Hasidic groups as it is the similarities that bind Hasidim together in the reification of mainstream Jewish religion.[12] Each Hasidic branch adopted its own particularistic court culture, ranging from R. Naḥum Twersky of Czarnobyl's (1730–1787) embrace of asceticism as a path to Divine attachment to R. Israel Friedman's (1796–1850) belief that physical elevation engendered spiritual revelation. The astounding breadth and encyclopedic nuance among Hasidic "things" served to create a sense of spiritual and material identification with a particular master even as this desire projected a dialectic character on the part of Hasidism in general.

How, for example, would we approach the Hasidic adoption of the Baal Shem Tov's use of a decorative silver collar (*atara*) on the prayer shawl (*tallit*)? What immediately becomes clear is that the Jewish-studies privileging of textual proscription yields understandings anachronistic to those people who use the *atara* and imbue it with meaning.[13] Since the sixteenth-century kabbalist Yitzḥak Luria eschewed the embellishment of the *tallit*, whatever theological meanings are associated with the *atara* are innovations of modern Jewish religious thought and practice, but shifting away from literary sources does not mean that the *atara* is divorced of ideology. Art historian Batsheva Goldman-Ida has identified the ways that the *experiential* world of Hasidic things shapes theological meanings. She has explored how the material and performative aspects of the Hasidic prayer shawl remind worshippers to cleave to their master during Divine service. Even in cases where the original *Rebbe* is no longer at the center of the custom, Goldman-Ida shows that the adornment of the *atara* on the prayer shawl serves as a mnemonic to worshippers to attend to the spiritual task at hand, and the motif of the rosette on the Hasidic *atara* and its braided silver threading technique embed kabbalistic numerology of the Divine Name.

From a sociological perspective, scholars might analyze a specific prayer shawl, such as the Baal Shem Tov's prayer shawl and *atara*, for its signification of discipleship and, in the aftermath of the Baal Shem Tov's life and the splitting off of Hasidic branches around individual tsadikim, for its signification of inherited spirituality.[14] As such, the adoption of the *atara* ties Hasidim together as followers of the Baal Shem Tov. After the followers of R. Shneur Zalman of Lady (1745–1812) sold theirs to obtain his release from the tsarist government in 1798, it became customary in the Chabad branch to abstain from wearing an *atara*, which allowed the unadorned prayer shawl to signify and reinforce the specific and unique master-disciple relationship of Chabad Hasidism.

Just as the traditional Jewish-studies methodologies often do not broach the core of Hasidic culture, conventional art-historical methodologies yield tangential conclusions. From an aesthetic point of view, Hasidim claim no inherent value to the objects they venerate, and without the cultural standard of "beautification" as an impetus for media production, methodologies designed to investigate cultural standards of taste (for example, iconography, provenance, stylistic influence) are often irrelevant to the study of Hasidic visual culture. Thus, the art-historical model might be useful when the object in question is the magnificent silver menorah and its now lost diamond-studded gold crown made by a Russian blacksmith in 1860 for the tsadik of the Sadagura dynasty because it might reveal the role that Russian culture played in Hasidic aesthetics, but this is rarely the case.[15] Rather, when the object is a modest prayer shawl or even a mass-produced silver ornament whose value is far more difficult to quantify, new approaches, such as those developed by the burgeoning field of visual studies, are necessary.

In the process-oriented approach to the study of Hasidic objects, whether the architecture of the court, the interior space, the *Rebbe's* things, the ceremonial objects, or the costume of court life, it is not so much the objects that we need to understand but the objectification of the *Rebbe*. In analyzing the processes of meaning-making in the master-disciple relationship, it would be incorrect to assume that the tsadik controlled his objectification. If the *Rebbe's* things offer Hasidim mediated access to a spiritual master, it is the beholder who beatifies objects as "belonging" to the tsadik. It is not enough for a *Rebbe* to sacralize the object through physical contact (although that is a prerequisite) since his followers can only access this consecration through their intentional use of the object (*kavanah*). The processes of embodying the *Rebbe* and his teachings into objects ultimately in the possession of the follower affects how the believer then looks at his tsadik in the flesh.

Returning to Hasidic ideology—whether those reflecting Gershom Scholem's preference for mystical works or Martin Buber's preference for the tsadik's miracle stories—the praxis of ideas reconstitutes the tsadik into "things," which, perhaps counterintuitively, gives us more access into the life of the followers than that of the *Rebbe*. The *Rebbe's* disciples mediate the spiritual achievements of their *Rebbe* through their own media practices, such as the preservation of his handwriting as charms or amulets, or the melting down of his blessed coins (*shmire*) into ceremonial objects such as one kiddush cup in the collection of the Israel Museum inscribed as a "cup of *shmires*."[16] The belief that the *Rebbe's* hand imbues objects with blessing allowed individual disciples with the ability to transform and disseminate such amulets and objects said to contain *shmire* coins in their own right. Even women, such as the famous example of Hanna Rokhel Verbermacher (c. 1815–1888), known as the "Maiden of Ludmir," participated in the exchange of spirituality through things.[17] Even non-Hasidim, such as R. Avraham Yehoshua Heshel Bick, styled himself the "Mezhibuzer Rav" through his post-Soviet patronage of the reconstruction of the Baal Shem Tov's destroyed synagogues on the site of its original location in Międzybóż (Mezibozh/Medzhybizh), Ukraine.[18]

Indeed, even the tsadik's literary trove—his letters (*kitvei kodesh*), transcribed public addresses (*sihot*), and authorized broadsides (*pashkevilim*)—often functioned as objects in the home, in the synagogue, and on the street in ways that reconstructed, sometimes even contradicted, the content of the tsadik's words.[19] In some circles, the objectification of the *Rebbe's* literary legacy extended to the practice of looking for guidance by opening a posthumous *Rebbe's* book to a random page and treating the passage as the *Rebbe's* answer.[20] This randomization of the *Rebbe's* words by the hand of the Hasid shifts autonomy to the Hasid, who can claim his *Rebbe's* authority.

The tsadik, whose persona Hasidic literature portrays as timeless, ends up in the fickle hands of his followers and admirers, who reshape the tsadik's legacy in succeeding generations to address contemporary needs and tastes. An example of this layered approach to Hasidic media practices is the posthumous treatment of the *Rebbe's* things by the Bratslav (Bracław) Hasidic branch. After the death of their founder, R. Naḥman (1772–1810), his followers refused to adopt a successor. Since R. Naḥman's court in Bracław was destroyed by fire and he moved to the Ukrainian city of Uman (Humań), where he died the same year, his followers had no court to flock to or to rebuild in America or Israel after immigration. Sometimes referred to as "Dead Hasidim," Bratslav Hasidim chose to authenticate their history through veneration of R. Naḥman's grave. Citing the precedent established by R. Naḥman's disciple R. Natan Sternharz (1780–1844), Bratslav Hasidim adopted the practice of pilgrimage to R. Naḥman's gravesite in Uman, where their persecution at the hands of both the government and other Hasidic groups with a living leader formed a unique Bratslav identity.

Rather than approaching Bratslav's pilgrimage practices as a continuum of religious tradition, there is more benefit to studying them within their immediate context. The contemporary pilgrimage shares little with travel practices in R. Naḥman's time but also diverges from contemporary models of tourism in which the tourist travels to experience foreign traditions and delights. Bratslav travel memoirs often take pride in comparing the beauty of the renowned local landmark of Sofiefka Park to the seemingly simple, but spiritually more arresting, gravesite of R. Naḥman.[21] In the post-Soviet era, following decades of heavily restricted accessibility to the gravesite, the Bratslav movement built a megastructure to accommodate the thousands of Hasidic tourists that annually flock to Uman on Rosh Hashanah, the Jewish New Year. The overwhelming presence of Hasidim on Ukrainian territory during these tours also negates the Ukrainian host culture; visiting Hasidim prefer their own performance of elaborate ritual, costume, song, and dance, as Ukraine culture is still identified with a history of antisemitic violence.[22] These rejectionist cultural performances allow Bratslav tourists to fight acculturation, demonstrate against antireligious policies, and mourn the annihilation of religion in the modern world.[23] Attention to the heavily storied social life of objects turns the analytic lens on the Hasidim who radically reformed traditional Judaism through the introduction of these objects into religious Jewish life and preserve them as part of the efforts to curb assimilation.

Thinging: The Religious-Materialism Approach

The other major category of research into Hasidic visual culture concerns the investigation of the religious implications of materialism. If "things" express the material of religion, "thinging" refers to the religion of the material world. Likewise, students of "thinging" must attend to the internalization and performance of Hasidism.[24] To some degree these are parallel processes, but if the study of "things" includes the stages of production, interpretation, consumption, and reception, the study of "thinging" is another subset of those processes and not an entity unto itself, and certainly not an a priori concept that informs the former.

At the core of "thinging" is the Hasidic embrace of the idea of "worship through materiality" (*avoda be-gashmiyut*), which maintains that the world contains more than the sum of all physical matter and that the believer must liberate the "shells" (*klipot*) concealing the holy sparks (*nitsotsot ha-kedushah*) of the Divine Presence (*Shekhinah*).[25]

A full understanding of "worship through materiality" is beyond the scope of this chapter, but what is pertinent is the ways that the late eighteenth-century popularization of the sixteenth-century Lurianic idea called for more accessible hermeneutic models than Isaac Luria's Tree of Life diagram with its ten circles representing Divine emanations (*sefirot*) and connecting pathways corresponding to the twenty-two Hebrew letters. "Worship through materiality" required the development of a new sensory regime to hone the worshipper's recognition of the illusory physical world and experience of the Divine Presence trapped within it. Worship through materiality first required Hasidim to *see* the world as a *material parable*, which Buber interpreted as representing higher-level existence and Scholem interpreted as a nihilistic drive against reality.[26] The Baal Shem Tov and the early Hasidic masters modeled this parable-perception and parable-making by delivering their teachings to their disciples primarily through the mode of parable, whether through tales, melody, or dance. In the context of the visual culture that developed during the institutionalization of Hasidism, the beholder divested the physical vessel of its material skin and redirected the material parable by imbuing everyday objects and acts (e.g., the court, *tallit*, *atara*, and eating, dancing, singing) as ideal vehicles for attachment (*devekut*) to the Divine Presence.[27] Focusing on the perceptual, behavioral, and communicative properties of parable-perception and parable-making offers new perspective on long-enduring debates such as the Hasidic approach to the mind-body dualism inherent in Lurianic Kabbalah. Whereas medieval kabbalists sought to focus on the permeability of boundaries between cosmological and material life through visualization of the Divine Name, Hasidim trained their focus on more tangible parables, such as the production of moral geographies in the mind of the body during sex.[28]

It is relevant to our discussion that the embodied materialism that defines Hasidic "thinging" and the requisite perceptual model of parable share key aspects with the aesthetic theories of contemporary German critics that paved the way for the Romantic cult of art as embraced by Kant and Hegel. While comparing intellectual systems often yields little clarity on either system, it is nonetheless useful to consider the Hasidic opposition to the hypertextual religious authority of traditional Judaism and the literary secularism that characterized the Jewish Enlightenment (Haskalah) as *both* actively engaging with contemporary European discourses.[29] As is so often the case in intellectual historical trends, German Jewish philosopher Moses Mendelssohn was conceptualizing Judaism as a rational behavioral system (conceptually in step with Lithuanian rabbinical culture) while East European Hasidic leaders were conceptualizing Judaism as an emotional terrain (conceptually in step with German Romanticism). Although profound differences characterized the Hasidic and German Romantic treatments of key issues (such as the mind-body split), several scholars have noticed overlapping inspirations between the two, such as the folklore publications of both R. Naḥman's *Sipurei ma'asiyot* and the Grimm Brothers's *Kinder- und Hausmärchen* in the same year (1812).[30] While there is nothing surprising about a shared cultural zeitgeist between Central European and East European intellectuals, much can be learned from understanding the connections between the Hasidic conceptualization of the physical world as a veil of illusion and the then-burgeoning field of aesthetics.

At the very least, finding overlaps between the philosophical conceptualization of Hasidic theology and what Heinrich Heine called the "art-religion" of his era reinforces the need to consider the visual dimensions of Hasidism seriously and contextually.[31] For eighteenth-century German thinkers, the pinnacle of the aesthetic experience was the recognition of the "sublime," a metaphysical state in which the observer is overwhelmed by a feeling of shapeless and unbounded expansiveness.[32] While the analogies between the raptures over the sublime by aestheticians and *devekut* by Hasidic masters are self-evident, it is the fine-tuning of these transcendental infinities that more convincingly calls for a reconsideration of Hasidism on aesthetic lines. For example, German Protestant thinker Karl Philipp Moritz's notion of "self-forgetting" (*das angenehme Vergessen unsrer selbst*) in contemplation of the work of art shares discursive similarities to the Hasidic concept of self-nullification (*bitul ha-yesh*) in contemplation of reality as popularized by R. Shneur Zalman of Lady in the same decade.[33]

While German philosophers sought to imbue secular art with the aura of religion, and East European Hasidic masters sought to imbue religion with the transcendence of the aesthetic experience, the two movements shared many discursive properties in their characterization of the transcendent power that the beholder can enact. This connection to German aesthetic ideas helps to frame our understanding of the impassioned description of European paintings by the fifth tsadik of Chabad Lubavitch as well as the embrace of a Hasidic mentality in R. Avraham Yitzḥak ha-kohen Kook's (1865–1935) claim that Rembrandt's paintings in London's National Gallery captured "the very light that was originally created by God Almighty."[34]

Re-thinging: Collecting and Exhibiting Hasidism

Since objects possessed by the tsadik were believed to retain mystical power indefinitely—to construct master-disciple relationships and to signify dynastic inheritance—Hasidic groups (most notably Bełz and Chabad) have established impressive object collections.[35] The same logic, however, explains why Hasidim tend to be averse to the collection, appropriation, formal analysis, and public exhibition of Hasidic material culture by secular scientific institutions such as museums and universities and by entertainment industries such as theaters and the cinema.[36] Stories record the purposeful destruction of objects by the tsadik himself so that they would not fall into the hands of the wrong people, who could reap their spiritual effects.[37]

In the modern museum model, the predominant ideological drive of collection and exhibition is the notion of the secular state and its authority over civilization rather than, say, attachment to the tsadik or the Divine.[38] In keeping with the structure of this chapter on the scholarly study of "things" and "thinging," I will focus on the museum's decontextualization of Hasidic "things" from Hasidic "thinging." Consequently, the institutionalized collection, conservation, and restoration of Hasidic objects has been primarily undertaken by non-Hasidic collectors and institutions. In fact, so many non-Hasidic private collectors, such as Polish émigré Michael Zagayski and American investor Michael Steinhardt, have amassed Hasidic objects that the field can only be fairly considered as part of the broader Judaica market.[39] In including a discussion on the re-thinging of Hasidic objects, I run a parallel risk to those outdated Jewish art surveys that include antisemitica. However, when the external reconstruction of the subject is so strong that it interacts with or affects the internal image of the self—as the museum has done with Hasidic visual culture—it enters the analysis in new and important ways.

The museological presentation of Hasidic things was undertaken for a number of reasons that speak to how the objects of Hasidism played a constructive role in non-Hasidic identity. In the wave of ethnographic projects that swept the Russian Empire in the first decades of the twentieth century, S. An-sky's ethnographic expedition (1911–1914) to the area of the Pale of Settlement amassed a treasure trove of phonographic recordings, photographs, and *kvitlekh*, artifacts belonging to tsadikim from Hasidic households for the State Ethnographic Museum, now divided between the collections of the Israel Museum in Jerusalem and the Judaica Center and European University in St. Petersburg.[40] An-sky believed that the Hasidim could, due to their passion for preserving their own history through folklore, music, and objects, inspire the amateur or semiprofessional secular collector (*zamler*) and serve as a vehicle for a modern rehabilitation of Jewish culture.[41] "More than any of his contemporaries," asserts Nathaniel Deutsch, "An-sky turned Hasidism into an object of ethnography."[42] Quite differently, Simon Dubnow's disappointment in Hasidism's turn to materialism speaks to his historicization of early Hasidism as a radical countercultural movement that launched a critique on "Rabbinism" at the same time as it offered an alternative path to spiritual regeneration.[43] After the Sovietization of the State Ethnographic Museum, the collection went on exhibit as a testament to the diverse nationalities that lived in "friendship with the peoples" under the Soviet flag, and the Jewish holdings were displayed among Belarusian, Latvian, and Lithuanian materials with typical nationalist flare.[44]

If the ideological role of state authority in museological re-thinging strayed from Hasidic thinging, Israel's museums were especially problematic as they were institutions that explicitly promoted Jewish national rather than religious identity. The largest institutional collections in the interwar period were initiated by secular leaders in Palestine who sought to preserve and exhibit the Old World they left behind in more than fifty kibbutz museums. Like the Soviet ethnographic collections, the Israeli museological exhibition of Hasidic objects is bound by national ideologies that were antithetical to mainstream Hasidic ideologies. East European immigrants to the Yishuv (the Jewish communities in pre-1948 Palestine) conceived of the development of a new "Hebrew" culture in relationship with the diasporic past and put what they identified as relics of that heritage on display.[45] Kibbutz object-collections played out identity tensions not only among themselves but in relationship to those "literary" Zionists still in Europe. While kibbutz curators were apt to shape the legacy of the so-called Litvak model of Judaism, a model that also opposed Hasidism under the name of mitnagedim as a world of darkness and catastrophe, the objects of Hasidism offered a more acceptable example of a lived Jewish culture through which kibbutz ideologues could project a nostalgia for the world they left behind. Just as the Hasidic court signaled a rupture with Lithuanian rabbinical structures to devotees, the Hasidic image likewise offered cultural Zionists a usable precedent of Jewish cultural innovation in the face of regressive traditionalism. This impulse to represent Hasidism as a critique on an enervated Jewish diaspora culture was at the heart of Martin Buber's revival of Hasidic tales, the best-known effort on behalf of an early twentieth-century spiritual renaissance.

With the development of Holocaust museums, Hasidic objects took a turn that Hasidim would come to integrate into their own visual culture. In the context of Hasidic remembrance, the Hasidic image came to signal a "vanished world," an irretrievable past stamped out by racial antisemitism that serves to remind viewers in Israel of the import of their own national homeland and in America of the values of tolerance and democracy. As James Young has argued, the representation of Hasidim in American Holocaust museums portray a peaceful, family-loving people whose ignorance of the coming storms elicit pathos in their victimization, while Israeli museums emphasize the heroic struggle waged by secular Jews on behalf of their religious brethren.[46] It is in this capacity that Hasidim have not only actively participated in Old World nostalgia but invited ethnographers and artists to represent their communities as belonging to that bygone world as it reinforced their self-identification as "surviving remnants" (*sha'arit ha-pleitah*) of an otherwise annihilated East European traditional life.[47] Indeed, the predominant "republishers" of YIVO archive photographs have been Hasidic and ultra-Orthodox media outlets, which continue to trace the individual genealogies of their leaders and model contemporary life after Jewish visual representations of prewar Eastern Europe.[48]

In 2012, the Israel Museum mounted the largest exhibition of Hasidic objects to date in *A World Apart Next Door: Glimpses into the Life of Hasidic Jews*, presenting 270 photographs, drawings, engravings, video and music clips, articles of clothing, headdresses, and ceremonial objects to represent Hasidism as not only alive but flourishing in contemporary Israel.[49] The exhibition, unique in its focus on the materialism of Hasidic life, was staged in the museum's ethnographic wing. Since my discussion here focuses on the role that media plays in Hasidic life, my critique of the exhibition addresses new directions that Hasidic studies might take in view of the current state of the field. While the ethnographic approach has been the typical course of Hasidic "re-thinging" since the times of An-sky, *A World Apart Next Door* relies heavily on professional artists seeking artistic status, not *zamlers*. Without acknowledging the role that the media consciously plays in the Hasidic stylization of the self, the exhibition presented the photographs as vignettes of everyday Hasidic life. That is, the exhibition treated the highly constructed objects as ethnographic artifacts.

The different attitudes toward the cultural construction of space that Hasidim, artists, and museums assume in the representation of Jewish life are made explicit by one of the six videos on display. Displayed on a larger-than-life screen, a bride participates in a "*mitsve-tants*," a dance with her father, the Rachmistrivke (Rotmistrzówka) *Rebbe*, in an elaborate performance meant not only for the vast audience of male Hasidim that sit on bleachers but also for the professional non-Hasidic videographer, whose access to his subjects was contingent on his acceptance of their mores of representation. The bride is both concealed under a nearly opaque veil and on display in the highly choreographed scene. Her contained movements are out of step with the ecstatic motions of her father, but her modest performance is a sign of her spirituality as much as the tsadik's ecstatic dance is a sign of his. The video lens allows no other women to enter the frame and emphasizes the *Rebbe's* movements, the thousands of attentive Hasidim dressed in black, and the singularity of the bride bedecked in white. In contrast to this choreographed organization of social bodies along gender and familial dynastic lines, the Israel Museum created a space in which religious and secular men and women democratically inhabit the exhibitionary complex.

Just as the objectification of the tsadik's words transforms both the tsadik and his disciples, the non-Hasidic collection and institutionalization of Hasidic things transforms both the Hasidic subject and the non-Hasidic viewer. Inquiry into the practices and principles of re-thinging throws light onto the ways that the Hasidic image has shaped American multiculturalism, Israeli nationalism, diaspora Judaism, and so on.

An Example

The Russian-cum-American Hasidic movement of Chabad is currently the most widely represented Hasidic group in global popular culture, and its last leader, R. Menaḥem Mendel Schneerson (1902–1994), is the most visible and publicly recognized *Rebbe* of the twenty-first century despite his passing at the end of the twentieth. His highly successful media campaigns have cornered the market on the Jewish image worldwide, and it is worth considering the origins of Chabad's embrace of rabbinical life-portraiture, which began in 1935 with a highly unusual series of watercolor portraits of R. Menaḥem Mendel Schneerson's predecessor and father-in-law, R. Yosef Yitzḥak Schneersohn, by the Viennese Jewish artist Gertrud Elise Zuckerkandl-Stekel (1895–1980; see figures 10.1–10.4). The series is extraordinary in part because few Hasidic portraits survive from the 1930s. Further, no other rabbinical portraits that I know of takes the form of a series with multiple poses, and no other tsadik life-portrait has been attributed to a female artist prior to World War II.

Initially, I did not have much to go on in establishing the origins and provenance of the portraits. I knew that Gertrud Zuckerkandl-Stekel was an academ-

Figures 10.1–10.4. Gertrud Zuckerkandl-Stekel, portraits of R. Yosef Yitzḥak Schneersohn, 1935, watercolor, paper. Source: Collection of AGUCH. Photos by Maya Balakirsky Katz.

ically trained artist and that the paper on which she painted the portraits was stamped "1935" and "Vienna." From accessible public records, I was able to establish that the year and city matched those of R. Yosef Yitzḥak Schneersohn's stay in the famous Purkersdorf Sanatorium, and that the artist and her husband had inherited the sanatorium only months before R. Yosef Yitzḥak's stay. This was truly extraordinary and raised two interrelated questions only the portraits themselves could ultimately answer: How did a wealthy, intellectual Jewish artist see an East European rabbi in Vienna? How did a Hasidic *Rebbe* feel about being observed and represented by a nonreligious Jewish woman? If I were going to find any answers to these questions, I knew that I would have to begin to look at the portrait series as embedding the competing claims that tsadikim, followers, and outsiders make on the Hasidic image.

In my desire to learn more about the life-world of the artist, I turned to Gertrud's prolific father, the psychoanalyst Wilhelm (Wolf) Stekel (1868–1940), and discovered, as unlikely as it seems, that Stekel had analyzed R. Yosef Yitzḥak's father in 1903 under the supervision of Freud.[50] Research into the portraits revealed that this was no chance meeting in Purkersdorf in 1935, but that the Stekel and Schneersohn families had known each other for two generations in a mental-health-care capacity. I came to wonder what, if anything, did this second generation know about Stekel's analysis and case history of Schneersohn, and how, if at all, did their own relationship as sanatorium proprietor and patient play a role in the creation of the portraits. With more research into Vienna's artistic and medical cultures at the time, I learned that Jewish women artists were being pushed into the margins while Austrian male artists were shaping aesthetic principles around the convergence of Freudian psychoanalysis as a science and expressionism as an art form.[51] This must have been a hard pill to swallow for the daughter of one of Vienna's most prolific psychoanalysts (second only to Freud) who grew up in Freud's inner circle and who painted many of her father's patients. I began to understand that, for Gertrud, whether or not she knew of her father's case history of R. Yosef Yitzḥak's father, R. Shalom Dovber Schneersohn, the portraits exemplified her engagement with the modernists' interest in psychological interiority, which by 1935 was considered a prerequisite to Viennese modernism. Even after her turn to abstraction following World War II, Gertrud insisted that "the psychological portrait always held the greatest fascination for me, especially the expression of the eyes."[52]

I began to consider the possibility that I was not looking at a series of rabbinical portraits but at psychological patient studies. The various threads of the Viennese art world helped me see Gertrud's portraits of R. Yosef Yitzḥak as revealing character studies of a sanatorium patient by an artist who habitually painted psychiatric patients. In an era when art was considered "the handmaiden of medical diagnosis," and the aesthetic principles of the sanatorium, down to the design of the chess pieces, were believed to be "good for the nerves," the creation of the portraits belonged both to the history of the Purkersdorf Sanatorium and to a Viennese art world steeped in working relationships with psychiatrists.[53] If, as art historian Mary Bergstein argues, portrait series were believed to record psychological states, contemporaneous viewers would have readily read R. Yosef Yitzḥak's successive facial expressions as the record of distinct *emotional* states progressing toward a "final" pose in a way parallel to how images in clinical contexts would be used as material ripe for the medical gaze.[54]

But when my research shifted from Gertrud's life-world back to R. Yosef Yitzḥak, I grew conscious of just how far the series had strayed from conventional Hasidic representations of the tsadik. Gertrud's use of delicate pink pastels for R. Yosef Yitzḥak's lips and the overlapping shades of rose hues for his cheeks interiorized the subject from a Viennese perspective but would be objectionable to a Hasidic audience. The unconventional use of color, such as the blue watercolor that spreads into the armpits of the tsadik's robe, bestows the tsadik's body with a musky physicality out of step with Hasidic "thinging" vis-à-vis the spiritual holiness of the tsadik. The very notion of a portrait series with its multiple dressings, alternating space between artist and sitter, and direct eye contact between the artist and the tsadik is unique to Hasidic representations of the *Rebbe.*

Yet, if we follow the process of the artist-sitter relationship, we get a very traditional set of Hasidic practices. In R. Yosef Yitzḥak's face-to-face private sitting with Gertrud, in the artist's gifting R. Yosef Yitzḥak the work of her hands, and in R. Yosef Yitzḥak's preserving the paintings in his private collection, tsadik and artist were drawn together in the most fundamental aspect of Hasidic visual culture.

Furthermore, although the portraits remained in R. Yosef Yitzḥak's private collection and were unpublished for his entire life, the genre of the character portrait nonetheless began to play a key role in R. Yosef Yitzḥak's public persona after he left Vienna and returned to Poland. R. Yosef Yitzḥak, who never officially published any portraits of himself prior to 1935, authorized the first of what would become many portraits upon his return to Otwock, Poland, in his journal, *Ha-tamim.*[55] Although Hasidic movements had produced several Yiddish periodicals in the interwar period, such as *Emek halakha*, *Degel haze'irim*, *Ha-kerem*, and *Beit Avraham*, R. Yosef Yitzḥak's journal held the distinction of publishing the first photographic portrait of a tsadik. To justify his decision despite his father's and grandfather's apparent aversion to portraiture during their leadership tenures, the caption below the photograph explains that the portrait is not simply an external likeness but captures something of "the presence and holiness (*pnei kodesh*) of the master."[56] R. Yosef Yitzḥak appears alone behind his consciously disorganized desk in his private chamber in his makeshift court in the Tomchei Temimim Yeshiva, where he settled after being exiled from the Soviet Union in 1927. In displaying a highly privileged space within what appears to be the interior of a traditional Hasidic court, the photograph implies that R. Yosef Yitzḥak remains in a position of spiritual leadership despite his distance from his Hasidim. His authorization of the portrait established a precedent to own and display rabbinical portraits in Chabad life, which would cast all tsadikim's portraits—future and past—as devotional portraits of dynastic spiritual masters.

It is notable that rabbinical portraiture would come to define the public persona of his successor, R. Menaḥem Mendel Schneerson, who regularly referenced R. Yosef Yitzḥak's portrait legacy to articulate his own position within the patriarchal principle of Hasidic dynasty.[57] In public addresses and personal letters written during the year following R. Yosef Yitzḥak's death, R. Schneerson advised his Hasidim "who did not merit to see" him in life that they could "do so by looking at a picture," and this visualization "requires only our will to do so."[58] In his tenure as *Rebbe* from 1951 to 1994, R. Schneerson charged his followers to disseminate a material Jewish culture not only among themselves but to the world at large, proving transformative to the broader modern Jewish consciousness.

The study of Hasidic visual culture is still in its infancy, and no one can know what new directions Jewish studies will assume with a true understanding of visual culture, but it is my hope that this brief example on rabbinical portraits demonstrates that we should approach material sources not as a repudiation of textual ones, but as revealing new layers of legitimate experiences through the fields of *vision* and *perception*.

SUGGESTED READING

The visual culture Hasidism has produced is vast and storied, but the scholarly literature is still only taking shape. The following resources will offer a solid overview of the current field.

Assaf, David, *The Regal Way: The Life and Times of Rabbi Israel of Ruzhin* (Stanford, CA: Stanford University Press, 2002)—a biohistory of the tsadik of Ruzhin [Rużyn], R. Israel Friedman, that takes into account his attitude toward materialism. Includes many contemporaneous descriptive passages of the architecture, décor, and atmosphere of this magnificent court.

The Bezalel Narkiss Index of Jewish Art—online resource that includes 676 entries under the search term *Hasidic*. Includes architectural drawings and photographs of Hasidic courts, synagogues, schools, and ritual baths as well as more modern portraits and ceremonial objects.

Goldman-Ida, Batsheva, *Hasidic Art and the Kabbalah* (Leiden and Boston: Brill, 2018)—takes the phenomenological approach to Hasidic ceremonial objects with detailed critical analyses of key Hasidic objects, such as R. Naḥman's red chair, *shmire*, the *atara*, among others.

Katz, Maya Balakirsky, *The Visual Culture of Chabad* (New York and Cambridge: Cambridge University Press, 2010)—book-length study on the visual culture of Chabad Hasidism from the mid-nineteenth century to the present. Analyzes the portraits of the *Rebbe*, the objects of religious outreach, and the social constructions of space during the late tsarist era, Sovietization, and Americanization.

Levine, Shalom Dovber, *Treasures from the Chabad Library: The Central Chabad Lubavitch Library and Archive Center* (Brooklyn: Library of Agudas Chasidei Chabad, 2009)—an illustrated and annotated catalogue of the Chabad library collection (AGUCH), including portraits, objects belonging to the *Rebbe*, and photographs of famous disciples.

Muchawsky-Schnapper, Ester, *A World Apart Next Door: Glimpses into the Life of Hasidic Jews* (Jerusalem: The Israel Museum, 2012)—a book-length museum catalogue on the fashions, customs, and visual culture of modern Hasidism in Israel. Includes useful bibliography.

Shandler, Jeffrey, *Jews, God, and Videotape: Religion and Media in America* (New York: New York University Press, 2009), 230–269—explores the ways that Chabad Hasidim employed media as a tool of their religious-outreach programs to engage nonreligious Jews and to create a virtual *Rebbe* for themselves.

Wertheim, Aaron, *Law and Custom in Hasidism*, trans. S. Himelstein (Hoboken, NJ: Ktav, 1992)—an erudite analysis of the fashions, holiday observances, liturgical practices, and master-disciple customs (footnoted, largely within the religious context).

NOTES

1. Visual studies were predominantly launched on behalf of Christianity. For a review essay on the current scholarship on religion and media, see David Morgan, "Religion and Media: A Critical Review of Recent Developments," *Critical Research on Religion* 1 (2013), 3:347–356.

2. See, for example, Cecil Roth and Bezalel Narkiss, eds., *Jewish Art: An Illustrated History* (New York: Vallentine Mitchell, 1971); Joseph Gutmann, ed., *Beauty in Holiness: Studies in Jewish Customs and Ceremonial Art* (New York: Ktav Publishing House, 1970).

3. Erwin R. Goodenough, *Jewish Symbols in the Greco-Roman Period*, 13 vols. (New York: Pantheon Books, 1953–1968).

4. Barbara Kirshenblatt-Gimblett and Jonathan Karp, eds., *The Art of Being Jewish in Modern Times* (Philadelphia: University of Pennsylvania Press, 2008), 2.

5. Gershom Scholem singled out the theoretical literature while Martin Buber singled out folklore at the center of essential Hasidism. See Scholem's *Major Trends in Jewish Mysticism* (New York: Schocken Books, 1941); Buber's *Tales of the Hasidim*, trans. O. Marx (New York: Schocken Books, 1948).

6. The first Hasidic book, Ya'akov Yosef of Polnoe [Połonne], *Toldot Ya'akov Yosef* (Korzec: R. Tsevi Hirsh, 1780), attacks "rabbinism," including the arrogance of book writing. See Zeev Gries, "The Hasidic Managing Editor as an Agent of Culture," in *Hasidism Reappraised*, ed. A. Rapoport-Albert (London: The Littman Library of Jewish Civiliation, 1997), 141–155.

7. Some items of the *geniza* were displayed in a 1960 exhibition on Hasidism. See *Katalog ta'arukhat ha-ḥasidut* (Tel Aviv: Beit HaSofer, 1960). On the forgeries, see Ada Rapoport-Albert, "Hagiography with Footnotes: Edifying Tales and the Writing of History in Hasidism," *History and Theory* 27 (1988), 4:119–159.

8. See Aaron Wertheim, *Law and Custom in Hasidism*, trans. S. Himelstein (Hoboken, NJ: Ktav, 1992).

9. For a discussion of Hasidic spatial practices, see Adam Teller, "Hasidism and the Challenge of Geography: The Polish Background to the Spread of the Hasidic Movement," *AJS Review* 30 (2006), 1–29; Alla Sokolova, "The Podolian Shtetl as Architectural Phenomenon," in G. Estraikh and M. Krutikov, eds., *The Shtetl: Image and Reality* (Oxford: Oxford University Press, 2000), 36–79.

10. Immanuel Etkes, "The Early Hasidic 'Court,'" *Text and Context* (2005), 157–186. On the synagogues that served as models for Hasidic courts, see Rachel Wischnitzer, *The Architecture of the European Synagogue* (Philadelphia: Jewish Publication Society, 1964). For a case history of one court and its culture, see David Assaf, *The Regal Way: The Life and Times of Rabbi Israel of Ruzhin* (Stanford, CA: Stanford University Press, 2002), 276, 334. On the Chernobyl court, see Gadi Sagiv, *Ha-shoshelet: Bet Chernobil u-mekomo be-toledot ha-ḥasidut* (Jerusalem: Zalman Shazar Center, 2014). For more, see chapter 12 of this book.

11. Jeffrey Shandler, *Jews, God, and Videotape: Religion and Media in America* (New York: New York University Press, 2009), 230–269.

12. For a comparative study of Bratslav [Bracław] and Chabad Hasidism, see Joseph Weiss, *Studies in East European Jewish Mysticism and Hasidism* (London: Littman Library of Jewish Civilization, 1997).

13. Batsheva Goldman-Ida, *Hasidic Art and the Kabbalah* (Boston: Brill Press, 2017).

14. Moshe Rosman, *The Founder of Hasidism: A Quest for the Historical Baal Shem Tov* (Berkeley: University of California Press, 1996); David Assaf, ed., *Tsadik ve-'edah: Hevetim historiyim ve-ḥevratiyim be-ḥeker ha-ḥasidut* (Jerusalem: Zalman Shazar Center, 2001); Glenn Dynner, *Men of Silk: The Hasidic Quest of Polish Jewry* (Oxford: Oxford University Press, 2006); Avram M. Ehrlich, *Leadership in the HaBaD Movement: A Critical Evaluation of the HaBaD Leadership, History, and Succession* (Northvale, NJ, and London: Jason Aronson, 2000); Maya Balakirsky Katz, *The Visual Culture of Chabad* (New York and Cambridge: Cambridge University Press, 2010).

15. For photographs of the menorah, see Mattis Goldberg, *Gedolei Yisroel: Portraits of Greatness* (Jerusalem: Feldheim Publishers, 2006), 254–255.

16. For a volume that reproduces samples of handwriting, portraits, and photographs of gravesites, see Yitzḥak Alfasi, *Ha-ḥasidut* (Tel Aviv: Bnei Berit, 1974).

17. See Nathaniel Deutsch, *The Maiden of Ludmir: A Jewish Holy Woman and Her World* (Berkeley: University of California Press, 2003). Other famous Hasidic women include Merish, daughter of R. Elimelekh of Lizhensk [Leżajsk] (1717–1787); Perele, daughter of R. Israel of Kuznits [Kozienice] (1733–1814); Malkale, daughter of R. Avraham of Trisk [Turzysk] (1806–1889).

18. A discussion of secular artists whose work was informed by their own Hasidic backgrounds is not included here because they chose channels of communication that were not adopted by Hasidism, such as Yiddish theater, puppetry, toy-making, photography, and cinematography.

19. On the use of broadsides, see Hananel Rosenberg and Tsuriel Rashi, "And Ye Shall Bring Forth the Old (Medium) before the New: Wall Posters (Pashkevilim) in the Struggle for Legitimacy of Kosher Cell Phones," *Israel Studies in Language and Society* 6 (2014), 2:71–95.

20. In Chabad, the practice is supported, in part, on the *Rebbe's* ruling on the permissibility of seeking answers from holy books in Menaḥem Mendel Schneerson, *Shaarei halakhah u-minhag*, vol. 5 (Brooklyn, NY: Kehot Publication Society, 1993). For a recent example, see the story by Yehudis Litvak, "The Baal Shem Tov's Sefer Torah: A Special Journey," *Tachlis Magazine*, June 17, 2016, 41.

21. Gedaliah Fleer, *Against All Odds* (Israel: Breslov Research Institute, 2005); Yitzḥak Ayzik Zilberman, *'Ir ha-gaguim* (Jerusalem: self-published, 1988).

22. Jack Kugelmass, "The Rites of the Tribe: The Meaning of Poland for American Jewish Tourists," *YIVO Annual* 21 (1993), 395–453; Mitsuharu Akao, "A New Phase in Jewish-Ukrainian Relations? Problems and Perspectives in the Ethno-Politics over the Hasidic Pilgrimage to Uman," *East European Jewish Affairs* 37 (2007), 2:137–155.

23. David Assaf, *Untold Tales of the Hasidim: Crisis and Discontent in the History of Hasidism*, trans. D. Ordan (Waltham, MA: Brandeis University Press, 2010), 149–152.

24. On visuality and materialism in Hasidic ideology, see Elliot Wolfson, *Through a Speculum That Shines: Vision and Imagination in Medieval Jewish Mysticism* (Princeton, NJ: Princeton University Press, 1994); Daniel Boyarin, "The Eye in the Torah: Ocular Desire in Midrashic Hermeneutics," *Critical Inquiry* 16 (1990), 534–543.

25. Gershom Scholem, "Devekut or Communion with God," in Scholem, *The Messianic Idea in Judaism and Other Essays on Jewish Spirituality* (New York: Schocken Books, 1971), 203–226.

26. Gershom Scholem, "Martin Buber's Interpretation of Hasidism," in *The Messianic Idea in Judaism*, 227–250.

27. On the use of parable in the Hasidic tale, see Joseph Dan, *Ha-sipur ha-ḥasidi* (Jerusalem: Keter, 1975). On the use of parable in Hasidic dance, see Michael Fishbane, "The Mystery of Dance according to R. Nahman of Bratslav," in *Be-ma'agelei ḥasidim: Kovets meḥkarim le-zikhro shel profesor Mordekhai Wilensky*, ed. I. Etkes et al. (Jerusalem: Mosad Bialik, 1999), 335–350. On the use of parable in Hasidic music, see Chani Haran Smith, *Tun-*

ing the Soul: Music as a Spiritual Process in the Teachings of Rabbi Nahman of Bratzlav (Boston and Leiden: Brill, 2010).

28. Yehudah Liebes, "Ha-Tikkun Ha-Kelali of R. Nahman of Bratslav and Its Sabbatean Links," in *Studies in Jewish Myth and Jewish Messianism*, ed. Y. Liebes, trans. B. Stein (Albany: State University of New York Press, 1993), 115–150; David Biale, *Eros and the Jews: From Biblical Israel to Contemporary America* (Berkeley: University of California Press, 1997), 121–148.

29. Samuel Abba Horodetzsky, "Rabbi Nahman, Romanticism, and Rationalism," in *God's Voice from the Void: Old and New Studies in Bratslav Hasidism*, ed. S. Magid (Albany: State University of New York Press, 2002), 263–276.

30. Marianne Schleicher, *Intertextuality in the Tales of Rabbi Nahman of Bratslav: A Close Reading of Sippurey Ma'asiyot* (Leiden and Boston: Brill, 2007), 58 n119.

31. Kirk Pillow, *Sublime Understanding: Aesthetic Reflection in Kant and Hegel* (Cambridge, MA: MIT Press, 2000).

32. Immanuel Kant, *Observations on the Feeling of the Beautiful and Sublime*, trans. J. T. Goldthwaite (Berkeley: University of California Press, 2003 [1764]).

33. Karl Philipp Moritz, *Schriften zur Äesthetik und Poetik*, ed. H. Schrimpf (Tübingen: Max Niemeyer, 1962). See the related discussion by Naftali Loewenthal, *Communicating the Infinite: The Emergence of the Habad School* (Chicago and London: University of Chicago Press, 1990), 139–179.

34. On RaSHaB's interpretation of a painting, see Yosef Yitzḥak Schneersohn, *Sefer ha-Siḥot 5696—Khoref 5700* (Brooklyn: Kehot Publication Society, 1989), 46–47. On attitudes toward Rembrandt, see A. Melnikoff, "Rembrandt and Divine Light," *London Jewish Chronicle*, September 13, 1935, 21.

35. Some of these have even been put on display by Hasidic groups. In his forthcoming essay "Hasidism in the Museum from a Social History Perspective," David Assaf identifies the first exhibition of Hasidic objects as sponsored by Hasidim in 1960: "Hasidism in the Museum: The Social History Perspective," in *New Directions in the History of the Jews in the Polish Lands*, eds. Antony Polonsky, Hanna Węgrzynek, and Andrzej Żbikowski (Boston: Academic Studies Press, 2018), 93–104. See also Shalom Dovber Levine, *Treasures from the Chabad Library: The Central Chabad Lubavitch Library and Archive Center* (Brooklyn, NY: Library of Agudas Chasidei Chabad, 2009).

36. One notable exception is Chabad's Jewish Children's Museum in Crown Heights, Brooklyn.

37. For the legend of R. Shneur Zalman of Lady's setting fire to his own court in Lady in 1812 so that Napoleon's advancing armies could not appropriate its tangible spirituality, see Yosef Yitzḥak Schneersohn, *Likkutei Dibburim: An Anthology of Talks*, trans. U. Kaploun (Brooklyn, NY: Kehot Publication Society, 1987).

38. For the article that opened the field of political museology, see Carol Duncan and Alan Wallach, "The Universal Survey Museum," *Art History* 3 (1980), 448–469.

39. For one recent large-scale auction, see *Catalogue of Fine Judaica: Printed Books, Manuscripts, Autograph Letters, Ceremonial Objects, and Graphic Art from the Estate of a Chassidic Scholar* (New York: Kestenbaum & Co., 2013).

40. See the essay on An-sky's collection in Valerii Dymshits, "The First Jewish Museum," in *Photographing the Jewish Nation: Pictures from the S. An-sky's Ethnographic Expeditions*, ed. E. M. Avrutin et al. (Waltham, MA: Brandeis University Press, 2009).

41. Sh. An-sky, *Ḥurban ba-yihudim be-Polin, Galicia, ve-Bukovina*, part I (Berlin: A. I. Shtibel, 1929). An-sky's wedded view of ethnographic collecting and cultural revitalization bears out in his play *The Dybbuk*. On Hasidic-themed plays on the Polish stage preceding An-sky, see Marcin Wodziński, *Haskalah and Hasidim in the Kingdom of Poland: A History of Conflict* (Oxford: The Littman Library of Jewish Civilization, 2005), 241–247.

42. Nathaniel Deutsch, *The Jewish Dark Continent: Life and Death in the Russian Pale of Settlement* (Cambridge, MA: Harvard University Press, 2011), 50.

43. Simon Dubnow, *History of the Jews in Russia and Poland from the Earliest Times until the Present Day*, trans. I. Friedlander (New York: Nabu Press, 1975), 1:384.

44. Judith Belinfante and Igor Dubov, eds., *Tracing An-sky: Jewish Collections from the State Ethnographic Museum in St. Petersburg* (Zwolle: Waanders, 1992), 17. For a discussion of other interwar Jewish museum projects in Eastern Europe, see Renata Piatkowska, "Skarby naszej przeszłości: Muzea żydowskie w Polsce," *Studia Judaica* 16 (2013), 3–45.

45. Galia Bar-Or, *Hayenu mehaivim omanut: Banyan tarbut ke-vinyan ḥevrah, 1930–1960* (Sedeh-Boker: Ben Gurion University Press, 2010).

46. James Young, *The Texture of Memory: Holocaust Memorials and Meaning* (New Haven, CT: Yale University Press, 1994). See, for example, Lucjan Dobroszycki and Barbara Kirshenblatt-Gimblett, *Image before my Eyes: A Photographic History of Jewish Life in Poland, 1864–1939* (New York: Schocken Books, 1977). For the ways that photographic technology came to evoke a broader "freezing" of Orthodoxy before the Holocaust, see Jeffrey Shandler, "The Time of Vishniac," *Polin* 16 (2003), 332.

47. See, for example, Philip Garvin, *A People Apart: Hasidism in America* (New York: Dutton, 1970).

48. See, for example, the large-format illustrated tome published by Agudath Israel, *Ashes to Renewal: The Story of a Nation's Immortality* (New York: Agudath Israel of America, 1995).

49. Ester Muchawsky-Schnapper, *A World Apart Next Door: Glimpses into the Life of Hasidic Jews* (Jerusalem: The Israel Museum, 2012).

50. For the article that identifies Stekel's case history of "der rabbiner" as R. Shalom Dovber Schneersohn, see Maya Balakirsky Katz, "An Occupational Neurosis: A Psychoanalytic Case History of a Rabbi," *AJS Review* 34 (2010), 1:1–31. For the article that deals with some of the inconsistencies in the writing of the case history, see Maya Balakirsky Katz, "A Rabbi, a Priest, and a Psychoanalyst: Religion in the Early Psychoanalytic Case History," *Contemporary Jewry* 31 (2011), 1:3–24.

51. See Julie M. Johnson, *The Memory Factory: The Forgotten Women Artists of Vienna 1900* (West Lafayette, IN: Purdue University Press, 2012), 112.

52. See the exhibition of Gertrud's art in conjunction with the French printing of her father's *Technik der analystischen Psychotherapie* in Jacqueline Baron, "Gertrude Stekel: Des tableaux lumineux et tragiques," *La Suisse*, October 21, 1976.

53. Leslie Topp, "An Architecture for the Modern Nerves: Josef Hoffmann's Purkersdorf Sanatorium," *Journal of the Society of Architectural Historians* 56 (1997), 4:414–437.

54. Mary Bergstein, *Mirrors of Memory: Freud, Photography, and the History of Art* (Ithaca, NY, and London: Cornell University Press, 2010), 89.

55. This was the first published portrait, although R. Yosef Yitzḥak did have postcards of himself printed in 1927, the year that he was exiled from Russia. It is impossible to distinguish between the editors of *Ha-tamim* and their *Rebbe* as he and his son-in-law oversaw the journal's content.

56. Photograph and caption in *Ha-tamim* (1936), 1:7.

57. See the explanation of individual portraits of Chabad's leaders throughout the Chabad library collection in Levine, *Treasures from the Chabad Library.*

58. Eliezer Zaklikofsky, *Mekadesh Yisrael: Talks and Images at Wedding Celebrations (1943–1963)* (Brooklyn, NY: Kehot Publication Society, 2000), 19.

CHAPTER 11

Music

Edwin Seroussi

"Hasidism brought about a veritable renaissance of Jewish music."[1] This is the most widespread, almost axiomatic trope in the modern literature about Jewish music. It stems from Hasidic and neo-Hasidic sources as well as from scholarly writings on Hasidism. The regenerative energy of this musical renaissance was also the impulse for the central place Hasidic music attained in diverse streams of modern Jewish culture, from Zionism to postmodern American Jewish spiritualism. This modern idea can be traced back to various sources emanating from diverse intellectual streams based in German-speaking countries and in the Russian Empire. The first stream, stemming from German Jewish circles, is aptly summarized in the young Martin Buber's dictum that "Hasidism is the birth of a new Judaism" and that the "synagogal and popular music" which remained alive in the (Hasidic) ghetto "adapt[s] easily to the new forms [of musical composition]."[2] The second stream emanates from ideas about Hasidism as the last "authentic" trace of traditional Judaism that developed among the Jewish intelligentsia in the Russian Empire around 1900 (see more below). Berlin and St. Petersburg soon became centers for the documentation, publication, arrangement, and distribution of Hasidic music amid other emergent Jewish centers from Vienna to New York City.

Part of this widening modern interest in Hasidic music is grounded on the perception that "musicking" was a hallmark of Hasidism.[3] Early research on Hasidism also noticed the prominence of music in Hasidic rituals and thought, as evidenced in the oral and written literature about music in all genres, folk tales, homilies, commentaries of scripture, and more. Hasidism's acerbic opponents, mitnagedim and maskilim, as well as its romantic and admiring promoters shared this perception of the centrality of music in Hasidism, though for different reasons. This enthusiastic approach to Hasidic music has generated ample literature and a constant interest in this repertoire from the early twentieth century to the present. At the same time, this literature led to misperceptions about the nature, origins, and characteristics of Hasidic music and dance that continue to be perpetuated.

An ontology of Hasidic music is impossible because the span of musical styles, genres, performance practices, and discourses deployed by Hasidim refuse simple characterizations. One has to consider in this regard the different stages in the development of Hasidic music. In the rather limited geographical area where Hasidim developed in the eighteenth century, one can assume that the repertoire was rather homogenous. During the consolidation of Hasidism as a major movement of Judaism throughout Eastern Europe in the nineteenth century, repertoires diversified with the creation of local traditions by "court composers" and cantors associated with each tsadik, although family networks between the tsadikim did promote the sharing of niggunim along vast distances. With the emergence of parallel Hasidic diasporas outside Eastern Europe, first in Ottoman Palestine, later in Western Europe, and finally in the Americas, the repertoires of each court diversified even more and were enriched by newer local musical accretions. The Holocaust dislocated and erased many Hasidic musical memories, and their recovery had to lean on those diasporas that were spared annihilation.

The post-World War II period witnessed an impressive regrouping of Hasidic remnants from the ashes, the re-creation of many courts in the Americas, Western Europe, and Israel, and subsequently the recovery of lost musical repertoires amid intensive creativity and "inventions of tradition." Moreover, as we shall notice, the massive distribution of commercial recordings after the war catapulted some Hasidic niggunim from specific courts (especially Modzits [Modrzyce] and Chabad) into universal fame in Hasidic and non-Hasidic circles as well. Thus, the dynamics of standardization and diversification nurtured each other in a dialectic process.

Hence, the contemporary concept of "Hasidic music" has developed throughout the modern period, reflecting practices and aesthetic choices that often bear no relation to the music performed by Jews who define themselves as Hasidic. In turn, not all contemporary "Hasidic music" is Hasidic, and not all the music performed by Hasidim is necessarily unique to them inasmuch as Hasidim are part of the Ashkenazi world and share many musical practices with non-Hasidic Ashkenazi Jews. Finally, not all Hasidic music as presented nowadays by Hasidim themselves as "historically authentic" is indeed so.

"Hasidic music" is usually supported by a discourse of Hasidic musical exceptionalism that emerged among scholars of Jewish music from the beginnings of ethnography. Sonic exceptionalism is a component of the general trend to exoticize Hasidism as a unique spiritual form of Judaism, a trope that became a staple of Jewish modernity. As we shall see, Hasidic music and musical theory have roots in previous Jewish practices and ideas about music and its powers.

Nevertheless, Hasidism also deployed music in a novel fashion that reflects the time and place of its appearance. In its own manner, then, "real" Hasidic music is a modern musical phenomenon too.

It must be stressed that Hasidic music was (and still is to a certain extent) transmitted orally. Therefore, tangible data about the music itself appear only in the early twentieth century, when ethnographic efforts to capture Hasidic music emerged and when the movement was already well advanced in its history. As noticed, the Holocaust erased musical memories too, and therefore one cannot know the extent to which available data reflect past Hasidic musical practices. On the other hand, writings about music by Hasidic masters and descriptions of Hasidic musical life by their opponents are available from the beginnings of the movement. These statements allow for a fragmentary incursion into the ways Hasidism approached, created, and mobilized music since its inception.

To summarize, any attempt to set boundaries to a corpus of music or of ideas about music defined as "Hasidic" is problematic. This statement, however, does not imply that Jewish communities defining themselves as Hasidic in the present do not perform musical repertoires and possess ideas about music that are particular to them. However, as much as Hasidism is a variegated and multifaceted strand of Judaism, so are the musical repertoires and theories of music associated with it. Since Hasidism is a dynamic process, so are its musical repertoires and practices.

Five basic tenets will guide this chapter:

1. Hasidic music is Ashkenazi music. Therefore, the degree to which Hasidic music departs from non-Hasidic Ashkenazi music practices is a question to be addressed.
2. The geographical span of the Hasidic movement during its European peak in the late nineteenth century covered a vast territory whose musical cultures varied. The vastness of the boundaries of Eastern Europe calls for an approach that stresses the multiplicity of Hasidic musical cultures in terms of localized genres, styles, and performance practices, and this is in spite of their shared Ashkenazi liturgical heritage and language.
3. As it consolidated toward the second third of the nineteenth century and exists now, Hasidism is a phenomenon of the modern era. All the images that modern Jewish secular culture (from the maskilim of all types to Zionists to diasporic nationalists) and the non-Jewish imagination have imposed upon Hasidism—such as "traditional," "Orthodox," "authentic," "spiritual," "ecstatic," "revolutionary"—distanced Hasidism from its modern observers. However, the adaptability of Hasidism to modernity is remarkable also in terms of music research. Contemporary Hasidim share the modern anxieties of forgetting, documenting, and archiving music, and they entertain basic value concepts of modernity, such as "tradition" and

"authenticity," and avidly recruit the late capitalist economy of music by using modern technologies of music preservation and distribution such as music notation or music portals in the internet. One has to distinguish then a musicology of Hasidism (the external gaze) from Hasidic musicology (the internal one).

4. Even though every aspect of Hasidic life has a religious import and thus all musical performances imply a religious experience, not all music heard in Hasidic courts was necessarily earmarked to the divine service. Certain genres, especially marches, were also used as symbols of status, as part of the aristocratic pomp and circumstance that surrounded some tsadikim, although these too could be interpreted as a component of the worship of a revered spiritual master.
5. Hasidic music also exists outside Hasidism. It became part of the Zionist musical culture as well as the modern Jewish revivalist movements in America, especially after World War II. Even more poignant from a historical perspective, Hasidic music has conquered significant portions of the Ashkenazi Orthodox camp, as well as non-Ashkenazi Sephardic and Oriental Jews in Israel who "converted" to Hasidism. Thus, a musicology of Hasidism has to look beyond the borderlines of the established Hasidic communities.

Research on Hasidic Music

As mentioned, research on Hasidic music is multifaceted, going back to the late nineteenth century. Many scholars reviewed here had direct personal roots in Hasidic families or ties to Hasidic courts through family connections. Therefore, they had the advantage of having access to inside information but at times the disadvantage of lacking the more detached gaze of the outsider. We will start with the impact of new paradigms of research on Hasidism on musicological research before moving into a review of the literature. Following a distinction presented in the introduction, Hasidic musicology, or the Hasidic writings on music, appear in a separate section.

Hasidic Music and New Research on Hasidism

New paradigms of interpretation that developed in the study of Hasidism in the past three decades are pertinent to Hasidic music research. By anchoring Hasidism to subterranean currents within Judaism, some of them going back to antiquity, and contextualizing it within the economic, social, and ideological shifts taking place in Eastern and Central Europe since the mid-eighteenth century outside the Jewish community, scholars have pointed out the complexities of this movement and its impressive, if at times overemphasized, dissemination. Hasidism has also been deconstructed into a variety of movements, at times contrasting, with diverse agendas and models of leadership. Music reflects such a variety as well.

Although addressing mostly music in pre-Hasidic kabbalistic and mystical Jewish circles, the musical scholarship of Moshe Idel has set an agenda for the study of Hasidic music that was internalized by musicologists.[4] Idel's critique of Martin Buber and of Gershom Scholem emphasized the following conceptual tools that guided the approaches of these two scholars to Hasidism: proximism, reductionism, Kabbalah as Gnosticism, existentialism versus historicism, stable essences versus emphasis on change, and reactive versus continuative.[5] All these concepts can be projected into music research. They lead to questions such as:

1. Does Hasidic music depart from its antecedent Ashkenazi music?
2. Do Hasidic ideas about music emanate from immediate Lurianic, Cordoverian, or Sabbatean precedents, or do they disclose deeper currents going back to antiquity and the early Middle Ages?
3. Is the idea of the textless niggun a Hasidic innovation or a continuation or expansion of previous Ashkenazi practices?
4. To what degree does Hasidic music dialogue with musical practices of surrounding non-Jewish peoples such as Ukrainian folk music or Romantic Polish opera, or is it a sui generis repertoire?
5. How do the present-day Hasidic repertoires that were consolidated after World War II relate to those of the past?

Music's slippery nonverbal signification challenged the dichotomy between phenomenological versus intellectual experience as the focus of a musicology of Hasidism. Moreover, as mechanical recordings and printed scores proliferated, the musicology of Hasidism also drowned in the vast ocean of niggunim, attempting to domesticate a repertoire that defies classifications. Even when "native" musical terminologies appeared, such as in the case of Chabad, they offered contradictory criteria, such as the mixed classification of niggunim by their composers, social function, and musical style.

Idel stressed Hasidism as an aural culture, one in which sound plays a crucial role rather than the written word. For example, the sounds of prayer and Torah study are "the substrata whereupon the supernal voices cleave and announce future things, which also reach man by hearing."[6] The voice of the tsadik is a primal element that can influence supernal processes, such as the vocal performance of the Book of Enoch by the Besht while teaching the Maggid of Mezrich (Międzyrzecz).[7]

The relational models of Hasidism are quintessential to musical performances. Man-God and man-community are relations forged through sonic communication, mostly by niggun. These direct relations obliterated (on the surface, as we shall see) intermediaries. The tsadik or any spiritually inspired layman could chant the liturgy, substituting the vocally trained cantor and his assistants who were so prominent in large Ashkenazi synagogues when Hasidism emerged.[8]

Other ideas proposed by Idel, even if not accepted *tout court* by all scholars of Hasidism, opened new vistas for musicology. The idea that Hasidic thought was closer to Muslim than to Christian mysticism, for example, is interesting if one considers the proximity of the cradle of Hasidism, Podolia and Volhynia, to the lands controlled by the Ottoman Empire, such as Moldavia.[9] Some of the ideas about the transformative power of music in attaining a state of cleaving to the Divine (*devekut*) may have percolated into Hasidism via the writings of Jewish masters and kabbalists active in the Ottoman Empire, such as R. Menaḥem di Lonzano, or the oral traditions carried back to Eastern Europe by occasional Hasidic visitors to the Levant. Moreover, these "Eastern" ideas about prayer techniques as well as the social structure of the Hasidic courts (including the centrality of the tsadik) suggestively resonate with those of Ottoman Sufi orders.

In addition, Idel's remarks regarding the binary opposition between the participatory experience of *communitas* in Hasidism versus the focus on the individual tsadik's performance have musical implications too.[10] Individual mystical experience was the focus of activities by early Hasidic masters, although their final aim was to project this experience into their community. Musical performances will therefore move over time from solo to group performance, as is hinted by the vivid description, one of the first of its kind, of the Shabbat table at the court of the Maggid of Mezrich by Salomon Maimon: "We sat down to table and during the meal a solemn silence reigned. After the meal was over, the superior (*hohen Obern*) struck up a solemn inspiring melody, held his hand for some time upon his brow, and then began to call out 'Z. of H.!' 'M. of R.!' 'S.M. of N.!' and so forth. Every new comer was thus called by his own name and the name of his residence."[11] The musical performance of a slow or meditative niggun by the Maggid (if we can interpret "solemn inspiring melody" in this way) therefore induced his clairvoyance. This incident, whose ethnographic authenticity cannot be discarded in spite of Maimon's overall animosity toward the whole experience, suggests a synthesis between the extreme mystical and the extreme magical claims of the tsadikim that Idel also suggests.[12]

A most colorful description of this irresistible attraction that Hasidic singing held on "innocent" souls, again coming from Hasidism's opponents, draws from none other than Homer's *Odyssey*:

> When the naïf arrives, he hears their tunes and their pleasant voices, for the majority of them have fine voices and know how to sing. This melodious sweetness leads him to attach himself to them with great love. . . . His fate in this is like that of the inexperienced sailor. There is a certain creature that lives in the sea: its upper half has the appearance of a female human being, while below

> it is fishlike. It sometimes appears to those who sail the seas, showing only its upper half. It sings to them in a sweet and seductive voice. The foolish and inexperienced sea captain will be drawn closer to hear her better and to enjoy her singing. The sweetness of the song will be fatal because it is oversweet.[13]

If one applies these new approaches to Hasidism suggested by Idel and many other scholars to the field of music, one can start by stressing continuities in the musical terminology of Hasidism and Jewish antiquity, Kabbalah in its many facets (especially but not exclusively Lurianic), and neo-Platonic ideas.[14] For example, the influential corpus of texts stemming from the ascetic Jewish circles in the Rhineland during the twelfth and thirteenth centuries known as *Sefer ḥasidim* may be a source for the centrality of niggun (a recurrent concept in *Sefer ḥasidim*) as a transformative medium, especially during statutory prayer. Exposure of early Hasidic masters to the musical ideas of *Sefer ḥasidim* may have been direct (the compendium was printed in 1538) or through quotations in texts that Hasidim read, such as Menaḥem di Lonzano's *Shetei yadot*, which treats the concept of niggun extensively under the authority of *Sefer ḥasidim*.[15]

Moving beyond Judaism, the ecstatic experience of niggun in Hasidism, including variants of trance and even possession, cannot be separated from similar phenomena that have been studied from a cross-cultural perspective.[16] Even if the early Hasidic masters did not pick up their enthusiastic patterns of renewing the religious experience of prayer through music and dance from non-Jewish models such as ecstatic Christian sects in the Russian Empire, they were cognizant of these powers of music and dance from ancient Jewish sources.[17]

The act of borrowing niggunim from the surrounding gentile cultures as an act of redeeming their lost original holiness, a central topos of many writings about Hasidic music, also needs historical contextualization and moderation. Considered to be one of the most exciting and infuriating novelties of early Hasidism by its sympathizers and opponents respectively, this idea has, however, a long pedigree in Judaism. What is remarkable is the extent to which Hasidism delved into the concept of niggun redemption (even if the actual number of "acquisitions" is proportionately much lower than what the literature tends to emphasize), and its practical consequences are namely a stylistically diverse repertoire.

For example, the Imrei Ḥayim, R. Ḥayim Moshe Hager of Vizhnitz (Vijniţa) (1887–1972), whose musical gifts are well documented, as is the elaborate musical pageantry of his renewed court in Israel, elaborated a famous commentary on Genesis 43:11. In this verse, Jacob says to his sons, "Take of the best produce of the land [*mi-zimrat ha-ʿarets*] in your vessels, and take an offering to the man." For the Imrei Ḥayim, "of the best produce of the land" are songs and melodies (*zemirot ve-nigunim*) from a "low place"—from the earthly realm. Those songs and melodies are uploaded "in your vessels," thus are raised by the tsadik who makes them holy by revealing their concealed holiness. "The man" (*ish*) who receives this "melodious present" is God, as written (Exodus 15:3): "God is a man (*ish*) of war." The Imrei Ḥayim makes a point of positioning himself in a musical lineage by recalling his predecessors in this musical practice, R. Yitzḥak Aizyk Taub of Kaliv (Nagykálló) (1744–1821) and his own father, R. Israel ben Barukh Hager of Vizhnitz (1860–1936). Both these holy men heard melodies and songs from simple shepherds and elevated these songs from their overflowing holiness. The Imrei Ḥayim just perpetuated this established practice.[18]

However, the midrash by the Imrei Ḥayim has deep roots and goes back as far as Rashi's eleventh-century commentary on the expression *mi-zimrat ha-'arets*, which reads as follows: "of the best produce of the land: Targumim [Aramaic translations] render *midebeshabḥa ba-ar'ah* [lit.], from what is praised in the land, that which each one sings about when he comes into the world." Moreover, sixteenth- and seventeenth-century Ottoman Sephardic rabbis and poets, such as the aforementioned Menaḥem di Lonzano, supported the idea of borrowing the most attractive melodies from non-Jewish society as an act of deploying their emotional affects to the true sacred service. Other earlier Hasidic writings also elaborated this argument, departing from the same biblical verse, most famously those by R. Naḥman of Bratslav (Bracław).[19]

Some scholars claim, on the other hand, Hasidic exceptionalism on the subject of melodic acquisitions from the "lowest" strata of the surrounding society. Glenn Dynner proposes to interpret this borrowing of music as a case of the power of transgression as a religious deed particular to Hasidism.[20]

Another cross-cultural perspective calls for attention to how general trends in European music history relate to Hasidic music. In the modern imagination, Hasidic music is linked to the experience of the imagined shtetl at the expense of the urban one. The dichotomy between city and shtetl (in its noticeably different variants throughout time and space) is, however, problematic. Hasidism emerged at a time of fast urbanization, when substantial changes in the conceptualization, practice, and economy of music materialized in German-speaking Europe, including such "Eastern" cities as Vienna and Prague. Cities of the Austro-Hungarian Empire experienced accelerated Hasidic presence after the partition of Poland. Russian-controlled Warsaw offered Hasidim access to sophisticated urban music as early as the second third of the nineteenth century.[21] Leaders of early nineteenth-century Hasidism were exposed to large cities and their powerful soundscapes, whether because of a forced journey, such as that of R. Shneur Zalman of Lady to his St. Petersburg imprisonment, or advanced medical treatment, as in the case of R. Naḥman of Bratslav.

The Napoleonic wars contributed to the exposure of Hasidim to imposing military music that became a model for the music of other imperial armies. "Hasidic armies" spiced wedding processions of groom and bride and regal receptions of visiting tsadikim with military formations of young Hasidim dressed as Cossacks (or in more modern American versions, dressed as American soldiers of the Revolutionary War) striding to the sounds of Russian marches.

In addition, modern cathedral-like synagogues, which offered expanded choral services, rose in the nineteenth century one after another in large European cities. They became a yardstick against which Hasidim would react by rejecting these new aesthetics of worship and strengthening their "sonic difference" or by internalizing some of their features. This period also marks the beginning of Jewish European musical literacy with musicians of Jewish pedigree getting access to prestigious music schools and stages in Berlin, Paris, Vienna, and later on St. Petersburg. The rise of the German romantic idea of "absolute" instrumental music as a transformative art of high spiritual power percolated into the large urban centers of western Poland and Russia by the beginning of the nineteenth century, reaching also Hasidic ears. Warsaw opera houses, for example, were, according to rumors, frequented by Hasidic singers in disguise eager to learn new melodies.[22] This effervescent European sonic atmosphere that enveloped Hasidic music in the nineteenth century is the source, for example, of the presence of the waltzes in the Hasidic repertoires of "urban" courts such as Ger.

The evolving idea of the Hasidic court with its urban overtones invited a permanent musical apparatus that would include cantors, singers, and instrumentalists. While the *shtibl* could be compared to an inn, projecting intimacy and therefore the idea of "chamber music," the court's musical needs grew exponentially, as pilgrimages to tsadikim and assemblies on Shabbats and holy days became larger. This growth in musical activity further complicates the concept of "Hasidic music" and its city/shtetl binary opposition.

Ethnographies and Studies of Hasidic Music

We have seen that the modern, non-Hasidic Jewish gaze on Hasidism paid utmost attention to the Hasidic niggun and its performance practices as one of the major novelties of the movement since its inception. This interest led to the ethnography of the niggun carried out at first by sympathetic maskilim and later by Hasidim who joined these ventures out of similar motivations: the modern anxiety of disappearance and the recruitment of new technologies to advance cultural, religious, and political agendas. Niggunim were assiduously collected, transcribed into musical notation, published in journals, arranged for concert performances, and recorded by an array of practicing musicians and scholars.

Among the earliest important writings is an article of 1907 (published in installments in the Zionist Hebrew newspaper *Ha-ʿolam*) by the cantor, composer, and music teacher Avraham Ber Birnbaum (1864–1922), scion of a Hasidic family from Pułtusk near Warsaw and for most of his adult life a "modern" chief cantor in Częstochowa. An "insider/outsider" witness who experienced Polish Hasidism during its peak, Birnbaum wrote an essay that is a notable contribution duly recognized by Abraham Zvi Idelsohn, who quoted him copiously.[23] Especially interesting is Birnbaum's lachrymose opening perception of the "cooling off of 'poetical Hasidism' that has almost disappeared," which triggered his ethnographic endeavor. "[Music] is important for the historian [of Hasidism] because it has utmost importance in Hasidism, on the lectern [of the synagogue], on the *tish* [he uses the Hebrew *shulḥan*] and after it. Without *zemirot* it is impossible to think about the Hasidic *act* [his word in Hebrew too]. You can give up the '*torah*' [sayings of the *Rebbes*] and the *tish* but not the *zemirot*; for this reason [I hope] these articles will be useful for the historian."[24] Birnbaum offers firsthand accounts of Hasidic musicians, tsadikim as well as their court singers and cantors (*ḥazanim*), transmitted to him by eyewitnesses or whom he heard directly, especially from the courts of Ger and Kock. Also, what stands out in his text is the mobility of Hasidic leaders and their flock, which turns the homology between court and musical repertoire problematic.

Systematic research on the musical cultures of Hasidism started at about the same time that Birnbaum published his essay. Broadly speaking, these enterprises took place in two centers working in parallel and usually in isolation from each other, one in the Russian Empire and later on in Poland and the USSR, and the other in Palestine. In Russia, the interest in Hasidic music emerged as a by-product of an overall reshuffling of Jewish distinctiveness within the complex politics of identity in the empire, as well as of the late romantic interest in the cultures of "the folk" as a source for the regeneration of national culture. The idea (not unlike Buber's) that Hasidic folklore can revitalize modern Jewish music was central to these circles of mostly acculturated Russian Jews.[25] These concerns led to the establishment of organizations and projects, of which the S. An-sky (Shloyme Zaynvl Rapoport) Jewish ethnographical expeditions of 1912–1914 to the Pale of Settlement are relevant to Hasidic music research. Distinguished Russian Jewish musicologists and folklorists, most notably Yoel Engel and Sussman Kisselgoff, took part in these expeditions and recorded niggunim and instrumental music in areas amply inhabited by Hasidic communities.[26] World War I and the Bolshevik revolution disrupted these endeavors, although their echoes resound in many musical compositions by Russian Jewish composers who draw Hasidic melodies from the materials collected in the An-sky expeditions.

During the interwar period, the ethnographic musical efforts initiated by An-sky moved to independent Poland and to Lithuania, where the interests of folklorists leaned more toward secular Yiddish song. However, many of these songs share their melodies with Hasidic niggunim, and hence the relevance of the work of singer, journalist, and ethnographer Menachem Kipnis in Warsaw, and even more relevant the *Musikalischer Pinkas* (Vilna, 1927) by the Vilna cantor and scholar Abraham M. Bernstein (1866–1932). In the Soviet Union the Ukrainian Jewish music teacher and scholar Moisei Beregovskii took over where the

St. Petersburg ethnographers stopped. In 1927, he founded the Commission for Jewish Folk Music Research at the Department of Jewish Culture of the Ukrainian Academy of Sciences, and from 1929 to 1949, he headed the Cabinet for Jewish Musical Folklore of the Institute of Jewish Proletarian Culture in Kiev. He established the Archives for Jewish Folk Music, adding his own impressive ethnography of Hasidic music to the earlier recordings by Engel and Kisselgoff. Beregovskii transcribed hundreds of Hasidic niggunim and published some of the most valuable studies in this field.[27]

Born, raised, and educated in the Baltic countries and Germany and married to a scion of a Hasidic family, Abraham Zvi Idelsohn, considered by many to be the "father" of modern Jewish music research, embarked on his research on Hasidic music in his youth in Europe and especially after settling in Ottoman Jerusalem in 1907. In Jerusalem and its environs, Idelsohn met Hasidim from diverse dynasties who had settled in the Holy Land from the early nineteenth century, and he recorded them. His contributions to the study of Hasidic music are foundational. They encompass three main publications: chapter 19 of his *Jewish Music in Its Historical Development* (New York, 1929), his 1931 article "Ha-neginah ha-ḥasidit," and volume 10 of his *Thesaurus*, titled *Gesänge der Chasidim*.[28] These three publications drew from each other and from other published and unpublished writings by Idelsohn (especially his unpublished volumes of *Toledot ha-neginah ha-ʿivrit*).

Chapter 19 is a rather schematic discussion of the basic tenets of Hasidic music, spiced with quotations from primary sources, followed by musical analyses of a rather limited selection of niggunim. His target audience was a lay English-speaking readership. The article in Hebrew, on the other hand, is Idelsohn's most detailed exposition of the subject. It is a dense condensation of Hasidic texts about music gleaned from primary and secondary sources. It stresses the role of the tsadik as a singer, composer, instrumentalist, producer, and music patron. The discussion of the music itself, however, is minor because the target audience for this article was Hebrew-reading Jewish-studies scholars. Volume 10 of *Thesaurus* is a major music publication, the largest of its kind published up to that time. It includes 250 niggunim, notes on many of them regarding their provenance and authorship, analyses of the general stylistic characteristics of the repertoire, and a substantial introduction that is a slightly abridged version of the 1931 article in Hebrew.

In his preface to volume 10 of the *Thesaurus*, from April 1931, Idelsohn points out that he had been collecting Hasidic songs for about forty years, starting in his youth in the Hasidic synagogues of Libau (then part of the Russian Empire, today Liepāja in western Latvia), the town where he grew up. Hasidim from Lithuania, Belarus, Poland, and southern Russia had settled there. More than half of his collection he accumulated from Hasidim in Jerusalem between 1907 and 1921. He collected other items during trips to Europe, South Africa, and the

United States up to 1931. Moreover, he drew many niggunim from the family of his wife, Zilla Shneider (1882–1957), whose father, cantor Hillel Schneider (1860–1941), from Sidra in northeastern Poland, leaned to Hasidism while employed in Leipzig. Idelsohn was close to R. Israel Friedman (1878–1951), the son of the Boianer *Rebbe*, who established his court in Leipzig. His volume also incorporates items published by previous ethnographers, such as Kisselgoff, Kipnis, and Bernstein. Another major contribution of Idelsohn in this field is the location of the earliest specimens of niggunim of probable Hasidic origins in manuscripts of East European cantors who settled in the West in the first half of the nineteenth century.

Another performer/scholar insider from this period is Chemjo Vinaver. His posthumously published *Anthology of Hasidic Music*, superbly edited, introduced, and commented on by Eliyahu Schleifer, is one of the most important scholarly works on Hasidic music. Born in Warsaw in 1895, Vinaver was a grandson of R. Yitzḥak of Vorke (Warka), one of the most notable tsadikim of the mid-nineteenth century. He collected niggunim from an early age while also developing a full career as a "modern" musician. He learned niggunim from R. Moishe-Noah Shtraymelmacher of Łódź and from R. Israel Taub, the tsadik of Modzits, whom he met when he was eighteen years old (1913). His unique career took him out of Poland to Berlin (from 1920), where he was active in the Kulturbund under the Nazi regime. In Berlin, Vinaver published niggunim in local Jewish journals that he transcribed from his memory. This ethnography became the basis for his anthology. In 1938 he managed to immigrate to the United States, where he pursued his career and research on Hasidic music, moving to Israel in 1959 where he spent the rest of his life. He continued to collect niggunim, especially among the Karlin Hasidim in Jerusalem. As Schleifer remarks, Vinaver's assemblage of Hasidic music (*nusaḥ* for synagogue services, *zemirot* and niggunim for prayers, niggunim with Hebrew words, wordless niggunim, music for weddings and Jewish theaters, and choral arrangements of music on "Hasidic motives") is sui generis and subjective.[29]

An important contemporary of Vinaver was Meir Shimon Geshuri (born Bruckner in Myslowitz/Mysłowice, then in Prussian Silesia, 1897–1977), scion to a family with ties to the tsadik of Khentshin (Chęciny), a grandson of the Seer of Lublin. A fervent Zionist, he moved to Palestine in 1921 after studying music in Berlin and Gdańsk (Danzig). He was an active music critic and scholar. His prolific output (see sources below), part of which remained unpublished, is of outmost importance to Hasidic music research.

Another forerunner of the study and publication of the Hasidic niggun in Israel of the same generation of Vinaver and Geshuri was the distinguished composer and cellist Joachim Stutchewsky (1891–1982). A scion of a notable klezmer dynasty from Ukraine, Stutchewsky was a driving force in Jewish music circles in Vienna before moving to Israel in 1938.

In the mid-1950s the Institute of Religious Music established by the Ministry of Education and Culture of Israel, under the directorship of Hungarian-born ethnomusicologist Avigdor Herzog, started recording Hasidic music in Israel on a more systematic basis. However, a turning point in the musicology of Hasidism was the establishment in 1964 of the Jewish Music Research Centre and the National Sound Archives at the Jewish National and University Library (today the National Library of Israel). In this framework, Yaakov Mazor and Andre Hajdu carried out a massive ethnographic enterprise in Hasidic courts in Israel. Based on these rich materials, they attempted to outline systematically the stylistic characteristics of niggun.[30] Hajdu and Mazor's entry on music appended to the "Hasidism" article of the *Encyclopedia Judaica* remains the standard survey on the subject.[31]

Mazor's publications are among the most informed ones. From a prestigious Hasidic family from Jerusalem, Mazor had access to the inner works of Hasidic courts, and thus continued a long-standing tradition of insiders/outsiders in Hasidic music research.[32] Mazor offers a unique amalgam of textual analysis and actual practices—such as the style of performance of niggunim in prayer and Hasidic *tish*—based on his massive ethnography.

Another scholar associated with the same institutions, Uri Sharvit (1995), compiled a valuable collection of niggunim from Galicia based on the lore of one Hasid only, El'azar Sharvit, the father of the author, a Hasid closely associated with the court of Bełz.[33]

Innovative interdisciplinary methodologies by an emerging generation of scholars from Israel are starting to render new vistas. To test the claims that R. Levi Yitzḥak of Berditchev indeed composed the niggunim that are attributed to him, Michael Lukin and Matan Wygoda examined in detail the various musical and multilingual lyrical components of his niggunim, comparing versions scattered in assorted Hasidic courts.[34] In this specific case, the rabbi/composer was not a leader of a Hasidic dynasty. Therefore, a cross-dynastical search for niggunim attributed to him had to be carried out in different courts. The researchers also examined his religious philosophy, and crisscrossed musical and lyrical evidence with his surrounding cultural and social settings. Defining the tsadik's compositional style as a combination of traditional East European Ashkenazi prayer and study tunes with instrumental melodies (some borrowed from Ukrainian sources), ranging from folk to high culture, allowed these young scholars to identify previously unknown niggunim by the tsadik of Berditchev.[35] Furthermore, Lukin and Wygoda claim that R. Levi Yitzḥak in fact developed an already existing genre of Ashkenazi folk songs and endowed them with Hasidic content.

Israeli research on Hasidic music, based on the unprecedented reality of Hasidism operating in the sociopolitical ecology of a Jewish national state, is conditioned by its unique local contingencies. This does not mean the absence of continuities with the pre-Holocaust world in Europe but rather that an autochthonous Palestinian Hasidic music tradition took shape even before the arrival of the remaining Hasidim after the war. A clear example of this locality is the Hillulah of Lag ba-Omer in and around the tomb of R. Shimon Bar-Yoḥai in Meron in Upper Galilee. This event led to the appearance of the concept of *nigunei Meron* in Israeli scholarship as a staple of the local Hasidic musical scene.[36] In Meron, two traditions converge: the cult of the saintly dead tsadik (which Hasidim in Meron share with North African Jews), and the cult of the living one as more and more tsadikim attend this event. Pilgrimage at such a nationwide scale has become a transformative pan-Hasidic Israeli experience. While the original privilege to the site's main (and mystically loaded) event, the lighting of the first fire torch, was acquired by the Boian Hasidim already in the late nineteenth century, more and more tsadikim claim their own space on Mount Meron. They do so also by massive niggun performances as a means to enhance their presence on a national level.

With all its achievements, Israeli-based scholarship does not account for the music of Hasidim in the United States or on a global scale. Ethnomusicologist Ellen Koskoff's *Music in Lubavitcher Life* (2001) still stands as the only monograph on music in a contemporary Hasidic community based on fieldwork reflecting the American Hasidic experience. Moreover, as the only study of Hasidic music written by a woman and addressing the musical experience of Hasidic women as well, it points to the remarkable absence of publications on Hasidic music by and for women.

Finally, traditional Hasidic music scholarship has hardly addressed its neo-Hasidic expressions within and outside the Hasidic courts. Mark Kligman penned an initial survey of some trends in Hasidic pop music in America, while Abigail Wood addressed the appropriation of Hasidic materials by new generations of American Yiddish singers.[37] These two studies address the reverberations that Hasidic music has in contemporary American Jewish life, attending to the role the music industry and the aesthetics of pop-rock, funk, and hip-hop have in relation to it.

Another venue to which Hasidic music is central is the revivalist Jewish movements, especially those of R. Shlomo Carlebach (who was not a scion of a Hasidic family) and R. Zalman Schachter-Shalomi (of Bełz background) as their most representative and influential figures. Both rabbis became disciples of R. Yosef Yitzḥak Schneersohn (1880–1950), the sixth *Rebbe* of Chabad-Lubavitch, and eventually they made music the main instrument of their religious mission. The recent work by Ophir on Carlebach along with Schachter-Shalomi's chapter on niggun in his autobiographical reminiscences are the beginning of studying the turn of Hasidic niggun into a transformative experience for modern American Jews who were removed from Orthodox Judaism. This "turn" is contemporary to wider musical trends in the American society, especially the so-called "folk-song revival" movement, and therefore has to be analyzed in this wider historical context.[38]

The Concept of Niggun

Any study of Hasidic music is a study of niggun. Niggun (plural *niggunim*) is a vocal song, usually but not always without words, performed by a solo singer or by a congregation in unison. On occasions and places where it is allowed (especially in weddings), it is sung with instrumental accompaniment. We can summarize the main features of niggun as follows:

1. Niggun performance is an integral part of Hasidic rituals. It can appear in the normative liturgy, special religious events such as the lightening of the Hanukah candles, community gatherings around the tsadik (called *tish*, one of the most important innovations of Hasidism where singing and dancing are essential) taking place on Shabbats, holy days, and memorial days of previous tsadikim, more private smaller gatherings dedicated to spiritual strengthening (*hitva'aduyot*), and life-cycle festivities (circumcisions, weddings, etc.).
2. However, a niggun can also appear in a very intimate occasion, as an outburst of the individual in a moment of introspection. It may be an element of meditation or a vehicle to attain spiritual uplifting and overcome a stressful situation. These contemplative niggunim, many of which are attributed to tsadikim, are generally more complex in their compositional structure than the communitarian ones.
3. A niggun is linear but also circular because it is repeated many times during a performance until its beginning and end lose their binary difference.
4. Repetition is not mechanic but variable in terms of tempo, absolute pitch, dynamics, and melodic contour. Moreover, different performances of the same niggun in different contexts and occasions may also cause variants.
5. A niggun is a musical "text" whose structure can encode a teaching of Hasidism or recall an event of the past whose meaning is decoded by the intellect of the tsadik.
6. A niggun can be very short (just one phrase), average in length (usually four short sections), long, or exceptionally long, depending on the context of performance, composer, place, and period of composition. It can be very rhythmic (e.g., niggunim accompanying dance) or without a clear beat (e.g., contemplative niggunim sung by individuals), either fast or slow.
7. Niggun and dance go hand in hand in Hasidism. Dancing (or other types of concerted movements) is usually communal. At times, the tsadik participates actively, most especially in the *mitsve tans* at the end of weddings.[39]

8. Some niggunim have an oral or written metatext: a text that clarifies the deep meaning of the musical text, its history, or the circumstances of its conception.
9. Hasidic masters first perceived fixation of the niggun, in musical notation and later on in sound recordings, as detrimental and undesirable. Whatever the dangers of these techniques of capturing (in fact "freezing") a niggun may have been, Hasidim eventually embraced both practices wholeheartedly. However, listening to a commercially recorded niggun, even if recorded by Hasidic musicians for the daily consumption of a Hasidic audience, is a radically different experience from participating in a live performance in a Hasidic context.
10. Reproductions led to the creation of canons of niggunim. Yet the repertoires of Hasidic niggunim of each dynasty remain an open canon. New items can enter the repertoire via borrowing or original composition, while others were probably forgotten.

These characteristics challenge some parameters found in writings on Hasidic music. The niggun is not exclusively a "song without words," as Beregovskii phrased it.[40] Many niggunim have a text (in Hebrew, Aramaic, Yiddish, or, much more rarely, in a local vernacular such as Ukrainian or Hungarian) that is actually sung or is implied in the minds of the singers during the act of singing. Moreover, the textless niggun is not a unique Hasidic innovation. The Ashkenazi liturgy since the Middle Ages contained extensive vocalizations without text, located in special sections of the services in which the cantor expressed himself with mystical devotion.[41] Second, the ubiquitous Western idea of the niggun as a "piece," with its fixed structure, rhythms, and musical modes, conceals the real significance of musical performance in Hasidism as worship, as a process of psychological transformation experienced by the worshippers while moving from one state of mind to another. There is more here than a phenomenological approach to niggun performance, for certain branches of Hasidism developed complex "theories of niggun," language-texts that unfold music-texts. Some of these texts introduce the secrets of the niggun, while others theorize its transformative powers. In both cases, knowledge about niggun is part of the niggun experience. Third, the essence of niggun performance practice, its circularity, entails development. The parallel growing in the intensity of pitch, dynamics, and tempo is an essential component of the niggun experience as religious worship. In many cases, the tsadik initiates the performance by introducing the community to the niggun by the power of his own voice into the proper mood. Then the community takes over, at times growing in intensity by slightly, sometimes imperceptibly, raising the pitch, and singing louder and faster. After reaching the peak of intensity, whence one cannot go higher, there is a fall in all the parameters, either to start a new cycle, to move into another niggun, or to make room for a sermon by the tsadik.

Hasidic Prayer

An observant Jew is commanded to pray a fixed set of prayers at fixed times. Prayers have always been a congregational effort carried at a community location, a synagogue, or a study house (*bet midrash*). Congregational prayer could be guided by a *sheli'aḥ tsibur*, a representative of the congregation, but during the era when Hasidism developed and spread more intensively (late eighteenth and early nineteenth century), prayers at Ashkenazi synagogues were usually led by an accomplished cantor supplemented by two or more assistants (*meshorerim*) called *zinger* and *bas*. These assistants to the cantor improvised harmonies, drones, and filled in the cadences with responses. This Ashkenazi musical practice has roots in the late medieval period but was upgraded by cantors leading to more formal choirs to match the changing musical tastes of the eighteenth century.

Hasidim of the first generations took part in these practices, and the question is to what extent Hasidic prayer became indeed exceptional. In its earlier phases, the sui generis approaches to prayer of certain Hasidic circles (unconventional hours, individual expression, crying, shouting, clapping of hands, extreme body movements, or intense concentration without moving, etc.) became the most overt expression of a new aesthetics of Jewish worshipping. This intense manner of praying led to the physical separation of Hasidim from the rest of the Jewish congregation in many towns, creating the *shtibl*, the humbler place of studying and praying that eventually characterized Hasidism.

The vitriolic reactions of the early mitnagedim to Hasidic praying practices reflect the shocking effects caused by the visibility and audibility of these new practices. Sonic difference was one of the earliest distinctive features of Hasidism in comparison to the customs of other Ashkenazi Jews. This difference was radical and entailed either absolute silence and immutability or loudness and stark movement. Much of these earliest sonic practices of Hasidism can be gleaned from the literature of their opponents, who addressed the unique sonic dimension of early Hasidism. Such descriptions come in the form of accusations that blamed Hasidim for turning every day into a holiday and allowing their joy to overcome any sorrow.

Among the earliest such descriptions are the ones emanating from the circles of R. Eliyahu, the Gaon of Vilna. In the anonymous Hebrew epistle suggestively titled *Zamir 'aritsim ve-ḥaravot tsurim* (The Song of Tyrants and Flint Knives, 1772), one reads about "strange movements and gestures during prayer, creating separate prayer halls in order to distinguish themselves from the rest of Israel, not observing standard practices, using loud voices, stopping in the middle of prayers and smiling and amusing themselves unceasingly."[42] Moreover, they are criticized for changing the order of the prayers, by adopting the customs of the "other" Jews, the Sephardim, "who dwell far away and have their own ways in all their practices according to their illustrious sages of old." More crucial, "there is no sorrow for him [the Hasid] and his voice is sweet and his look is handsome," and "when they pray they sing without restraint and their voices are heard from afar."[43] In another pamphlet, *Shever posh'im*, they are accused of singing obscene songs all the time (*shire 'agavim*), while in *Sefer ha-vikuaḥ*, by R. Israel Loebel of Słuck (1799), the Besht is accused of reciting very long prayers: "He sings, and raises his voice and hits with his fist and swings himself like stalk in stormy wind, and the Ar"i [R. Yitzḥak Luria] argues that all this aborts intention (*kavanah*)."[44]

These deviations from established traditions of worshipping are tendentiously exaggerated.[45] Hasidism is depicted as anticantorial, individualistic, and disrespectful of traditional Ashkenazi synagogue repertoires. The truth is, as often, somewhere in the middle. These new forms of worship indeed created tensions between more radical and conservative Hasidim. Different relations to the traditional liturgy in Hasidism throughout its history reveal how diverse subterranean currents in ancient and medieval Judaism resurface in early modernity. As an example, one might mention the creative, individualistic approach to prayer hinted at in the aforementioned *Sefer ḥasidim* (Bologna 1538, par. 158), which suggests that the devotee choose his own melodies and even the language of prayer if he does not command Hebrew well. On the other hand, there are the venerable and immutable musical traditions of Ashkenaz transmitted in *Sefer ha-Maharil* in the name of R. Ya'akov ben Moshe Levi Moelin (Maharil; c. 1365–1427). This source suggests a more rigid and controlled liturgical musical diet in the hands of experienced cantors, especially during the High Holy Days.

Schleifer discussed the Hasidic attitude to the Ashkenazi musical traditions, distinguishing between "two theories."[46] Idelsohn asserted that Hasidim "paid but little attention to the musical tradition of the synagogue,"[47] while Geshuri maintained that "the Hasidic precentor did not change the niggunim from Sinai, but sang new tunes side by side with the old ones."[48] Schleifer stresses that Hasidim of many dynasties still prefer a simple precentor to a professional cantor, whose vanity they reject. Neeman proposes that most Hasidim share a *nusaḥ* (in the sense of "mode of praying"), which he calls "Vohlinian," with non-Hasidic Ashkenazi Jews.[49] Did the Hasidim invent new formulas, or did they draw them from an old melodic repertoire that coexisted in Eastern Europe with the Ashkenazi one and emphasized their choice to stress sonic differences from non-Hasidic communities? This question requires research.

Louis Jacobs, in a comprehensive study on Hasidic prayer, summarized these tensions as they appear in diverse Hasidic and mitnagedic sources. One can see that the performance of the statutory prayers divided the more "intellectual" R. Ya'akov Yosef of Polnoe (Połonne) from the "spiritualist" Maggid of Mezrich.[50] The former sided, implicitly, with the Maharil and unequivocally criticized the late eighteenth-century non-Hasidic Ashkenazi cantors who enhanced their musical performances as ends in themselves. At the same time, R. Ya'akov Yosef suggested devotedly maintaining the traditional melodies associated with specific texts of the High Holy Days' liturgy.[51] This critique may also be read as a rebuke to his contemporaneous Hasidim, who may have broken away from established liturgical music practices. This is clear from sources such as the very early ban on Hasidim issued by the Jewish community of Kraków in 1786. The Hasid is accused there of "constructing a stage for himself changing, God forbids . . . the *neginah* [a term that can be read as Biblical cantillation or musical mode] and praying with different movements . . . and whistling with their lips and clapping hand on hand."[52]

Structural tensions between individual devotion and community effort are inherent to any enthusiastic religious movement. Echoes of this tension in Hasidism between creativity and continuity, untrained spiritual leaders of prayer and professional cantors and choirs, small *shtiblekh* and large synagogues were constant. They continued into the twentieth century, as shown by the writings of R. Aharon Rote (Roth; known as R. Arele), the founder of one of the most idiosyncratic Hasidic courts in Jerusalem and a scholar of niggun.[53] R. Rote insists that "our sweet *nusaḥ* can awaken the experience of kavanah" and forbids changing "the melodic movements (*kol ha-tenu'ot*) that are customary." This *nusaḥ* "is connected to the essence of the Godhead." He warns especially against changing the melodies for Rosh Hashanah and Yom Kippur, "whose melodic motifs were given at Sinai." At the same time, R. Arele composed new melodies for prayers and Yiddish songs to exercise what is written, *shiru le-Adonai shir ḥadash* (Psalms 149:1).[54]

Mazor suggests that Hasidic prayer emerged out of the abandonment (or ignorance) of the formalized Ashkenazi cantorial art.[55] A story about "the cantor of the Besht," however, still recalls this practice at the time of the Besht and his followers. The following story, which contains details pertinent to our discussion, was brought from "a manuscript by the Holy Rabbi of Komarno" in the name of R. Avraham Mordekhai Horowitz of Pintchev (Pinczów) (1762–1824), a disciple of R. Elimelekh of Lizhensk (Leżajsk).[56] Apparently, this is a reference to the collection of stories about the Besht, *Sefer ma'aseh ha-shem*, by R. Avraham's disciple and son-in-law, R. Yitzḥak Aizik Yehudah Yeḥiel Safrin of Komarno (1806–1874) and is embedded in his *Megilat setarim*.[57]

The Besht appointed one of his disciples as a cantor. This anonymous disciple refused the position, out of either humility or anxiety over his master's presence, saying that his musical capabilities were meager (*eyn ani yakhol lenagen*). His master insisted and told him that he would "connect him to the realm of music (*'olam ha-nigun*)." And so, by the magical powers of the Besht, this cantor became one of the best of his time. He once came to R. Elimelekh's court, apparently as a "gift" from the Besht. His arrival caused an uneasy feeling, because R. Elimelekh and his son, R. Eliezer, did not know if they should allow him to conduct the service to welcome in the Shabbat, fearing that the cantor would distract R. Elimelekh from his holy deeds. Why? Because the cantor had two assistants accompanying him, a *bas* and a *zinger*. After the first moments of discomfort, R. Elimelekh and his son decided to allow the cantor to perform the service out of respect for the Holy Besht, and "whatever will be, will be." When the cantor started the service, R. Elimelekh ordered the *zinger* to leave, saying that "only the cantor and the *bas* will continue." He later ordered the two of them to leave for "fear that he will cut himself from reality by the sheer volume of the light and the upper holy thoughts and the high illuminations that opened before our Rabbi by the singing of this tsadik, and afterwards our Rabbi honored the cantor during all the Shabbat, but [the cantor] did not lead the prayers from the lectern out of fear [of the Rabbi] of all the above." At the end of Shabbat, the cantor transmitted to R. Elimelekh all the praises and miracles of the Besht from his firsthand experience.

An interesting follow-up to the story appears after all the praises of the Besht. The cantor died after a while. During the thirty-day period of mourning, the *bas* returned home on the eve of Shabbat after the ritual bath of purification and told his wife to prepare for his imminent death. "My cantor," said the *bas* to his wife, "was honored in the Garden of Eden with leading the welcoming of the Shabbat and he does not want [to lead the prayers] but [only] with me. And he laid down on his bed and died."

This episode teaches us the following:

1. According to Hasidic tradition, the Besht kept a capable cantor and assistants around him, as in the Ashkenazi custom.
2. Cantors were sent by tsadikim from one court to another.
3. R. Elimelekh and his son were suspicious of cantors accompanied by assistants, but abided by the authority of the Besht.
4. The tsadik may have been distressed by the assistant's performance, leading him to "deconstruct" the traditional cantorial three-voice texture of older Ashkenazi practice.
5. The cantor's voice (remember that the voice was "trained" by the Besht himself) was so psychologically transformative that it had to be ceased for fear of R. Elimelekh losing touch with reality.
6. The *bas* was a pious Jew (hinting that the *zinger* was not) who had a synergetic relationship with "his cantor" and died with him.

The teachings of this story thus provide a complex picture of continuity and change in the field of liturgical music during the early days of Hasidism.

Mazor calls the individualist approach to Hasidic prayer performance "the Chabad model," wherein each individual is free to calibrate how "sonic" his prayer is, as well as to determine the speed of his tempos.[58] The result of such an approach is a rather boisterous sound cloud generated by the freedom allowed to the individual worshipper. Another model stresses togetherness, particularly in the liturgical sections that by tradition are "musicalized." Wertheim emphasizes that "the whole purpose of the song was to bring to the awakening (*hit'orerut*) of the soul of the singer and for this reason it is the duty of the participants to participate in the prayer."[59]

Schleifer has discussed at length the evolution of cantorial art music in Hasidic courts, tracing the process from rejection to embracement.[60] The critique of "high-synagogue" practices by early Hasidim gave room in the nineteenth century to the (re)establishment of larger synagogues at affluent Hasidic courts, the engagement of the best cantors accompanied by choirs, and the composition of new liturgical music in contemporary styles. Exchanges of musical personnel between Hasidic and non-Hasidic courts became more frequent as the "Orthodox" camp consolidated against the shared threats of modernization, secularization, and acculturation. The Hasidic niggun made inroads into modern Ashkenazi cantorial art music. Some of the stylistic features of cantorial art music as it consolidated toward the end of the nineteenth century are formalized versions of Hasidic sonic gestures. Many distinguished cantors who achieved wide success throughout the Jewish world in the early twentieth century grew up in Hasidic families or served in Hasidic courts. For example, Zeidel Rovner (Jacob Shmuel Margowsky, 1856–1943), orphaned of his father at an early age, was "discovered" by R. Ya'akov Yitzḥak Twersky of Makarów (d. 1892) and remained under this tsadik's influence even after developing an international career in Eastern Europe and later in the United States.

Hasidic Music and Klezmer Music

The lines dividing the instrumental (klezmer) from vocal repertoires performed in Hasidic courts were never clear cut. Klezmorim were certainly a fundamental feature of Ashkenazi musical culture, and Hasidim just continued to employ their services, especially at weddings. Moreover, the practice of singing vocal songs without text probably emerged, among other reasons, from the desire to listen to pieces from the cherished klezmer repertoire on Shabbat and holy days, when instrumental music is proscribed. Whether this practice is uniquely Hasidic or has antecedents in earlier Ashkenazi practices is still a conjectural matter. On the other hand, the klezmer genre known as *chosidl* reflects the opposite move, from vocal niggun to instrumental music. The vocal/instrumental dichotomy is at times equated to the spiritual/material one. R. Ya'akov Yosef of Polnoe, speaking about material rejoicing as the basis for spiritual rejoicing, mentions that the spiritual rejoicing of groom and bride is awakened by the material music emanating from the instruments.[61] The rejoicing is fulfilled when both the material and the spiritual blend.

Due to the blurred borderlines between vocal and instrumental Hasidic repertoires, Idelsohn and Beregovskii included in their respective collections of Hasidic niggunim items that could derive from one medium or another. For example, Vinaver documented in writing a niggun from David Bergelson (Berlin, 1926/7) and testifies that his informant "sang with mimics as the klezmorim [played] a freilachs."[62] On the other hand, klezmer collections include items that are also known as vocal niggunim.

The Tsadik as a Musician

Many tsadikim play a central role in the musical life of their congregation as composers, players of instruments, conductors of musical performances at the *tish*, musical instructors, and critics. Chronicles about the wonders of niggun in relation to the exceptional powers of tsadikim to alter or challenge inner or outer psychological moods and thus change mental reality have appeared since the beginning of Hasidism. They continue even now to reverberate in different variants. These narratives circulate today in websites that clamp together sayings and stories about tsadikim from diverse sources in a genre similar to the traditional Hasidic stories (as described in chapter 3). As R. Zvi Freeman states, "A *tsadik* is one who has mastered the animal inside and achieved a higher state of being. In a niggun, a tsadik encodes his soul. When we sing a niggun of a tsadik, we connect with the innermost garments of the tsadik's soul, and from there come to union with the light that tsadik has found. That is why each note and nuance of a niggun must be precise. As the words of a sacred text, they must be learnt and repeated in perfect form. Because the tsadik's mind and soul are held within them."[63]

A story about the Imrei Ḥayim, R. Ḥayim Moshe Hager of Vizhnitz, told by R. Shmuel Ya'akov Kahan and appearing in an online collection called *Toledot ha-Imrei Ḥayim*, , exemplifies this genre of narratives about a tsadik's exercise of his unique spiritual strength through a niggun:

> I heard from my father my teacher [R. Abraham Yitzḥak Kahan], may he be blessed with long and good days amen, a wondrous case of worshiping through rejoicing (*'avodat ha-simḥah*) that he saw from our revered saintliness the *Imrei Ḥayim*, may his memory protect us, when he [Rabbi Abraham Yitzḥak] was called to Safed on the eve of the Ninth of Av, 5729 [1969] to drive our revered saintliness Our master, teacher and rabbi of blessed saintly memory, to the funeral of Our master, teacher and rabbi of Chust of blessed saintly memory [who was the *Imrei Ḥayim*'s son-in-law] . . . and when the rabbi

> entered the car, he was broken and exhausted, and he did not stop crying over the death of his son-in-law for a long while. All of the sudden he stopped himself abruptly [from crying], and leapt into profound and mysterious thoughts, and immediately after he uttered some flowery words, and sang for himself a niggun of rejoicing, and he returned to experience a quite extraordinary ecstatic joy. He remained in this state even after he returned to his home in Safed and this was a wonder to all those surrounding him, how he controlled himself in order not to forsake the state of worshiping God with joy [even in a moment of deep personal sorrow].[64]

Musical Dynasties: The Case of Modzits

Hasidic lore attributes unique musical skills to certain dynasties and to their leaders. Without doubt, the story of the Modzits (Modrzyce/Dęblin) dynasty as a "musicalized" one due to the exceptional abilities of its tsadikim as composers and performers is one of the most accepted tenets in writings on Hasidic music. R. Israel ben Shmuel Eliyahu Taub (1849–1920), a grandson of R. Yeḥezkel Taub of Kuzmir (Kazimierz), became the first tsadik of Modzits in 1891. He was a gifted composer, and one of his compositions, the "Great Ezkera," attained a unique status among his Hasidim to this day. Stories related to the conception of this niggun transmit several teachings. R. Israel's son, R. Shaul Yedidya El'azar Taub (1886–1947), who left Poland for New York at the outbreak of World War II and to whom close to one thousand niggunim are attributed, relates in his *Imrei Shaul* that his father, when suffering from severe diabetes, traveled to Berlin in 1913 to have his leg amputated.[65] While suffering severe pain after the effect of the anesthesia dwindled, he looked through the window and saw the beauty of Berlin. His consciousness was overridden with another type of pain that made him forget his physical agony. He thought of how despised and debased the city of Jerusalem was, and during the operation he composed a thirty-minute niggun on the text of the *piyut* for the service of Yom Kippur, *Ezkera elohim ve-ehemayah* ("I shall remember God and bemoan when seeing every city intact while the city of Jerusalem lies destroyed and empty"). Later versions of the story circulating among the Hasidim tell an even more heroic version, that R. Israel in fact demanded from his doctors not to receive anesthesia.

The story has a spin off that emphasizes the power of the tsadik to control the course of musical events. Vinaver heard this niggun from the tsadik himself and wanted to transcribe it, but the tsadik forbade him from doing so. Later, someone else transcribed the niggun, but his score mysteriously disappeared. The same happened to a field recording that Vinaver made many years later in New York from a Modzits Hasid. The willpower of the tsadik not to have his niggun fixed in notation or recording continued to operate after his death.[66] Indeed, even though the score of the niggun can be obtained in several publications, the Modzitser Hasidim do not allow it to be recorded during the once-a-year performance on the *yortsayt* of R. Israel.[67]

This episode about musical notation as a taboo in Hasidic musical thought is not unique. It reveals a long-standing Hasidic reticence from fixating what by definition cannot be fixed because the niggun is, as we have seen, a process. Moreover, musical notation was a powerful symbol of the music of the "others," be they Western culture, maskilim, or professional cantors. In this context, the decision by R. Yosef Yitzḥak Schneersohn of Chabad to start the systematic written documentation of the dynasty's repertoire appears as a revolutionary step that was accepted due to the uncontested clairvoyance of this tsadik.[68]

Yet another teaching from the story about the "Great Ezkera" niggun of the tsadik of Modzits is the redemptive role of the niggun in moments of martyrdom.[69] The most oft-repeated modern version of this motif is the composition of the famous niggun "Ani ma'amin," attributed to R. Azriel Dovid Pastag, a cantor from Warsaw close to the Modzits court, when he was being transported to Treblinka. Once again, this martyrdom story has acquired mythical proportions in spite of solid historical evidence, as it appears that the tune was in fact composed in the Warsaw ghetto before the deportation.[70] This niggun is now part of official Holocaust memorials worldwide.

Hasidic Musicology

Of all Hasidic dynasties, Chabad provides the most systematic musicology emerging out of Hasidic thought. This *torat ha-nigun* appears in the teachings of all the Chabad tsadikim. It was summarized by Shmuel Zalmanov in the introduction to the *Sefer ha-nigunim* and worked out in several variants in later texts and virtual spaces.[71] Following in Zalmanov's steps is R. Lev Leibman, a young Jewish musician (b. 1982), educated in Moscow and Tel Aviv, who became an active Chabadnik musicologist at the Hasidic Music Institute (Makhon Neginah le-Or ha-Hasidut) established by him in Kfar Chabad (Israel). Leibman has published several books, and his presence in the virtual scene of Chabad music through writings and performances is very noticeable.[72]

Chabad's musicology considers the niggun a path to higher consciousness and transformation of being. This teaching about the privileged status of music is summarized in the often-quoted formulation by R. Shneur Zalman of Lady, "If words are the pen of the heart, then song is the pen of the soul." As R. Zvi Freeman synthesizes this idea, "while words carry meaning downwards from God's own primal consciousness into the minds of sages and the lips of prophets to inscribe them upon human hearts, song carries the soul upwards to be absorbed within the Infinite Light. That is why niggunim generally have no words. Words limit and define, but the niggun tears the soul beyond all bounds."[73]

Chabad is not the only court engaged in Hasidic musicology. Another systematic piece of Hasidic musicology can be found in the important monograph *Hekhal ha-neginah*, compiled by the Ger Hasid Dovid Abraham Mandelbaum and published by the composer of the Ger court, Zvi Meir Goldknopf.[74] The book is a hybrid collection of Hasidic texts about music, legends about the origins of certain niggunim, biographies of Hasidic singers, musical transcriptions (many are handwritten drafts), and photographs. Despite emanating from the Ger court, the author addresses the musical lore of many other Hasidic courts. Moreover, the book reveals the musical interactions between the different courts in relatively early periods in the history of the movement. An entire musical edifice also surrounds the thought of R. Naḥman of Bratslav, whose musicology can be gleaned from publications stemming from the institutions of Bratslav Hasidim as well as from the detailed academic research conducted by Chani H. Smith.[75]

Members of younger generations of Hasidim in Israel, exposed to modern ideas such as conservation, archives, and ethnography, are among the important collectors and scholars of niggunim. In pursuit of materials, they have no qualms about visiting such "off-limits" institutions as the National Library in Jerusalem. The niggun is also central to the thinking of Hasidic-oriented sectors of the National Religious movement in the West Bank settlements. Clarinetist Yechiel ("Chilik") Frank, one of the most in-demand klezmorim in Israel, is one researcher/performer who imparts "musical Hasidism" in spiritual assemblies taking place in locations such as the "musical yeshiva" in Otniel near Hebron.[76] As pointed out, in an ironic twist of history, the Hasidic niggun has nowadays a stronghold among the younger generations of students in Lithuanian yeshivot in Israel, namely among the heirs of the mitnagedim who so fiercely derided Hasidic musical devotions more than two centuries ago.

Hasidic Niggun beyond the Hasidic Realm

Building on the idea of Hasidism as a regenerative force of modern Judaism advanced by Buber and others, niggunim appear in a variety of Jewish stages beyond the boundaries of Hasidism. We have already mentioned the niggun presence in compositions of the St. Petersburg Jewish school, in Zionist musical culture, and among revivalist movements in America. Printed scores, the staging of Hasidic musical scenes (both serious, e.g., Ans-ky's *Dibbuk*, and parody) in interwar Jewish theater and film, and later commercial recordings are evidence of this wide dissemination. Witnessing the propagation of pseudo-Hasidic niggunim, Idelsohn, reflecting a "purist" standpoint, complained, "there is a kind of Hasidic niggunim, that are a sort of harming plague, and these are the parodic and satiric niggunim about the tsadikim and their oddities; these are caricatures not only of the life of the Hasidim, but also of true Hasidic music, as jazz is [a caricature] of classical music. To the regret of every educated person, there are many who, out of sheer shallowness, think about these acts of mockery as the real Hasidic music."[77] Idelsohn applies here to pseudo-Hasidic music the widespread early twentieth-century American trope of "jazz" as corrupted (and corrupting) music.

Hasidic music academic purism could not contain, however, the unruly diffusion of Hasidic repertoires, "real" or "invented" outside Hasidism. Zionist songsters circulated Hasidic niggunim among Jews in British Palestine, Germany, and America. An early specimen is the collection *Echoes of Palestine*, notated and arranged with piano accompaniment by Thelma Goldfarb (Brooklyn, 1929). As the title indicates, the songs originated in the Jewish community of British Mandate Palestine. The section of *zemirot Shabbat* consists mostly of Hasidic niggunim, and another one, titled "Songs without Words," includes not only Hasidic niggunim but also klezmer tunes reflecting the pervasive presence of the Hasidic repertoire in the Yishuv and its transfer over the Atlantic. In the same year, 1929, a major Zionist Hebrew songster, *Mizimrat Haaretz*, appeared (published by the Jewish National Fund in Warsaw), edited by Salomon Rosowsky, from the St. Petersburg circle of Jewish musicians who had settled in Palestine.[78] This songster included a special section on Hasidic niggunim, as did, a few years later, Jacob Schoenberg's *Shirei Eretz Israel* (Berlin, 1935), a Hebrew songbook that had a great impact in Europe and was even reprinted after World War II.[79] Around the same time, the copious and widely circulating publications of the educator and composer Harry Coopersmith introduced Hasidic niggunim, mostly tunes from the Shabbat *zemirot* repertoire (defined as "Chasidic," "Chasidish," "Chasidic adapted H.C.," or attributed to specific tsadikim), to American Jewish educational institutions.[80] All these printed products and many more attest to the deep internalization of the Hasidic niggun as an "authentic" component of the modern Jewish sonic experience in the interwar period outside the cradle of Hasidism in Eastern Europe.

This pattern persisted after the Holocaust, but in a different guise. A patent example is the successful 1968 Israeli musical *Ish ḥasid haya*, compiled and edited by playwright and scholar Dan Almagor (and restaged on Broadway in 1971), which heralded "the return to the roots" that would characterize Israeli society many years later. Staged precisely at the peak of power of secular Israeliness, this musical and its niggunim became a landmark of the "return to the roots" by Israeli Ashkenazim. The secular Hasidic Song Festival produced by the Israel Broadcasting Authority from 1968 to 1977 and the appearances of R. Shlomo Carlebach in them further expanded this Hasidic revivalism in Israel and linked it to the American scene.[81] Hasidic niggunim or musical themes reappear in other quintessential Israeli productions, such as the Givatron's *Shirim mi-beit Abba* (meaning songs from the previous generations), a restaging of Shabbat ceremonies in the kibbutzim of the 1930s and 1940s, and in Naomi Shemer's song "Shirat ha-ʻasavim," from 1976 (based on *Likkutei Moharan*, second part, 63).

Post-Holocaust America presented a different picture in relation to "Hasidic" music among non-Hasidic Jews beyond Orthodox circles. In 1954, Isadore Freed, a composer associated with the Reform movement in America, a nemesis of Hasidism, composed his *Hassidic Service for the Sabbath Eve*, heralding a renewed interest in Hasidic music. However, despite its innovation, Freed's *Service* did not have an auspicious reception in Reform congregations and certainly not beyond them. Other, more popular products, such as imported commercial recordings of the Pirchei London children's choir of Yigal Calek, catered to the postwar American Jewish nostalgic longing for music of the "Old World," conceptualized as "Hasidic" music.

East European Jewish instrumental music, klezmer, was eventually the focus of a post-1960 generation of young American Jews living in the age of "ethnic pride" in America. Also interested in the "Old World," members of this generation were reticent about the Jewish establishment's musical resources and tastes, such as the publications of, for example, Coopersmith, or the LPs of the "Pirchei" choirs, or the overt centrality of Israel and Israeli music. They sought their musical regeneration in more "authentic," old 78-rpm records and among the few remaining East European Jewish immigrant musicians who had moved to America in the early twentieth century. Through the agency of klezmer music, the Hasidic niggun found its indirect return to the scene of mostly secular American Jewish audiences and eventually to non-Jewish audiences worldwide.

A renewed interest in and fascination with Hasidic niggunim and the Hasidic courts that flourished in the backyards of great cities, notably New York City, was also noticeable among secular young American Jews. The grandiose productions of the Purim plays (*purimshpil*) by the Bobov (Bobowa) court in Borough Park (Brooklyn) became a focus of attraction for a new generation of scholars.[82] The publication of two large volumes of niggunim by Hasidic music connoisseur Velvel Pasternak *Songs of the Chasidim*, which offered a large repertoire to the general American public, is another expression of this renewed interest. Pasternak's association with the Modzits court established in New York in 1940 by R. Shaul Yedidya El'azar Taub is remarkable. It explains why the vast musical repertoire of Modzits, continued in Israel by R. Shaul's son and successor, R. Shmuel Eliyahu Taub (1905–1984), received such a central place in Pasternak's many publications on Hasidic music. Finally, the central role of the Hasidic niggun in the writings and teachings of the late Elie Wiesel attests to the pertinence of this revered musical repertoire at so many registers of the modern American Jewish experience.[83]

SUGGESTED READING

Avenary, Hanoch, "The Hasidic Nigun: Ethos and Melos of a Folk Liturgy," *Journal of the International Folk Music Council* 16 (1964), 60–63. Reprinted in *Encounters of East and West in Music* (Tel-Aviv: Tel Aviv University, 1979), 158–164.

Barzilai, Shmuel, *Chassidic Ecstasy in Music* (Frankfurt: Peter Lang, 2009).
Ben-Moshe, Rafi, *Experiencing Devekut: The Contemplative Niggun of Habad in Israel* (Jerusalem: Jewish Music Research Centre, the Hebrew University of Jerusalem, 2015).
Beregovski, Moshe, *Old Jewish Folk Music: The Collections and Writings of Moshe Beregovski*, ed. M. Slobin, 2nd ed. (Syracuse, NY: Syracuse University Press, 2000).
Birnbaum (Birnboyim), Abraham N., "Ha-shirah veha-zimrah be-hatserot ha-tsadikim be-Polin," *Ha-Olam* 1 (1907), 20–22, 30–31, 44–45, 69–70, 81–82, 105–106, 129–130.
Dale, Gordon A., "Music in Haredi Jewish Life: Liquid Modernity and the Negotiation of Boundaries in Greater New York" (Ph.D. diss., City University of New York, 2017).
Friedland Ben-Arza, Sara, "Ha-nigun be-ḥasidut Modzits," accessed September 4, 2016, http://old.piyut.org.il/articles/761.html.
Geshuri, Meir Shimon, *Ha-nigun veha-rikud ba-ḥasidut*, 3 vols. (Tel Aviv, 1955–1959).
Geshuri, Meir Shimon, *La-hasidim mizmor: A Collection of Literature and Folk Music of Chasidim with Tunes, Pictures, and Facsimiles* (Jerusalem: Hateḥiyah, 1936).
Geshuri, Meir Shimon, *Neginah ve-ḥasidut be-vet Kuzmir u-venoteha* (Jerusalem: Ha-ḥevrah lehafaẓat ha-ḥasidut u-neginatah, 1952).
Hajdu, Andre, "Le Niggun Meron: Description d'un Patrimonie Instrumental Juif," *Yuval* 2 (1971), 73–97.
Horodezky, Samuel A., "Hasidic Song and Dance," trans. A. Regelson, in *An Anthology of Hebrew Essays*, compiled by I. Cohen and B. Y. Michali (Tel Aviv: Institute for the Translation of Hebrew Literature, 1966), 472–482.
Idel, Moshe, "Conceptualization of Music in Jewish Mysticism," in L. E. Sullivan (ed.), *Enchanting Powers: Music in the World's Religions* (Cambridge, MA: Harvard University Press, 1997), 159–188.
Idel, Moshe, *Hasidism: Between Ecstasy and Magic* (Albany: State University of New York Press, 1995).
Idel, Moshe, "The Magical and Theurgic Interpretation of Music in Jewish Sources from the Renaissance to Hasidism," *Yuval* 4 (1982), 33–62.
Idelsohn, Abraham Zvi, "Ha-neginah ha-ḥasidit," *Sefer Hashanah: The American Hebrew Yearbook* 1 (1931), 74–87.
Idelsohn, Abraham Zvi, *Jewish Music in Its Historical Development* (New York: Tudor Publishing Company, 1929).
Jacobs, Louis, *Hasidic Prayer* (Oxford and Portland, OR: Littman Library of Jewish Civilization,,1993).
Kligman, Mark, "Contemporary Jewish Music in America," *American Jewish Year Book* 101 (2001), 88–141.
Koskoff, Ellen, *Music in Lubavitcher Life* (Urbana: University of Illinois Press, 2001).
Loewenthal, Naftali, "Spirituality, Melody and Modernity in Habad Hasidism," in *Proceedings of the First International Conference on Jewish Music*, ed. S. Stanton (London: City University of London, 1997), 62–78.
Lukin, Michael, and Matan Wygoda, "Darei ma'alah 'im darei matah: Nigunei R. Levi Itzhak mi-Berditchev be-perspektivah historit," in *Rabbi Levi Yitschak of Berdichev: History, Thought, Literature and Melody*, ed. Z. Mark and R. Horn (Rishon LeZion: Yedi'ot Aharonot, 2017), 426–581.
Malkah, Shai, ed., *Pirkei shirah, nigun ve-zikaron* (Otni'el: Yeshivat Otni'el, 2006).
Mandelbaum, Dovid Abraham, *Hekhal ha-neginah* (Jerusalem: Z. Goldknopf, 2005).
Mazor, Yaakov, Ha-shoshalot ha-ḥasidiyot veha-tekstim shebe-fihen, accessed March 12, 2016, www.piyut.org.il/articles/910.html#habad.
Mazor, Yaakov, "Hasidism: Music," in *YIVO Encyclopedia of Jews in Eastern Europe*, accessed May 15, 2016, www.yivoencyclopedia.org/article.aspx/Hasidism/Music.

Mazor, Yaakov, "Koḥo shel ha-nigun ba-hagut ha-ḥasidit ve-tafkidav ba-ḥavai ha-dati veha-ḥevrati," *Yuval* 7 (2002), 23–53.
Mazor, Yaakov, "Merkaziyuto shel ha-admor be-hitḥadshut ha-ḥayim ha-musikaliyim be-ḥatser Vizhnits bi-Bene-Berak, 1949–1972," *Dukhan* 12 (1989), 130–158.
Mazor, Yaakov, "Min ha-nigun ha-ḥasidi el ha-zemer ha-yisra'eli," *Katedra* 115 (2004), 95–128.
Mazor, Yaakov, Bathja Bayer, and Andre Hajdu, "The Hasidic Dance-Niggun: A Study Collection and Its Classificatory Analysis," *Yuval* 3 (1974), 136–266.
Mazor, Yaakov, and Edwin Seroussi, "Towards a Hasidic Lexicon of Music," *Orbis Musicae* 10 (1991), 118–143.
Mazor, Yaakov, and Moshe Taube, "A Hasidic Ritual Dance: The *Mitsve Tants* in Jerusalemite Weddings," *Yuval* 6 (1994), 164–224.
Naḥman of Bratslav, *Azamra!* (Brooklyn, NY: Breslov Research Institute, 1984).
Neeman, Yehoshua L., *Nusaḥ la-ḥazan* (Jerusalem: Israel Institute for Sacred Music, 1969).
Ophir, Natan, *Rabbi Shlomo Carlebach: Life, Mission, and Legacy* (Jerusalem: Urim Publications, 2013).
Pasternak, Velvel, *Hasidic Music: An Annotated Overview* (Cedarhurst: Tara Publications, 1999).
Regev, Motti, and Edwin Seroussi, *Popular Music and Israeli National Culture* (Berkeley: University of California Press, 2004).
Schachter-Shalomi, Zalman, "Niggun! A Soul in Song," in Z. Schachter-Shalomi and J. Segel (eds.), *Davening: A Guide to Meaningful Jewish Prayer* (Woodstock, NY: Jewish Lights Publishing, 2012), 28–57.
Schwartz, Dov, *Kinor nishmati: Music in Jewish Thought* (Ramat Gan: Bar Ilan University Press, 2013).
Smith, Chani H., *Tuning the Soul: Music as a Spiritual Process in the Teachings of Rabbi Naḥman of Bratzlav* (Leiden: Brill, 2010).
Werner, Eric, *A Voice Still Heard: The Sacred Songs of the Ashkenazic Jews* (University Park: Pennsylvania State University Press, 1976).
Wood, Abigail, "Stepping across the Divide: Hasidic Music in Today's Yiddish Canon," *Ethnomusicology* 51 (2007), 2:205–237.

Recordings

Historic Collection of Jewish Music, 1912–1947, 6 vols. (Kiev: National Library of Ukraine, Institute for Information, 2001–2013). Rare historical documentation of Hasidic music from Ukraine, mostly from before the Holocaust.
L'Chaim Tisch, 18 vols. (2005–2012). One of the most ambitious Hasidic recording initiatives of recent times, produced by R. Yosef Moshe Kahana. Includes niggunim from most Hasidic courts.
Mazor, Yaakov, ed., *The Hasidic Niggun as Sung by the Hasidim*, 2 CDs (Jerusalem: Jewish Music Research Centre, The Hebrew University of Jerusalem, 2004). A comprehensive selection of field recordings from the Sound Archives of the National Library of Israel, with copious annotations.

Scores with Annotations and Commentaries

Beregovskii, Moisei, *Evreiskie napevy bez slov* (Moscow: Kompozitor, 1999).
Coopersmith, Harry, *Songs of My People* (Chicago: Anshe Emet Synagogue, 1937).
Hajdu, Andre, and Yaakov Mazor, *Hasidic Treasury: 101 Hasidic Dance Tunes*, 3rd ed., rev. and enl. by Yaakov Mazor (Jerusalem: Renanot, 2000).
Idelsohn, Abraham Z., *Songs of the Chassidim*, vol. 10 of the *Thesaurus of Hebrew Oriental Melodies* (Leipzig: F. Hofmeister, 1932).

Pasternak, Velvel, *Songs of the Chasidim*, vol. 1 (New York: Tara Publications, 1968), vol. 2 (Cedarhurst: Tara Publications, 1971).
Sharvit, Uri, *Chasidic Tunes from Galicia* (Jerusalem: Renanot, 1995).
Stutschewsky, Joachim, *120 nigunei ḥasidim* (Tel Aviv: Ha-histadrut ha-klalit, c. 1950).
Vinaver, Chemjo, *Anthology of Hasidic Music*, ed. E. Schleifer (Jerusalem: Jewish Music Research Centre, The Hebrew University of Jerusalem, 1985).
Zalmanov, Shmu'el, ed., *Sefer ha-nigunim*, 3 vols. (Brooklyn: Nichoach, 1948, 1957; Kefar Chabad: Nichoach, 1985).

Websites

The massive use of the internet by Hasidim allows today for easier access to recordings of niggunim as well as to the literature on the subject. A comprehensive guide to the virtual network of the Hasidic niggun is beyond the scope of this chapter. Here are few recommendations only. The website Heichal Menachem-Heichal Haneginah is in fact a virtual continuation of the massive documentation of the Chabad repertoire published in the *Sefer ha-nigunim*. The recordings of each niggun frequently include a spoken introduction, similar to the notes included in *Sefer ha-nigunim*, about the history behind the melody, its transmitters, and its spiritual and mystical significance. Its counterpart is the website of the Institute for the Conservation and Documentation of the Modzitz Niggun, which also includes scores, recordings, and texts. The blog *Heichal HaNegina* appeared in August 2005 and was active intermittently until 2014. It is a rich repository of original materials leaning toward the Modzits court and offers access to other websites maintained by institutions related to different Hasidic dynasties or by individuals.

NOTES

1. Tzvi Rabinowicz, *Hasidism: The Movement and Its Masters* (Northvale: Jason Aronson Inc. Publishers, 1988), 330; Rabinowicz, *Encyclopedia of Hasidism* (Northvale: Jason Aronson Inc. Publishers, 1996), 332. I would like to acknowledge the contributions of my colleagues Jonathan Garb, Walter Zev Feldman, and Neil Levin, and of my students Michael Lukin and Matan Wygoda to the improvement of this text.

2. Martin Buber, "Jüdische Künstler," trans. in Martin Buber and Gilya G. Schmidt, *The First Buber: Youthful Zionist Writings of Martin Buber* (Syracuse, NY: Syracuse University Press, 1999), 104.

3. Christopher Small, *Musicking: The Meanings of Performing and Listening* (Hanover, NH: University Press of North England, 1998). The earliest sources about Hasidic circles already stress music as a hallmark of their ritual practices. R. Shlomo of Chełm in his introduction to *Sefer Mirkevet ha-mishneh* (Frankfurt on the Oder: Be-vet ha-defus shel doctor Grilo, 1751) depicts the "sect" praying with "songs and melodies, in voices and tunes" (*be-shir ve-renanim, kolot ve-nigunim*). Quoted in Gershon Scholem, "Shetei ha-eduyiot ha-rishonot al ḥavurot ha-ḥasidim veha-Besht," *Tarbiz* 20 (1950), 233.

4. Yaakov Mazor, "Koḥo shel ha-nigun ba-hagut ha-ḥasidit ve-tafkidav ba-ḥavai ha-dati veha-ḥevrati," *Yuval* 7 (2002), 23–53.

5. Moshe Idel, *Hasidism: Between Ecstasy and Magic* (Albany: State University of New York Press, 1995).

6. Ibid., 181.

7. *In Praise of Baal Shem Tov [Shivhei Ha-Besht]: The Earliest Collection of the Legends about the Founder of Hasidism*, trans. and ed. D. Ben-Amos and J. R. Mintz (Bloomington: Indiana University Press, 1970), 83.

8. Ibid., xxii; Idel, *Hasidism*, 353 n.3; Louis Jacobs, *Hasidic Prayer* (London: Littman Library of Jewish Civilization, 1993), 58. It is important to point out, however, that also in

non-Hasidic synagogues, any *ba'al tefilah* (i.e., a member of the congregation who was conversant in the performative *nusaḥ* of the prayers) could lead services regardless of his having formal vocal or musical training. Knowledgeable *ba'alei tefilah* in non-Hasidic synagogues had ample room for a personal import, but their basic compliancy with the accepted rules of *nusaḥ* separates them from "inspired" Hasidic lay prayer leaders who did not abide by those rules.

9. Idel, *Hasidism*, 27.

10. Ibid., 210.

11. Solomon Maimon, *An Autobiography*, trans. J. Clark Murray (Urbana and Chicago: University of Illinois Press, 2001), 167–168. For a more extensive quote see chapter 1.

12. Idel, *Hasidism*, 211.

13. "Shever posh'im," in Mordecai Wilensky, *Ḥasidim u-mitnagedim: Le-toledot ha-pulmus she-benehem 1772–1815* (Jerusalem: Mosad Bialik, 1970), 2:173–174. Translation is mine.

14. Moshe Idel, "The Magical and Theurgic Interpretation of Music in Jewish Sources from the Renaissance to Hasidism," *Yuval* 4 (1982), 33–62; Idel, "Conceptualization of Music in Jewish Mysticism," in *Enchanting Powers: Music in the World's Religions*, ed. L. E. Sullivan (Cambridge, MA: Harvard University Press, 1997), 159–188.

15. Edwin Seroussi, "Rabbi Menchem di Lonzano: Ethnomusicologist," in *Prof. Meir Benayahu Memorial Volume*, ed. M. Bar Asher, Y. Liebes, M. Assis, and Y. Kaplan (Jerusalem: Carmel, 2019); see also Idel, *Hasidism*, 36.

16. For a valuable if a bit outdated summary, see Gilbert Rouget, *Music and Trance: A Theory of the Relations between Music and Possession* (Chicago: University of Chicago Press, 1985); for Hasidism, see Jonathan Garb, *Shamanic Trance in Modern Kabbalah* (Chicago: University of Chicago Press, 2011); Garb, *Yearnings of the Soul: Psychological Thought in Modern Kabbalah* (Chicago: University of Chicago Press, 2015).

17. Yehudah Halevy, *Kuzari*, trans. H. Hirschfeld (New York: E.P. Dutton, 1905), 2:50.

18. Aharon Perlow, "Toledot ha-Imre Ḥayim mi-Viznits," *Yidishe Velt Forum*, accessed January 21, 2019, http://www.ivelt.com/forum/viewtopic.php?t=26250, quoted from *Bita'on Vizhnitz*, Kislev 5764, p. 63.

19. Nahman of Bratslav, *Likkutei Moharan* (Jerusalem, New York: Breslov Research Institute, 1975) second part, f. 29b, teaching 63.

20. Glenn Dynner, *Men of Silk: The Hasidic Conquest of Polish Jewish Society* (New York: Oxford University Press, 2006), 220–225.

21. See Abraham N. Birnbaum (Birnboyim), "Ha-shirah veha-zimrah be-ḥatserot ha-tsadikim be-Polin," *Ha-Olam* 1 (1907), 20–22, 30–31, 44–45, 69–70, 81–82, 105–106, 129–130; Chemjo Vinaver, *Anthology of Jewish Music* (New York: Edward B. Marks Music, 1955), 258–265.

22. See Birnbaum, "Ha-shirah veha-zimrah."

23. Abraham Zvi Idelsohn, "Ha-neginah ha-ḥasidit," *Sefer Hashanah: The American Hebrew Yearbook* 1 (1931), 74–87; Idelsohn, *Thesaurus of Hebrew Oriental Melodies*, vol. 10: *Gesänge der Chasidim* (Leipzig: B. Harz Verlag, 1932), introduction.

24. Birnbaum (Birnboyim), "Ha-shirah veha-zimrah," 20–22.

25. See James Loeffler, *The Most Musical Nation: Jews and Culture in the Late Russian Empire* (New Haven, CT: Yale University Press, 2010).

26. The publications by Lyudmila Sholokhova on the Russian-Jewish ethnography of Hasidic music are fundamental. See, for example, "Jewish musical ethnography in Russian Empire: ideology and chronology," in *Jüdische Kunstmusik im 20. Jahrhundert: Quellenlage, Entstehungsgeschichte, Stilanalysen*, ed. J. Nemtsov (Wiesbaden: Harrassovitz, 2006), 217–223.

27. Moshe Beregovski, *Old Jewish Folk Music: The Collections and Writings of Moshe Beregovski*, ed. M. Slobin, 2nd ed. (Syracuse, NY: Syracuse University Press, 2000).

28. Idelsohn, "Ha-neginah ha-ḥasidit"; Idelsohn, *Thesaurus of Hebrew Oriental Melodies.*

29. Schleifer in Vinaver, *Anthology of Jewish Music*, 18.

30. Yaakov Mazor, Bathja Bayer, and Andre Hajdu, "The Hasidic Dance-Niggun: A Study Collection and Its Classificatory Analysis," *Yuval* 3 (1974), 136–266.

31. A[ndre] Hajdu and Y[aakov] Mazor, "Musical Traditions of Hasidism," in *Encyclopedia Judaica*, 2nd ed., ed. F. Skolnik and M. Berenbaum (Detroit: Mcmillan Reference Press in association with Keter, 2007), 8:425–434.

32. See esp. Yaakov Mazor, "Koḥo shel ha-nigun"; Mazor, "Min ha-nigun ha-ḥasidi el ha-zemer ha-yisra'eli," *Katedra* 115 (2004), 95–128.

33. Uri Sharvit, *Chasidic Tunes from Galicia* (Jerusalem: Renanot, 1995).

34. Michael Lukin and Matan Wygoda, "Darei ma'alah 'im darei matah: Nigunei R. Levi Yitzḥak mi-Berditchev be-perspektivah historit," in *Rabbi Levi Yitchak of Berdichev: History, Thought, Literature and Melody*, ed. Z. Mark and R. Horn (Rishon LeZion: Miskal, 2017).

35. Compare also Idelsohn, *Thesaurus of Hebrew Oriental Melodies.*

36. Andre Hajdu, "Le Niggun Meron: Description d'un Patrimonie Instrumental Juif," *Yuval* 2 (1971), 73–97.

37. Mark Kligman, "Contemporary Jewish Music in America," *American Jewish Year Book* 101 (2001), 88–141; Abigail Wood "Stepping across the Divide: Hasidic Music in Today's Yiddish Canon," *Ethnomusicology* 51 (2007), 2:205–237.

38. Natan Ophir, *Rabbi Shlomo Carlebach: Life, Mission, and Legacy* (Jerusalem: Urim Publications, 2013); Zalman Schachter-Shalomi and Joel Segel, "Niggun! A Soul in Song," in *Davening: A Guide to Meaningful Jewish Prayer* (Woodstock, VT: Jewish Lights Publishing, 2012), 28–57.

39. See Yaakov Mazor and Moshe Taube, "A Hasidic Ritual Dance: The *Mitsve Tants* in Jerusalemite Weddings," *Yuval* 6 (1994), 164–224.

40. Moisei Beregovskii, *Evreiskie napevy bez slov* (Moscow: Kompozitor, 1999).

41. For the phenomenon of vocalization in the Ashkenazi liturgical practice, see Geoffrey Goldberg, *Between Tradition and Modernity: The High Holy Days Melodies of* Minhag Ashkenaz *According to Ḥazzan Maier Levi of Esslingen* (Jerusalem: Jewish Music Research Centre, 2019).

42. Wilensky, *Ḥasidim u-mitnagedim*, 1:39–41.

43. Ibid., 1:53–54.

44. Ibid., 2:60, 75, 302–303.

45. Marcin Wodziński, *Hasidism and Politics: The Kingdom of Poland, 1815–1864* (Oxford: The Littman Library of Jewish Civilization, 2013), 80–85.

46. Vinaver, *Anthology of Hasidic Music*, ed. E. Schleifer (Jerusalem: Jewish Music Research Centre, 1985), 32.

47. Idelsohn, *Thesaurus of Hebrew Oriental Melodies*, ix.

48. Meir Shimon Geshuri, *Ha-nigun ve-ha-rikud ba-ḥasidut* (Tel Aviv: Netsah, 1955–1959), 1:24.

49. Yehoshua L. Neeman, *Nusaḥ la-ḥazan*, vol. 2 (Jerusalem: Israel Institute, for Sacred Music 1969); see Yaakov Mazor, "Ha-shushalot ha-ḥasidiyot veha-tekstim shebe-fihen," note 15, on the Hasidic concept of "*velt nusaḥ*," i.e., "universal prayer mode," *Hazmanah le-piyyut*, accessed January 21, 2019, http://old.piyut.org.il/articles/910.html.

50. Jacobs, *Hasidic Prayer.*

51. Avraham Kahana, *Sefer ha-ḥasidut: Min Rabi Israel Besht ad Rabi Naḥman mi-Braslav* (Warsaw: Levin-Epstein, 1922), 138–139.

52. Wilensky, *Ḥasidim u-mitnagedim*, 2:137–141.

53. See Mazor, "Koḥo shel ha-nigun," 43.

54. Aharon Rote, *Sefer takanot ve-hadrakhot de-ḥevrat Shomrei emunim* (Jerusalem: [s.n.], 1933), 17a, 37b, 48a.

55. Mazor, "Koḥo shel ha-nigun," 42–43.

56. Aharon Rote, *Sefer shomer emunim*, first part, 2nd ed. (Jerusalem [s.n.], 1959), 32b–33a. A different version of this tale appears in Abraham Rechtman, "Le-toledot shenei nigunim," *Yeda 'Am* 6 (1955), 1–2:44–47. According to a note in the opening of this article, this version was recorded in 1913 in Międzybóż (Mezhbizh), the city of the Besht, during the An-sky expedition. The informant was R. Chaim Mikhl Bik (1889–1964), the last rabbi of Międzybóż who moved to the USA in 1925. This version is much more elaborate. The story refers to a rich merchant from Piława (today Pylyavka, Ukraine) a village near Międzybóż whose son-in-law, Mendel, a Hasid, used to accompany him to periodic visits to the Besht. When his father-in-law and sustainer died, Mendel went to the Besht for counseling. The Besht commanded him to stay over Shabbat, attend his services, and memorize his new *niggun* to "Adonay malakh ge'ut labesh" (from *Lekha dodi*). After Shabbat, the Besht tests Mendel and is astonished by his musical memory and quality of voice, appointing him on the spot as cantor in his own kloyz. Before departing, he tells Mendel that he will be a cantor all his life but will perish on the first occasion in which he will be removed from the pulpit. After the Besht's death, Mendel hires a *meshorer* and becomes a wandering cantor, reaching the court of R. Elimelekh of Lizhensk, where the story unfolds similarly to the version by R. Rote.

57. See *Megilat setarim* (Jerusalem: Mosad Harav Kook, 1944).

58. Mazor, "Koḥo shel ha-nigun."

59. Aaron Wertheim, *Law and Custom in Hasidism*, trans. S. Himelstein (Hoboken, NJ: Ktav Publishing House, 1992).

60. Vinaver, *Anthology of Hasidic Music*, 269–272.

61. Ya'akov Yosef of Polnoe, *Toledot Ya'akov Yosef*, "Shlaḥ lekha," 137a; quoted in Mazor, "Koḥo shel ha-nigun," 37.

62. Vinaver, *Anthology of Hasidic Music*, 252.

63. Tzvi Freeman, "Music, Spirituality and Transformation," *Chabad.org*, accessed January 21, 2019, www.chabad.org/library/article_cdo/aid/67814/jewish/Music-Spirituality-and-Transformation.htm.

64. Aharon Perlow, "Toledot Ha-Imre Ḥayim mi-Viznits," *Hidabrut*, accessed January 21, 2019, www.hidabroot.org/article/77391, quoting from R. Yidele Horowitz of Dzików, *Zikhron Yehuda*, (Jerusalem, 2003), 156.

65. *Imrei Shaul*, p. 311, par. 22–p. 312, par. 23.

66. Vinaver, *Anthology of Hasidic Music*, 156–163; see also Meir Shimon Geshuri, *Neginah ve-ḥasidut be-vet Kuzmir u-venoteha* (Jerusalem: Netsah, 1952), 69–75.

67. Sara Friedland Ben-Arza, "Ha-nigun be-hasidut Modzits," *Hazmanah le-piyyut*, http://old.piyut.org.il/articles/761.html, accessed January 21, 2019. The *Ezkera* niggun was eventually recorded by the late composer of the Modzits dynasty in America, R. Ben Zion Shenker (1925–2016).

68. See Shmuel Zalmanov, ed., *Sefer ha-nigunim*, 2 vols., 3rd ed. (Kefar Chabad, 1985); for detailed analysis of this episode, see Naftali Loewenthal, "Spirituality, Melody and Modernity in Habad Hasidism," in *Proceedings of the First International Conference on Jewish Music*, ed. S. Stanton (London: City University, Department of Music, 1997), 62–78.

69. This motif in Judaism goes back to the story about the composition and singing of the *piyut* "U'netane tokef" by a spurious eleventh-century sage, R. Amnon of Mainz, at the moment he returned his soul to his creator in the synagogue under indescribable pain after refusing to convert to Christianity and undergoing inhuman physical punishment. Although research has repeatedly shown this episode to be a constructed myth, it continues to be recycled to this day in countless printed texts and oral statements. The literature on this myth is vast. For a useful summary, see Lawrence A. Hoffman, *Who by Fire, Who by Water—Un'taneh Tokef* (Woodstock, VT: Jewish Lights Publications, 2010).

70. Friedland Ben-Arza, "Ha-nigun be-ḥasidut Modzits."

71. Zalmanov, ed., *Sefer ha-nigunim*; for a scholarly dissent, see Rafi Ben-Moshe, *Experiencing Devekut: The Contemplative Niggun of Habad in Israel* (Jerusalem: Jewish Music

Research Centre, 2015). See also Freeman, "Music, Spirituality and Transformation"; Garb, *Yearnings of the Soul*, 201n.15.

72. His last book is a tour de force essay dedicated to one of the most sacred niggunim of Chabad, the "Arba Bavot" (Four Gates), by R. Shneur Zalman of Lady. See Lev Leibman, *Niggun Arba Bavot* (Kfar Chabad: Makhon Neginah Le'Or Ha-Hasidut, 2015).

73. Freeman, "Music, Spirituality and Transformation."

74. Dovid Abraham Mandelbaum, *Hekhal ha-neginah* (Jerusalem: Z. Goldknopf, 2005).

75. Naḥman of Bratslav, *Azamra!* (Brooklyn, NY: Breslov Research Institute, 1984); Chani H. Smith, *Tuning the Soul: Music as a Spiritual Process in the Teachings of Rabbi Nahman of Bratzlav* (Leiden: Brill, 2010).

76. Shai Malkah, ed., *Shirat kol ḥai: Perakim be-nigun shirah ve-ḥasidut* (Otni'el: Yeshivat Otni'el, 2006).

77. Idelsohn, "Ha-neginah ha-ḥasidit," 86.

78. Salomon Rosowsky, *Mi-zimrat ha-arets* (Warsaw: Keren Kayemet Le-Israel, 1929); 2nd ed. (Paris: Editions Salabert, 1935), 144–156.

79. Jakob Schönberg, *Shirei Erets Israel* (Berlin: Jüdische Verlag, 1935).

80. See, e.g., Harry Coopersmith, *Songs of My People* (Chicago: Anshe Emet Synagogue, 1937).

81. Motti Regev and Edwin Seroussi, *Popular Music and Israeli National Culture* (Berkeley: University of California Press, 2004), 126–29.

82. Shifra Epstein, "Drama on a Table: The Bobover Hasidim Pirimshpiyl," in *Judaism Viewed from Within and Without: Anthropological Studies*, H. E. Goldberg (Albany: State University of New York Press, 1987), 195–217; Barbara Kirshenblatt-Gimblett, "Performance of Precepts/Precepts of Performance: Hasidic Celebrations of Purim in Brooklyn," in *By Means of Performance: Intercultural Studies of Theatre and Ritual*, ed. R. Schechner and W. Appel (Cambridge: Cambridge University Press, 1990), 109–117.

83. Velvel Pasternak, *Songs of the Chasidim*, vol. 1 (New York: Bloch Publishing Co., 1968); vol. 2 (Cedarhurst, NY: Tara Publications, 1971). Wiesel used to open many of his talks with a Hasidic niggun he remembered from his childhood. A concert in his honor and with his participation as performer, titled *Elie Wiesel:Memories and Melodies of My Childhood*, was held in New York City in 2010 at the 92nd Street Y and circulates as a DVD.

CHAPTER 12

Material Culture

Vladimir Levin

Everyone seeing contemporary Hasidim in Jerusalem, New York, London, or Antwerp immediately recognizes that they look different from other people. Their distinct appearances imply that their material culture differs from that of other Jewish communities. Notwithstanding this difference, Hasidism did not invent new types of objects and buildings, but adopted those that existed in the traditional culture of the Eastern Ashkenazi diaspora.

A main concept of Hasidism is worship through materiality (*avodah be-gashmiyut*), in which any profane activity—eating, drinking, smoking, sexual relations—attains sacred meaning. In this way, regular objects become religiously significant and attain a degree of sacredness. Thus, the Hasidic material culture is characterized not by innovation, but by investing existing objects with new, mystical meaning. The most fruitful approach to Hasidic material culture is phenomenological, applied by Batsheva Goldman-Ida in her research on Hasidic ceremonial objects. As she formulates, "the attitude towards the object becomes part of the definition of the object itself."[1]

The major novelty that distinguishes Hasidism is the concept of the tsadik—a righteous man who mediates between simple Hasidim and the Divine.[2] Many objects of material culture are connected directly to the tsadik and his functioning in the Hasidic milieu. He is considered a holy man, and all material objects he uses attain holiness in the eyes of his followers. The mystical connection of a Hasid's soul to the soul of the tsadik is also expressed through material means: Hasidim give tsadikim written notes with their requests (*kvitlekh*), accompanied by monetary gifts (*pidyon*) that create mystical ties; the tsadik may give a Hasid a blessed coin (*shmirah*) and other objects as amulets; during the festive meeting of the tsadik with his Hasidim (*tish*), the latter eat food blessed by him (*shirayim*).[3] The graves of the deceased tsadikim are venerated and visited by the Hasidim, who pray there and leave *kvitlekh*.

In this chapter, we will discuss the material objects that are important and sometimes indispensable for the Hasidic worship and way of life: a tsadik's court, graves, a Hasidic synagogue, ceremonial and personal objects, and Hasidic clothing. As we will show, attention to the material objects, combined with research on ideas and rituals, allows for a better and more comprehensive understanding of the phenomenon of Hasidism.

Courts

From the time of the Maggid of Mezrich (Międzyrzecz) (d. 1772), the tsadik acted mainly in his dwelling place, known as the court. The court became the place of pilgrimage for Hasidim willing to spend time in the proximity of their master.[4] The most important attempt to describe the physical appearance of the court was made by David Assaf, who researched the courts of the dynasties that developed "the regal way" of life.[5]

Not many Hasidic courts have been physically preserved in Eastern Europe.[6] Courts were destroyed by frequent fires in the nineteenth century, or fell victim to the destruction caused by World War I, the Bolshevik rule in the USSR, the Holocaust, and Communist regimes after World War II. To the best of my knowledge, none of the courts from the second half of the eighteenth century and from the first half of the nineteenth century are extant. None was even photographed; hence, our knowledge about those courts is derived mostly from sparse written sources. A tiny minority of the later courts survived the turbulent twentieth century.

The best-preserved courts are those of the Ruzhin dynasty. While nothing remained from the court of R. Israel Friedman in Rużyn (Ruzhin), three courts of his descendants are still extant: the kloyz (prayer house) and palace of R. Avraham Ya'akov in Sadagura (Sadhora, Ukraine);[7] the kloyz of R. David Moshe in Czortków (Chortkiv);[8] and the kloyz of R. Yitzḥak in Buhuşi, Romania.[9] The kloyzn in Sadagura and Czortków, as well as the kloyz of R. Israel's son-in-law, R. Menaḥem Mendel Hager of Vizhnitz (Vijniţa/Vyzhnytsa), known only from photographs (see figure 12.1), have two towers flanking the main façade. The palace in Sadagura also had two towers.[10] The two-tower scheme might refer to the Jachin and Boaz columns, which stood in the Jerusalem Temple, and thus equate the tsadik's kloyz (and his palace) with the temple. Indeed, Hasidim perceived the kloyz as the temple and the tsadik as the high priest officiating there.[11]

More modest complexes of a tsadik's court are preserved in the tiny town of Zinków (Zinkiv, Ukraine). The large two-story house of R. Moshe Heshel and his small single-story kloyz nearby are situated in the center of town (figure 12.2), while the small house and large kloyz of his brother R. Pinḥas can be found at its northern part.[12]

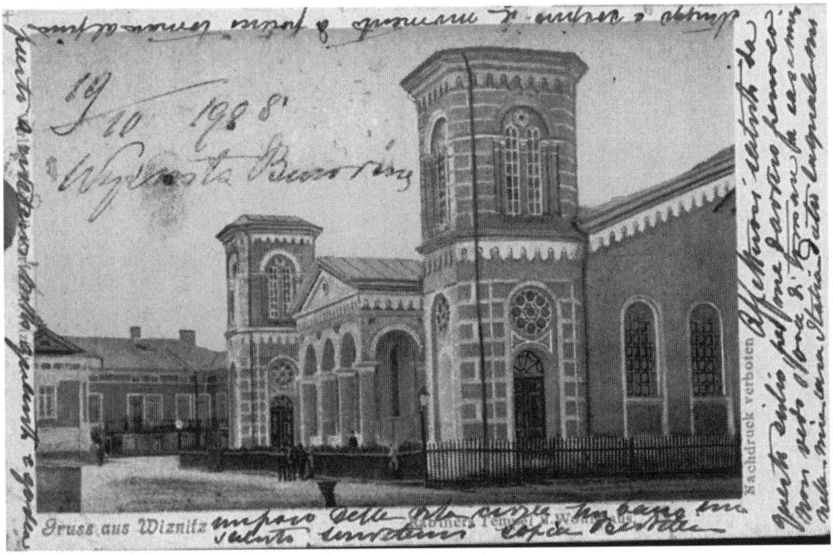

Figure 12.1. Kloyz with two towers and tsadik's house (on the left) in Vizhnitz (Wyżnica, Vyzhnytsa); postcard, early twentieth century. Courtesy of Gross Family Collection, Tel Aviv.

Figure 12.2. House (on the right) and kloyz (on the left) of R. Moshe Heshel in Zinkiv, 2002. Photo courtesy of the Center for Jewish Art, the Hebrew University of Jerusalem.

During the nineteenth century, Hasidic leaders settled mostly in small towns,[13] and the majority of their courts were organized in a similar way. The court was a fenced space that contained the dwelling house of the tsadik and his family, his prayer house, a *mikveh*, and services needed for the functioning of the court: kitchens, stalls for horses and cows, sheds for carriages, firewood, and so on. In many courts, separate houses for tsadik's adult sons and sons-in-law were built. The courts of the Ruzhin-Sadagura dynasty usually had gardens, open only to the tsadik family. Thus, the court was clearly separated—spatially and socially—from the town.[14]

The separation of the tsadik's court resembled the model of a nobleman's manor house, which was separated from the village or town and acted as an independent economic and social unit.[15] However, the placement of some courts in the towns' centers (e.g., Zinków or the preserved tsadik's house in Stolin; IJA 6106) points to another model—the homes of wealthy Jews. This issue has not yet been studied, but at least one feature of a tsadik's court—the private synagogue—originated in the houses of the Jewish elite. Starting at least from the seventeenth century, prominent members of the Jewish community had their own prayer rooms in their houses.[16] As Rachel Manekin stresses, "the public synagogue seems almost to be a place serving the less fortunate Jews, those with lower socio-economic or intellectual status."[17] Therefore, the custom of having a kloyz in the houses of tsadikim not only allowed them to conduct prayer and learning in the Hasidic mode and to develop distinctive customs characteristic of a certain branch of Hasidism, but also stressed the tsadik's prominence and emphasized the high level of social and religious prestige.[18] The kloyz was the central and most important structure in the court, which, in contrast to the dwelling houses, was open to all visitors.

In the late nineteenth century, tsadikim began to leave small towns and move to larger cities, where they tried to keep their courts but under completely different spatial and social conditions. For example, R. Ḥaim Meir Yeḥiel Shapira established his court in Drohobych in 1885. A drawing, made by his son (figure 12.3), features a two-story dwelling house situated in a garden; the large semicircular windows on the upper floor provide light for the tsadik's *bet midrash*.[19] Thus, the tsadik combined two models: the model of a separate manor house with a garden, and the model of a city house, where the living apartment and the bet midrash unite under the same roof.

Less affluent tsadikim could not afford such comfortable living spaces. Like other city dwellers, they had to live in rented apartments. For example, R. Mordekhai Zusya Twersky from the Trisk (Turzysk) dynasty moved to Iaşi, Romania, in 1905 and settled there in a small apartment. The only difference from other apartments was that his included a "synagogue" that also served as a waiting room for those who came to see him.[20]

Figure 12.3. Bet midrash of R. Ḥayim Meir Yeḥiel Shapira in Drohobych. Source: N. M. Gelber, ed., *Sefer zikaron le-Drohobich, Borislav veha-svivah* (Tel-Aviv, 1959), plate xix.

World War I caused, among other things, the destruction of Hasidic courts in small towns and their transfer to the cities. With scant academic research, this phenomenon and its architectural dimension are almost unknown.[21] Two interesting examples of such new courts were located in Stanisławów (now Ivano-Frankivsk, Ukraine). One is the court of R. Ḥaim Hager of Ottynia (Vizhnitz dynasty), who settled in Stanisławów after World War I, buying an existing large dwelling house and building a kloyz in its courtyard in 1926 (IJA 11532). Hager thus reestablished the scheme typical for the Hasidic courts in small towns, where the house of the tsadik and his kloyz were two separate buildings situated near each other.[22] Another example is the court of R. Ḥaim Leifer of Nadvorna (Nadwórna), which was situated in a single building and included the tsadik's apartment, the kloyz, and the *mikveh* (IJA 11528).

The combination of the dwelling and prayer spaces under a single roof, or the designation of a large room in the tsadik's apartment for prayer, became, apparently, typical for Hasidic courts situated in the cities, where it was impossible to develop the infrastructure of the "traditional" court. This combination stressed the importance of two main spaces of the court: the tsadik's dwelling and his kloyz.

Tsadik's Dwelling House

According to Hasidic principles, the tsadik interacts with heavenly spheres not only when he performs rituals, but also at every moment of his life. Therefore, the home of the tsadik bears a high degree of holiness, which emanates from him. For example, the room in a hotel in the village of Pena, where R. Shneur Zalman of Lady died in 1812, immediately became a pilgrimage place for Chabad Hasidim.[23] One of the early depictions of R. Israel the Maggid of Koznits (Kozienice), printed in the mid-nineteenth century, shows him in either his study or his bedroom, surrounded by books and Hasidim (figure 12.4). Both rooms are inside his home, a venue presented as the place where the tsadik acts.[24]

Not many tsadikim's houses are preserved in Eastern Europe. In addition to the palace in Sadagura and the house in Stolin (IJA 6106), we can point to the houses of tsadikim in Kock, Tarłów, and Góra Kalwaria (Ger) in Poland, and in Bursztyn and Kosów in Ukraine.[25] When these houses ceased serving Hasidic masters, they became regular buildings, not differing from their surroundings and not containing special features. Other tsadikim's houses, known only from photographs, were also simple town houses.[26] The importance of these buildings derived from their functioning as the tsadikim's abode and not from their architectural or structural features.

The interiors of the tsadik's houses are little known. After in-depth research, Assaf could write about the house of R. Israel in Sadagura: "We know almost nothing of the interior, for the privacy of the tsadik's family life was jealously guarded, and nobody besides close relatives or the staff of servants was permitted to enter."[27] This assessment probably characterized the courts of the tsadikim living in the "regal way." For simpler courts the statement of Nehemiah Polen is more appropriate: "The Hasidic court was not characterized by sharp delineations between the public and private, between domestic and communal. Hasidim, as least Hasidic intimates, came into the family residence all the time."[28] In both cases, however, the houses reflected the "bourgeois" way of life, which the majority of tsadikim lived. The houses of the Friedman and Twersky "regal" dynasties were larger and richer; the houses of other tsadikim smaller and less affluent. Some houses had a semipublic space—the room where the tsadik met his Hasidim for personal interviews. The study room of R. Menaḥem Mendel of Lubavitch, where he worked, studied Torah, prayed, ate, and met his Hasidim, was connected to his apartment as well as to the bet midrash.[29] R. Avraham Mordekhai Alter of Ger had a similar arrangement: he met his Hasidim in a large room on the ground floor of his house, which was connected to the bet midrash; he recited his morning prayers in the same room.[30] In other courts, however, such as Trisk and Sadagura, the room where the tsadik met Hasidim was not part of his house but was attached to the kloyz.[31]

תמונה פנים האינּאן מופת הדור בופינא קדישא איש אלקי קדוש מהורר
ישראל מנוח מהו עבתי זל מגיד מישרים דקק קאובין עם בנו טמילא מקן זו

MAGITA Z KORZENIEC I SYN IEGO KTORY ZOSTAL NA
STĘPCA PO OYCU SWOIEM RABINEM.

Figure 12.4. Lithograph showing R. Israel of Kozienice blessing his son Moshe;
mid-nineteenth century. Courtesy of the Museum of Jewish History in Russia, Moscow.

Kloyz

The kloyz—a most sacred space—held distinct significance. Prayer had a special meaning in Hasidism. Through mystical prayer, Hasidic leaders had contact with the divine world; therefore, the physical place of their prayer was also
considered special.[32] It is thus not surprising that the bet midrash of the Besht—a
small wooden communal bet midrash standing near the Great Synagogue—was

preserved in Międzybóż (Medzhybizh) in its eighteenth-century form until it was annihilated during World War II[33] (it was built anew at the same place in 2005; see IJA 10220). The Old Synagogue in Piatra Neamţ, Romania, presents itself as the place where the Besht once prayed (notwithstanding that it was built six years after his death, in 1766).[34]

Like all communal batei midrash, the kloyzn in tsadikim's courts, besides being locations of prayer and study, could serve as clubs where Hasidim engaged in storytelling, celebrating, and even slept. R. Ḥaim of Sanz (Nowy Sącz), for example, ruled that "the sanctity of the *bet midrash* should not be applicable" to the kloyzn of the tsadikim.[35] At the same time, none of those activities were allowed in the kloyz in Sadagura.[36] In Lubavitch of the mid-nineteenth century, the kloyz known as the "great hall" stood closed all the year, except for the High Holidays and important events.[37] In 1901, however, that "hall" was repaired to accommodate the yeshiva Tomchei Temimim, not only as a place of learning, but also as the area for students to sleep.[38]

While the ruling of R. Ḥaim of Sanz denied the sanctity of court's bet midrash, in Bełz that sanctity was increased beyond the regular degree prescribed by the Talmud and was extended to the mystical sphere. The founder of the Bełz dynasty, R. Shalom Rokeaḥ, participated in the building of its synagogue and bet midrash, since "the laws of the synagogue" were revealed to him from the heaven and he invested the building process with kabbalistic meanings.[39]

The kloyz in the court almost did not differ from other synagogues, either structurally or stylistically (for the special features in Sadagura, Czortków, and Vizhnitz, see above). Its liturgical space was typical: the Torah ark was at the eastern wall, the *bimah* in the center,[40] benches and tables in the remaining space. The question about the existence of women's sections is not yet sufficiently researched.[41] As historic photographs and measured drawings in the archives of the Center for Jewish Art show, many court's kloyzn had no place for women at all (Ştefăneşti, Buhuşi, Ger), while others had women's sections (Bełz, Sadagura, Czortków). The feature that particularly distinguished the court kloyz from other synagogues was the existence of a special room where the tsadik prayed alone or with a minyan of his close people and family, thus keeping him in close proximity to the Hasidim, but not causing him to intermingle with them.[42]

Another feature singling out some kloyzn in Hasidic courts from regular synagogues was special arrangements that allowed large numbers of people to attend court rituals, since many *kloyzn* served as the public meeting place for the tsadik and the Hasidim. The bet midrash in Trisk, for example, had, in its northern side, special tribunes for Hasidim participating in a *tish*, which reached the ceiling and shielded the windows.[43] In other courts, such as Sadagura, the *tish* ceremony was carried out in a special building, not in the kloyz.[44]

Mikveh

Immersing in a *mikveh* plays an important role in the Hasidic way of life; many Hasidim immerse each day before the morning prayer.[45] As Marcin Wodziński notes, "The group's social experience in the *mikveh* created a sense of solidarity and a shared identity among the men."[46] While every community had a *mikveh* of its own, the tsadikim were not eager to use them and had their separate *mikvaot* in the courts.

Due to the *mikveh*'s nature as an underground structure and the privacy it requires, little is known about *mikvaot* in general and about their role in Hasidic courts in particular. Few photographs of historic *mikvaot* exist, and they are seldom preserved in Eastern Europe. Recently, with the development of Hasidic pilgrimages to former Hasidic centers, several attempts were made to find and uncover the *mikvaot* built and used by Hasidic leaders. For instance, the *mikveh* arranged in the house of R. Shalom Duber Schneersohn in Rostov on Don was uncovered in 1998,[47] and that of Bełz, built by R. Shalom Rokeaḥ, was excavated and renovated in the 2000s.[48]

Symbolic Memory of Hasidic Courts

With the post-Holocaust reestablishment of Hasidic centers in Israel and the United States, the houses of tsadikim in Eastern Europe lost their significance, while some *kloyzn* continued to serve as important identification marks. For example, the synagogue of the Bełz Hasidim in Bnei Brak, Israel, built in the 1950s, was modeled after the synagogue in Bełz,[49] and the new spacious Bełz complex in Jerusalem, erected in 2000, also resembles that synagogue. The bet midrash in Kiryat Vizhnitz in Bnei Brak (built in the 1950s) was symbolically modeled after the kloyz in Vizhnitz, with two towers flanking the main entrance.[50] The Vizhnitz *kolel* in front of it, the Vizhnitz Talmud Torah on its side, the new huge bet midrash built in the place of the old one in the 2000s (figure 12.5), and the current Vizhnitz House under construction all feature two flanking towers. The Hasidim of Ger built a diminished replica of the façade of the *Rebbe's* bet midrash in Góra Kalwaria, near the grave of R. Avraham Mordekhai Alter in Jerusalem.

The tsadik's residence, which plays a special symbolic role in the contemporary Hasidic experience, is embodied in the house of the Lubavitcher Rebbe at 770 Eastern Parkway, Brooklyn, replicated in at least eleven locations. However, this case should be dealt with separately: on the one hand, the *Rebbe's* house also included the bet midrash; on the other hand, the replicas were built in the framework of the distinct messianic context that marks contemporary Chabad from other Hasidic branches.[51]

Figure 12.5. Bet midrash in Kiryat Vizhnitz in Bnei Brak. Its two towers resemble the two towers of the tsadik's kloyz in Vizhnitz (Wyżnica) in Ukraine, which is depicted on the façade of a temporary lobby, built for the High Holidays. Photo by V. Levin, Sukkot 2016.

Graves of Tsadikim

The passing away of a Jew does not imply his or her complete disappearance; one only passes to another world and is still open to communication with the living. The best place to communicate with the deceased and to ask for their assistance is at their graves. After tsadikim pass away, their power becomes even greater than during the lifetime. Hasidim pray at the graves of their deceased masters and place *kvitlekh* at the spot, just as they gave *kvitlekh* to living tsadikim.[52]

Any Jewish cemetery is considered holy,[53] but the graves of righteous men and women have a higher degree of holiness. To protect a tsadik's grave, a special small house—*ohel*—was often erected above it. Our knowledge about *ohalim* is limited, as the majority of them were destroyed during and after the Holocaust.[54] One rare structure that was preserved intact is the *ohel* of R. Yehoshua Gottlieb of Ludmir (Włodzimierz Wołyński) in Olewsk, Ukraine (figure 12.6). The massive stone building was probably erected soon after the tsadik died in 1889.[55] Several original *ohalim* are preserved in the Okopowa Street Cemetery in Warsaw as well as in several towns in Romania. The majority of *ohalim* existing today in Eastern Europe were erected after the collapse of the Communist regimes in the 1990s, by various Hasidic organizations or families. Tombstones in the *ohalim* sometimes preserve traditional polychromic colors, as they are not exposed to rain and sunshine.[56]

Figure 12.6. *Ohel* of R. Yehoshua and R. Levi Yitzḥak Gottlieb of Ludmir in Olewsk. Photo by V. Rogozov, 2013, courtesy of the Center for Jewish Art, the Hebrew University of Jerusalem.

Although the *ohel* became closely associated with Hasidism, the grave of the founder of the movement, the Besht, located in Międzybóż, did not have an *ohel*. Instead, a wooden shed was constructed there long after his death.[57]

During the nineteenth century, the custom of erecting *ohalim* on tsadikim's graves became widespread. Some, like that in Olewsk, were built of stone and bricks, while others, like the *ohel* of R. Ḥayim Shneur Zalman Schneerson in Lady (Belarus), captured in a photograph of 1930, were wooden (IJA 26312).

To be buried in the proximity of tsadik's grave was considered respectful. Therefore his descendants were usually buried in the *ohel*, thus producing a family mausoleum. Hasidic dynasties had no unanimous approach to gender segregation of graves. In some places, like in Lubawicze (Lubavitch) or Buhuşi, women were buried in a separate *ohel* (IJA 26937; 26267; 26269); in other places, such as Góra Kalwaria, the women of the Alter family were buried around the *ohel* (IJA 26922). In many other *ohalim*, one can find graves of men and women together, as in Zabłotów (Ukraine), Radomsko (Poland), or Roman (Romania) (IJA 26921; 15337; 26929).

Judaism generally does not allow the moving of a grave to another place, particularly with regard to the holy graves of tsadikim. Therefore, the original graves in Eastern Europe attract Hasidic pilgrimage, although the majority of the Hasidim live in the United States or Israel.[58] The most famous place of pilgrimage is the grave of R. Naḥman of Bratslav in Humań (Uman). Since the fall of the Iron Curtain, the destroyed grave of R. Naḥman was restored and it attracts thousands of pilgrims, especially during Rosh Hashanah—in accordance with R. Naḥman's testament. The popularity of the pilgrimage to Uman (Humań) today reaches all segments of religious Jews, far beyond adherents of Hasidism.

Synagogues

A major means for forming a Hasidic community was to establish a separate Hasidic prayer house, usually known as *shtibl* or kloyz.[59] However, it seems that the most commonly used word for Hasidic prayer house in the formative stage of the Hasidic movement was *minyan* (the quorum of ten adult male Jews needed for public prayer), a term usually applied to groups gathering for prayer in a private house, without special architectural arrangements.[60] This name persisted in Lithuania, where Hasidism spread only marginally, well into twentieth century.

Shaul Stampfer has recently shown that "the *shtibl* played a key role in the spread of Hasidism as a mass movement and greatly facilitated its expansion and growth."[61] Stampfer's analysis takes into account the late eighteenth century and the first half of the nineteenth century. He stresses that the establishment of a Hasidic shtibl in a given locality provided Jews who might have been interested in a new religious movement with the opportunity to experience it without obligation and without expensive travel to the courts of Hasidic leaders. Belonging to the shtibl also had social advantages, since the liturgy was conducted according to *nusaḥ sefarad*, previously restricted to elitist groups of kabbalists, and the shtibl "attracted newcomers by creating an enjoyable atmosphere that was less formal and more inviting than the atmosphere in the traditional synagogues or *batei midrash*."[62]

The first Hasidic shtiblekh were rooms in dwelling houses or other unpretentious buildings. The erection of large Hasidic synagogues was the next step, which legitimatized the Hasidic mode of religious life and attested to the growing place the Hasidim held in a Jewish community. The importance of Hasidic public synagogues is exemplified by the history of constructing such a synagogue in Lwów (Lviv/Lemberg). To get the support of the official community to establish a Hasidic synagogue in 1840–1843, Jacob Glanzer, a leader of Lwów's Hasidim, even donated money for the building of the Progressive Temple in the city, as well as agreeing that the new synagogue would be under the control of the community council and that prayers would be conducted according to *nusaḥ ashkenaz* and not the Hasidic *nusaḥ sefarad*. His efforts bore fruit, and when all governmental restrictions on Hasidic worship were removed in Austria in 1848, the synagogue became a major Hasidic center.[63]

The location of a Hasidic shtibl in a town might serve to indicate the prominence of Hasidim (or a certain branch of Hasidism) in a community. However, the geographic situation can serve only as a partial indicator, since traditionally almost all houses of prayer in old Jewish settlements were concentrated around the Great Synagogue: either in the *shulhoyf* or nearby.[64] Thus, in the stronghold of Lithuanian Judaism, Vilna (Vilnius), the Hasidic shtibl (often called *minyan*) and the shtibl of the Chabad Hasidim were situated in the *shulhoyf*, in proximity to the Great Synagogue and the Vilna Gaon's kloyz.[65] The placement of the Hasidic shtibl in the communal *shulhoyf*—and not in a private house—certified the legitimization of Hasidism and its inclusion in the "sacred realm" of the community.

No differences between Hasidic and non-Hasidic synagogues are indicated by their architecture. The major features—Torah ark and *bimah*—are present in both types of synagogues. Large Hasidic and non-Hasidic synagogues usually had a women's section, while very small prayer houses of the Hasidim as well as those of non-Hasidim might have lacked space designated for women.[66] What differentiated the Hasidic synagogue from others was the prayer according to *nusaḥ sefarad*, special Hasidic customs, and "after-prayer" activities. Glenn Dynner notes that "liturgical and stylistic innovation served as territorial markers" and created new power relations.[67] Information about selling alcohol in a synagogue (as in Ostróg) or about a bottle of vodka kept in the Torah ark (as in Krzemieniec) may testify to worshippers' adherence to Hasidism,[68] but it had nothing to do with structural or decorative features of the building.

In his recent book, Boris Khaimovich attempts to establish a connection between Boian Hasidism and the elaborate wall paintings of the Bet Tfilah Benyamin Synagogue in Cernauti (Chernivtsi) (1923)[69] and the New Great Synagogue in Nowosielica (1919–1920).[70] Although neither of these synagogues was associated with the Boian Hasidim, Khaimovich found indirect connections between the model for the decoration of both synagogues, which became a "regional canon," and the Boian court. In his mind, this "most extensive and holistic decoration program" among all known synagogue wall paintings is ideologically connected to the "regal way" of the Ruzhin-Sadagura dynasty.[71] The major logical problem with this conclusion is that the regal way of life was reserved for the tsadikim and not for their Hasidim. However, if this claim is to be supported by other evidence, it may point to a connection between Hasidism and a certain type of program for synagogue decoration.

A contrasting approach has recently been formulated by Sergey Kravtsov. He cites how the Russian Jewish writer Isaac Babel described a Hasidic synagogue: "There are no adornments in the building, everything is white and plain to the point of asceticism, everything is fleshless, bloodless, to a grotesque degree" and concluded that Hasidic groups "minimally cared about the external visible exquisiteness of the sacred space."[72] While Babel (and Kravtsov after him) contrasted modest Hasidic shtiblekh to the magnificent communal Great Synagogues, the modesty of the prayer houses was not an exclusively Hasidic feature. It seems that the majority of small non-Hasidic synagogues in Eastern Europe were also very modest, without exterior or interior decorations.

Ceremonial and Personal Objects

Like the buildings, personal objects of tsadikim have holiness transmitted to them from their holy owners. Even in the formative stage of the Hasidic movement, the objects—especially ritual ones—belonging to Hasidic masters were considered sacred. This is clearly evident in a report about the meeting of R. Shneur Zalman of Lady with R. Baruch of Medzhybizh (Międzybóż), a grandson of the Besht, in 1810. R. Baruch used the tefilin of the Besht, and R. Shneur Zalman reprimanded him for not examining their validity because of their holiness.[73] In contrast to R. Baruch, R. Israel of Ruzhin indeed examined and repaired the tefilin, which had belonged, in sequence, to all his ancestors and later became the possession of his son, R. David Moshe of Czortków.[74] Tsadikim often had their own Torah scrolls, which were also considered special: a Torah scroll of R. Levi Yitzḥak of Berdyczów (Berdichev) came to the hands of R. Avraham Yehoshua Heshel of Apt (Opatów) and later was kept in the kloyz in the Sadagura court;[75] a small Torah scroll of R. Aharon of Czarnobyl belonged to his descendant R. Mordekhai Israel Twersky of Ozarinets-Khotin.[76] Objects inherited from great tsadikim of previous generations were a means to establish a tsadik's legitimacy, as they stressed his direct connection to his holy ancestors.

Ritual objects produced by famous Hasidic figures also possessed special value. For example, a Torah scroll written by Efraim Sofer, the scribe of the Besht, was kept in the Old Kloyz in Równe (Rivne), and R. Israel Perlov, the Yanuka of Stolin, always went to that kloyz in order to read from this specific scroll during his yearly visits to the city.[77] Similarly, the profane objects of famous tsadikim were also held in high esteem. Thus, R. Avraham Yehoshua Heshel of Kopychinets (Kopyczyńce) used the pipe of R. Barukh of Medzhybizh (Międzybóż).[78] R. Mordekhai Twersky of Shpikov kept in "ironbound chests" a knife of the Besht, a coat of R. Naḥum of Czarnobyl, and—not less important—a golden snuffbox of Shaul Wahl, a mythological one-day king of Poland from the sixteenth century.[79] The walking stick of the *Rebbe* of Trisk, transferred after World War II to the Jewish Historical Institute in Warsaw, has a silver plaque engraved with the words *me-Trisk* (from Trisk). The attachment of such a plaque converted an ordinary item of everyday use into a Hasidic memorial object.[80] Walking sticks, often seen in the photographs of tsadikim in the interwar period, served as symbols of high status.[81]

Among profane objects, the chairs of the tsadikim took a special place, as they were usually connected to the tsadik's prayer. For example, the bench and reading desk (*shtender*) of the Maggid of Mezrich were preserved in the old kloyz in Równe, where he presumably studied in his youth.[82] Many such objects perished during the Holocaust, together with the synagogues and private homes.[83] As with other cases described here, the special importance of the chair was known to pre-Beshtian kabbalists, who used their synagogue chairs and reading pulpits for their funeral biers.[84] The same custom was adopted for the funeral of R. Naḥman of Bratslav.[85]

The most famous tsadik's chair is that of R. Naḥman of Bratslav. It was produced for him in 1808 and smuggled from Soviet Russia to Jerusalem in 1936. Batsheva Goldman-Ida demonstrates how the chair, decorated with traditional Jewish themes, inspired R. Naḥman's dream, sermon, and tale. According to Goldman-Ida, R. Naḥman "designated it as a birthing chair, relating it to a mythic image of the divine Throne of Glory" and invested it with messianic significance. Contemporary Bratslav Hasidim, in contrast, use it as the Elijah chair for circumcision ceremonies, thus changing the meaning of this object.[86]

Besides the universal tendency to preserve objects belonging to great people, Hasidim had a special interest in memorabilia. The concept of worship through materiality allowed making every profane activity and every profane object part of the worship. David Assaf noticed that the tsadikim who behaved in the regal way considered their luxury items—good horses, splendid carriages and furniture, and so on—as equal to prayers and other normative religious actions; they were "seen as ritual objects in every sense."[87] Goldman-Ida stresses that "[the] tendency to elevate everyday acts and objects to a higher, spiritual level is characteristic of Hasidism."[88]

Besides objects made of *shmirah* coins, dealt with below, all other Hasidic objects did not differ from objects used by non-Hasidic Ashkenazi Jews or by certain groups among them (e.g., kabbalists). What makes the object Hasidic is its usage, as certified by oral tradition or by an inscription.

Checking the dedicatory inscription is the easiest way to identify a Hasidic object. Many objects belonging to the tsadikim were gifts from their Hasidim. Sometimes such gifts were inscribed so that the name of the donor was constantly before the eyes of the tsadik, reminding him to bless the donor. For example, a glass Passover cup preserved in the National Museum in Kraków bears the inscription "Given as a present to His Honor, admor . . . R. Moshe Horovitz shlita, the rabbi of Rozwadów, from me, the young Yeraḥmiel son of Leah Rivka for success."[89] The inscription mentions the name of the donor with his mother's name and contains a request to pray for his success, as was customary in the *kvitlekh* submitted to the tsadik. In this case, the object presented to the tsadik acted as a "long-lasting" *kvitl*.

Likewise, the objects given by the tsadik were sometimes inscribed, like a goblet presented by R. Aharon Yeḥiel of Koznits, now in the collection of the Jewish Historical Institute in Warsaw.[90] However, the majority of Hasidim's gifts to tsadikim and tsadikim's gifts to Hasidim were not inscribed, and their provenance is testified solely by oral tradition.[91]

The complicated relations between inscriptions and oral traditions are seen in the case of the fifteenth-century handwritten illuminated prayer book known as the *Siddur* of the Rabbi of Ruzhin in the collection of the Israel Museum. The manuscript bears only one owner's inscription, which states that R. Moshe Efrayim inherited it from his uncle R. Avraham Dov of Owrucz (a Hasidic leader who died in 1840 in Safed). The ownership of the manuscript by R. Israel of Ruzhin was stated only by "the Friedman family of Buhuşi," who sold the item to the Bezalel National Museum (precursor of the Israel Museum) in 1951.[92]

The oral traditions about ownership of objects by illustrious Hasidic personalities are mostly preserved in families or among Hasidim of a certain tsadik. The Holocaust put an end to many such traditions: the objects were looted, and the bearers of the traditions were murdered. For example, a splendid nineteenth-century Passover plate that arrived from Poland to the Ein Harod Museum in Israel without any information (IJA 435) was identified by Goldman-Ida as the Passover plate of R. Avraham Ya'akov of Sadagura (see figure 12.7), presented to him by his Russian Hasidim after his recovery from illness in 1859 (the identification is based on the verbal description of the plate by a Hasid).[93]

Oral traditions, by their nature, are consciously or unconsciously invented and modified. Thus, a nineteenth-century Hanukkah lamp given to the Bezalel National Museum in Jerusalem was described by the donor as belonging to the Besht. Since the publication of its photograph in 1939, this type of lamp has been known as a Besht Hanukkah lamp.[94] Even taking into account that some objects were replicated, we cannot claim that this type of the Hanukkah lamp was especially popular among Hasidim.[95]

Many tsadikim's personal objects are still preserved in the homes of their successors. Some objects are found in the Judaica market, sold mostly to rich Hasidic collectors, for whom their provenance has a special value. Only rarely do objects connected to famous Hasidic leaders find their way to museums.

The only items that have no parallels among non-Hasidim are *shmirah* coins and objects made of them. The *shmirah* is a regular silver coin that the tsadik blesses and gives to a Hasid. They were considered to have magical power and were used as amulets. They were worn on the neck, put under the pillow of an ill person, and placed under the head of the deceased during their funeral.[96] *Shmirah* coins were often melted and used for making kiddush cups, Hanukkah lamps, and other ceremonial objects.[97] Those objects were researched by Goldman-Ida;[98] the selection of kiddush cups made of *shmirah* coins from the collection of the Israel Museum was published by Ester Muchawsky-Schnapper.[99] Some such objects were inscribed "made of the *shmirot*," or "*shmirot* of the tsadikim," or "silver of

Figure 12.7. Passover plate of R. Avraham Ya'akov of Sadagura, 1859. Source: Mishkan Museum of Art, Ein Harod. Photo by N. Salmon, 1994, courtesy of the Center for Jewish Art, the Hebrew University of Jerusalem.

tsadikim," while others mentioned the name of the tsadik.[100] Probably the most impressive cup is kept in the Museum of Historical Treasures of Ukraine, in Kiev (figure 12.8). According to the engraved inscription, this single cup was made of coins received from eight tsadikim (IJA 260). The transformation of coins into ritual objects helped to perpetuate their sacredness. While a regular coin blessed by the tsadik had no external signs of its having been the *shmirah*, the items made of it and properly inscribed preserved their magical features for eternity. A common subject in Hasidic tales about *shmirah* coins is that they disappear after a miracle is performed or after the death of the tsadik who presented them.[101] Thus, production of durable objects from those coins had an effect of preserving the amulet and its magical qualities.

Another object characteristic only of Hasidim was a polished knife for the slaughtering of animals. The controversy about Hasidic use of polished knives and their refusal to eat from the slaughtering by mitnagdim evolved in the late eighteenth century and waned in the middle of the nineteenth. Shaul Stampfer points out that the end of the dispute came thanks to the appearance of knives made of steel, which could be sharp without losing their strength.[102] I do not know of any example of a Hasidic slaughtering knife kept in a museum. The only collector who published a catalogue of his collection of knives, Heshil Golnitzky, differentiated between knives made of iron and those made of steel, but he did not specify which belonged to Hasidic ritual slaughterers.[103]

Another object usually omitted when speaking about Hasidic material culture is the tefilin of Rabenu Tam. They differ from the commonly accepted European tefilin of Rashi by the order of placement of the Torah verses written on parchment. Pre-Beshtian Kabbalists wore two pairs of tefilin, that of Rashi and that of Rabenu Tam, and this custom become widespread among the Hasidim.[104] Therefore, it seems that all tefilin of Rabenu Tam found in Eastern Europe could be Hasidic objects, but to the best of my knowledge museums do not check the tefilin in their collections (the difference becomes apparent only through opening the leather box).

The final Hasidic object—portraits of tsadikim—is discussed in chapter 10 of this book.

Clothing

Dress is the feature that today immediately distinguishes Hasidim from other Orthodox Jews. The most recent research into Hasidic dress was undertaken by Ester Muchawsky-Schnapper for an exhibition in the Israel Museum in 2012. This is an ethnographic study concentrating on contemporary Hasidic customs and especially on the forms of dress and their variations among different courts. Muchawsky-Schnapper stressed the religious meaning of the dress: "Symbolic, often mystical, interpretations are given to explain the name, shape, or color of

Figure 12.8. Kiddush cup made from *shmirah* coins, 1885–1888. Source: Museum of Historical Treasures of Ukraine, Kiev. Photo by Z. Radovan, 1992, courtesy of the Center for Jewish Art, the Hebrew University of Jerusalem.

an item of clothing. Numbers assume great significance, with the number of parts or motifs in a garment corresponding to the numerical value of the Hebrew letters in words with relevant religious meaning. . . . In this way, clothing constitutes another example of the Hasidic attribution of spiritual value to material objects."[105]

Historical Clothing

Research on historical Hasidic clothing could be based on material, visual, and textual sources; all have serious faults. Not many pieces of clothing are preserved from the nineteenth century (even fewer from the eighteenth century), and only some of them could be directly associated with Hasidism.[106] As is the case with ritual objects, the nineteenth-century clothing said to belong to a tsadik can be surely defined as Hasidic.[107] Like buildings and ritual objects, the garments of tsadikim have special holiness, which is why they were often preserved by their successors and used during wedding ceremonies.[108] The Hasidic origin of other nineteenth-century garb is implicated by scholars and museum curators from their contemporary experience.

Visual sources also could be misleading. Before the arrival of photography in the mid-nineteenth century, the only visual depictions were made by artists in painting or drawing. The accuracy of such images must always be questioned.[109] As Muchawsky-Schnapper notes, the widely known depiction of a Hasid by Léon Hollaenderski in 1846 (see figure 12.9) presents him wearing a white fringed garment underneath his coat, which "appears to be some imaginary combination of *kitl* [white shirt-like ritual robe] and *tallit* [prayer shawl]."[110] To the best of my knowledge, this is one of a handful of nonphotographic depictions of Jews labeled "Hasid" by their authors.[111] There are many paintings by Isidor Kaufmann that intend to show Hasidim, but we cannot establish how faithfully the artists rendered the dress.[112] The same reservation must be applied to numerous postcards showing Jewish customs in Poland—they were generally staged and should be dealt with as artistic works and not as real-life photographs.[113] Depictions of tsadikim, notwithstanding the question of whether they were actual portraits or idealized images, may serve as a better source about Hasidic dress, since their authors wished to produce an ideal image of the Hasidic leader acceptable to his followers.

Photographs also should be dealt with cautiously since only some of them indicate that the photographed persons are Hasidim. Others could be almost certainly defined as images of Hasidim, and judgments about their dress could be made—for example, postcards showing young men standing in front of the tsadik's kloyz in Vizhnitz,[114] or Roman Vishniac's photographs of Jews around the court of R. Barukh Yehoshua Yeraḥmiel Rabinovich in Munkács.[115] Yet the majority of photographs showing, for instance, Jews in traditional attire on the streets of Polish cities could be considered images of Hasidim only through a false implication that all traditionally dressed Jews in Poland were Hasidim.

Textual sources on Hasidic dress describe reality in words.[116] The major problem with textual sources is that they call certain pieces of clothing by names not easily understood by contemporary readers, or with poetic language difficult to translate into the exact items of clothing.[117] A verbal description usually lacks

Figure 12.9. "A Hasid and his wife," plate in Léon Hollaenderski, *Les Israélites de Pologne* (Paris, 1846). Source: Léon Hollaenderski, *Les Israélites de Pologne* (Paris, 1846), tabl. after p. 240 [nlb]. Collection of the National Library of Israel in Jerusalem.

the details that could be discerned in visual sources. For example, a story by the Yiddish writer Ayzik Meir Dik (d. 1893) describes five kinds of Jewish hats worn in the first half of the nineteenth century. One is called *halbe-levona* (half a moon) or *khabadnitse* (literally, a Chabad-thing) and is described as a smaller version of a round sable fur hat named the *keylekhdike hitl*.[118] Is this the fur hat that appears in the above-mentioned engraving of a Hasid by Hollaenderski (figure 12.9)? Do the Hasidim standing in front of R. Israel of Koznits wear the *khabadnitse* (figure 12.4)? Or are their hats *keylekhdike hitl*, also described by Dik as a round sable hat, worn on minor holidays (in contrast to the *shtrayml* used on Shabbat and major holidays)? Although the name *khabadnitse* directly points to Hasidim, the explanation given by Dik is much larger: "Hasidim, *kloyzner* and *batlonim* used to wear it."[119] The last two words mean Torah scholars studying for a whole day and were usually used in non-Hasidic context. Should one understand that Dik, who lived in Vilna, described the hats used in Lithuania and that were irrelevant to other regions of eastern Europe?[120] The name of the hat refers to the Chabad Hasidim, which would hardly have been seen in Congress Poland, Galicia, Podolia, and Volhynia. Was this hat characteristic (if at all) for Chabad or for other "Lithuanian" Hasidim as well? The only clear statement in Dik's description is that fur hats were worn by Jews in summer and winter alike.[121]

Distinct Hasidic Dress

Three major questions that should be asked when dealing with Hasidic clothing are its difference from the dress of other Jews, the difference between the clothing of various branches of Hasidism, and the religious meanings connected to it.

At least from the time of the Maggid of Mezrich, tsadikim wore a dress distinct from that of other Jews. According to the memoirs of Salomon Maimon, who visited the Maggid, he was "clothed in white satin; even his shoes and snuffbox were white."[122] Anti-Hasidic bans and polemical works of the late eighteenth century mention the white clothing the Hasidim wore on Shabbat and prohibit it.[123] The white clothes of R. Zusya of Hanipoli (Annopol) were preserved at the Talne court,[124] and R. Israel of Koznits was described in 1814 as "dressed completely in white."[125] According to Kabbalah, white represents mercy; white clothing was worn on Shabbat by pre-Beshtian kabbalists and was subsequently adopted by the first generations of Hasidic masters. It is unclear when the white clothes of the tsadikim disappeared.[126] A tradition among the Bełz Hasidim states that the Seer of Lublin (d. 1815) was the last tsadik to wear a white coat (*bekeshe*), and the founder of the Bełz dynasty, R. Shalom Rokeaḥ, changed the color into black.[127] However, this tradition might represent Polish-Galician Hasidism, while in Lithuania-Belarus white clothes survived much longer. The famous portrait of R. Menaḥem Mendel Schneersohn of Lubavitch (d. 1866) shows him dressed in white;[128] a coat of a tsadik from Kojdanów in the Russian Museum of Ethnography is also white (the first tsadik of Kojdanów, R. Shlomo Ḥayim, died in 1862).[129]

Whereas the white dress was worn by first generations of tsadikim and disappeared some time in the nineteenth century, a preference for silk fabric has survived to our days. It was mentioned in a letter of the Russian governor of Vilna from 1800, who wrote that "the most learned among them" wear "*kitaichatoe*" (silk clothes) and explained that therefore Hasidim were called also "*kitaevtsy*" (the name of the fabric is derived from the Russian word *Kitai*, meaning China).[130] The preference for silk was intended to avoid a risk of *sha'atnez* (mixture of wool and linen), prohibited by the Torah. Silk garments were expensive, and wearing them on Shabbats and holy days evolved social prestige.

Hasidic—as well as non-Hasidic—prayer shawls (tallitot) were usually made of wool. Like other members of Jewish elite, tsadikim used to attach an *atara* to them—a collar made of silver threads. In some dynasties a tsadik's tallit was decorated also with an additional *atara*, which implied mystical significance.[131] From the late nineteenth century, the Hasidim of Radzyń began wearing fringes (*tsitsit*) with one cord in blue color (*tkhelet*), since their tsadik, R. Gershon Ḥanokh Leiner, found a way to produce dye as prescribed by the Talmud. This innovation was not accepted by other Hasidic groups, except for Bratslav.[132]

The most prominent part of today's Hasidic attire is a fur hat, called *shtrayml* in Yiddish. It will be discussed in the next section.

The only specifically Hasidic clothing item is the *gartl*—a belt, today made of silk cords. Talmud and *Shulḥan Arukh* prescribe wearing a belt during the prayer to create a "partition between his heart and his private parts." Ashkenazi Jews wearing trousers already have a belt fulfilling this demand, but Hasidim wore the second belt, *gartl*, during prayers.[133] The *gartl* is often used during the *mitzvah-tantz* in Hasidic weddings: a bride holds one end, while the other end is held by a male relative, who thus dances with the bride without physical contact.[134]

Women's attire occupies a less prominent place in the Hasidic experience and has less distinctive religious meanings.[135] Hasidim preserved the East European custom of shaving the heads of married woman. Today different Hasidic courts established clear rules concerning the acceptability of wigs (*sheytl*) or headscarves, but their historical development has not yet been researched.[136]

In general, it remains unclear when the distinctive Hasidic dress finally emerged and became "obligatory" for the majority of Hasidim. Probably this process occurred at different paces in different regions.

Case Study: Shtrayml

The object that today is exclusively associated with Hasidim is a special fur hat called the *shtrayml*. According to Dov Sadan, the word *shtrayml* is derived from *Streim*, which in Middle High German meant a strip.[137] Thus, the *shtrayml* or *shtraym-hitl* is a cap with a strip of fur around it. The majority of male Hasidim receive a *shtrayml* as a present for their marriage and wear it on Shabbat, holy days, and important events. Boys in some Hasidic groups in Jerusalem (especially Toledot Aharon) start to wear a *shtrayml* after bar mitzvah. The Hasidim of the Polish courts (Ger, Alexander, Modzits, etc.) wear another type of fur hat, *spodek* (see below). Chabad Hasidim do not use the *shtrayml*, but this is a custom of the last half century; before World War II, as seen in old photographs, they also wore *shtraymlekh*.[138] A *shtrayml* was a clear sign of masculitity, as indicated by a folk saying discussed by Sadan: *zi geyt in shtrayml* (literally "she wears *shtrayml*"), meaning she is a strong woman who rules her husband.[139]

A folktale describes the origins of the *shtrayml* in an anti-Jewish decree aimed at humiliating the Jews by forcing them to wear the tail of a fox (or other non-kosher animal) attached to their hats. The Jews succeeded in converting a humiliating sign into a sign of nobility and pride and began to wear fur hats.[140] We do not know of any document that prescribes that the Jews are obliged to wear tails on their hat. It seems that the *shtrayml* originated from a fur-rimmed hat worn by the Polish and Russian nobility in the seventeenth century. There, however, could be another source for this headgear, since portraits of German rabbis in the eighteenth century show them wearing fur hats as well.[141]

The *shtraymlekh* preserved in museum collections or known from old photographs are low velvet caps rimmed with fur in such a way that the tails of the animals are visible. The number of tail tips is usually symbolic: seven, thirteen, or eighteen.[142] In the second half of the twentieth century, however, the form of the *shtrayml* changed. Now the *shtrayml* is higher, its velvet cap is visible only from above, and the fur rim has a uniform outer surface so that the tips of the tails—of fox, marten, or sable—are not seen.[143] Since the cost of a *shtrayml* can reach five thousand dollars, there are special round boxes for storing and transporting *shtaymlekh*[144] and special plastic bags that protect them from rain while they are being worn.

Two additional types of fur hats are used today by Hasidim: *spodek* and *kolpik*. *Spodek*—a high hat made of dark fur—was considered more prestigious in the nineteenth century.[145] Dov Sadan repeats a proverb: *Az der rov geyt in shtrayml, geyt di rebetsen in spodek* ("When a rabbi wears a *shtrayml*, his wife wears a *spodek*"), which indicates the leading role of the *rebetsen*.[146] He also discusses in detail a saying recorded in his native Brody: *A shtraymele vil ikh nisht, a spodikl vil mikh nisht* ("I do not want a [bearer of] *shtrayml*, [the bearer of] *spodek* does not want me"). The meaning of the saying is that a bride with some *yikhes* or dowry does not want to marry a simple middle-class Jew (*balabayt*) who wears a *shtrayml*, but prominent Jews wearing *spodek* would prefer somebody with better *yikhes* or a larger dowry. Among those Jews Sadan counts rabbis, *dayanim*, Hasidic tsadikim, but also Torah scholars and ritual butchers (*shoḥatim*). His Hasidic great-grandfather used to wear *spodek* when he prepared his knife for ritual slaughter.[147] Sadan also recalled that on both Saturdays and weekdays the rabbi of Brody wore "a *spodek* that had a form of *kolpik*."[148]

The *kolpik* is a fur hat similar to the *spodek*, but made of light-brown sable with a darker horizontal stripe in the middle. Today tsadikim of certain courts wear *kolpik* on minor holidays and special occasions. Sons and grandsons of the tsadikim wear *kolpik* on Saturdays and holidays from the age of bar mitzvah until their wedding.[149]

One might ask, why and when did the *shtrayml* become the distinct Hasidic object? Scarce visual materials from the nineteenth century suggest that the *shtrayml* was not a Hasidic feature from the beginning. Even if rare nineteenth-century depictions of tsadikim show them wearing *shtrayml* or *spodek*,[150] many non-Hasidic rabbis wore *spodek* as well, as part of distinct "rabbinic attire." It seems that at least in the first half of the nineteenth century, the *shtrayml* was characteristic for all East European Jews who could afford it; it was a dress of the elite.[151] The most "anti-Hasidic" figure, the Vilna Gaon, was depicted in 1825 and 1858 as wearing a *spodek*.[152] A flag for Simḥat Torah, probably printed in Lwów in the 1860s, stresses the social hierarchy implicated by this headgear: Avraham sacrificing his son wears a *shtrayml*, while his servant holding the camels wears a wide-brimmed hat (IJA 2366). Avraham Ber Gottlober, born in 1811 in Volhynia, mentioned a *shtrayml*, together with a tallit, pearls, and *shterntikhl* (bejewelled headdress worn by married women) as presents exchanged by the parents—apparently affluent—of groom and bride.[153] Dov Sadan stated that artisans—the lowest social strata of Jewish society—did not wear *shtraymlekh*.[154]

Why and when did non-Hasidim abandon the *shtrayml*, then? We may suppose that the restrictions on traditional Jewish clothing imposed by the Russian government in the 1840s and 1850s caused a sharp divide.[155] It is logical to suggest that in the Russian Pale of Settlement and Congress Poland, non-Hasidim reconciled and developed new forms of Jewish dress, thus Hasidim faithful to the old style remained the only wearers of the *shtrayml* (as well as of the long coats that button on the left, in contrast to the Western convention about men's and women's clothes).[156] We may also suppose that in addition to general Hasidic conservatism and traditionalism in the late nineteenth century, the mystical symbolism with which objects of traditional Jewish dress were invested in Hasidism provided a good cause for their continuous usage.

However, those suggestions are not without problems. It seems that the Hasidim in the Pale of Settlement reacted to the restrictions on traditional Jewish dress differently than in Congress Poland. In Poland the Hasidim adopted Russian merchant attire: long coats, high fur hats, and—most importantly—the possibility not to shave the beard. Thus the Hasidim of the Polish courts adopted the *spodek*, similar to Russian merchants' fur hat, as their headgear. In the Hasidic regions of the Pale of Settlement, the development went another way.

Israel Aksenfeld, who lived in Odessa, stated in his 1861 novel *Dos shterntikhl* that the *shtrayml* was used no more: "Maybe a *shtrayml* and *spodek*, for the sake of memory should also be put in alcohol, to be exhibited one day."[157] A similar statement was made by Gottlober in his memoirs published in 1879–1880: "in our days, the *shtrayml* and the *shterntikhl* in our country fell by the decree of the emperor Nicholas I in 1844, fell and did not resurrect!"[158] Yeḥiel Ravrebe, in his description of a wedding between a daughter of the tsadik of Makarów (not far from Kiev) and a son of R. Ya'akov of Novominsk (Mińsk Mazowiecki) in Congress Poland around 1900, stressed that the groom's father wore "a high sable fur hat," implying that the "Volhynian tsadikim" were dressed differently.[159]

It also seems that in Volhynia, Podolia, and Kiev province of the late nineteenth century, *shtraymlekh* were reserved for tsadikim and their entourage and not worn by rank-and-file Hasidim.[160] For example, Shmuel Kofman, a merchant from Podolia, would visit tsadikim in the Russian Empire. When in the 1880s he came to Galicia and attempted to visit the tsadik of Husiatyn, just across the Russo-Austrian border, he discovered with great surprise that it was impossible to come to him without a *shtrayml*, which Kofman did not have.[161]

There is another fault in our explanaition, since the non-Hasidim outside of the Russian Empire also abandoned *shtrayml*. Dov Sadan, for example, mentioned that "old mitnagdim" in Brody in Galicia of the early twentieth century did not wear *shtraymlekh*, in contrast to Hasidic *balabatim* in the town.[162] Was it a reaction to the exclusive adoption of the *shtrayml* by Hasidim, or a sign of relative openness to modern non-Jewish dress habits? The latter suggestion seems false since Sadan stated that the children and grandchildren of those "old mitnagdim" already wore *shtraymlekh* and prayed according to *nusaḥ sefarad* in Hasidic prayer houses. In general, non-Hasidic Orthodox Jews in Galicia and Hungary were not less determined to preserve traditional Jewish dress than the Hasidim.[163] Nonetheless, the *shtrayml*, *spodek*, and *kolpik* became the hallmarks of Hasidism.

This short case study of Hasidic headgear demonstrates that the object unambiguously associated today with Hasidism and Hasidim was originally part of the dress of Jewish elite. Its adoption by Hasidic leaders and Hasidic masses was diachronic and differed in different regions. Thus, consideration of material culture makes it impossible to speak about Hasidism as a whole without paying attention to chronology and geography. More than anything else, material objects are anchored in time and space.

Conclusion

As we have seen, Hasidic material culture did not differ significantly from that of traditional East European Jews. Taking into account the Hasidic dominance—whatever it means numerically—among traditional Jews in several regions (Podolia, Volhynia, Galicia, Congress Poland, Bessarabia, Romanian Moldavia, and the Hungarian Unterland later on), it could be stated, with a significant degree of exaggeration of course, that Hasidic material culture is the traditional Jewish material culture of those East European regions. Hasidim instituted only minor novelties: persistence on silk garments and *gartl* in the field of clothing, objects made from the *shmirah* coins in the field of ritual objects, separate prayer rooms of tsadikim attached to their kloyzn, and tribunes in those kloyzn in the field of architecture.

In the majority of cases, special features do not make an item a Hasidic object, but rather its usage by Hasidim and the mystical symbolism invested in it. In the beginning, Hasidim adopted many customs characteristic of the kabbalistic elite of the seventeenth and eighteenth centuries, and the objects related to them. Besides the mystical meaning of those customs and objects, social prestige was important. In the course of the nineteenth century some distinct Hasidic objects, such as white coats and polished knives, were abandoned, while other items, like *shtraymlekh*, became closely associated with Hasidism.

The objects and buildings connected to the tsadikim played a special role in Hasidism. A tsadik's contact with ritual and ordinary objects "elevated" them into the status of holy ones; Hasidim venerated them as a means of connection to the living or deceased tsadik and secured their sacral meaning by oral tradition and sometimes by inscriptions.

It is important to remember that the history of Hasidism and its theology have been researched for a century, and Hasidic mysticism and social organization have been dealt with for several decades. Research into Hasidic material culture, in contrast, is only beginning, and many aspects of this culture await scholarly attention.

SUGGESTED READING

As a useful introduction to the topic, one might consult David Assaf, *The Regal Way: The Life and Times of Rabbi Israel of Ruzhin* (Stanford, CA: Stanford University Press, 2002), in which the author discusses aspects of material culture. Also, Ilia Lurie, *Edah u-medinah: Ḥasidut ḥabad ba-imperiyah ha-rusit, 1828–1883* (Jerusalem: Magnes Press, 2006) contains details on the physical appearance of the Lubavitch court. Many legends about Hasidic leaders, their synagogues, and their graves were recorded by S. An-sky on his expedition to Volhynia and Podolia and published in Yiddish in Avrom Rekhtman, *Di yidishe etnografie un folklor* (Buenos Aires: YIVO, 1958). The memoir of Yitzḥok Even, *Funem rebens hoyf: Zikhroynes un mayses gezehen, gehert un nokhdertselt* (New York: Isaac Even, 1922) contains descriptions of material objects, too.

The largest, although by no means representative collection of images of Hasidic objects and buildings is the Bezalel Narkiss Index of Jewish Art (IJA) at the Center for Jewish Art, Hebrew University of Jerusalem, accessible online (http://cja.huji.ac.il/browser.php; choose "Browse by community" and select "Hasidic"). Many more objects can be found in the catalogues of Jewish museums and private collections, as well as in the catalogues of Judaica auctions. An example of such a catalogue is Elżbieta Długosz, *Czas chasydów/Time of the Hasidim* (Kraków: Muzeum Historyczne Miasta Krakowa and Katedra Judaistyki Uniwersytetu Jagellońskiego, 2005).

Hasidic architecture has not yet been dealt with as a whole. A pathbreaking article about Hasidic influence on a town is Eleonora Bergman, "Góra Kalwaria: The Impact of a Hasidic Cult on the Urban Landscape of a Small Polish Town," *Polin* 5 (1990), 3–23. Information on Hasidic synagogues can be also gathered from the following: Rita Bogdanova, *Latvia: Synagogues and Rabbis, 1918–1940* (Riga: Shamir, 2004); Eleonora Bergman, *"Nie masz bóżnicy powszechnej": Synagogi i domy modlitwy w Warszawie od końca XVIII do początku XXI wieku* (Warszawa: DiG, 2007); A. Cohen-Mushlin et al., eds., *Synagogues in Lithuania: A Catalogue* (Vilnius: Vilnius Academy of Arts Press, 2010–2012); Sergey Kravtsov and Vladimir Levin, *Synagogues in Ukraine: Volhynia* (Jerusalem: the Zalman Shazar Center and the Center for Jewish Art, 2017).

The architecture of the courts of the Ruzhin dynasty is discussed in Sergey Kravtsov, "Jewish Identities in Synagogue Architecture of Galicia and Bukovina," *Ars Judaica* 6 (2010), 81–100; the replication of the house of Lubavitcher Rebbe is dealt with in Gabrielle A. Berlinger, "770 Eastern Parkway: The Rebbe's Home as Icon," in *Jews at Home: The Domestication of Identity*, ed. S. J. Bronner, (Oxford: The Littman Library of Jewish Civilization, 2010), 163–187.

One of the first works on the topic of Hasidic clothing is Tamar Somogyi, *Die Schejnen und die Prosten: Untersuchungen zum Schönheitsideal der Ostjuden in Bezug auf Körper und Kleidung unter besonderer Berücksichtigung des Chassidismus* (Berlin: Dietrich Reimer Verlag, 1982).

The book by Batsheva Goldman-Ida *Hasidic Art and the Kabbalah* (Leiden and Boston: Brill, 2017) discusses prayer books with kabbalistic features; special cups for kiddush in the form of an apple, which were popular among Hasidic leaders; splendid plates for Passover Seder, on which the three matzot are placed under the "signs of the seder" as prescribed by the Lurianic kabbalah; hanging Shabbat lamps; collars for prayer shawls; pipes of the tsadikim; *shmirah* coins; and the chair of R. Naḥman of Bratslav.

Another important book on the subject is the richly illustrated catalogue of an exhibition in the Israel Museum by Ester Muchawsky-Schnapper, *A World Apart Next Door: Glimpses into the Life of Hasidic Jews* (Jerusalem: The Israel Museum, 2012), which discusses various aspects of historical and contemporary Hasidic dress and objects.

A popular description of modern Hasidic dress and its variations according to courts is a newspaper article by Lipa Schmeltzer, "She-lo shinu et malbusham," *Ba-kehilah - musaf pesaḥ*, April 24, 2006, 3–47.

Hasidic struggle against "clothing decrees" of the Russian tsars is dealt with in Glenn Dynner, "The Garment of Torah: Clothing Decrees and the Warsaw Career of the First Gerer Rebbe," in *Warsaw. The Jewish Metropolis: Essays in Honor of the 75th Birthday of Professor Antony Polonsky*, ed. G. Dynner and F. Guesnet (Leiden: Brill, 2015), 91–127. The struggle over knives for *sheḥitah* is discussed by Shaul Stampfer in *Families, Rabbis and Education: Traditional Jewish Society in Nineteenth-Century Eastern Europe* (Oxford: The Littman Library of Jewish Civilization, 2010), 342–355.

NOTES

1. Batsheva Goldman-Ida, "The Birthing Chair: The Chair of Rabbi Nahman of Bratzlav, A Phenomenological Analysis," *Ars Judaica* 6 (2010), 115.

2. Arthur Green, "The Zaddiq as Axis Mundi in Later Judaism," *Journal of the American Academy of Religion* 45 (1977), 328–347.

3. On *pidyon*, see David Assaf, *The Regal Way: The Life and Times of Rabbi Israel of Ruzhin* (Stanford, CA: Stanford University Press, 2002), 288–296; Haviva Pedaya, "Le-hitpatḥuto shel ha-degem ha-ḥevrati-dati-kalkali ba-ḥasidut: Ha-pidyon, ha-ḥavurah veha-aliyah la-regel," in *Dat ve-kalkalah: Yaḥasei gomlin*, ed. M. Ben-Sasson (Jerusalem: The Zalman Shazar Center, 1995). On an important collection of *kvitlekh* preserved from

the mid-nineteenth century, see Glenn Dynner, "Brief Kvetches: Notes to a 19th-Century Miracle Worker," *Jewish Review of Books* 18 (Summer 2014), 33–35. For kerchiefs given by tsadikim in Volhynia, see Lev Aizenberg, "Mestechko Kamenka i ego obitateli," *Evreiskaia letopis'* 4 (1926), 80, 82–83. On *shirayim*, see Allan Nadler, "Holy Kugel: The Sanctification of Ashkenazic Ethnic Foods in Hasidism," in *Food and Judaism*, ed. L. J. Greenspoon, R. A. Simkins, and G. Shapiro (Omaha, NE: Creighton University Press, 2005), 193–214.

4. On the role of the Maggid in the establishment of Hasidic court, see Pedaya, "Le-hitpatḥuto shel ha-degem ha-ḥevrati-dati-kalkali ba-ḥasidut," 321–324. On the pilgrimage to Hasidic court as a rite of passage, see Ilia Lurie, *Edah u-medinah: Ḥasidut ḥabad ba-imperiyah ha-rusit, 1828–1883* (Jerusalem: Magnes Press, 2006), 15.

5. Assaf, *The Regal Way*, 269–278.

6. On the geography of Hasidic courts, see Marcin Wodziński and Uriel Gellman, "Toward a New Geography of Hasidism," *Jewish History* 27 (2013), 171–199.

7. Photo: "Rebbe's Kloyz in Sadhora," Bezalel Narkiss Index of Jewish Art (IJA), accessed January 9, 2019, http://cja.huji.ac.il/browser.php?mode=set&id=10438. Here and further when referring to the IJA (http://cja.huji.ac.il/browser.php), I will give only the Object ID, e.g., IJA 10438. All objects were accessed January 9, 2018. See also Sergey Kravtsov, "Jewish Identities in Synagogue Architecture of Galicia and Bukovina," *Ars Judaica* 6 (2010), 94.

8. "Kloyz of R. David Moshe Friedmann in Chortkiv," IJA 15296. See also Kravtsov, "Jewish Identities," 96.

9. "Rebbe's Kloyz in Buhuşi," IJA 3354. See also Aristide Streja and Lucian Schwarz, *Synagogues of Romania* (Bucharest: Hasefer, 1997), 80.

10. For a photograph clearly showing the tower of the palace in Sadagura, see Gérard Silvain and Henri Minczeles, *Yiddishland* (Paris: Hazan, 1999), 409. For a verbal description, see S. Ansky, *The Enemy at His Pleasure: A Journey through the Jewish Pale of Settlement during World War I*, trans. J. Neugroschel (New York: Metropolitan Books, 2002), 279.

11. Yitzḥok Even, *Funem rebens hoyf: Zikhroynes un mayses gezehen, gehert un nokhdertselt* (New York: Isaac Even, 1922), 83–85. See also Assaf, *The Regal Way*, 271.

12. "House of Rabbi Moshe Heshel in Zin'kiv," "Rabbi Pinhas Heshel's Kloyz in Zin'kiv," "Rabbi Moshe Heshel's Kloyz in Zin'kiv," IJA 7523; 7524; 7528. See *Pinkas Zinkov*, ed. Sh. Aizenshtadt (Tel Aviv: Vaad Zinkov, 1966), map on 26; Beniamin Lukin and Boris Khaimovich, *100 evreiskikh mestechek Ukrainy: Istoricheskii putevoditel'*, vol. 1 (Jerusalem and St. Petersburg: Ezro, 1997), 105–106.

13. See discussion in Wodziński and Gellman, "Toward a New Geography of Hasidism," 197.

14. See Assaf, *The Regal Way*, 275–276; Marcin Wodziński, *Historical Atlas of Hasidism* (Princeton, NJ: Princeton University Press, 2018), maps 4.1.1, 4.1.3.

15. On the resemblance between tsadikim and Polish noble magnates, see Adam Teller, "Hasidism and the Challenge of Geography: The Polish Background to the Spread of the Hasidic Movement," *AJS Review* 30 (2006), 18–24.

16. For private prayer houses in Vilna, see Vladimir Levin, "Synagogues, Batei Midrash and Kloyzn in Vilnius," in *Synagogues in Lithuania: A Catalogue*, ed. A. Cohen-Mushlin et al. (Vilnius: Vilnius Academy of Arts Press, 2010–2012), 2:281. For private prayer houses in Volhynia, see Vladimir Levin, "The Legal History of Synagogues of Volhynia," in *Synagogues in Ukraine: Volhynia*, Sergey Kravtsov and Vladimir Levin (Jerusalem: The Zalman Shazar Center and the Center for Jewish Art, 2017), 21–22.

17. Rachel Manekin, "Praying at Home: The Minyan Laws of the Habsburg Empire," *Polin* 24 (2012), 66.

18. On the differences between courts, see Aaron Wertheim, *Law and Custom in Hasidism* (Hoboken: Ktav, 1992), 148–149.

19. Shimon Segal, "Ele ezkerah (batei-kneset ve-kloyzn be-Drohobych)," in *Sefer zikaron le-Drohobych, Boryslav veha-sevivah*, ed. N. M. Gelber (Tel Aviv: Irgun yotsei drohobych,

boryslav veha-sevivah, 1959), 93; Yosef Kitai, "Ha-rabi mi-Drohobych - rabi Ḥaim Meir-Yeḥiel Shapira," in ibid., 153.

20. Gad Sagiv, *Ha-shoshelet: Bet Chernobyl u-mekomo be-toledot ha-ḥasidut* (Jerusalem: The Zalman Shazar Center, 2014), 393–394.

21. For the most recent scholarship, see Marcin Wodziński, "War and Religion; or, How the First World War Changed Hasidism," *Jewish Quarterly Review* 106 (2016), 290–299.

22. Similarly, when after World War I the tsadik of Boian, R. Menaḥem Naḥum, settled in Cernăuți [Chernivtsi/Czernowitz], he bought a large dwelling house and built a kloyz nearby. See "House of the Boyaner Rebbe in Chernivtsi," "Kloyz of the Boyaner Rebbe in Chernivtsi," IJA 10645; 22232.

23. Ḥaim Meir Ḥeilman, *Bet rabbi* (Berdichev: Sheptel, 1902), 1:91–92.

24. The portraits of R. Menaḥem Mendel Hager of Vizhnitz [Vijnița/Vyzhnytsa] and R. Menaḥem Mendel Schneersohn of Lubavitch [Lubawicze], made in the mid-nineteenth century, also present them in their study rooms.

25. Tadeusz Rolke and Simon Schama, *Tu byliśmy: Ostatnie ślady zaginionej kultury* (Berlin-Warszawa: edition.fotoTAPETA, 2008), 129, 177; Maria and Kazimierz Piechotka, *Landscape with Menorah: Jews in the Towns and Cities of the Former Rzeczpospolita of Poland and Lithuania* (Warsaw: Salix alba Press, 2015), 165; Eleonora Bergman, "Góra Kalwaria: The Impact of a Hasidic Cult on the Urban Landscape of a Small Polish Town," *Polin* 5 (1990), 14–15; Svetlana Amosova, "'Evreiskaia zhizn' bez evreev: Vospominaniia o dovoennoi zhizni v g. Burshtyn Ivano-Frankovskoi oblasti," in *Svoio sredi chuzhogo, chuzhoe sredi svoego*, ed. E. E. Zhigarina and Iu. N. Naumova (Moscow: Forum, 2016), 59–61. For photographs, see "Rebbe's House in Burshtyn," "Rebbe's House in Kosiv," IJA 11718; 7891.

26. For Bobowa, see Elżbieta Długosz, "Hasidic Customs and Their Traces in Museum Collections," in *Czas chasydów/Time of the Hasidim*, ed. E. Długosz (Kraków: Muzeum Historyczne Miasta Krakowa and Katedra Judaistyki Uniwersytetu Jagellońskiego, 2005), 97; for Khotin, see Yitzḥak Meir Twersky, *Mi yar'enu tov: . . . toledot . . . rabi Mordekhai Yisrael Tversky . . . ha-admor mi-Ozarinets-Khotin* (New York: Genealogy Research Center of the Twersky Chernobyl Dynasty, 2001), 9; for Ottynia, see Silvain and Minczeles, *Yiddishland*, 409; for Kopychinets [Kopyczyńce], see Yitzḥak Alfasi, *Ha-ḥasidut mi-dor le-dor* (Jerusalem: Makhon Daat Yosef, 1995), 220.

27. Assaf, *The Regal Way*, 274. For descriptions of the tsadikim houses in Ştefăneşti and Buhuşi, see ibid., 276–277.

28. Nehemia Polen, "Rebbetzins, Wonder-Children, and the Dynastic Principle in Hasidism," in *The Shtetl: New Evaluations*, ed. Steven T. Katz (New York: New York University Press, 2007), 71.

29. Lurie, *Edah u-medinah*, 11–12.

30. Bergman, "Góra Kalwaria," 14; Aharon Surasky, *Rosh golat ariel: Toledot ḥayav u-fo'alo shel . . . rabi Avraham Mordekhai Alter mi-Gur* (Jerusalem: Makhon Amudei Ha-or, 1990), 2:179, 181.

31. Assaf, *The Regal Way*, 272; Kravtsov and Levin, *Synagogues in Ukraine: Volhynia*, 687.

32. See Louis Jacobs, *Hasidic Prayer* (London: The Littman Library of Jewish Civilization, 1993), 126–139.

33. For its photographs, see Zoya Yargina, *Wooden Synagogues* (Moscow: Image, 1993), plates 333–335; Stefan Taranushenko, *Synahohy Ukrainy* (Khar'kiv: Kharkivs'kyi pryvatnyi muzei mis'koi sadyby, 2011), 42–43; Maria and Kazimierz Piechotka, *Heaven's Gate: Wooden Synagogues in the Territories of the Former Polish-Lithuanian Commonwealth* (Warsaw: Krupski i S-ka, 2004), ill. 14.

34. Streja and Schwarz, *Synagogues of Romania*, 105. See also "Old Wooden Synagogue (Besht Synagogue) in Piatra Neamț," IJA 3368.

35. Quoted in Assaf, *The Regal Way*, 273.

36. Ibid.

37. Lurie, *Edah u-medinah*, 10.

38. Ilia Lurie, *Milḥamot Lubavich: Ḥasidut ḥabad be-Rusyah ha-tsarit* (Jerusalem: The Zalman Shazar Center, 2018), 99–100.

39. Moshe Tzvi Guterman, *Va-yakhel Shlomo* (Piotrków: Palman, 1909), 19; Avraham Ḥayim Simḥah Bunem Mikhelson, *Dover shalom* (Przemyśl: Simche Freund, 1930), 9.

40. In many contemporary synagogues in Hasidic courts, the *bimah* is a movable object that can be easily removed from the center of the prayer hall to make room for a huge table during the *tish* ceremony or an empty space for the tsadik's dancing on Simhat Torah. It is unknown if the *bimot* in the tsadikim kloyzn in Eastern Europe were movable as well.

41. For useful observations, see Marcin Wodziński, "Women and Hasidism: A 'Non-Sectarian' Perspective," *Jewish History* 27 (2013), 399–434.

42. Assaf, *The Regal Way*, 273–274. For the mention of separate tsadik's prayer rooms in Drohobych, Khotin, and Izbica, see Segal, "Ele ezkerah," 93; Twersky, *Mi yar'enu tov*, 17; Shlomo Zalman Shargai, *Be-netivei ḥasidut Izbitsa-Radzin* (Jerusalem: Sh. Z. Shargai, 1993), 80, 119.

43. Shloyme Keyzer, "Dem rebens hoyf," in *Pinkas ha-kehilah Trisk: Sefer zikaron*, ed. N. Livneh (Tel Aviv: Irgun yotsei trisk be-israel, 1975), 153; Shmuel Kofman, *Zikhronot (toldot yemei ḥayai)* (Tel Aviv: Hotsa'at ha-mishpakhah, 1955), 136.

44. Assaf, *The Regal Way*, 272.

45. Wertheim, *Law and Custom in Hasidism*, 102–105, 216.

46. Wodziński, "Women and Hasidism," 412.

47. Shalom Duber Levin, *Toldot ḥabad be-Rusiya ha-tsarit ba-shanim 1770–1920* (Brooklyn, NY: Kehat, 2010), 224.

48. I am grateful to Dr. Sergey Kravtsov for this information.

49. I owe this observation to Professor Yehoshua Kaniel z"l.

50. Alfasi, *Ha-ḥasidut mi-dor le-dor*, 569.

51. For the discussion of this case, see Gabrielle A. Berlinger, "770 Eastern Parkway: The Rebbe's Home as Icon," in *Jews at Home: The Domestication of Identity*, ed. S. J. Bronner (Oxford: The Littman Library of Jewish Civilization, 2010), 163–187.

52. For a useful introduction about Hasidic veneration of tsadikim's graves, see Assaf, *The Regal Way*, 321–324. For veneration of tsadikim's graves by local non-Jews, see Maria Kaspina and Svetlana Amosova, "Paradoks mezhetnicheskikh kontaktov: Praktika obrashcheniia neevreev v sinagogu (po polevym materialam)," *Antropologicheskii Forum Online* 11 (2009), 14–15; Svetlana Amosova, "There Are No Jews Here: From a Multiethnic to a Monoethnic Town of Burshtyn," *Cultural Analysis* 10 (2011), 121–122.

53. It was customary in Hasidic regions of Eastern Europe that a tsadik was invited to consecrate a new cemetery or a new burial ground in an existing cemetery. This action symbolized the connection between a certain community and a certain tsadik and added to the holiness of the cemetery.

54. On graves in the USSR, see Michael Greenberg, *Graves of Tzaddikim in Russia* (Jerusalem: Shamir, 1989); in Poland, see Marcin Wodziński, *Groby cadyków w Polsce: O chasydzkiej literaturze nagrobnej i jej kontekstach* (Wrocław: Towarzystwo Przyjaciół Polonistyki Wrocławskiej, 1998).

55. For the documentation of the *ohel* in Olewsk, see Kravtsov and Levin, *Synagogues in Ukraine: Volhynia*, 480–482, and "Ohel of Rabbis Yehoshua and Levi Yitshak Gottlieb in the Jewish Cemetery in Olevsk," IJA 23820.

56. For the painted tombstones in the *ohel* in Roman (Romania), see "Ohel in the Jewish Cemetery in Roman," IJA 26929; for the *ohel* in Radomsko (Poland), see "Ohel of the Rebbes in the Jewish Cemetery in Radomsko," IJA 15337.

57. Avrom Rekhtman, *Di yidishe etnografie un folklor* (Buenos Aires: YIVO, 1958), 115–118; for a picture, see p. 179.

58. A rare case of a tsadik's grave being transferred from Eastern Europe to Israel is the grave of R. Avraham Matityahu Friedman of Ştefăneşti, which was moved to Naḥalat Yitsḥak Cemetery in Givatayim in 1969.

59. For the recent discussion, see Marcin Wodziński, "Space and Spirit: On Boundaries, Hierarchies and Leadership in Hasidism," *Journal of Historical Geography* 53 (2016), 64–66. See also Wodziński, "The Hasidic 'Cell': The Organization of Hasidic Groups at the Level of the Community," *Scripta Judaica Cracoviensia* 10 (2012), 111–122; Wodziński, *Hasidism and Politics: The Kingdom of Poland, 1815–1864* (Oxford: The Littman Library of Jewish Civilization, 2013), 42–76; Wodziński, *Źródła do dziejów chasydyzmu w Królestwie Polskim, 1815–1867, w zasobach polskich archiwów państwowych* (Kraków and Budapest: Austeria, Institute for the History of Polish Jews and Poland-Israel Relations, Tel Aviv University, 2011); Glenn Dynner, *Men of Silk: The Hasidic Conquest of Polish Jewish Society* (Oxford: Oxford University Press, 2006), 59–70.

60. For such usage, see, for example, *Igerot kodesh me'et k"k admo"r ha-zaken, k"k amo"r ha-emtsa'i, k"k admo"r ha-Tsemaḥ Tsedek* (Brooklyn, NY: Kehat, 1987), 76.

61. Shaul Stampfer, "How and Why Did Hasidism Spread?," *Jewish History* 27 (2013), 218.

62. Ibid., 208.

63. Rachel Manekin, "Hasidism and the Habsburg Empire, 1788–1867," *Jewish History* 27 (2013), 288–290.

64. On *shulhoyf*, see Vladimir Levin, "Synagogues in Lithuania: A Historical Overview," in *Synagogues in Lithuania: A Catalogue*, 1:29.

65. Levin, "Synagogues, Batei Midrash and Kloyzn in Vilnius," 303.

66. For a discussion of women's sections in Hasidic *shtiblekh*, see Wodziński, "Women and Hasidism," 408–412. For example, among 107 prayer houses counted in Warsaw in 1815, 61 prayer houses occupied one room; that may point to the absence of women's sections. Among 111 prayer houses listed there in 1826, 36 had one room only. See Eleonora Bergman, *"Nie masz bóżnicy powszechnej": Synagogi i domy modlitwy w Warszawie od końca XVIII do początku XXI wieku* (Warszawa: DiG, 2007), 95–102, 107–114. Among 135 synagogues in mitnagedic Vilna (Vilnius) in the late nineteenth century to the first half of the twentieth century, at least 15 had no women's section. See Levin, "Synagogues, Batei Midrash and Kloyzn in Vilnius," 296, 303, 304, 307, 309–312, 317, 321, 324, 336.

67. Dynner, *Men of Silk*, 58.

68. Kravtsov and Levin, *Synagogues in Ukraine: Volhynia*, 347, 505.

69. On this synagogue, see Boris Khaimovich, *"The Work of Our Hands to Glorify": Murals of Bet Tfilah Benyamin Synagogue in Chernovits: Visual Language of Jewish Artist* (Kyiv: Dukh i litera, 2008).

70. See Boris Khaimovich, *The Murals in the Novoselitsia Synagogue* (Kyiv: Dukh i litera, 2016).

71. Khaimovich, *The Murals in the Novoselitsia Synagogue*, 41–48.

72. Sergey Kravtsov, "Synagogue Architecture of Volhynia," in Kravtsov and Levin, *Synagogues in Ukraine: Volhynia*, 113–114.

73. Avraham Ber Gottlober, *Zikhronot u-masa'ot* (Jerusalem: Mosad Bialik, 1976), 1:172; Rekhtman, *Di yidishe etnografie*, 344–347; David Assaf, *Ne'ehaz ba-svakh: Pirkei mashber u-mevukhah be-toledot ha-ḥasidut* (Jerusalem: The Zalman Shazar Center, 2006), 104 and bibliography there.

74. Reuven Zak, *Bet Yisra'el* (Piotrków: Mordechai Cederbaum, 1913), 16, 145. According to another version, the Chortkover *Rebbe* inherited the tefilin of R. Israel written by R. Moshe of Przeworsk—see Rekhtman, *Di yidishe etnografie*, 334.

75. "Sadagora," *Ha-levanon*, July 20, 1881, 400.

76. Twersky, *Mi yar'enu tov*, 20–21.

77. Kravtsov and Levin, *Synagogues in Ukraine: Volhynia*, 589.

78. Avraham Yehoshua Heshel, *Ḥasidei Moshe Kopychinits: Zmirot le-shabat kodesh u-le-yom-tov, minhagim* (Brooklyn, NY: Mifal torah ve-hesed "Hasdei moshe kopyczynyts", 2003), second pagination, 21; Batsheva Goldman-Ida, *Hasidic Art and the Kabbalah* (Leiden and Boston: Brill 2017), 301 and fig. 125.

79. Yoḥanan Twersky, *He-ḥatser ha-penimit: Korot mishpaḥah* (Tel Aviv: N. Twersky, 1954), 35.

80. Długosz, "Hasidic Customs," 95; *Muzeum Żydowskiego Instytutu Historycznego: Zbiory artystyczne* (Warszawa: Auriga, 2000), ill. 69.

81. Długosz, "Hasidic Customs," 95. A collection of walking sticks of tsadikim was kept in the court of Talne—see Twersky, *He-ḥatser ha-penimit*, 28.

82. Kravtsov and Levin, *Synagogues in Ukraine: Volhynia*, 589.

83. After the Holocaust, new objects connected to the surviving tsadikim appeared. For example, the chair and *shtender* of R. Aharon Rokeaḥ of Bełz are preserved in the Bełz synagogue in Jerusalem. See Ester Muchawsky-Schnapper, *A World Apart Next Door: Glimpses into the Life of Hasidic Jews* (Jerusalem: The Israel Museum, 2012), 17.

84. See, e.g., Menaḥem Mendel Biber, *Mazkeret le-gedolei Ostroha* (Berdichev: Sheftel, 1907), 339–340.

85. Natan Sternharz, *Yemei moharnat* (Jerusalem: Makhon Torat Hanetzah Breslov, 1997), 130, siman 66; Goldman-Ida, "The Birthing Chair," 118.

86. Goldman-Ida, "The Birthing Chair"; Goldman-Ida, *Hasidic Art and the Kabbalah*, 345–376.

87. Assaf, *The Regal Way*, 238.

88. Goldman-Ida, *Hasidic Art and the Kabbalah*, 304.

89. IJA 812; Stanisława Odrzywolska and Monika Paś, *Judaica in the Collection of the National Museum in Krakow* (Kraków: The National Museum in Kraków, 2018), 261–262. A selection of objects presented to the tsadikim by their Hasidim and kept in the Israel Museum was recently published by Muchawsky-Schnapper, *A World Apart Next Door*, 45.

90. Długosz, "Hasidic Customs," 92; *Muzeum Żydowskiego Instytutu Historycznego*, ill. 37.

91. Many ritual objects in Ukrainian synagogues also did not bear the name of the donors. This may point to the importance of orally transmitted knowledge as compared with the knowledge transmitted in writing, as well as to the mystical features of donations. See Vladimir Levin, "The Social Function of Synagogue Ceremonial Objects in Volhynia," in Kravtsov and Levin, *Synagogues in Ukraine: Volhynia*, 143–146.

92. Iris Fishof, "The Origin of the Siddur of the Rabbi of Ruzhin," *Jewish Art* 12–13 (1987), 81–82; Bezalel Narkiss, *Hebrew Illuminated Manuscripts* (Jerusalem: Keter, 1969), 128, plate 44.

93. Goldman-Ida, *Hasidic Art and the Kabbalah*, 137–146; Even, *Funem rebens hoyf*, 213.

94. Muchawsky-Schnapper, *A World Apart Next Door*, 34.

95. Among five Hanukkah lamps of tsadikim published in Alfasi, *Ha-ḥasidut mi-dor le-dor*, 52, 112, 155, 215, 542, none belongs to the Besht type.

96. See, e.g., Even, *Funem rebens hoyf*, 195–201; Aizenberg, "Mestechko Kamenka," 82; Heshil Golnitzky, "Yikrat kos ha-berakha u-matbe'a ha-segulah," in *Sefer Zeevi*, ed. Y. Siegelman (Haifa: Beitenu Literature and Folklore Club, 1966), 119–126; Maria Kaspina, "Pochitanie Shtefaneshtskogo rebbe: Proshloe i nastoiashchee," in *"Staroe" i "novoe" v slavianskoi i evreiskoi kul'turnoi traditsii*, ed. O. Belova (Moscow: Sefer, 2012), 126–128.

97. For a tray with inlaid Austrian and Russian coins, inscribed "it is made from holy shmirot," see Hillel Kazovsky and Boris Khaimovich, eds., *Museum of Jewish History in Russia* (Moscow: Museum of Jewish History in Russia, 2015), 76. For a Hanukkah lamp with Austrian and Russian coins at the bottom of each, see "Hanukkah Lamp of Rabbi Levi Yitzhak Gottlieb of Ludmir-Olevsk with Shmirot Coins," IJA 26128.

98. Goldman-Ida, *Hasidic Art and the Kabbalah*, 306–344.

99. Muchawsky-Schnapper, *A World Apart Next Door*, 44.

100. A cup made of the coins from the Sadagura Rebbe belongs to the Gross Family Collection in Tel Aviv. For a cup made of the coins from the Boian Rebbe, see "Kos Shmirot," IJA 26919.

101. See, e.g., Even, *Funem rebens hoyf*, 197; Kaspina, "Pochitanie Shtefaneshtskogo rebbe," 128.

102. Shaul Stampfer, *Families, Rabbis and Education: Traditional Jewish Society in Nineteenth-Century Eastern Europe* (Oxford: The Littman Library of Jewish Civilization, 2010), 342–355.

103. Heshil Golnitzky, *Be-maḥzor ha-yamim: Mo'ed va-ḥol ba-omanut u-va-folklor ha-yehudi* (Haifa: Hug yedidei ha-folklor ha-yehudi, 1963), 71–72, fig. 86. For another example of a knife, see "Slaughtering Knife," IJA 17136.

104. Wertheim, *Law and Custom in Hasidism*, 120–123.

105. Muchawsky-Schnapper, *A World Apart Next Door*, 67–68.

106. The exhibition "The Time of the Hasidism" in the Historical Museum in Kraków in 2005 could present only three Hasidic coats and two *shtraymlekh* collected in Polish museums, all made in the interwar period. See Długosz, *Czas chasydów*, 105, 116–119. Three *shtraymlekh* in the Museum of the History of Jews in Russia (Moscow) are dated to the early twentieth century. See Kazovsky and Khaimovich, *Museum of Jewish History in Russia*, 78–79. Some pieces of clothing identified as Hasidic in the collection of the Israel Museum also could be dated to the early twentieth century, while the rest are from the late twentieth and early twenty-first centuries. See Muchawsky-Schnapper, *A World Apart Next Door*, passim.

107. For a cap (yarmulke) of a tsadik from Yampol and a white coat of a tsadik from Kojdanów, see Liudmila Uritskaia and Semion Yakerson, *Evreiskie sokrovishcha Peterburga: Ashkenazskie kollektsii Rossiiskogo etnograficheskogo muzeia* (St. Petersburg: Arca, 2009), 134; Muchawsky-Schnapper, *A World Apart Next Door*, 94–95.

108. Muchawsky-Schnapper, *A World Apart Next Door*, 94, 106, 108, 153.

109. For example, Sergey Kravtsov has discussed depictions of synagogues that differ from their real appearance as seen in photographs in order to visualize the meaning implied by the viewer (but not necessarily by the builders). See Sergey Kravtsov, "Juan Bautista Villalpando and Sacred Architecture in the Seventeenth Century," *Journal of the Society of Architectural Historians* 64 (2005), 323; Kravtsov, "Synagogue Architecture of Volhynia," 69, 72.

110. Muchawsky-Schnapper, *A World Apart Next Door*, 71.

111. The others are Isidor Kaufmann's "Der Sohn des Wunderrabbi von Belz" and "Sohn des Wunderrabbi von N." See G. Tobias Natter, ed., *Rabbiner, Bocher, Talmudschüler: Bilder des Wiener Malers Isidor Kaufmann, 1853–1921* (Wien: Jüdisches Museum der Stadt Wien, 1995), 231, 351. A painting of Józef Schneider titled "In a Hasidic Synagogue" is published in Kazovsky and Khaimovich, *Museum of Jewish History in Russia*, 81.

112. For example, Kaufmann's "Karaite from Halicz" wears a *shtrayml* exactly as Jews in his other portraits. See Natter, *Rabbiner, Bocher, Talmudschüler*, 237. It could be that Kaufmann dressed his models in the clothing items he possessed, similarly to his numerous Jewish home scenes, which were painted in the "Shabbat room" he set up in the Jewish Museum of Vienna. Kaufmann's "Beth Hamidrash" shows a small prayer room with people wearing *shtraymlekh* and *spodeks* and wrapped in tallitot with silver collars. In reality, it is a prayer room in Holleschau (Holešov) in Moravia, where Hasidim and *shtraymlekh* hardly were found (Natter, *Rabbiner, Bocher, Talmudschüler*, 266–271, 306–307).

113. Shalom Sabar, "Between Poland and Germany: Jewish Religious Practices in Illustrated Postcards of the Early Twentieth Century," *Polin* 16 (2003), 141–144.

114. Silvain and Minczeles, *Yiddishland*, 364; Vladimir Likhodedov, *Synagogues* (Minsk: Riftur, 2007), 95.

115. E.g., Roman Vishniac, *A Vanished World* (Harmondsworth: Penguin Books, 1986), passim.

116. A good introduction to the topic is Tamar Somogyi, *Die Schejnen und die Prosten: Untersuchungen zum Schönheitsideal der Ostjuden in Bezug auf Körper und Kleidung unter besonderer Berücksichtigung des Chassidismus* (Berlin: Dietrich Reimer Verlag, 1982).

117. For an example of such a description of a rich Hasid of R. Israel of Ruzhin [Rużyn] in the 1820s, see Gottlober, *Zikhronot u-masa'ot*, 1:110.

118. Cited in Noaḥ Prilutski, *Dos gevet: Dialogen vegn shprakh un kultur* (Warsaw: Kultur-Lige, 1923), 37. See also Somogyi, *Die Schejnen und die Prosten*, 142; Olga Goldberg-Mulkiewicz, "Dress," in *The YIVO Encyclopedia of Jews in Eastern Europe*, ed. G. D. Hundert (New Haven, CT: Yale University Press, 2008), 423.

119. Cited in Prilutski, *Dos gevet*, 37.

120. Tamar Somogyi states that it is a Lithuanian item. See Somogyi, *Die Schejnen und die Prosten*, 142.

121. Cited in Prilutski, *Dos gevet*, 38. Sadan mentions that such Jews were ridiculed by a Talmudic verse that says "An ass feels cold even in the summer solstice" (Shabbat 53a, Soncino translation)—Dov Sadan, "Tsvishn shtrayml un spodek," *Isroel shtime* 19, September 19, 1973, 5.

122. Solomon Maimon, *An Autobiography* (New York: Shocken Books, 1947), 54.

123. Mordecai Wilensky, *Ḥasidim u-mitnagdim* (Jerusalem: Mosad Bialik, 1990), 1:37, 47, 54, 56.

124. Twersky, *He-ḥatser ha-penimit*, 28.

125. Dynner, *Men of Silk*, 74.

126. Wertheim, *Law and Custom in Hasidism*, 217–218.

127. Lipa Schmeltzer, "She-lo shinu et malbusham," *Ba-kehilah—musaf pesaḥ*, April 24, 2006, 16. I am grateful to Prof. Shaul Stampfer for bringing this source to my attention.

128. For the oil portrait painted in the late nineteenth century and a woodblock on paper printed in 1891 in Odessa, see, e.g., Boris Khaimovich, Hillel Kazovsky, and Maria Kaspina, *Videt' i pomnit': Estetika sakral'nogo v evreiskoi visual'noi kul'ture* (Moscow: Museum of Jewish History in Russia, 2012), 104; Kazovsky and Khaimovich, *Museum of Jewish History in Russia*, 72–73.

129. Muchawsky-Schnapper, *A World Apart Next Door*, 95.

130. Semion Dubnov, "Vmeshatel'stvo russkogo pravitel'stva v antikhasidskuiu bor'bu (1800–1801)," *Evreiskaia starina* 3 (1910), 260–261.

131. Goldman-Ida, *Hasidic Art and the Kabbalah*, 232–276.

132. Wertheim, *Law and Custom in Hasidism*, 114–120; Muchawsky-Schnapper, *A World Apart Next Door*, 110; Gadi Sagiv, "Mabat ḥadash al pulmus ha-tkhelet be-sof ha-me'ah ha-19," *Zion* 82 (2017), 59–95.

133. Wertheim, *Law and Custom in Hasidism*, 113; Muchawsky-Schnapper, *A World Apart Next Door*, 118.

134. For the description of this custom, see Muchawsky-Schnapper, *A World Apart Next Door*, 46–57; Nava Vasserman, *Mi-yamai lo karati le-ishti: Zugiyut be-ḥasidut Gur* (Sde Boker: The Ben-Gurion Research Institute for the Study of Israel and Zionism, 2015), 277–278 and bibliography cited there.

135. It can be clearly seen in Muchawsky-Schnapper, *A World Apart Next Door*, where 63 pages are devoted to male attire and only 28 to female's, notwithstanding that the majority of the author's contacts were with women (ibid., 19).

136. Ibid., 134–145.

137. Sadan, "Tsvishn shtrayml un spodek," *Isroel shtime* 20, October 3, 1973, 5.

138. Muchawsky-Schnapper, *A World Apart Next Door*, 83. See also illustration in chapter 10.

139. Sadan, "Tsvishn shtrayml un spodek," *Isroel shtime* 24, December 5, 1973, 5.

140. Muchawsky-Schnapper, *A World Apart Next Door*, 80; Schmeltzer, "She-lo shinu et malbusham," 46–47.

141. Richard I. Cohen, *Jewish Icons: Art and Society in Modern Europe* (Berkeley: University of California Press, 1998), 116, 124, 130.

142. Aizenberg, "Mestechko Kamenka," 95; Sadan, "Tsvishn shtrayml un spodek," *Isroel shtime* 20, October 3, 1973, 5; Muchawsky-Schnapper, *A World Apart Next Door*, 82.

143. Muchawsky-Schnapper, *A World Apart Next Door*, 82.

144. A metal box of the early twentieth century is preserved in the Museum of Jewish History in Russia; see Kazovsky and Khaimovich, *Museum of Jewish History in Russia*, 78.

145. Somogyi, *Die Schejnen und die Prosten*, 137–140. According to Gottlober, however, the *spodek* was a headgear of a teacher's assistant, which implies low position in society. Gottlober, *Zikhronot u-masa'ot*, 1:67. See also Muchawsky-Schnapper, *A World Apart Next Door*, 84–87.

146. Sadan, "Tsvishn shtrayml un spodek," *Isroel shtime* 20, October 3, 1973, 5.

147. Ibid., *Isroel shtime* 19, September 19, 1973, 5.

148. Ibid., *Isroel shtime* 24, December 5, 1973, 5.

149. Muchawsky-Schnapper, *A World Apart Next Door*, 84. According to Dov Sadan ("Tsvishn shtrayml un spodek," *Isroel shtime* 19, September 19, 1973, 5), "tsadiks' grandchildren" wore *spodek*. For an example of historical *kolpik*, see Kazovsky and Khaimovich, *Museum of Jewish History in Russia*, 79.

150. The portrait of R. Menaḥem Mendel Schneersohn of Lubavitch, which might have been painted in the middle of the nineteenth century, shows him in white garb and white *shtrayml*. R. Menaḥem Mendel Hager of Vizhnitz is also depicted in *shtrayml* in his study room. The depictions of R. Aharon of Czarnobyl and R. Ya'akov Yitzḥak of Makarów from the second half of the nineteenth century show them wearing *shtrayml*, while R. David of Talne and R. Avraham of Trisk are shown in *spodek*. The portraits of R. Eliyahu Guttmacher of Greiditz (Grodzisk Wielkopolski, d. 1874) and of R. Meir Ḥayim Katsenelenbogen of Stepań (d. 1902) also show them wearing *shtrayml*. See, e.g., Khaimovich, Kazovsky, and Kaspina, *Videt' i pomnit'*, 104, 110, 121; Kazovsky and Khaimovich, *Museum of Jewish History in Russia*, 72–73, 75.

151. Three engravings of Jews published in 1846 by Léon Hollaenderski show "a Lithuanian Jew" in a *shtrayml*, "a Warsaw Jew" in a *spodek*, and "the Hasid" in a round, high fur hat, but with a pipe, a bottle of alcohol, and a red nose, figure 12.9. Another engraving, entitled "Lithuanian Stock Exchange," presents Jews either in *shtraymlekh* or in wide-brimmed hats. The Jews in Warsaw and Odessa—supposedly more connected to Hasidism—were depicted in the same attire in 1826 and 1840. See Léon Hollaenderski, *Les Israélites de Pologne* (Paris: Chez Dageteau et Cie, 1846), 188, 210, 222, 280. For the Odessa picture, see Alfred Rubens, *A History of Jewish Costume* (New York: Funk and Wagnalls, 1967), 117; Hundert, *The YIVO Encyclopedia of Jews in Eastern Europe*, 451. For the synagogue in Warsaw, see Bergman, "*Nie masz bóżnicy*," 185.

152. Rachel Schnold, ed., *The Gaon of Vilna: The Man and His Legacy* (Tel Aviv: Beth Hatefutsoth, 1998), 37–38.

153. Gottlober, *Zikhronot u-masa'ot*, 1:89. Cf. Stampfer, *Families, Rabbis and Education*, 20–21.

154. Sadan, "Tsvishn shtrayml un spodek," *Isroel shtime* 19, September 19, 1973, 5.

155. Cf. David Assaf and Gad Sagiv, "Hasidism in Tsarist Russia: Historical and Social Aspects," *Jewish History* 27 (2013), 260. On clothing decrees in Congress Poland, see Glenn Dynner, "The Garment of Torah: Clothing Decrees and the Warsaw Career of the First Gerer Rebbe," in *Warsaw. The Jewish Metropolis: Essays in Honor of the 75th Birthday of Professor Antony Polonsky*, ed. G. Dynner and F. Guesnet (Leiden: Brill, 2015), 91–127.

156. Wertheim, *Law and Custom in Hasidism*, 297–298; Muchawsky-Schnapper, *A World Apart Next Door*, 88.

157. Yisroel Aksenfeld, *Dos shterntikhl* (Moscow: Emes, 1938), 49; English translation: Barbara Kirshenblatt-Gimblett, "Folklore, Ethnography, and Anthropology," in Hundert, *The YIVO Encyclopedia of Jews in Eastern Europe*, 522.

158. Gottlober, *Zikhronot u-masa'ot*, 1:89.

159. Yeḥiel Ravrebe, "Svad'ba Makarovskogo tsadika," *Vestnik evreiskogo universiteta v Moskve*, no. 2 (1993), 185.

160. E.g., see the description of "tsadik R. Gershele" of Kamenka (Volhynia, probably meaning R. Avraham Yehushua Heshel) in the 1870s, as dressed in "an atlas coat and a seven-tails *shtrayml*," which implies that other Jews in the synagogue were dressed differently—Aizenberg, "Mestechko Kamenka," 95.

161. Kofman, *Zikhronot*, 70. Dov Sadan, born in Brody on the Galician side of the Russo-Austrian border, also mentions that Jews in Russia (Volhynia) did not wear *shtrayml*, but a different hat called *boyke*—Sadan, "Tsvishn shtrayml un spodek," *Isroel shtime* 19, September 19, 1973, 5.

162. Ibid.

163. On Hungarian Orthodoxy and its stress on traditional dress, see Michael Silber, "The Emergence of Ultra-Orthodoxy: The Invention of a Tradition," in *The Uses of Tradition: Jewish Continuity in the Modern Era*, ed. J. Wertheimer (New York: The Jewish Theological Seminary of America, 1992), 23–84.

CHAPTER 13

Big Data

Marcin Wodziński

Today the digital humanities (DH) represent some of the most frequently used and overused concepts in the academic world, and undoubtedly the issues related to the field produce some of the most heated discussions. Voices range the gamut from enthusiastic eulogists of revolution to frustrated seekers of global conspiracy. This is hardly surprising. The DH arouse both the greatest hopes among current scholars for radically new discoveries and new lines of academic inquiry, and the greatest fears for the future of the humanities and their institutions of higher learning.

Supporters point out that the DH enable research to be made into great social and cultural phenomena hitherto invisible to the naked eye, or inaccessible to the "analog" scholar with limited resources. They also point out that the DH can transcend temporal boundaries and examine phenomena in long historical cycles, thus fulfilling the dreams of modern historiography's founding fathers. For the first time in history, the DH also exceed the limitations of the typical humanities scholar working in isolation and enables, or even forces, her or him to work collaboratively. Finally, the DH can not only present research findings in a form accessible to a small group of initiated specialists, but can also respond to the noble requirements for democratizing scholarship.

Opponents point to the unfulfilled promise of earlier phases of quantitative research, principally to the so-called cliometrics of the 1970s and 1980s and to this school's spectacular failures, and above all to the illusory promises of greater objectivity and "scientific rigor" of research into the humanities. They claim, too, that the greatest research issues in the humanities have, and have always had, an interpretive dimension that cannot be quantified at all, thus eluding the tools of the new quantitative school. Attention is often drawn to the connection between the crisis of traditional, increasingly underfunded humanities departments and the interests of university authorities or state sponsors in the development of more "objective" and "practical" quantitative research.[1] The resistance to DH is interesting not just because it points to the problems in this line of research (after all, what new method does not have its problems?), but because it proves, even more than its supporters' claims do, that DH really is one of the greatest challenges in the humanities today. If that is the case, then we need to consider how much the most typical sources and methods of the DH are in use in studies of Hasidism. The most important are certainly quantitative sources and their research methods.

Of course the term *big data* is not completely suitable for studies into Hasidism, nor indeed for nearly all of the humanities, for DH very rarely uses truly large-scale sources comparable to those used in the hard sciences or the social sciences. But even if the *big data* of the title were to be very small, and even truly microscopic, as in the case of research on Hasidism, it is doubtless worth asking what large-scale resources a student of Hasidism has or might have at her or his disposal, what use has been made hitherto of this type of source in work on Hasidism, and what use could be made in the future.

What Are the Digital Humanities?

Before, however, tackling the issue of large-scale sources in studying Hasidism, we must first define the DH phenomenon. For some it is "the next big thing" and the inevitable future of "the humanities as they are now practiced and as they will increasingly be practiced in the future."[2] For many others it simply means using the internet or basic computer skills in their daily research and teaching work. This extended definition appears to be inadequate, for a concept applied too widely loses its force. Today the term *DH* usually means any and all research activities using digital information resources and computer-based tools in the widest sense (computers, software, digital media, the internet). DH usually also encompasses computer-enhanced learning and humanities content available online, as well as new editorial practices, including open-access online publishing, posting and discussing research results on social media, and, above all, moving away from the printed word as the sole means of presenting research results. In place of the traditional text, DH scholars are proposing charts and posting online sources, interactive presentations, and, more frequently of late, maps.

In the research aspect that interests us the most, we understand DH usually to be the online accessibility of data and various sorts of internet data bases, mainly textual source materials (digital libraries); new forms of visualizing research results, mainly charts and maps; quantitative research tools such as text mining, data modeling; successively developed systems for handling metadata; and finally—at the most advanced level—the creation of new analytical tools and platforms that facilitate the introduction of advanced automated quantitative research. Altogether this means that the DH are currently a field with greatly varied research practices, ranging from the simple use of the internet or the use of it to make sources available online, right up to the application of advanced tools for the analysis of text, images, and sound.

Naturally, not all these techniques are represented equally in the modern DH suite. Despite great hopes and even greater investments, the overwhelming majority of research practices still focus on the relatively straightforward cataloguing and sharing of data, and not on quantitative analysis, not to mention projects that build on the developed bodies of metadata and analytical tools. Unfortunately, the latter often do not treat their results as true research tools geared toward answering the questions asked of them, but simply as an example of possibilities which, perhaps, someone else might exploit in the future. Even the most interesting projects from the research perspective, such as, for instance, Digital Harlem (http://digitalharlem.org), provide limited possibilities for new searches, generating new research possibilities unforeseen by their authors during the building process.[3]

Perhaps the most promising are projects using mapping, above all the GIS (geographic information system), since they allow for studying key, yet hitherto poorly perceived, geotemporal correlations, thus ensuring that the "spatial turn" announced in humanities studies becomes reality and not just a theory. Space and place are indeed categories ever more frequently present in the work of current humanities scholars. A good example is the project Mapping the Republic of Letters (http://republicofletters.stanford.edu/), which maps the thousands of connections found in letters of people from the Enlightenment era. However, even this project, though one of the best known, reveals in equal measure DH's potential and limitations: in reality the project really effectively describes only the network of connections of the best-known figures chosen by the team, and only through links selected by it.[4] What is worse, like many such undertakings financed by the wealthiest research centers, the project sins by its imperial perspective, focusing on figures from Western Europe and North America, and almost completely ignoring letters and writers from other parts of the world, other cultures, or other languages. For example, one would search the project's website in vain for writers of the Jewish Enlightenment and for contacts in Eastern Europe. In this way, DH strengthen the pathology of the contemporary humanities, becoming an instrument for perpetuating the "imperial map of the world" created by the wealthy and mighty citizens of the center, thanks to which they become even more central, even wealthier, and even more powerful. Thus, despite great expectations, DH still all too rarely lead to results that respond to the central questions of contemporary humanities, whether in the form of publications or in other ways. Therefore, those critics of the new tools who point out that DH still promise more than they deliver are correct, and that what they do produce often provides results at variance with those promised.

The same is more or less true for Jewish studies. The majority of works focus on bibliographical, cataloguing, and digitizing projects. Over the last twenty years, incredible progress has been made in gaining remote access to ancient epitaphs and manuscripts, and lately a greater emphasis is being laid on old prints, journals, and nontextual sources. On its website, the National Library of Israel (http://web.nli.org.il) has splendid bibliographical tools, the most important being RAMBI (http://web.nli.org.il/sites/NLI/English/infochannels/Catalogs/bibliographic-databases/rambi/Pages/rambi.aspx) and Kiryat Sefer (http://web.nli.org.il/sites/nli/english/infochannels/catalogs/bibliographic-databases/pages/qsefer.aspx), often linked to access to complete texts, as well as dozens of databases allowing access to millions of documents. Similarly, all the major Jewish archives and libraries, such as the Center for Jewish History (http://www.cjh.org/) in New York City, the Yad Vashem Institute (https://www.yadvashem.org) in Jerusalem, and the United States Holocaust Memorial Museum (https://www.ushmm.org) in Washington, DC, are making ever greater parts of their collections electronically accessible. The Rothschild Foundation Europe has initiated a major project entitled Yerusha (http://yerusha.eu), which aims eventually to collect data on all the key archival collections containing information on the history and culture of Jews throughout Europe. A great deal of information on valuable resources for the history of Hasidism has already been made available thanks to this project. Many non-Jewish libraries and archives have equally valuable collections of Hasidiana. For example, the Russian State Library holds huge collections of the Schneersohn family (https://search.rsl.ru/en/index#ef=1&af=1&c=shn).

The more advanced digital tools that could facilitate access not only to historical content but also to their automated analysis are much rarer. The best represented in this small group are tools using geolocation, which once again confirms the growing significance of spatial analysis in the modern humanities, including Jewish studies (and research into Hasidism, of which more later). One of these interesting projects is Footprints: Jewish Books Through Time and Place (https://footprints.ccnmtl.columbia.edu/), whose aim is to trace the circulation of Jewish books using advanced statistical analyses, reconstructions of readership circles, tracking lost books, inferential statistical analysis, and the visualization of a network of connections. Unfortunately, the project is still in its initial stages, and for the time being it is difficult to judge whether it will achieve its ambitious goals. If it does then it will be the first such advanced project in the field of Jewish studies. For a scholar of Hasidism, it is already making available information on the fate of books from the important Chabad library in Moscow.

The Daat Hamakom (http://www.daat-hamakom.com) project—really a platform for more than a dozen linked projects focused on mapping phenomena of Jewish culture, ranging from the cult of R. Shimon Bar-Yoḥai, by way of the history of the Jews in Kraków, up to rabbinic responsa as a communications network—is similarly advanced on the technological side, but it is relatively behind in terms of actual implementation. The project already has undoubted educational merit, yet it is still hard to define just to what extent it will allow innovative independent exploration of sources and spatial analyses of the sources thus assembled.

Finally, it should be mentioned that there are many digital projects accessible on the web whose cognitive value is minimal and which would never have got past the reviewers' sieve had there been a question of publishing in the traditional academic manner. Some of them are located on the websites of academic institutions and pretend to be scholarly projects, which exposes the dark side of the democratization of the modern humanities.

Big Data and Hasidism

The sources used in quantitative research into the humanities can be generated in the process of gathering and digitizing traditional sources, or they can be "born digital" in that they arise directly from the digital world. This second variety is of course easier to identify, since it arises daily on the internet, and is also relatively easier to work on, since it is already in a digital format, but its extent is limited in time to the last two decades and is thus used more in research into contemporary societies than in historical studies. In the case of studies of Hasidism, this relates above all to internet sites dedicated to ultra-Orthodox communities, the so-called *ḥaredim*. The most popular are Behadrey Haredim (http://www.bhol.co.il/), Kikar ha-Shabat (https://www.kikar.co.il), and KaveShtiebel (http://www.kaveshtiebel.com), providing thousands of texts and images on contemporary life in this community. An equally popular form of ultra-Orthodox participation in the internet is the blog. The most popular of them, FailedMessiah (https://failedmessiah.typepad.com), was sold in 2016 by Shmarya Rosenberg to a new owner, but its full archive, a priceless resource for DH research, is still available online.[5] The ultra-Orthodox press, such as *Ha-Modia* (https://hamodia.com), is a similarly valuable online resource. Another invaluable large-scale source of information on the present-day Hasidic community is the internet sites of active online groups, the most active among them being Chabad-Lubavitch, which carries out intensive missionary work both online and off. In addition to its official sites, Lubavitch.com and Chabad.org, this group runs dozens of other sites dedicated to various lesser communities and needs. Of such sites, Chabad Library (http://chabadlibrary.org/books/) seems of greatest significance for potential research. The large community of Bratslav Hasidim (cf. breslov.org and breslov.com) is quite active online, too. Unfortunately, internet activity by Hasidic groups is more the exception than the norm. Many groups—among them the large Satmar (Szatmár), Ger (Góra Kalwaria), and Bełz groups—are more or less absent from the internet, or at least do not set up official or open websites. Online materials, especially those created by Chabad-Lubavitch, have already been analyzed by scholars interested in DH and the new media, but as a rule their attention has focused on the internet as a medium of missionary activity, and hitherto they have not used the tools of quantitative analysis.[6]

If we turn to large-scale sources of nondigital provenance for the history of Hasidism, an excellent repository of such sources is the previously mentioned platforms that make Hebrew or Yiddish books accessible. Among the most noteworthy is HebrewBooks (http://hebrewbooks.org), an open-access platform of more than forty thousand religious books, mainly in Hebrew, as well as the commercial Otzar HaHochma (https://www.otzar.org), with eighty-seven thousand religious books. Both these platforms make it possible to select Hasidic books from among the categories of searched texts (HebrewBooks also has a separate category of Chabad books), and they offer free automatic searches of the contents of these books.[7] Naturally these platforms are widely used by scholars of Hasidism, but as far as I know they have not yet been studied as a quantitative resource.

Similarly, the Historical Jewish Press (http://web.nli.org.il/sites/JPress/English), an excellent project of the National Library of Israel, has made available dozens of old press titles in textual form, scanned en masse and formatted using OCR (optical character recognition), including the most important nineteenth- and twentieth-century journals from Eastern Europe, filled with as yet unused information on the Hasidic movement.[8] The platform also provides simple statistical data on the subject of searched phrases and words, for instance informing in tabular form that out of 6,177 occurrences of the word *Hasidism* (*ḥasidut*) throughout the whole database, as many as 46 percent appear between 1950 and 1969, the most (6 percent) occurring in 1960. Of course, these data can be analyzed further; a simple example is figure 13.1, which juxtaposes the use of the same word, *Hasidism*, in the three most important Hebrew journals of nineteenth-century Eastern Europe. The table presents a total number of appearances of the word *Hasidism* in successive time grids of five years each, starting in 1860–1864 and ending in 1900–1904. This very simple table illustrates splendidly the differences in attitude toward Hasidism of the three maskilic centers grouped around these journals and of their editors in chief, for instance the influence of Nahum Sokolow on the growth of interest in Hasidism on the editorial board of *Ha-tsefirah*.[9] The analysis could of course be pursued further.

In this context we should mention the database created in the project New Sources for the Research of Hasidism: The Hebrew Press in Eastern Europe (https://tau-primo.hosted.exlibrisgroup.com/primo-explore/collectionDiscov

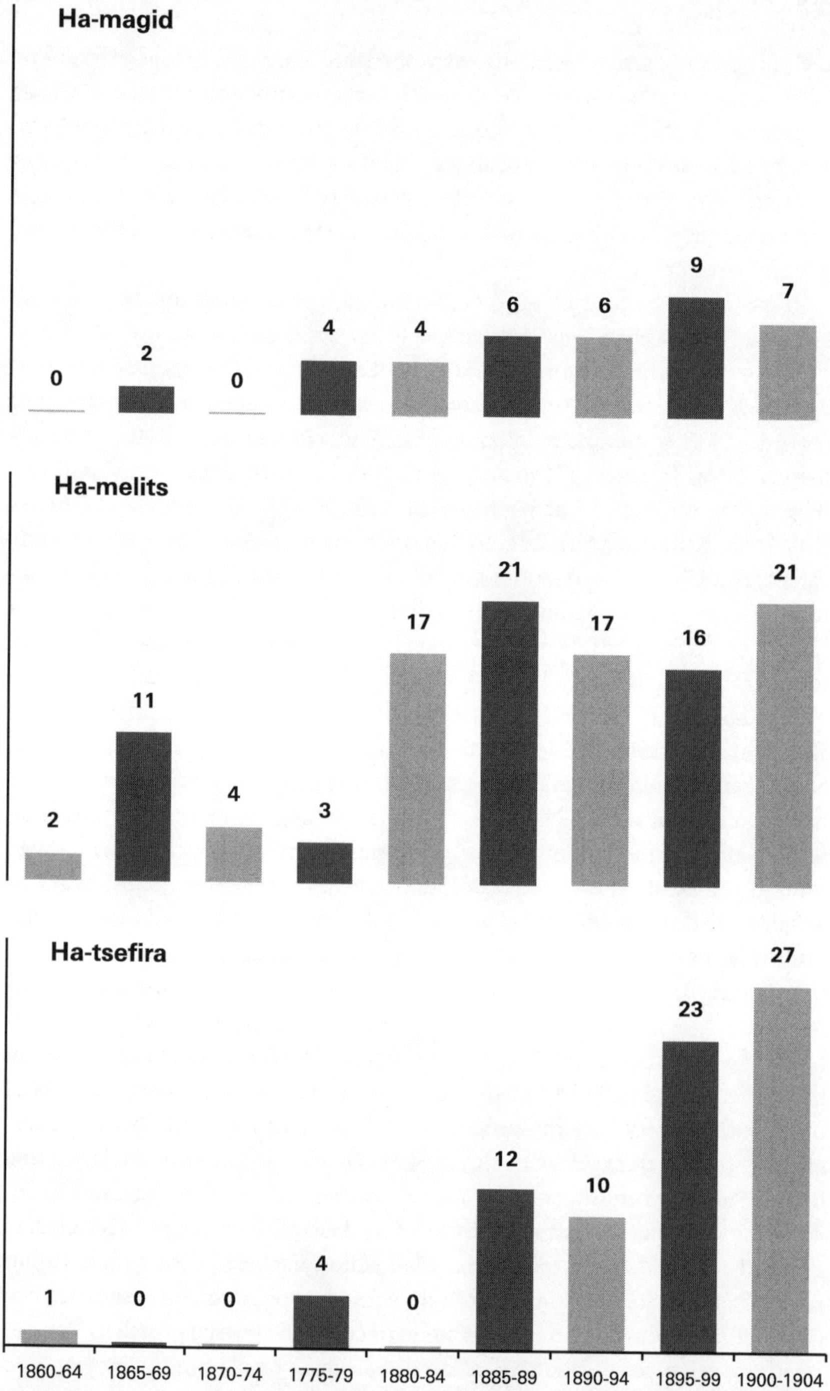

Figure 13.1. Appearance of the word *Hasidism* (*ḥasidut*) in the East European Hebrew periodicals *Ha-magid*, *Ha-melits*, and *Ha-tsefirah*, 1860–1904. Data source: *Historical Jewish Press*; http://web.nli.org.il/sites/JPress/English/Pages/default.aspx.

ery?vid=TAU&collectionId=81264597260004146&lang=en_US), carried out by David Assaf at Tel Aviv University. The project is meant to make available structured, annotated, and cross-referenced sources for the history of Hasidism mined by a team of historians from the extensive, hitherto nondigitized body of the Jewish press from the nineteenth and early twentieth centuries. If the project lives up to its expectations, this will be the only academic database on the internet devoted exclusively to sources for the history of Hasidism. Let us hope that the platform will also enable quantitative research, distant reading, and that it will enable visualization.

Finally, we should mention an exceptionally valuable large-scale resource: local Jewish communities' memorial books (*yisker bikher* or *pinkasim*). Chapter 6 discusses them briefly as a type of ego-document. Here I should simply like to note that memorial books are the collective memoirs of former Jewish inhabitants of the towns and villages of Eastern Europe, describing their lives before World War II, sometimes going back to the nineteenth century, and their deaths during the Holocaust. These memorial books are all the more precious because they contain, by virtue of their nature, unique large-scale testimony of daily life written by nonelite authors. This extensive material now runs to eight hundred works, often in many volumes; all told, the genre includes more than 350,000 large-format pages of text (and illustrations) in several languages. Close reading, or classical historical textual criticism, is powerless when faced with this volume of material. Even reading 100 to 150 pages daily, in Hebrew, Yiddish, Hungarian, Spanish, German, English, and Polish, it would take about ten years to get through all the books. The only way to achieve a detailed analysis of this source is by applying distant reading, with the help of automated text scanning and quantitative techniques as an essential first step in this analysis.[10] Unfortunately, the memorial books, although digitized and available on the New York Public Library website (https://www.nypl.org/collections/nypl-recommendations/guides/yizkorbooks), cannot be textually searched as they are not in OCR format. Fortunately, the wonderful genealogical portal JewishGen (https://www.jewishgen.org/Yizkor/) provides a worthy alternative, which will not, however, replace a full textual search, but will enable an initial analysis of most of these books in either a partial or full English translation. An automated search of these English translations was, for instance, one of the first stages in building a database of 2,854 Hasidic places of worship (*shtiblekh*), which became the basis of an analysis of the spatial dimensions of the Hasidic movement from the start of the twentieth century to the Holocaust. In order to illustrate the potential possibilities of this type of work in both its quantitative and spatial aspects, it is worth briefly presenting the main findings of this research. Given that this issue has been covered in detail in two other places, here I shall cite only the most important conclusions.[11]

Spatial Analysis

The shtibl was the basic institution of the Hasidic movement. Unlike spontaneous prayer groups, the shtibl was a relatively stable institution with a well-developed social structure and extensive membership requiring a material infrastructure and economic backing. This means that the shtibl is a reliable gauge of the relatively well-developed and enduring influences of Hasidism. At the same time, the shtibl was an institution small enough to reflect even minute divisions between Hasidic groups, and is thus a relatively accurate instrument. Thanks to this, the shtibl is the ideal analytical tool for a great many phenomena occurring in the Hasidic community.

The first observation emerging from the assembled database of 2,854 shtiblekh in 858 locations, the ideal analytical tool for a great many spatial phenomena occurring in the Hasidic community, is a strong correlation between the boundaries of the Hasidic groups' spheres of influence and the political borders of nineteenth-century Eastern Europe. The question was how many shtiblekh of a given court were located in the same nineteenth-century province as the court with which they were affiliated. The average was 83 percent. With few exceptions, just about all the courts limited their influence to territory within the borders of nineteenth-century administrative entities. In other words, twenty years after the political border between Central Poland (formerly under Russian rule) and Galicia (formerly under Austrian rule) was removed, there were almost no shtiblekh of tsadikim from Central Poland set up in Galicia, nor those of tsadikim from Galicia on the territory of Central Poland. The same happened with all the other boundaries. This provides a powerful argument in favor of the durability of the phantom borders of nineteenth-century Europe in the structure of the influence of interwar Hasidism (and, we might add, beyond).

Another observation concerns the hierarchy of influence: in each of the areas, two dominant groups controlled about half the shtiblekh in an area; 20 percent of the groups controlled almost 80 percent; and half of all the groups controlled 90 percent of all the shtiblekh. This allows us to divide the groups into several categories: the dominant (in Central Poland they were Ger and Alexander [Aleksandrów]), the medium-sized, the small, and the ephemeral groups with two or three shtiblekh and minimal influence.

Maybe most interesting, the number and distribution of shtiblekh affiliated with a given tsadik also provide indirect information on the type of leadership exerted by this tsadik, and thus on a fundamental question for Hasidic spirituality. In order to trace this, our analysis needed to introduce another variable: the median distance between the courts and the shtiblekh. The relationship between the number of shtiblekh and the median distance for each of the groups is shown in figure 13.2, whose smoothed mean plot follows the logarithmic regression model of the relationships between these two parameters. The relationship

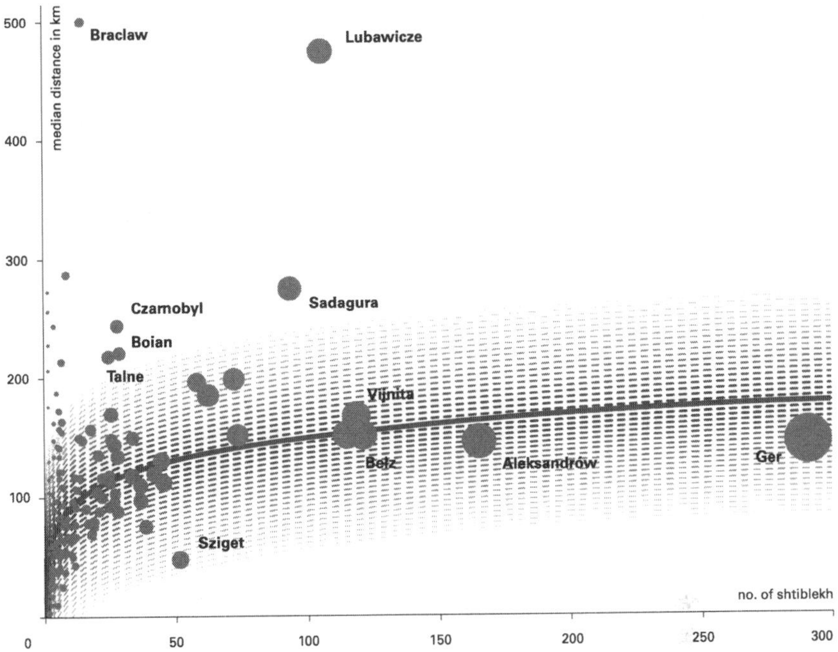

Figure 13.2. Number of shtiblekh and median distance between shtiblekh and courts, 1900–1939. Source: Wodziński, "Space and Spirit."

clearly follows the natural correlation of the number of shtiblekh and the average distance between a court and the shtiblekh, which have to be distributed over a greater area. For example, for the large group of Ger (294 shtiblekh), the median distance between the court and the shtibl was 145 kilometers; for mid-size Radomsko (42 shtiblekh), it was 97 kilometers; and for small Krimlov (Kromołów; twelve shtiblekh), only 40 kilometers.

However flat and impersonal these correlations might sound, they have in fact profound implications for understanding the type of spiritual relationship between Hasidic leaders and their followers. Simply put: the greater the number of shtiblekh and the greater the physical distance, the greater the social and emotional distance between the Hasidim and the tsadik. This was seen most clearly at the dominant courts, at which the tsadikim attracted thousands of followers. This mass dimension and thus the power of the group was one of the sources of pride and group identity for their followers, but the inevitable cost was that contact between the tsadikim and their Hasidim had to be minimal. Among the thousands of followers of the tsadikim of Ger or Bełz, a huge majority never spent more than a few holy days at their courts and never had any meaningful personal contact with their tsadik. And the tsadik did not know most of his followers personally.

At the other extreme were the ephemeral groups with two or three shtiblekh. In their cases there was no difference between Hasidic experience at a tsadik's court and the life of Hasidim far from the court, for often the court was also a shtibl, where all the followers' religious needs were met—or it was at most a few kilometers away.

A spectrum of medium-sized groups existed between these two extreme types of dominant and ephemeral ones. Significantly, they differed not only in the size of the group and median distance between the court and the shtiblekh, but also in their historical-spatial development and, often, type of leadership. One such type was made up of groups with fewer shtiblekh than in the dominant groups, but with similarly high average distances; this type is composed mostly of regressive groups, such as Kock or Vorke (Warka), which historically were dominant groups but had lost this position, though their shtiblekh continued to be scattered over a large area that had formerly been under their dominion. Another type was that of regional groups having an average number of shtiblekh and with average distances between the court and the shtiblekh. Bobowa, for example, controlled only 0.8 percent of all shtiblekh. However, in Kraków province, in which most of them lay, it controlled 16 percent, which made it a dominant group there. Another similar type, but on a still smaller scale, was provided by local groups. Their radius of influence was limited to one or two districts, but in that area their influence was high, often similar to the influence of dominant national groups.

This reveals a key distinction between dominant groups and regional and local ones, whose territorial limitations should be seen not as a relative weakness, but as an expression of another model of leadership. In those groups in which shtiblekh lay within a radius of thirty or forty kilometers from the court, every Hasid was able to reach his tsadik many times a year, remaining in close, intimate contact. Numerous memoirs emphasize this type of interpersonal relationship—radically different from that at dominant courts—and the warm, intimate atmosphere of small Hasidic groups. The tsadik of Pinchev (Pińczów), with six shtiblekh and a median distance of twenty-six kilometers, made a point of knowing all his Hasidim well and of assuring an intimate atmosphere at his court, while the tsadik of Wąchock, with two shtiblekh and a median distance of four kilometers, gathered all his Hasidim for weekly Shabbat meals.[12]

The relationship between the size of a group and the distance between a tsadik and a Hasid differed in each of these models. But it did not diminish the leadership potential of any of them. Leadership charisma can be developed on the basis of great physical and social distance and low interaction (as in Ger), just as well as it can on close social relations and intense interaction (as in Wąchock).[13] The full spectrum between these two provides a useful typology of Hasidic leadership, clearly correlated with the size and geographical dispersion of the groups. What is perhaps most significant is the fact that these typological differences can be successfully mapped and quantified.

Hasidic Telephone Books: A Case Study

Perhaps the most fascinating aspect of the DH is that they can draw their sources both from quantitative data traditionally used in social research and from new, hitherto unknown and surprising types of mass data that might ultimately transform our research practices. Such data might deliver information on aspects of history, social life, and culture that have thus far remained beyond the reach of historians. Examples of traditional source corpora include census polls, school records, and tax registers, analyzed in the quantitative research of Hasidism mainly by sociologists and geographers interested in the demography and spatial distribution of the contemporary Hasidic movement. It would be an overstatement to claim that they have already established a new trend in scholarship. While still the exception, they have heralded the possibility of significant quantitative research on Hasidism and bring some hope for more such studies in the future.[14]

It appears that a good example of the latter category of unusual sources could be Hasidic phone books. Hitherto there has been rather marginal use of this source, mostly as supportive evidence for geographic research.[15] The largest project to date that is based on Hasidic phone books is the *Historical Atlas of Hasidism*, in which they were used for the study of demography and spatial dispersion of contemporary Hasidism. What follows is a summary of these findings.[16]

What exactly are the Hasidic phone books? All the large and many of the medium-sized Hasidic groups publish telephone books that list all the families of the followers of that specific group. These directories are relatively accurate, given that they fulfill the role of a substitute membership list. Additionally, it is important for many large groups to demonstrate their size; hence, they are careful to get the list right. On the other hand, also due to demographic competition, the groups police each other so that rivals do not list in their telephone books families who do not belong there.[17] The result is that telephone books are a reasonably reliable source, although of course they are not error-free. They also vary in quality: some are very accurate, while others consciously inflate their numbers, and some are visibly incomplete. Moreover, not all groups have books, so the sources are by definition incomplete. And yet despite all their shortcomings, the telephone directories, once acquired, are among the most accurate and reliable sources for describing contemporary Hasidism, both in terms of the macroscale picture of the worldwide distribution and in terms of internal divisions, hierarchies, settlement patterns, and more.

Telephone books for thirty-four Hasidic groups for the years 2012–2016 were collected for research on the *Historical Atlas of Hasidism*.[18] In addition, in the case of eleven groups, data from auxiliary materials have been drawn.[19] This allowed for the construction of a large database of 116,290 Hasidic domestic households, including data on their affiliation, sometimes size, and exact location in one of 1,350 localities. This is possibly the largest, most detailed, and most accurate database we possess on the number, affiliation, and geographical dispersion of contemporary Hasidim.

One of the most pressing questions is that of the demographic extent of Hasidism, and it has not been answered accurately despite its potentially explosive nature.[20] Based on the reasonable assumption that the database accounts for some 90 percent of all Hasidim, the combined total of all the Hasidic families in the world in 2016 can be calculated as circa 130,000. With the average size of a Hasidic household totaling 5.5 persons, we can roughly calculate that overall there are between 700,000 and 750,000 Hasidim in the world today, approximately 5 percent of all Jews worldwide. This proves quite clearly that fears of a supposed domination by Hasidim of the Jewish community are seriously exaggerated. The data also show that, despite spectacular resurgence since the Holocaust, Hasidism is still demographically far removed from its glory years of the mid-nineteenth century, when regionally it accounted for more than half the Jewish population.[21]

As for geographical distribution, roughly half of the world's Hasidim reside in the United States (about 41 percent of all Hasidim), and roughly half in Israel (about 48 percent of all Hasidim). This corresponds closely with the dominance of both countries in the Jewish population's general structure: around 40 percent and 44 percent of all the Jews in the world are found in the United States and Israel respectively.[22] Table 13.1 provides general data on Hasidic distribution by country of residence.

As the table shows, in the United States, Canada, and Israel, Hasidim represent 5 percent of the Jewish population, very close to the average percentages worldwide. But in Great Britain they total 10 percent, and in Belgium they represent as many as 33 percent of the local Jewish population. As in Austria and Switzerland, the high percentage of Hasidim in Great Britain and Belgium is the result of the existence of a single large Hasidic community, usually located in one of the great centers of the modern world and business. Today London represents that center in Great Britain, Antwerp in Belgium, Zurich in Switzerland, and Vienna in Austria.

Altogether, the telephone books show the presence of Hasidim in 1,350 locations, including 369 locations in Israel and the West Bank, and 526 in the United States. Of these, the vast majority are localities with one or two Hasidic families of Chabad-Lubavitch or Bratslav affiliation—two groups with especially high degrees of spatial dispersion. The greatest concentration of Hasidim is in New York, home to thirty-four thousand Hasidic families, or 26 percent of all Hasidim worldwide. A total of 75 percent of all Hasidim live in the ten largest communities, and 95 percent of Hasidim live in 10 percent of the largest communities. This confirms the continuing dominance of metropolitan centers, above all New York, Jerusalem, and greater Tel Aviv. This is not surprising and corresponds to the

TABLE 13.1

HASIDIC SETTLEMENT BY COUNTRY, 2016

Country	*Number of Hasidic Families*	*Core Jewish Population in the Country*	*% of World Jewry*	*Share in Country's Jewish Population (%)*	*Share in World Hasidic Population (%)*	*Dominant Group (%)*
Israel	62,062	5,700,000	43.5	5	48	Ger 16
USA	53,485	6,227,400	39.8	5	41.4	Satmar 40
UK	5,519	290,000	2	10	4.3	Satmar 28
Canada	3,392	386,000	2.7	5	2.6	Satmar 22
Belgium	1,791	29,800	0.2	33	1.4	Belz 24
Australia	1,002	112,800	0.8	5	0.8	Chabad 80
France	552	467,500	3.3	1	0.4	Chabad 88
South Africa	343	69,800	0.5	3	0.3	Chabad 90
Switzerland	219	18,900	0.1	6	0.2	Ger 32
Austria	153	9,000	0.1	9	0.1	Satmar 24
Brazil	144	94,500	0.7	1	0.1	Chabad 55
Argentina	99	181,000	1.3	0	0.1	Chabad 75
Ukraine	94	60,000	0.4	1	0.1	Chabad 74
Russia	93	183,000	1.3	0	0.1	Chabad 90
Uruguay	47	17,100	0.1	2	0	Satmar 87
Italy	32	27,600	0.2	1	0	Chabad 88
Other	188	436,100	3	0	0.1	
TOTAL	129,215	14,310,500	100	5	100	

Source: Marcin Wodziński, *Historical Atlas of Hasidism*; cartography Waldemar Spallek (Princeton, NJ: Princeton University Press, 2018).

general demographic tendencies today in Jewish society, the overwhelming majority of which lives either in Israel or in the greatest metropolises of the modern world.[23]

Three other models of settlement can also be seen. These have been described in existing scholarly literature, so there is no need to go into detail here.[24] What the phone-books database provides that is new in this regard is greater precision in the overall picture. For example, scholars have described a phenomenon of Israeli Hasidim resettling to new cities, often dominated by the populations of ultra-Orthodox enclaves, and often located in the Occupied Territories just beyond the Green Line, in, for example, Betar Ilit or Modi'in Ilit.[25] What the database highlights is that unlike American enclaves, those new cities have a very varied settlement structure and lack the clear dominance of any one group: in Betar Ilit, Boian Hasidim are the largest single group (15 percent), but there are almost the same number of Karlin-Stolin, Chabad, and Bratslav Hasidim, with slightly smaller numbers of Slonim, Amshinov, Sanz, and Vizhnitz. Overall, Hasidim from just about every group live there.

What is more, the database not only visualizes the general settlement structure of present-day Hasidim, as outlined above, but also allows one to follow settlement models of specific Hasidic groups, revealing how they differ from one another in this respect.

The first feature is size. Among the largest present-day Hasidic groups are Satmar (26,078 families), Chabad-Lubavitch (16,376), Ger (11,859), and Bełz (7,535). The second obvious feature is the degree of concentration. Some groups display a high degree of concentration in a single settlement area, while others are characterized by an even distribution. For instance, only 19 percent of Bełz Hasidim live in their largest center in Jerusalem, with almost the same number residing in Borough Park and Ashdod. Another feature of concentration appears in the percentage of families living in settlements of less than ten Hasidic families. This is on average very low, clearly less than 1 percent, which emphatically proves that Hasidim have avoided such settlements. This phenomenon is not, however, uniform. It appears that a general correlation exists between the degree of aversion to this type of settlement and the strictness (*ḥumra*) of a given group: whereas in the very restrictive Toledot Aharon there is not a single family that would live outside a Hasidic center, in the very eclectic Vasloi group there are as many as 6 percent.

The analysis can be even more precise when we examine both old and new telephone books.[26] For example, one can trace the birth rate of the groups we have such data for, or see developments in their distribution patterns such as the gradual movement of Israeli Hasidim to new enclaves and a growing concentration in the major Hasidic centers. There are also many other phenomena that can be investigated once the database is further scrutinized, including the patterns of territorial coappearance of various Hasidic groups, possible territorial coalitions, differences in spatial cohesion, and spatial strategies of various groups. If the data derived from the telephone books are juxtaposed with census-based information, one could possibly research nuances of the wealth, education, gender structure, and more of both the Hasidic community as a whole and its various subsets.

Conclusions

No doubt these and other studies will be undertaken before too long. What the example above demonstrates is that rich and valuable quantitative resources exist and, with the advent of DH, might be available for research of historical and contemporary Hasidism. Their potential use in the study of Hasidism is almost limitless. For example, in 1996, when Moshe Rosman published his groundbreaking biography of the putative founder of Hasidism, the Besht, the main point of contention was Rosman's narrow use of late traditions, attributed to the Besht, but recorded several decades after his death, in publications by other authors.[27] The simple resolution to this prolonged controversy could be the statistical analysis of authorship attribution, so called stylometry, which allows for high-probability attribution of anonymous texts, including those cited within larger texts by other authors. The same procedure could be applied to many other controversial authorship issues, of which the history of Hasidism is full. Similarly, the mainstream of intellectual history of Hasidism could greatly profit from relatively simple frequency analyses determining the predilection of specific authors for certain terms and phrases, their chronospatial variables, clustering, and so on. Imagine what we could gain from a simple frequency analysis of the word *devekut* or the phrase *'avodah be-gashmiyut*, tabulated by periods, authors, regions, and genres. With slightly more advanced techniques one could analyze cognitive stylistics of the canonical Hasidic texts, trace microcitations and text filiations across large corpora of Hasidic texts and authors, and much more. But even without these advanced research tools, one can easily imagine that an automated corpus of Hasidic stories could provide an authoritative list of all the narratives in all versions and all collections for any given Hasidic figure, large or small. With such a simple tool it would be far easier to move forward in all areas of Hasidic studies.

All this has yet to happen. One may find it discouraging that the "digital turn" is yet to take hold in the study of Hasidism. But one may also find it exciting to contemplate the changes that DH could bring to the field. Once those changes happen, scholars will be enabled to find radically new vistas on Hasidism, to provide much greater precision to what we already know, and to change the picture of Hasidism in ways that are not yet apparent.

SUGGESTED READING

There are a number of useful general introductions to DH that have nothing to do with the topic of Hasidism. Most of them are user-friendly and accessible to newcomers to the world of mathematical equations; some are available online.

Cohen, Daniel J., and Roy Rosenzweig, *Digital History: A Guide to Gathering, Preserving, and Presenting the Past on the Web* (Philadelphia: University of Pennsylvania Press, 2005)—free online version available at the site of the Roy Rosenzweig Center for History and New Media (http://chnm.gmu.edu/digitalhistory/).

Gardiner, Eileen, and Ronald G. Musto, *The Digital Humanities: A Primer for Students and Scholars* (New York: Cambridge University Press, 2015)—useful textbook for a wide range of readers.

Hillier, Amy, and Anne Kelly Knowles, eds., *Placing History: How Maps, Spatial Data, and GIS Are Changing Historical Scholarship* (Redlands: ESRI Press, 2008)—a classic for those seeking spatial analysis.

Schreibman, Susan, Ray Siemens, and John Unsworth, eds., *A Companion to Digital Humanities* (Oxford: Blackwell, 2004)—available online at www.digitalhumanities.org/companion/.

There are only few texts discussing the state of DH in Jewish studies. Even though they focus on the interconnections between new media and Judaism, and none of them deal specifically with Hasidism, they might be useful for providing a more general context.

Adlerstein, Yitzchok, "Digital Orthodoxy: The Making and Unmaking of a Lifestyle," in *Developing a Jewish Perspective on Culture*, ed. Y. Sarna (New York: Yeshiva University Press, 2014), 270–301.

Campbell, Heidi A., ed., *Digital Judaism: Jewish Negotiations with Digital Media and Culture* (New York: Routledge, 2015).

Chesner, Michelle, "JS/DH: An Introduction to Jewish Studies/Digital Humanities Resources," *Judaica Librarianship* 20 (2017), 194–196.

For examples of the use of quantitative research in the study of Hasidism, see:

Cahaner, Lee, "Expansion Processes of the Jewish Ultra-Orthodox Population in Haifa," *Themes in Israeli Geography* (2012), 70–87 (expanded Hebrew version in *Ofakim* 73–74 [2010], 214–240)—interestingly combines qualitative and quantitative methods of analysis.

Comenetz, Joshua, "Census-Based Estimation of the Hasidic Jewish Population," *Contemporary Jewry* 26 (2006), 35–74—so far the best use of the census polls in the demographic research of Hasidism.

Gonen, Amiram, *Between Torah Learning and Wage Earning: The London Experience and Lessons for Israel* (Jerusalem: Floersheimer Institute for Policy Studies, 2006)—the first study to use Hasidic telephone books.

Wodziński, Marcin, *Historical Atlas of Hasidism* (Princeton, NJ: Princeton University Press, 2018)—the first extensive DH study in the subfield of Hasidic studies.

Wodziński, Marcin, "Space and Spirit: On Boundaries, Hierarchies and Leadership in Hasidism," *Journal of Historical Geography* 53 (2016), 63–74—analysis of the distribution patterns of 2,854 shtiblekh.

On digital media in the missionary practices of Chabad-Lubavitch, see:

Blondheim, Menahem, and Elihu Katz, "Religion, Communications, and Judaism: The Case of Digital Chabad," *Media, Culture and Society* 38 (2016), 89–95.

Dein, Simon, "Internet Mediated Miracles: The Lubavitcher Rebbe's Online *Igros Kodesh*," *Jewish Journal of Sociology* 54 (2012), 27–45.

Golan, Oren, and Nurit Stadler, "Building the Sacred Community Online: The Dual Use of the Internet by Chabad," *Media, Culture and Society* 38 (2016), 1:71–88.

Pearl, Sharrona, "Exceptions to the Rule: Chabad-Lubavitch and the Digital Sphere," *Journal of Media and Religion* 13 (2014), 3:123–137.

NOTES

1. For a general introduction to DH, see the bibliography at the end of this chapter.

2. Richard Grusin, "The Dark Side of Digital Humanities: Dispatches from Two Recent MLA Conventions," *Differences* 25 (2014), 1:85.

3. For more on Digital Harlem, see Stephen Robertson, "Digital Mapping as a Research Tool: Digital Harlem: Everyday Life, 1915–1930," *American Historical Review* 121 (2016), 1:156–166; Joshua Sternfeld, "Harlem Crime, Soapbox Speeches, and Beauty Parlors: Digital Historical Context and the Challenge of Preserving Source Integrity," *American Historical Review* 121 (2016), 1:143–155.

4. See Dan Edelstein et al., "Historical Research in a Digital Age: Reflections from the Mapping the Republic of Letters Project," *American Historical Review* (2017), 2:400–424.

5. For several others see http://theantitzemach.blogspot.ca, http://ifyoutickleus.blogspot.ca, and http://katlekanye.blogspot.ca.

6. On digital media in the missionary practices of Chabad-Lubavitch, see the bibliography at the end of this chapter.

7. Of others, Responsa Project (https://www.responsa.co.il/home.en-US.aspx) provides, inter alia, a large body of Hasidic literature; Yiddish Book Center (https://www.yiddishbookcenter.org/) provides a number of mostly OCR-processed books in Yiddish, some of them related to Hasidism; DBS ha-Taklitor ha-Torani (http://www.dbs123.com/) is a useful resource for full text search in Hasidic literature.

8. On the press as a source for the history of Hasidism, see chapter 9.

9. On the attitudes of the editors of *Ha-tsefirah*, Chaim Zelig Słonimski and Nachum Sokołów, toward Hasidism, see Marcin Wodziński, *Haskalah and Hasidism in the Kingdom of Poland: A History of Conflict*, trans. S. Cozens (Oxford and Portland: The Littman Library of Jewish Civilization, 2005), 170–176, 231–234. On Alexander Tsederbaum, the editor of *Ha-melits*, and the stages of his interest in Hasidism, see David Biale et al., *Hasidism: A New History* (Princeton, NJ: Princeton University Press, 2017), 357, 489–490.

10. On distant reading, see Franco Moretti and Alberto Piazza, *Graphs, Maps, Trees: Abstract Models for Literary History* (London and New York: Verso, 2007); Franco Moretti, *Distant Reading* (London and New York: Verso, 2013).

11. See Marcin Wodziński, "Space and Spirit: On Boundaries, Hierarchies and Leadership in Hasidism," *Journal of Historical Geography* 53 (2016), 63–74; Wodziński, *Historical Atlas of Hasidism* (Princeton, NJ: Princeton University Press, 2018), 115–137.

12. For Pińczów, see *Undzer shtot Wolbrom*, ed. M. Sh. Geshuri (Tel Aviv: Irgun yotsei Wolbrom be-Israel, 1962), 197; for Wąchock, see *Sefer Virzbnik-Starakhovits*, ed. M. Shutsman (Tel Aviv: Yotsei Virzbnik-Starachowits ba-arets uva-tefutsot, „Sheyres Hapleyte" fun shtetl in Isroel un in der Welt, 1973), 44.

13. Boas Shamir, "Social Distance and Charisma: Theoretical Notes and an Exploratory Study," *Leadership Quarterly* 6 (1995), 19–47.

14. See esp. Lee Cahaner, "Expansion Processes of the Jewish Ultra-Orthodox Population in Haifa," *Themes in Israeli Geography* (2012), 70–87; Joshua Comenetz, "Census-Based Estimation of the Hasidic Jewish Population," *Contemporary Jewry* 26 (2006), 35–74.

15. See Amiram Gonen, *Between Torah Learning and Wage Earning: The London Experience and Lessons for Israel* (Jerusalem: Floersheimer Institute for Policy Studies, 2006); Beata Shulman, "Religijne, społeczne i historyczne uwarunkowania rozwoju osadnictwa chasydzkiego po II wojnie światowej na przykładzie grupy Bobov" (PhD diss., Jagiellonian University, 2012).

16. See Wodziński, *Historical Atlas of Hasidism*, 188–209.

17. See Ḥayim Shaulzon, "Ha-milḥamah be-Vizhnitz al sefer ha-telefonim mi mofiya be-reshimat mi?," blog post of April 18, 2013 at Be-olamam shel ḥeredim, accessed January 12, 2019, http://bshch.blogspot.co.il/2013/04/blog-post_6366.html.

18. These are the following: Alexander, Amshinov (R. Ya'akov Arie Milikovsky), Ashlag (R. Yankl Grenirer), Belz, Biala-Lugano, Bobov, Boian, Bratslav, Chabad, Duschinsky, Erloi, Ger, Karlin-Stolin, Krule, Makhnovka, Modzitz, Nadvorna, Pinsk-Karlin, Pupa, Rachmistrovka, Sanz, Satmar, Seret-Vizhnitz, Skvira, Slonim Weisse and Schwartze, Spinka (R. Israel Ḥayim Weiss), Strikov Bnei Brak, Toledot Aharon, Toledot Avraham Yitzḥak, Vasloi, Vizhnitz (R. Israel), Vizhnitz-Monsey, Zvihl Jerusalem (R. Shlomo Goldman).

19. Kahal hasidei Yerushalayim, Kretchniff, Lelov, Mishkenot ha-ro'im, Pittsburgh, Premyshlan, Pshevorsk, Shtutin, Tosh, Vien, and Vizhnitz (R. Mendel).

20. So far the best study of this kind is Comenetz, "Census-Based Estimation."

21. Estimations in Wodziński, *Hasidism: Key Questions* (New York: Oxford University Press, 2018), 133–163.

22. Here and below I refer to the data on the core, not expanded, Jewish population.

23. On the typology of the Hasidic settlements, see Hune E. Margulies, "The Spatial Culture of the Hasidic Community" (PhD diss., Columbia University, 2000).

24. See Margulies, "The Spatial Culture of the Hasidic Community," 40–60, 117–120.

25. See Amiram Gonen, "Temurot be-tifroset ha-ukhlusyah ha-ḥaredit-ashkenazit be-Yisrael: Mi-hitkansut be-shenei rikuzim gedolim le-hitparshut 'al penei ha-merḥav ha-artsi," in *Merḥavim be-shinuy: Temurot ge'ografiyot be-'Erets Yisra'el u-sevivotah*, ed. Y. Baleslav, Y. Katz, and Y. Schnell (Tel Aviv: Tel Aviv University Press, 2016), 349–374.

26. For a precise picture of the settlement structure of a few selected Hasidic groups, including the four largest, see Wodziński, *Historical Atlas of Hasidism*, maps 8.3.4–8.3.9.

27. For a fair summary of the controversy, see the introduction to the second edition of Moshe Rosman, *Founder of Hasidism: A Quest for the Historical Baal Shem Tov* (Oxford: The Littman Library of Jewish Civilization, 2013).

Acknowledgments

I am grateful to the Rothschild Foundation (Hanadiv) Europe and the Ministry of Science and Higher Education, Republic of Poland (grant No 11H 12 0290 81), within the National Program for the Development of the Humanities, 2013–2018, for financing the research project that led to the publication of this book. I express my deepest gratitude to these institutions, and even more to all of those who represent them. I am also indebted to two anonymous readers who shared with me their comments and advice. Their suggestions and opinions inspired me to revise critical parts of this study, especially the introduction. Most of all, however, I am grateful to the authors of the chapters in this book. Without their cooperation and much patience, the book would never have been possible.

Notes on Contributors

David Assaf (b. 1956) is a full professor in the Department of Jewish History at Tel Aviv University. His research focuses on traditional Jewish society in Eastern Europe with special attention to the social history of Hasidism. He lives in Jerusalem. Among his books in English are *The Regal Way: The Life and Times of Rabbi Israel of Ruzhin* (2002); *Journey to a Nineteenth-Century Shtetl: The Memoirs of Yekhezkel Kotik* (2002); *Untold Tales of the Hasidim: Crisis and Discontent in the History of Hasidism* (2010). He is one of the eight coauthors of *Hasidism: A New History* (2017).

Maya Balakirsky Katz (b. 1973) was born in Perm, Russia, but her people called Belaya Tserkov, Ukraine, their home for five generations. She is a professor of art history at Bar-Ilan University (Israel) and a senior candidate at the New Jersey Institute of Psychoanalysis. Her academic research focuses on the intersection of religion and media in the nineteenth century, and her clinical practice focuses on resolving internal conflicts in the present. She is the author of *The Visual Culture of Chabad* (2010) and *Drawing the Iron Curtain: Jews and the Golden Age of Soviet Animation* (2016). Of her creative productions, she is most proud of her five children: Ilan, Yair, Talia, Shai, and Dina Ronit.

Levi Cooper (b. 1973), originally from Melbourne, Australia, currently lives in Zur Hadassa, Israel, where he volunteers as the community rabbi. Levi teaches at the Pardes Institute of Jewish Studies in Jerusalem. His research focuses on legal history in the late modern period and the interplays between Jewish legal writing and the broader legal, intellectual, and cultural contexts. Besides his academic pursuits, Levi is an education advisor to the Jewish community of Istanbul.

Uriel Gellman (b. 1973) was born and raised in Israel. He teaches modern Jewish history at Bar-Ilan University in Israel. His main field of research is the cultural and social history of Jews in Eastern Europe, especially the history of Hasidism and Jewish Orthodoxy. He is coauthor of *Hasidism: A New History* (2017) and author of *The Emergence of Hasidism in Poland* (2018).

GALIT HASAN-ROKEM (b. 1945) was born and raised in Helsinki, Finland. She has served as Max and Margarethe Grunwald Professor of Folklore and Professor of Hebrew Literature at the Hebrew University of Jerusalem, where she now is Professor Emerita. Her main research interests are: folk literary, ethnographic, and intercultural aspects of late antique Rabbinic literature; theory of folklore; the proverb genre; Jewish motifs in European folklore; Israeli folklore. Publications include: *Web of Life: Folklore and Midrash in Rabbinic Literature* (2000); *Tales of the Neighborhood: Jewish Narrative Dialogues in Late Antiquity* (2003); *The Wandering Jew: Essays in the Interpretation of a Christian Legend*, with A. Dundes (1986); *Companion to Folklore*, with Regina F. Bendix (2012); *Louis Ginzberg's* Legends of the Jews*: Ancient Jewish Folk Literature Reconsidered*, with Ithamar Gruenwald (2014).

VLADIMIR LEVIN (b. 1971) was born in St. Petersburg and studied there and at the Hebrew University of Jerusalem. Currently he is the director of the Center for Jewish Art at the Hebrew University. His research interests include social and political aspects of modern Jewish history in Eastern Europe, synagogue architecture, and art. He authored *From Revolution to War: Jewish Politics in Russia, 1907–1914* (2016) and coauthored with Sergey R. Kravtsov *Synagogues in Ukraine: Volhynia* (2017).

SHAUL MAGID (b. 1958) was born and raised in New York. He is currently the Jay and Jeanie Schottenstein Professor of Jewish Studies and Professor of Religious Studies at Indiana University/Bloomington and a Kogod Senior Research Fellow at the Shalom Hartman Institute of North America. His work focuses mostly on Hasidism, Kabbalah, and American Judaism. His most recent publications are *Hasidism Incarnate* (2015) and *The Bible, The Talmud, and the New Testament: Elijah Zvi Soloveitchik's Commentary to the Gospels* (forthcoming 2019).

YOHANAN PETROVSKY-SHTERN (b. 1962) was born and raised in Kyiv, USSR. He obtained his MA in Romance and Germanic Philology from Kyiv Shevchenko University (KDU) and his PhD in Comparative Literature from Moscow Lomonosov University (MGU). He published more than sixty articles and edited three books on European and Latin American literature and philosophy before he switched to Jewish Studies and obtained his second PhD from Brandeis University. Currently he teaches early modern and modern Jewish history and culture at Northwestern University in Chicago, where he holds the Crown Family Chair in Jewish Studies. Among his six books, three are award-winning, and one, *The Golden Age Shtetl* (2014), was a nominee for the Pulitzer Prize and a winner of the National Jewish

Book Award. His books and articles appeared also in Ukrainian, Polish, Russian, Greek, Spanish, and Hebrew translations.

Gadi Sagiv (b. 1970) is a member of the Department of History, Philosophy and Judaic Studies at the Open University of Israel. His research focuses on the history of Jews in the modern period, in particular Hasidism. He is the author of *Dynasty: The Chernobyl Hasidic Dynasty and Its Place in the History of Hasidism* (2014), coeditor of *Habad Hasidism: History, Theology, Image* (2016), and coauthor of *Hasidism: A New History* (2017).

Edwin Seroussi (b. 1952) was born in Montevideo, Uruguay. In 1971, he moved to Israel. He teaches musicology at the Hebrew University of Jerusalem, where he also runs the Jewish Music Research Centre. His research focuses on the musical cultures of the Jews, especially in the Ottoman Empire and North Africa, as well as Israeli popular and folk music. His most recent publication is the comprehensive survey "Jüdische Musik," appearing in *Musik in Geschichte und Gegenwart* (2018).

Marcin Wodziński (b. 1966) was born and raised in Silesia, Poland. He works currently at the University of Wrocław, Poland, where he runs the Department of Jewish Studies. His research focuses on the history and culture of East European Jews in modern times, especially the Haskalah and Hasidism. Of his recent publications, he is most proud of *Historical Atlas of Hasidism* (2018) and *Hasidism: Key Questions* (2018).

Index